2 Corinthians

TEACH THE TEXT COMMENTARY

John H. Walton
Old Testament General Editor

Mark L. Strauss
New Testament General Editor

Volumes now available:

Old Testament Volumes

Exodus .... T. Desmond Alexander
Leviticus and Numbers .... Joe M. Sprinkle
Joshua .... Kenneth A. Mathews
Judges and Ruth .... Kenneth C. Way
1 & 2 Samuel .... Robert B. Chisholm Jr.
Job .... Daniel J. Estes
Psalms, volume 1 .... C. Hassell Bullock
Ecclesiastes and Song of Songs .... Edward M. Curtis
Jeremiah and Lamentations .... J. David Hays
Daniel .... Ronald W. Pierce

New Testament Volumes

Matthew .... Jeannine K. Brown
Mark .... Grant R. Osborne
Luke .... R. T. France
Romans .... C. Marvin Pate
1 Corinthians .... Preben Vang
2 Corinthians .... Moyer V. Hubbard
James, 1 & 2 Peter, and Jude .... Jim Samra
Revelation .... J. Scott Duvall

Visit the series website at www.teachthetextseries.com.

Teach the Text
Commentary Series

2 Corinthians

Moyer V. Hubbard

Mark L. Strauss and John H. Walton
GENERAL EDITORS

ILLUSTRATING THE TEXT
Kevin and Sherry Harney
ASSOCIATE EDITORS

Jeff Porte
CONTRIBUTING AUTHOR

a division of Baker Publishing Group
Grand Rapids, Michigan

© 2017 by Moyer V. Hubbard
Illustrating the Text sections © 2017 by Baker Publishing Group

Published by Baker Books
a division of Baker Publishing Group
P.O. Box 6287, Grand Rapids, MI 49516-6287
www.bakerbooks.com

Printed in the United States of America

All rights reserved. No part of this publication may be reproduced, stored in a retrieval system, or transmitted in any form or by any means—for example, electronic, photocopy, recording—without the prior written permission of the publisher. The only exception is brief quotations in printed reviews.

Library of Congress Cataloging-in-Publication Data
Names: Hubbard, Moyer V., author. | Strauss, Mark L., 1959– editor. | Walton, John H., 1952– editor.
Title: 2 Corinthians / Moyer V. Hubbard, author ; Mark L. Strauss and John H. Walton, general editors ; Kevin and Sherry Harney, associate editors ; Jeff Porte, contributing writer.
Other titles: Second Corinthians
Description: Grand Rapids : Baker Books, 2016. | Series: Teach the text commentary | Includes index.
Identifiers: LCCN 2016051159 | ISBN 9780801092367 (pbk.)
Subjects: LCSH: Bible. Corinthians, 2nd—Commentaries.
Classification: LCC BS2675.53 .H83 2016 | DDC 227/.307—dc23
LC record available at https://lccn.loc.gov/2016051159

Unless otherwise indicated, Scripture quotations are from the Holy Bible, New International Version®. NIV®. Copyright © 1973, 1978, 1984, 2011 by Biblica, Inc.™ Used by permission of Zondervan and Biblica. All rights reserved worldwide. www.zondervan.com; Biblica.com. Italics in the NIV text have been added by the author for emphasis.

The "NIV" and "New International Version" are trademarks registered in the United States Patent and Trademark Offices by Biblica, Inc.™

Scripture quotations labeled ESV are from The Holy Bible, English Standard Version® (ESV®), copyright © 2001 by Crossway, a publishing ministry of Good News Publishers. Used by permission. All rights reserved. ESV Text Edition: 2011

Scripture quotations labeled NASB are from the New American Standard Bible®, copyright © 1960, 1962, 1963, 1968, 1971, 1972, 1973, 1975, 1977, 1995 by The Lockman Foundation. Used by permission. (www.Lockman.org)

Scripture quotations labeled NET are from the NET BIBLE®, copyright © 2003 by Biblical Studies Press, LLC. www.netbible.com. Used by permission. All rights reserved.

Scripture quotations labeled NLT are from the *Holy Bible*, New Living Translation, copyright © 1996, 2004, 2015 by Tyndale House Foundation. Used by permission of Tyndale House Publishers, Inc., Carol Stream, Illinois 60188. All rights reserved.

Scripture quotations labeled NRSV are from the New Revised Standard Version of the Bible, copyright © 1989, by the Division of Christian Education of the National Council of the Churches of Christ in the United States of America. Used by permission. All rights reserved.

Scripture quotations labeled RSV are from the Revised Standard Version of the Bible, copyright 1952 [2nd edition, 1971] by the Division of Christian Education of the National Council of the Churches of Christ in the United States of America. Used by permission. All rights reserved.

Unless otherwise indicated, photos are copyright © Baker Publishing Group and Dr. James C. Martin. Unless otherwise indicated, illustrations and maps are copyright © Baker Publishing Group.

17 18 19 20 21 22 23   7 6 5 4 3 2 1

Contents

Welcome to the Teach the Text
   Commentary Series   vii
Introduction to the Teach the Text
   Commentary Series   ix
Abbreviations   xi

Introduction to 2 Corinthians 1
2 Corinthians 1:1–7 9
   Comfort in Affliction
2 Corinthians 1:8–11 15
   Learning to Trust
2 Corinthians 1:12–14 21
   Apostolic Integrity
2 Corinthians 1:15–2:4 26
   Changing Plans, a Faithful God
2 Corinthians 2:5–11 32
   Forgiveness and Restoration
2 Corinthians 2:12–17 38
   Led as Captives
2 Corinthians 3:1–6 44
   The New Covenant
2 Corinthians 3:7–11 50
   The Surpassing Glory of the Ministry of the Spirit
2 Corinthians 3:12–18 55
   New Covenant Transformation
2 Corinthians 4:1–6 62
   New Covenant Service

2 Corinthians 4:7–15 68
   Jars of Clay
2 Corinthians 4:16–5:5 74
   Fixing Our Eyes on the Unseen
2 Corinthians 5:6–10 81
   By Faith, Not Sight
2 Corinthians 5:11–15 87
   The Impelling Love of Christ
2 Corinthians 5:16–21 93
   The Ministry of Reconciliation
2 Corinthians 6:1–13 100
   An Appeal for Reconciliation
2 Corinthians 6:14–7:1 107
   An Appeal for Purity
2 Corinthians 7:2–4 113
   An Appeal for Reciprocated Affection
2 Corinthians 7:5–16 117
   Comfort, Repentance, and Reconciliation
2 Corinthians 8:1–7 124
   The Generosity of the Macedonians
2 Corinthians 8:8–15 131
   Finish the Work!
2 Corinthians 8:16–24 137
   Money Matters
2 Corinthians 9:1–5 143
   Giving Generously
2 Corinthians 9:6–15 148
   Giving Cheerfully

2 Corinthians 10:1–6 154
Demolishing Strongholds
2 Corinthians 10:7–11 161
Authority to Build
2 Corinthians 10:12–18 167
Boasting in the Lord
2 Corinthians 11:1–6 173
Divinely Jealous
2 Corinthians 11:7–15 180
True and False Apostles
Additional Insights 187
Paul, Patronage, and the Corinthians
2 Corinthians 11:16–21a 189
Playing the Fool
2 Corinthians 11:21b–29 193
Apostolic Credentials
2 Corinthians 11:30–33 200
Boasting in Weakness

2 Corinthians 12:1–10 205
Weakness as Strength
2 Corinthians 12:11–13 212
Not the Least Inferior
2 Corinthians 12:14–21 217
Ready or Not, Here I Come
2 Corinthians 13:1–4 224
Be Warned
2 Corinthians 13:5–10 230
Test Yourselves!
2 Corinthians 13:11–14 237
Finally, Brothers and Sisters . . .

Notes   243
Bibliography   249
Contributors   251
Index   252

Welcome to the Teach the Text Commentary Series

Why another commentary series? That was the question the general editors posed when Baker Books asked us to produce this series. Is there something that we can offer to pastors and teachers that is not currently being offered by other commentary series, or that can be offered in a more helpful way? After carefully researching the needs of pastors who teach the text on a weekly basis, we concluded that yes, more can be done; the Teach the Text Commentary Series (TTCS) is carefully designed to fill an important gap.

The technicality of modern commentaries often overwhelms readers with details that are tangential to the main purpose of the text. Discussions of source and redaction criticism, as well as detailed surveys of secondary literature, seem far removed from preaching and teaching the Word. Rather than wade through technical discussions, pastors often turn to devotional commentaries, which may contain exegetical weaknesses, misuse the Greek and Hebrew languages, and lack hermeneutical sophistication. There is a need for a commentary that utilizes the best of biblical scholarship but also presents the material in a clear, concise, attractive, and user-friendly format.

This commentary is designed for that purpose—to provide a ready reference for the exposition of the biblical text, giving easy access to information that a pastor needs to communicate the text effectively. To that end, the commentary is divided into carefully selected preaching units (with carefully regulated word counts both in the passage as a whole and in each subsection). Pastors and teachers engaged in weekly preparation thus know that they will be reading approximately the same amount of material on a week-by-week basis.

Each passage begins with a concise summary of the central message, or "Big Idea," of the passage and a list of its main themes. This is followed by a more detailed interpretation of the text, including the literary context of the passage, historical background material, and interpretive insights. While drawing on the best of biblical scholarship, this material is clear, concise, and to the point. Technical material is kept to a minimum, with endnotes pointing the reader to more detailed discussion and additional resources.

A second major focus of this commentary is on the preaching and teaching process itself. Few commentaries today help the pastor/teacher move from the meaning of the text to its effective communication. Our goal is to bridge this gap. In addition to interpreting the text in the "Understanding the Text" section, each unit contains a "Teaching the Text" section and an "Illustrating the Text" section. The teaching section points to the key theological themes of the passage and ways to communicate these themes to today's audiences. The illustration section provides ideas and examples for retaining the interest of hearers and connecting the message to daily life.

The creative format of this commentary arises from our belief that the Bible is not just a record of God's dealings in the past but is the living Word of God, "alive and active" and "sharper than any double-edged sword" (Heb. 4:12). Our prayer is that this commentary will help to unleash that transforming power for the glory of God.

The General Editors

Introduction to the Teach the Text Commentary Series

This series is designed to provide a ready reference for teaching the biblical text, giving easy access to information that is needed to communicate a passage effectively. To that end, the commentary is carefully divided into units that are faithful to the biblical authors' ideas and of an appropriate length for teaching or preaching.

The following standard sections are offered in each unit.

1. *Big Idea*. For each unit the commentary identifies the primary theme, or "Big Idea," that drives both the passage and the commentary.
2. *Key Themes*. Together with the Big Idea, the commentary addresses in bullet-point fashion the key ideas presented in the passage.
3. *Understanding the Text*. This section focuses on the exegesis of the text and includes several sections.
    a. The Text in Context. Here the author gives a brief explanation of how the unit fits into the flow of the text around it, including reference to the rhetorical strategy of the book and the unit's contribution to the purpose of the book.
    b. Outline/Structure. For some literary genres (e.g., epistles), a brief exegetical outline may be provided to guide the reader through the structure and flow of the passage.

c. *Historical and Cultural Background.* This section addresses historical and cultural background information that may illuminate a verse or passage.
   d. *Interpretive Insights.* This section provides information needed for a clear understanding of the passage. The intention of the author is to be highly selective and concise rather than exhaustive and expansive.
   e. *Theological Insights.* In this very brief section the commentary identifies a few carefully selected theological insights about the passage.
4. *Teaching the Text.* Under this second main heading the commentary offers guidance for teaching the text. In this section the author lays out the main themes and applications of the passage. These are linked carefully to the Big Idea and are represented in the Key Themes.
5. *Illustrating the Text.* At this point in the commentary the writers partner with a team of pastor/teachers to provide suggestions for relevant and contemporary illustrations from current culture, entertainment, history, the Bible, news, literature, ethics, biography, daily life, medicine, and over forty other categories. They are designed to spark creative thinking for preachers and teachers and to help them design illustrations that bring alive the passage's key themes and message.

Abbreviations

Old Testament

Gen.	Genesis	2 Chron.	2 Chronicles	Dan.	Daniel
Exod.	Exodus	Ezra	Ezra	Hosea	Hosea
Lev.	Leviticus	Neh.	Nehemiah	Joel	Joel
Num.	Numbers	Esther	Esther	Amos	Amos
Deut.	Deuteronomy	Job	Job	Obad.	Obadiah
Josh.	Joshua	Ps(s).	Psalm(s)	Jon.	Jonah
Judg.	Judges	Prov.	Proverbs	Mic.	Micah
Ruth	Ruth	Eccles.	Ecclesiastes	Nah.	Nahum
1 Sam.	1 Samuel	Song	Song of Songs	Hab.	Habakkuk
2 Sam.	2 Samuel	Isa.	Isaiah	Zeph.	Zephaniah
1 Kings	1 Kings	Jer.	Jeremiah	Hag.	Haggai
2 Kings	2 Kings	Lam.	Lamentations	Zech.	Zechariah
1 Chron.	1 Chronicles	Ezek.	Ezekiel	Mal.	Malachi

New Testament

Matt.	Matthew	Eph.	Ephesians	Heb.	Hebrews
Mark	Mark	Phil.	Philippians	James	James
Luke	Luke	Col.	Colossians	1 Pet.	1 Peter
John	John	1 Thess.	1 Thessalonians	2 Pet.	2 Peter
Acts	Acts	2 Thess.	2 Thessalonians	1 John	1 John
Rom.	Romans	1 Tim.	1 Timothy	2 John	2 John
1 Cor.	1 Corinthians	2 Tim.	2 Timothy	3 John	3 John
2 Cor.	2 Corinthians	Titus	Titus	Jude	Jude
Gal.	Galatians	Philem.	Philemon	Rev.	Revelation

General

AD	*anno Domini*, in the year of our Lord	ca.	*circa*, about	
		cf.	*confer*, compare	
BC	before Christ	chap(s).	chapter(s)	

e.g.	*exempli gratia*, for example	LAB	*Liber antiquitatum biblicarum* (Pseudo-Philo)
esp.	especially	Let. Aris.	Letter of Aristeas
etc.	*et cetera*, and others	Liv. Pro.	Lives of the Prophets
ibid.	*ibidem*, there the same	Pss. Sol.	Psalms of Solomon
i.e.	*id est*, that is	T. Job	Testament of Job
v(v).	verse(s)	T. Levi	Testament of Levi
		T. Sim.	Testament of Simeon

Ancient Versions and Manuscripts

LXX	Septuagint
m.	Mishnah
P.Oxy.	Oxyrhynchus papyrus
1QS	*Rule of the Community*

Modern English Versions

CEB	Common English Bible
ESV	English Standard Version
GNT	Good News Translation
KJV	King James Version
LEB	Lexham English Bible
NASB	New American Standard Bible
NET	The NET Bible (New English Translation)
NIV	New International Version
NJB	New Jerusalem Bible
NLT	New Living Translation
NRSV	New Revised Standard Version
RSV	Revised Standard Version

Apocrypha and Septuagint

Bel	Bel and the Dragon
2 Macc.	2 Maccabees
Sir.	Sirach
Wis.	Wisdom of Solomon

Old Testament Pseudepigrapha

Ascen. Isa.	Ascension of Isaiah
2–3 Bar.	2–3 Baruch
1–2 En.	1–2 Enoch
4 Ezra	4 Ezra
Jos. Asen.	Joseph and Aseneth

Greek and Latin Works

Aelius Aristides

Plat.	*To Plato*

Apostolic Fathers

Did.	*Didache*

Apuleius

Metam.	*Metamorphoses* (The Golden Ass)

Arius Didymus

Epit.	*Epitome of Stoic Ethics*

Dio Chrysostom

Or.	*Orations*

Epictetus

Diatr.	*Diatribai (Discourses)*

Horace

Odes	*Odes*
Sat.	*Sermones (Satires)*

Isocrates

Nic.	*Nicoles*

Josephus

Ant.	*Jewish Antiquities*
J.W.	*Jewish War*

Lucian

Alex.	*Alexander*
Fug.	*Fugitivi (The Runaways)*
Hermot.	*Hermotimus*

Merc. cond.	De mercede conductis (On Salaried Posts in Great Houses)	**Plutarch**	
		Adul. amic.	Quomodo adulator ab amico internoscatur (How to Tell a Flatterer from a Friend)
Rhet. praec.	Rhetorum praeceptor (A Professor of Public Speaking)		
		Aem.	Aemilius Paullus
		Mor.	Moralia

Martial

Epig.   Epigrams

Publilius Syrus

Sent.   Sententiae

Musonius Rufus

Disc.   Discourses

Quintilian

Inst.   Institutio oratoria (Institutes of Oratory)

Petronius

Sat.   Satyricon

Seneca

Cons. sap.   De constantia sapientis (On the Firmness of the Wise Man)

Philo

Agr.   On Agriculture
Flight   On Flight and Finding
Good Person   That Every Good Person Is Free
Migr.   On the Migration of Abraham
Planting   On Planting
Posterity   On the Posterity of Cain
QG   Quest. Gen.
Worse   That the Worse Attacks the Better

Dial.   Dialogi (Dialogues)
Ep.   Epistles

Suetonius

Tib.   Tiberius

Tacitus

Ann.   Annals

Modern Reference Works

BDAG   Frederick W. Danker, Walter Bauer, William F. Arndt, and F. Wilbur Gingrich. *A Greek-English Lexicon of the New Testament and Other Early Christian Literature*. 3rd ed. Chicago: University of Chicago Press, 2000
CIJ   *Corpus Inscriptionum Judaicarum*. Edited by Jean-Baptiste Frey. 2 vols. Rome: Pontifical Biblical Institute, 1936–52
LSJ   Henry George Liddell, Robert Scott, and Henry Stuart Jones. *A Greek-English Lexicon*. 9th ed. with rev. supplement. Oxford: Clarendon, 1996
Sel. Pap.   *Select Papyri*. Translated by A. S. Hunt and C. C. Edgar. 5 vols. Loeb Classical Library. Cambridge: Harvard University Press, 1932–35

Quotations of classical authors are from the Loeb Classical Library unless otherwise noted. Quotations of the Dead Sea Scrolls are from Florentino García Martínez and Eibert J. C. Tigchelaar, *The Dead Sea Scrolls*, study ed., 2 vols. (Leiden: Brill, 1999). Quotations from Arius Didymus are from Arthur John Pomeroy, ed., *Epitome of Stoic Ethics*, Society of Biblical Literature Texts and Translations 44 (Atlanta: Society of Biblical Literature, 1999). Quotations of Marsonius Rufus are from Cora E. Lutz, *Musonius Rufus: "The Roman Socrates"* (New Haven: Yale University Press, 1947). Quotations of the Cynic Epistles are from Abraham J. Malherbe, ed., *The Cynic Epistles: A Study Edition*, Sources for Biblical Study 12 (Missoula, MT: Scholars Press, 1977). Quotations of the Old Testament Pseudepigrapha are from James H. Charlesworth, ed., *The Old Testament Pseudepigrapha*, 2 vols. (Garden City, NY: Doubleday, 1983–85).

Introduction to 2 Corinthians

The City of Corinth

Corinth was one of the most illustrious city-states of ancient Greece. Its history stretches back to the eighth century BC and is marked by political, commercial, and cultural achievements. At the apex of Corinth's influence it became the leading city of the Achaian League, a federation of Greek cities aimed at securing the political fortunes of Achaia in the face of challenges from Macedonia, Sparta, and Rome. This alliance ultimately led to the destruction of Corinth and the final dissolution of the Achaian League in 146 BC by Rome. Corinth lay in rubble until it was refounded as a Roman colony in 44 BC by Julius Caesar.

Corinth's strategic position on the narrow isthmus joining the Peloponnese to the Greek mainland meant that it controlled the two harbors at nearby Lechaeum and Cenchreae. This maritime juncture connected Rome to its provinces in the East, which made the newly established Corinth a major center of commerce and travel. As the host of the biennial Isthmian Games—a Panhellenic athletic competition second in significance only to the Olympic Games—Corinth also benefited from related tourism and became a center of athleticism in the Mediterranean. Commerce, politics, and tourism contributed to Corinth's rapid growth; contemporary scholars commonly describe first-century Roman Corinth as "a boom town."[1]

When Paul first arrived in Corinth (ca. AD 51), he walked into a flourishing metropolis (including environs) of nearly one hundred thousand residents. In many respects this city was different from its ancient counterpart as it existed some three hundred years prior. Since Corinth was a Roman colony, the ruling elite were (largely) Roman, and Latin was the dominant language among the power brokers of the city. Corinth was the seat of the Roman provincial governor and therefore had a military presence. Yet the city also contained a large population of native Greeks, and so the designation Greco-Roman is truly applicable to the Corinth of the first century.

In recent years, a consensus has emerged in New Testament scholarship concerning a profile of Corinth and its citizens. This usually involves Corinth's relative wealth, status consciousness, devotion to rhetoric, emphasis on physical appearance, upward mobility, and licentiousness.[2] Paul confronts numerous manifestations of these cultural values throughout his letters to this church, and as a result we know more about the Christian community in Corinth than about any other New Testament assembly. We also know more about Paul's turbulent relationship with this church than with any other church he founded. Of the numerous letters that Paul wrote to Corinth, only two have survived, 1 and 2 Corinthians. Before we deal with important literary and historical issues crucial for interpreting 2 Corinthians, it will be helpful to situate this letter in the context of Paul's correspondence with the Corinthians and to understand the developments between 1 and 2 Corinthians.

Paul's Letters to Corinth and the Purpose(s) of 2 Corinthians

Paul's initial ministry in Corinth lasted approximately eighteen months (Acts 18:1–17). Sometime after leaving Corinth, Paul wrote to the Corinthians with further pastoral guidance. The content of this letter is unknown, except that it advised against associating with believers who continued to practice sexual immorality (1 Cor. 5:9). In scholarly discussions, this letter is sometimes referred to as "Letter A." Paul later spent an extended time in Ephesus (Acts 19), and during this period of ministry the apostle heard reports from "Chloe's household" of divisions in Corinth (1 Cor. 1:11).[3] He also received a letter from the Corinthians themselves with questions on matters such as marriage (1 Cor. 7:1), food sacrificed to idols (8:1), and other practical concerns. First Corinthians was written in response to Chloe's report and the Corinthians' questions. This letter, then, is actually (at least) Paul's second letter to Corinth (Letter B).

What precisely happened next is unclear, but it seems likely that Timothy returned from delivering this letter to the Corinthians (1 Cor. 4:17; 16:10–11; Acts 19:21–22) with news that the situation had deteriorated significantly. This caused Paul to abandon the itinerary he announced in 1 Corinthians 16:5–6 and to make an unplanned visit to Corinth (2 Cor. 1:15–24; 13:1–2). This visit did not go well; Paul calls it "painful" (2:1). Paul found himself personally attacked by a member of the community (2:5–11; 7:12), and he left in a state of grief over the Corinthians' sin (7:7–9). Upon returning to Ephesus, Paul composed an emotional letter, written "out of great distress and anguish of heart and with many tears" (2:4), which he conveyed through Titus (2:4, 12–13; 7:6–7). This letter, which is now lost, is often called "Letter C."

Titus eventually brought Paul the good news that the Corinthians had responded favorably to this strongly worded letter and had taken action against the offender (2:5–11; 7:5–12). However, he also brought news of a new threat: flamboyant missionaries from Judea had arrived in Corinth and were working to undermine Paul's credibility. Paul responded by dispatching Titus directly to Corinth with the letter before us, 2 Corinthians—Paul's fourth identifiable letter to this community—while Paul himself continued inland through Macedonia on his way to Corinth. He also tasked Titus with the responsibility of reinvigorating enthusiasm for the collection for the poor in Jerusalem, so that when Paul arrived with emissaries from the Macedonian churches, the Corinthians (to say nothing of Paul!) would not be embarrassed by their lack of support for this endeavor.

In light of this sequence of events, when Paul wrote 2 Corinthians he had several distinct but interrelated goals:

- to provide the full context for his change of travel plans, in order to refute the charge of fickleness from some in Corinth (chaps. 1–2);
- to provide a fuller perspective on his apostolic ministry, particularly his suffering and "weakness" (12:10), in order to counter those in Corinth—be they the Corinthians themselves or the intruders—who used Paul's hardships to undermine his apostolic credibility (chaps. 3–7);
- to assist Titus in his endeavor to motivate the Corinthians with respect to the collection for the poor in Jerusalem by providing further theological rationale and specific guidelines (chaps. 8–9);
- to directly confront the claims of intruding missionaries, to refute their defamation and expose their arrogance and duplicity (chaps. 10–12);
- to prepare the Corinthians for his third visit, which would include a thorough reckoning with regard to lingering sinful attitudes and actions (6:14–7:1; chap. 13).

The overarching purpose of 2 Corinthians can be described as *reconciliation and restoration*.[4] Paul's chief prayer for the Corinthians is for their "restoration" (13:9). The restorative work that needs to take place relates to God and to Paul, and also relates to relationships among the Corinthians themselves. Paul's hope is that this letter will prepare the ground for his impending visit, so that when he arrives he will not have to wield his authority in discipline but can use it for edification (13:10).

The Literary Integrity of 2 Corinthians

Given the multifaceted agenda behind 2 Corinthians, it should not be surprising that the unity of this letter has been seriously questioned. In fact, through the mid-1990s, the scholarly consensus held that 2 Corinthians was a composite document made up of at least two separate letters. Recent scholarship, however, has increasingly supported the unity of 2 Corinthians, which is the position adopted in this commentary. A detailed defense of this position is beyond the scope of this introduction,[5] but a few comments on both the positive arguments for the compositional unity of this letter and the most challenging aspects of this position are in order.

Arguments for the Unity of 2 Corinthians

Lack of textual support for a composite document. The first observation that should be made is that there is no textual evidence that 2 Corinthians ever existed in any form other than what we have today. If 2 Corinthians is a composite document made up of several letters, this would mean that the editorial process that produced the canonical form of 2 Corinthians must have been completed before any copies of the individual letters that contributed to its present form were circulated. We would also have to suppose that those letters were destroyed or lost after the composite document, canonical 2 Corinthians, was finished. We also have to provide a convincing motive behind editing and combining these letters. Combining multiple documents onto a single papyrus roll is not problematic, but the rationale behind eliminating introductions and conclusions and inserting fragments of one letter between segments of another letter requires a plausible explanation.

Unifying motifs. While it is certainly true that the major segments of 2 Corinthians (chaps. 1–7; 8–9; 10–13) deal with very different topics, it is also true that important themes permeate the letter as a whole, suggesting a rhetorically unified composition—for example, strength in weakness (2:14–16; 4:7–18; 11:30–33; 12:10; 13:3), Paul's style and philosophy of preaching (2:17; 4:2–5; 5:11–13; 10:10–12; 11:5–6; 13:2–3), proper and improper boasting (1:12, 14; 5:12; 7:4, 14; 8:24; 9:2; 10:8–17; 11:10–30; 12:1–10), and commendation (3:1–3; 4:2; 5:12; 7:11; 10:18; 12:11).

Chapters 1–9 prepare the ground for chapters 10–13. It is sometimes argued that the opponents of chapters 10–13 and the harsh rhetoric of this material are completely unprecedented based on the information of chapters 1–9, especially 7:4–16. On the other hand, in both sections of the letter Paul is defending himself before the Corinthians, and even the earlier chapters contain allusions to intruders (3:1), and to those who claim to be servants of God but who exploit others (2:17; 4:2) while preaching themselves (4:5). Moreover, when we connect these statements to Paul's lengthy reflection on the insufficiency of the Mosaic era and the law itself (3:1–18), we have virtually completed the profile of the Jewish-Christian intruders of chapters 10–13. In other words, it is simply not true that the apologetic of chapters 10–13 is completely unexpected based on the material of chapters 1–9.

Various issues, various strategies. According to 1 Corinthians, the fundamental problem in Corinth was the Corinthians themselves. In Paul's estimation, they were worldly, immature, and not ready for the "solid food" of mature discipleship (1 Cor. 3:1–4). While some progress had been made by the time Paul wrote 2 Corinthians, many of the same problems remained: dining in pagan temples (2 Cor. 6:14–7:2; cf. 1 Cor. 8; 10:14–22), sexual impurity (2 Cor. 12:21; cf. 1 Cor. 5:1–2), a carnal devaluation of Paul's rhetoric (2 Cor. 10:10; 11:6; cf. 1 Cor. 2:1–5), and factiousness (2 Cor. 10–12; cf. 1 Cor. 4:4–6). Quite apart from these lingering problems, as Paul composed 2 Corinthians he also had to address questions related to his altered travel itinerary, the stalled collection, and the recently arrived Jewish-Christian intruders. In other words, 2 Corinthians deals with a wide assortment of problems, and so to evaluate the integrity of this letter on the basis of contemporary standards of thematic consistency focused on a single objective is to fail to grasp the complexity of the situation on the ground in Corinth.[6]

Challenging Passages for Those Defending the Unity of 2 Corinthians

The literary seams in 2 Corinthians are widely agreed on: 1:1–2:13; 2:14–7:16 (interrupted by 6:14–7:1); 8:1–9:15; 10:1–13:13. Not all of these, however, are equally problematic with respect to the integrity of 2 Corinthians. For example, the abrupt thanksgiving at 2:14 and the excursus that follows are quite reasonably accounted for by Paul's mention of Titus in 2:13, which has reminded the apostle of the good news that Titus brought regarding the Corinthians' positive response to his forceful letter (2:1–4). This supposition is confirmed when Paul picks up this train of thought in 7:4–16. The emerging consensus on chapters 8 and 9 (even among those who do not regard the letter as a unity)[7] is that they belong together and were originally included in their present position, immediately following chapters 1–7. Two sections of 2 Corinthians, however, are particularly challenging to relate to the context in which they are found, and so they require brief comment.

2 Corinthians 6:14–7:1

Second Corinthians 6:14–7:1 appears to represent a dramatic shift of topic and also contains a high proportion of vocabulary not found elsewhere in Paul's letter. The call for separation and purity is reminiscent of the material from Qumran, and so some have concluded it is a Christianized Essene fragment.[8] Moreover, when this passage is removed, 6:13 connects to 7:2 quite seamlessly. Other scholars, however, have countered that this passage can be integrated into its present context either by correctly identifying the broader Jewish traditions Paul is relying on,[9] or by accurately discerning the issue in the context that Paul is addressing in this appeal,[10] or by adequately appreciating the rhetorical structure of Paul's argument.[11] Especially intriguing is the suggestion that 6:14–7:1 represents a concrete application of the appeal for reconciliation in 5:21–6:2.[12] Some of these proposals are quite complex and imaginative. At the end of the day, Barrett's solution may be the most attractive, if only by virtue of its simplicity: "Paul not infrequently allows himself to wander from his point, and then brings himself back to it with something of a jerk."[13]

2 Corinthians 10–13

Second Corinthians 10–13 is certainly the most difficult segment of the letter for anyone arguing for the integrity of 2 Corinthians. In fact, it would be difficult to imagine a more jarring shift in content and tone than what the reader finds when he or she moves from chapter 9 to chapter 10 in this letter. Paul becomes angry and sarcastic and is clearly in attack mode. We suddenly read of false apostles who are preaching a different Jesus (11:1–4), and it seems that the Corinthians' loyalty is genuinely torn (12:11–18). How can this be reconciled with what precedes, where Paul expresses his "complete confidence" in the Corinthians (7:16)?

In the opinion of this writer, there is no completely satisfactory answer to this question. However, as noted above, the earlier chapters do contain allusions to intruders who are exploiting the Corinthians (2:17; 3:1; 4:2, 4) and also imply the Jewish character of these intruders (3:1–18). This renders their appearance in chapters 10–13 a little less surprising. In fact, Sumney's comprehensive study of Paul's opponents in 2 Corinthians concludes that the evidence from chapters 1–7 and chapters 10–13 points to the same opponents in each section of the letter.[14] Moreover, Paul's "complete confidence" cannot be construed to mean there are no outstanding problems in Corinth. The apostle's expression of confidence in 7:16 relates primarily to the Corinthians' handling of the matter involving the brother who attacked Paul during his "painful" visit (2:1), which is the focus of 7:4–16.

We also need to bear in mind that a letter the size and scope of 2 Corinthians was certainly not written in one sitting. Given what we know of Paul's travel and teaching and the self-supported nature of his ministry, it is more reasonable to imagine that this letter took at least several days, if not several weeks, to complete. During this time Paul may have received further information about the seriousness of the situation in Corinth, which caused him to change his approach and demeanor in the latter chapters. The earlier chapters still addressed important and relevant matters and for this reason would not have been discarded. It is also possible that Paul dictated this letter over an extended period of time, addressing different concerns in each session. These various segments were then compiled and sent to Corinth in the form of the letter we call 2 Corinthians. In essence, 2 Corinthians appears to represent a single letter from Paul, but one that addresses several distinct issues and a very complex set of circumstances in Corinth.

Paul's Opponents in 2 Corinthians

The identity of Paul's opponents in 2 Corinthians remains one of the most vexing issues in Pauline studies. One recent treatment of this topic identified nineteen distinguishable profiles devised over the past century.[15] Many of these suggestions share common characteristics, and these various permutations can be organized into four basic groups: Judaizers, gnostics, Hellenistic "divine men," and pneumatics.[16] Deciding between these alternatives is a daunting task and is made more so by Paul's complicated interaction with the Corinthians. For example, while all scholars agree that 2 Corinthians 10–13 provides firm evidence of intruders, we also know from both 1 Corinthians and elsewhere in 2 Corinthians that Paul had many other naysayers in Corinth. So, just because we detect Paul opposing a particular viewpoint, that does not necessarily mean that the intruding opponents held that viewpoint. We must distinguish between Paul's opponents (the intruders of chaps. 10–13) and his "opponents" (the disaffected among the Corinthians themselves). Moreover, we must allow that Paul could occasionally critique or censure larger cultural values that were not in keeping with the gospel, without providing any useful information concerning his rivals. In other words, given the complex situation apparent in these letters, we cannot assume that everything Paul opposes counters only one group or that all of his polemically oriented statements are directed toward a single, unified front. What we do know about Paul's opponents in 2 Corinthians 10–13 can be summarized briefly:

1. They were Jewish (11:22), but there is no evidence that they were advocating obedience to the Mosaic law. We hear nothing of circumcision or dietary restrictions, or other Jewish distinctives, although they clearly took great pride in Jewish credentials.

2. They came from outside Corinth, probably Palestine (11:22), and were viewed by Paul as illegitimately encroaching on his ministry jurisdiction (10:13–17).
3. They professed Christ (11:23) and claimed the title "apostle" (11:5, 13; 12:11). Paul, however, seems to doubt the authenticity of their confession. He calls them false apostles, deceitful workers, and servants of Satan (11:13–14), and he implies that they are preaching a very different Jesus (11:4).
4. They relished oratorical display (11:5–6) and rhetorical technique (11:12).
5. They took money from the Corinthians (11:7–15, 20; 12:14–15).
6. They boasted excessively (10:12–17; 11:16–12:11) and were abusive in their leadership style (11:20). Interestingly, Paul never attacks their teaching or doctrine but focuses on their arrogant, bombastic style.

Based on what we certainly know about the interlopers of chapters 10–13, it would appear that they were Jewish-Christian evangelists who had adopted the methods and style of the popular Hellenistic sophist-philosophers for their own financial gain, and who severely compromised the gospel in the process. This commentary will proceed on the assumptions of this somewhat minimalist assessment and will attempt to distinguish between the various strands of opposition encountered in this letter on a case-by-case basis.

2 Corinthians 1:1–7

Comfort in Affliction

Big Idea
Paul (and Timothy) greets the believers in Corinth and thanks God for the comfort he provides in the midst of suffering.

Key Themes
- Paul's authority as an apostle comes from his divine commission.
- God comforts the afflicted so that they can, in turn, comfort others.

Understanding the Text

The Text in Content

Paul's opening salutation (1:1–2) follows the basic pattern of letters of this period, which consisted of "X greets Y" and often included a hope for good health or a prayer to the gods (see the sidebar). Paul adopts this formulaic greeting and expands it theologically. Characteristic of all Paul's greetings is an emphasis on the fatherhood of God, the lordship of Christ, and the grace and peace offered to believers. The greeting of 2 Corinthians also highlights Paul's apostolic authority, which was being challenged by some in Corinth.

Paul's introductory blessings and prayers of thanksgiving (1:3–7; see also the comments on 2:14) set the tone for what follows and provide important clues to the main themes of the letter or section they introduce. Important in this opening benediction is *comfort in affliction*, which is echoed throughout chapters 1–7 (see 2:14–16; 4:8–12; 6:2–12; 7:5–16). The reason for the prominence of this theme is not fully revealed until chapter 7, where we learn that Paul experienced great relief and comfort through the good news Titus brought him concerning the Corinthians' response to his strongly worded letter.

Interpretive Insights

1:1 *Paul, an apostle of Christ Jesus by the will of God.* Paul frequently introduces his letters with reference to his apostolic status, though not always (e.g., 1 Thessalonians, Philippians, Philemon). It is likely that its inclusion is intentional and reflects a concern to remind his readers of his apostolic credentials in situations where he faced challenges (Corinth, Galatia) or where he was not personally known (Rome, Colossae). The addition of "by the will of God" (see 1 Cor. 1:1; 2 Tim. 1:1) adds gravity to the assertion by stressing the origin of Paul's apostolate in God's call (see Gal. 1:1).

Timothy our brother. Timothy became Paul's closest co-worker (see Phil. 2:19–20; 2 Tim. 1:1–4) and was well known in Corinth (Acts 18:5; 1 Cor. 4:17). The argument and tone of 2 Corinthians suggest that Paul was the primary personality behind its composition. Timothy is listed as cosender probably because he was present with Paul when the letter was written.

To the church of God in Corinth, together with all his holy people throughout Achaia. Paul addresses the entire community of believers in Corinth—that is, all the individual household gatherings—along with believers in the surrounding communities. We know from Romans 16:1, for example, that a house church existed in nearby Cenchreae, and we can safely assume the presence of other household assemblies in the regions around Corinth. The phrase "church *of God*" denotes possession and is a common expression in Paul's Letters (e.g., 1 Cor. 1:2; 10:32; Gal. 1:13; 1 Thess. 2:14; 1 Tim. 3:5). Paul never uses the phrase "my church," even where he is exerting his divinely granted apostolic authority. The church belongs to God; Paul pictures his role as a servant laboring in his master's field (1 Cor. 3:5–6).

1:2 *Grace and peace to you.* See the sidebar.

1:3 *Praise be to the God and Father of our Lord Jesus Christ.* This strong exclamation is unusual for Paul in an introduction (elsewhere only in Eph. 1:3) and is indicative of the emotional tone undergirding chapters 1–7 (see 2:14; 3:2; 6:11–12; 7:6–14). The correlation of God the Father and Jesus the Messiah (Greek, *christos*) as the single source of grace and peace is characteristic of all Paul's opening salutations, with the exception of Colossians. This linkage implies parity of status and rank.

Grace and Peace

The customary opening greeting in Greek letters of this period included the word *chairein* ("Greetings!") followed by a prayer for the health of the recipients. This example from the second century is typical: "Apollinarius to Taesis, his mother and lady, very many greetings. Before all I pray for your health. I myself am well and make supplication for you before the gods of this place" (*Sel. Pap.* 111). In a clever play on words Paul Christianizes this standard greeting in his letters by exchanging *chairein* with the similar-sounding *charis* ("grace"). The addition of "and peace" echoes the salutation of Hebrew and Aramaic letters (*shalom*, "peace"). The combination likely represents an intentional coalescence of Hellenistic and Jewish literary conventions within a Christian theological framework.

the Father of compassion and the God of all comfort. Paul describes God in terms consistent with his experience of God: compassionate and comforting. In prayers and blessings of this nature the descriptive clauses (1:3–4) provide the basis for the exclamation of praise (1:3; cf. 2:14). Paul praises God (1:3) *because of* God's compassion (1:3) and comfort (1:4). Comfort in distress is an important theme in chapters 1–7, with the Greek vocabulary of "comfort" (verb and noun) occurring more frequently in 2 Corinthians than anywhere else in the New Testament. The words are particularly concentrated in 1:3–7 (ten occurrences) and in 7:4–13 (seven occurrences). The connection between these two passages is clear, which also accounts for the strong emotional tenor of these chapters: Paul was greatly relieved by the news he received from Titus concerning the Corinthians' reception of his strongly worded letter (see 1:23–2:11). The apostle is quite open about the matter: "But God, who comforts the downcast, comforted us by the coming of Titus. . . . He told us about your longing for me, your deep sorrow, your ardent concern for me" (7:6–7). Moreover, the theme of comfort in affliction is present even where the precise vocabulary is not (see 1:8–10; 2:13–15; 4:7–18; 5:1–8; 6:3–10).

1:4 *who comforts us in all our troubles, so that we can comfort those in any trouble.* "So that" may express either purpose or result, or it may hover somewhere in between. Be that as it may, Paul expects that receiving God's grace in the form of comfort should transform us into people who comfort others. In describing God as the God who comforts, Paul is drawing from a deep reservoir of Old Testament poetry and hymnody that celebrates God as the one who comforts his people (e.g., Isa. 40:1; 51:12; 66:13; Pss. 23:4; 119:50). The first-person plural pronouns in 1:5–6 ("we," "our") are probably limited to Paul and his associates in ministry; in 1:6 the readers are specifically brought into the equation ("you," "your"). However, it seems likely that Paul intends his readers to understand that he is articulating a broader principle that applies to them as well: comfort begets comfort.

1:5 *For just as we share abundantly in the sufferings of Christ, so also our comfort abounds through Christ.* Verses 5 and 6 clarify verse 4 by explaining how hardship results in comfort. The crucial element of this explanation is that Paul reckons his suffering as "the sufferings of Christ." Paul perceives that his own suffering as Christ's representative replicates and continues the suffering of Christ (cf. Phil. 3:10; Col. 1:24). But as suffering overflows into the Christian's life, so too does God's comfort through Christ. Paul is patiently instructing the Corinthians on the paradoxical divine calculus of the Christian life, in which suffering produces comfort, affliction produces glory (2 Cor. 4:17; Rom. 8:17), and death produces life (2 Cor. 4:10–12).

1:6 *If we are distressed, it is for your comfort and salvation; if we are comforted, it is for your comfort.* Paul expands the principle of 1:4–5 and continues the christological paradigm that came to the foreground in 1:5: as Christ's life was characterized by suffering for the benefit of others, so Paul's suffering in the service of Christ is also endured for the benefit of others. Paul will repeatedly emphasize to the Corinthians that his labor and hardship are for the purpose of advancing the gospel and strengthening believers (4:11–12, 13–15; 6:3–10; 11:7–9, 23–29; 12:14–15), most poignantly in 12:15: "I will most gladly spend and be spent for your souls" (ESV). It is puzzling that Paul says that his distress results in their "salvation." He may mean that his proclamation of Christ entails suffering but ultimately brings some to saving faith. Alternatively, "salvation" may be used here in the sense of "preservation" or "safe-keeping," the most common meaning of this word outside the New Testament, and occasionally found within the New Testament (Luke 1:71; Acts 7:25; 27:34; Heb. 11:7). The context favors the latter interpretation; the phrase "comfort and salvation" should probably be understood as a hendiadys: "deepest comfort."

the same sufferings we suffer. It is not likely that Paul intends to say that the Corinthians were experiencing precisely the same hardships that he was enduring. There are no other indications of suffering or persecution in Corinth, and some passages imply the opposite (1 Cor. 4:8–10). Rather, Paul is affirming that whatever difficulties the Corinthians may encounter because of their faith are, like his own, "the sufferings of Christ" (see 2 Cor. 1:5).

1:7 *And our hope for you is firm, because we know that just as you share in our sufferings, so also you share in our comfort.* In 1:7 Paul draws a conclusion from 1:3–6, which amounts to a hopeful affirmation of the Corinthians' spiritual state. Although Paul has some difficult issues to address in this letter, he prepares the ground for these admonitions by expressing his confidence that the Corinthians will join with him in suffering for the gospel; his strategy was similar in 1 Corinthians (see 1:4–9). Much of these early chapters consists of Paul building rapport with the Corinthians so that his later requests (chaps. 8–9) and reprimands (chaps. 10–13) will be heard more readily.

Theological Insights

"Comfort, comfort my people, says your God" (Isa. 40:1)—these words of the prophet Isaiah, while spoken to a different people in different circumstances, could appropriately serve as the heading for Paul's opening blessing in 2 Corinthians 1:3–7. When Paul praises "the God of all comfort" (1:3), he is echoing and applying the theological perspective of the Hebrew Bible, particularly the book of Isaiah, where God reveals, "I, even I, am he who comforts you" (51:12). The fundamental theological insight of this passage is that God hears and responds to the suffering of his people and works through his suffering children to allow them to embody his comfort to others. This biblical motif is brought to a climax in Revelation 21 when the voice from the throne proclaims, "Look! God's dwelling place is now among the people. . . . They will be his people, and God himself will be with them and be their God. 'He will wipe every tear from their eyes'" (21:3–4).

Teaching the Text

1. *God as the source of comfort.* Paul's candid reflection on the theme of comfort in this passage exposes the primary emotional element undergirding these opening chapters: a feeling of deep relief and comfort concerning the Corinthians' response to his strongly worded letter (see 7:6–7). In teaching this text, it would be important to emphasize precisely what Paul does as he begins: God is the ultimate source of the comfort Paul is experiencing, and the comfort we experience (1:3–4). This point is all the more striking when we understand that the immediate source of Paul's relief was the news from Titus about the Corinthians' response. Paul, however, sees beyond the intermediate agent who brought the news, to the ultimate agent responsible for the change of heart on the part of the Corinthians, God himself.

2. *Blessings to bless others.* Another point to emphasize in teaching this passage is that God's blessings, like the comfort he provides, are not ends in themselves but are a means by which we can bless and comfort others (1:4). God's blessings entail an obligation. The comfort or blessing that God gives us is intended to be passed on to others, so that the larger community becomes the recipient of the blessings graciously bestowed on an individual: "If we [Paul and his associates] are comforted, it is for your [the Corinthians'] comfort" (1:6).

3. *Spiritual reciprocity.* Finally, the principle of spiritual reciprocity is beautifully communicated through Paul's deliberations on the relationship between suffering, comfort, and character formation. To share in Christ's suffering is to share also in Christ's comfort (1:5, 7). Because the Christian life is lived in community, the comfort of one member benefits others (1:6b), and even the pain experienced by one segment of the body can lead to growth in another segment of the body (1:6a). The ultimate outcome of this spiritual mutuality is the growth of the community in endurance, as they suffer together and translate that suffering into mutual comfort (1:7).

Illustrating the Text

Suffering produces endurance and growth.

Personal Testimony: Consider sharing an excerpt from your life or having a member of your congregation tell of a time when suffering was turned into growth and hardship into triumph.

Sometimes it is helpful to admit that everything is not OK.

Television: ***Parenthood.*** A 2012 episode of the television show *Parenthood*, "Everything Is Not Okay," focused on the character Kristina Braverman, who was diagnosed with breast cancer. The gravity of Kristina's cancer is contrasted with her husband's cheery optimism. His attitude only makes her feel worse. The episode concludes with Kristina confronting Adam, her husband: "I know you're trying to make everything OK for me. You always have, our whole lives. And I love you so much for that. But you have to let me be scared today. And I just want you to hear it. I don't want you to tell me to think positive or that everything is gonna be great. 'Cause right now I'm not sure that it's going to be, and I just want to be able to feel scared. That's just what I need from you right now."[1]

The blessings that God gives us are meant to be passed on to others.

Movie: ***Pay It Forward.*** The main idea of 1:4, that we experience comfort so that we can, in turn, comfort others, seems to be very close to the theme of the film *Pay It Forward* (2000). In this film, eleven-year-old Trevor McKinney devises a plan to change the world for the better by doing a good deed for another person, who is then asked to do a good deed for another person, to pay it "forward" rather than pay it back. This captures one element of this passage, that the comfort or blessing we receive should be translated into comfort or blessing to others.

2 Corinthians 1:8–11

Learning to Trust

Big Idea
God uses hardships to teach us to rely on him, not ourselves.

Key Themes
- God's purpose in leading us through hardship is to mature us and draw us closer to him.
- God's deliverance is experienced as believers intercede and should result in thanksgiving by God's people.

Understanding the Text

The Text in Content

Having praised the God "who comforts us in all our trouble" (1:4), Paul now provides a concrete example of God's consolation and rescue in a particularly dire situation. This material illustrates the principle articulated in the previous section (1:3–7), that God comforts the afflicted, while also providing corroboration for the following argument (1:12–22), that Paul has conducted himself with complete integrity and so the Corinthians can have confidence ("boast," 1:14) in him. This passage presents the first of several important hardship catalogs in 2 Corinthians (see 4:7–11; 6:3–10; 11:23–33), which are aimed at demonstrating Paul's character as a servant of Christ.

Interpretive Insights

1:8 *We do not want you to be uninformed.* The conjunction "for" (untranslated by the NIV; cf. ESV) connects this passage to the previous material as an elaboration. The generic truth of 1:3–7 is now expressed in a specific example of God's comforting provision: God rescued Paul from peril in Asia. The disclosure formula ("We do not want you to be uninformed") might indicate that this was new information, as in Romans 1:13 and 11:25, where the identical expression is found. On the other hand, since Paul does not actually relate the details of the situation, it could be that he is placing this event—of which they may have some knowledge—in proper perspective. Paul's concern is not to focus attention on the particulars of this harrowing experience but to underscore the greatness of God's rescue and, perhaps more important, God's providence and purpose in such hardships (2 Cor. 1:9).

the troubles we experienced in the province of Asia. As a glance at Paul's later hardship catalogs will reveal (esp. 11:23–33), there is a lot about Paul's biography and travels that we do not know. The Greek word translated "troubles" by the NIV is singular, indicating Paul has a particular incident in mind. There have been numerous attempts to identify this episode, though none can marshal decisive evidence in its favor. Some have argued that Paul refers to the psychological distress that a ruptured relationship with the Corinthians would have caused. This would fit with Paul's description of this trauma as experienced internally (literally, "in ourselves," 1:9), and also with his later statement in 7:3 that the Corinthians "have such a place in our hearts that we would live or die with you" (cf. 1 Thess. 3:8). Yet, Paul's description of a "sentence of death" (2 Cor. 1:9) does not sound like a situation of emotional distress, nor does this proposal explain why Paul mentions his location (Asia) during this season of duress. Another suggestion is that Paul is referring to a physical illness, as may be the case with the "thorn in my flesh" of 12:7. This interpretation, however, fails to account for Paul's use of the first-person *plural* ("we," "our," "us"). Most scholars tend to prefer

The Roman province of Asia was situated between the Aegean Sea to the west and Galatia to the east, with Pontus and Bithynia on its northern border. Ephesus was its principal city and became a major center of Paul's missionary work.

2 Corinthians 1:8–11

the final option, which relates this hardship to some kind of severe persecution, be it imprisonment or mob violence, like that described as occurring in Ephesus in Acts 18.[1] There is ample evidence from Acts and Paul's Letters that incarceration and mob violence were regular occurrences during Paul's missionary endeavors, and this final proposal fits well with the language Paul employs to describe this incident.

1:9 *we felt we had received the sentence of death.* Paul depicts this harrowing event as "great pressure, far beyond our ability to endure," so that he "despaired [even] of life itself" (1:8). Paul is clearly underscoring the urgency of the situation and its potentially calamitous outcome, which allows God's deliverance to stand out in even bolder relief. The "sentence of death" may refer to an actual judicial verdict, or its use here may be metaphorical, along the lines of "fighting wild beasts" (1 Cor. 15:32) or "demolishing strongholds" (2 Cor. 10:4). The fact that Paul emphasizes the subjective side of this experience ("in ourselves," untranslated by the NIV; cf. KJV, LEB) might indicate that he has in mind not an official sentence from a magistrate but a deep sense of impending doom. In 11:23 Paul says that he has been "exposed to death again and again," and then he proceeds to list a number of traumatic events that he regularly endured (beatings, shipwrecks, bandits, etc.), any of which could, conceivably, provide the background for the peril described here. Paul's lack of concern with the historical particulars indicates that his primary intent is to focus attention on God's purpose in this hardship (1:9), his own strengthened confidence in God's provision (1:10), and the importance of faithful intercession by fellow believers (1:11).

But this happened that we might not rely on ourselves but on God. Paul now articulates what he understands as God's purpose in this trial, to teach him to abandon confidence in himself and to trust wholly in God. Paul recognizes that this experience of severe distress contained an important life lesson for him: to bring him to the end of himself (see "Theological Insights," below). Paul expresses this verbal idea with a construction (a perfect periphrastic) that lays stress on the continuing effects of this experience. Learning to abandon self and rely on God is a lesson Paul carried with him as he ministered to others (see 2:16b; 3:5).

God, who raises the dead. Paul describes God by using a phrase drawn from Jewish synagogal liturgy of this era, "the God who raises the dead." The phrase occurs, for example, in the Jewish prayer the Eighteen Benedictions, where its function was polemical, opposing groups like the Sadducees who denied the future bodily resurrection. Paul employs it here in a very different sense, to describe God's help in a situation that, from a human vantage point, was utterly hopeless. He uses the idea similarly in his portrayal of Abraham, whose "body was as good as dead," yet who believed "against all hope" in "the God who gives life to the dead" that he would have an heir (Rom. 4:17–21). Life from death is the supreme example of God's power, and this phrase encapsulates for Paul God's ability to rescue when all human endeavor would be futile, be it forming life in the "dead womb" of Sarah or granting a reprieve from a "sentence of death" in Asia.

1:10 *He has delivered us from such a deadly peril, and he will deliver us again. On him we have set our hope.* Paul summarizes the main point of verses 8 and 9 (God *has delivered* us) and draws two conclusions from God's saving action on his behalf: (1) God will continue to rescue and save, and (2) we can set our hope in this God. Paul's confidence in God's faithfulness is a direct result of seeing it at work in his life.

1:11 *as you help us by your prayers.* Paul underscores the link between the deliverance God brings and the intercession God's people offer. The apostle understood that God, in his sovereignty, allows his people to participate in his work in the world through prayer. Paul both sought prayer from his congregations (Rom. 15:30; Phil. 1:9; Col. 4:3) and offered prayer on their behalf. Most of Paul's Letters either begin with a prayer or reference his "unceasing" prayer for his spiritual children.

Then many will give thanks on our behalf for the gracious favor granted us. The appropriate response to divine intervention is thanksgiving. The Greek word translated "gracious favor" is *charisma*, which in Paul's Letters has the connotation of a divinely bestowed favor or ability. Here, this divinely bestowed favor has come in the form of a reprieve from the "sentence of death," which was God's gracious yes in response to the prayers of his children.

Theological Insights

One result of Paul's painful trial in Asia was that it helped him see more clearly the importance of placing his hope in God (1:10). For the apostle Paul, *hope* was one of the cardinal virtues of the Christian life (1 Thess. 1:3; 5:8; 1 Cor. 13:13), and Paul's Letters contain more references to hope than the rest of the New Testament combined. In fact, in Paul's view, hope is what distinguishes believers from unbelievers (1 Thess. 4:13; Eph. 2:12). "Hope" in Paul's Letters generally has a future, eschatological orientation: inheriting the glory of God (Rom. 5:1–3; Col. 1:27), the redemption of our bodies (Rom. 8:23–24), final salvation (1 Thess. 5:8; Titus 1:1–2), and so on. In a few instances, however, "hope" refers to confidence in God's provision or protection in this life: Romans 4:18–21; 1 Timothy 5:5 (and context); and here in 2 Corinthians 1:10. In declaring his hope in the God who rescues from adversity, Paul echoes, in particular, the vibrant testimony of the psalmists who exhorted the people of Israel to place their hope in the God who delivers from hostile foes (Pss. 42:9–11; 43:1–5; 62:3–5; 69:6; 71:4–5; 119:114–16;

etc.). Paul, like the psalmists, hopes in a God who rescues not only from final destruction but also from present calamity.

Teaching the Text

In this passage Paul provides a specific example of the message of 1:3–7, that when the "sufferings of Christ" overflow into our lives, so too does God's comfort. Paul's focus is not on the hardship itself but on God's purpose in this hardship, Paul's renewed confidence in God, and, to a lesser extent, the importance of intercession as the means through which God's saving power is actualized. This provides a helpful teaching rubric for this important opening theme.

1. *God's purpose in hardship.* Perhaps the most important truth this text reminds us of is that God has a purpose in allowing his children to face hardship, even the most severe, life-threatening kind. This truth is echoed throughout Scripture and biblical history, although sometimes, as in the case of Job, God's purposes may remain hidden. The lesson that Paul learned through this hardship he teaches explicitly in other letters, Romans in particular. In Romans 5:3–4 Paul argues that suffering produces perseverance and character, which lead to hope. In Romans 8:28–38 Paul reasons that God works for our good in all things and that neither trouble nor hardship nor persecution nor nakedness nor danger nor the sword is able to separate us from God's love. This is a truth Paul has learned through experience (see also James 1:2–3, 12; 1 Pet. 1:6–7).

2. *The outcome of this hardship.* Paul describes two results of the painful experience in Asia. The first is that he has learned to rely more fully on God rather than on himself (1:9), and the second is that his confidence and hope in God's deliverance have been bolstered (1:10). It may sound surprising to us that the venerated apostle to the gentiles, who had seen the risen Christ on the Damascus road, who was caught up to paradise and beheld wonders beyond words, and whose proclamation of the gospel was accompanied by signs and mighty powers (Acts 19:11; Rom. 15:16; 2 Cor. 12:12), would need to learn to rely on God and not on himself, but that is precisely what Paul says. As Jesus was made perfect through suffering (Heb. 2:10), so too are his followers.

3. *Prayer as the divinely ordained means of God's deliverance.* Paul qualifies his confident hope that God will continue to deliver him and his coworkers in the gospel (1:10) with the important acknowledgment that God's deliverance comes in response to the prayers of God's people. Paul's firm conviction, evidenced throughout his letters, is that prayer moves God and changes the world.

Illustrating the Text

We should not be surprised by suffering and struggles.

Story: A New York City–based Korean pastor was arrested along with Chinese church planters when he was preaching with them in one of China's largest cities. Understandably scared and uncertain of what the Chinese officials might do to him, he was shocked and humbled by the attitude of the young pastors arrested with him. They had an almost cavalier attitude about their arrest. Rather matter-of-factly they told him, "Of course we are ready to be imprisoned, and even die."[2]

Prayer changes things; don't stop praying.

News: Kayaker Jon Stockton was out in the ocean off the coast of Hawaii testing some new equipment when a storm hit. His kayak repeatedly capsized, and the persistent winds blew him out to sea. When he woke up after surviving the storm, he found himself about thirty-five miles out to sea. He called for help on his cell phone, which then died. Stockton was discouraged to see that rescue planes were circling on the horizon but couldn't see his small craft. In his discouragement, he pulled out a Gideon Bible and spent his time praying. Stockton was finally rescued after about five days adrift. He attributes his rescue to God, who answered his prayers.[3]

2 Corinthians 1:12–14

Apostolic Integrity

Big Idea
Paul and his co-workers have acted with complete integrity toward the Corinthians and therefore should be regarded with grateful esteem.

Key Themes
- Paul has always dealt with the Corinthians with the utmost sincerity, honesty, and authenticity.
- Paul's desire is to boast in the Corinthians in the day of the Lord, and that they may boast in him.

Understanding the Text

The Text in Context

These three verses open the body of the letter and encapsulate the argument of 2 Corinthians, much the way that Romans 1:16–17 summarizes the message of that letter.[1] One of the central issues Paul needs to confront is that some in Corinth have come to question his integrity and even doubt his apostolic credentials. Paul will be defending himself on several fronts in this letter: his change of itinerary (1:15–2:4), his suffering as an apostle (2:12–7:16), his handling of the collection (12:11–18), his decision to support himself through manual labor (11:7–15), and his apostolic status (chaps. 10–13). While directly introducing Paul's defense of his altered travel plans (1:15–2:4), these verses also furnish the operative thesis of the entire letter: Paul and his companions have acted with godly integrity in all their dealings with the Corinthians.

Interpretive Insights

1:12 *Now this is our boast.* As 1:15 clarifies, Paul's "boast" in this context refers primarily to his *confidence* before God of his conduct (cf. NLT, NASB). In 7:4 "boasting" and "confidence" are also paired synonymously (see LEB, NASB). The central claims of this verse are reiterated in 4:2; 5:11–12; and 7:2–4, underscoring the thematic character of this opening paragraph.

Our conscience testifies. In Paul's Letters, the "conscience" (*syneidēsis*) most commonly refers to the inner moral faculty that evaluates actions, thoughts, and feelings to determine if they conform to one's highest ethical standards. The conscience is not a divine voice, as it can err through incorrect knowledge (1 Cor. 8:7–10; 10:27–29). Paul affirms that even his own conscience is subject to God's scrutiny (1 Cor. 4:1–4). Yet the testimony of one's conscience is important for Paul (Rom. 2:15; 2 Cor. 4:2; 1 Tim. 1:5; Acts 24:16), and Paul's claim here is that his conduct toward the Corinthians is vindicated at the inner tribunal of his conscience.

in the world, and especially in our relations with you. Paul distinguishes two spheres of his life and interactions that, taken together, compose the totality of his existence. "In the world" may have in view unbelievers in particular (1 Cor. 1:21), or it may be shorthand for the mundane realities of his daily life among all people in all situations. The latter seems preferable, making "our relations with you" a subset of this larger category. In insisting that his conduct has been upright "especially" among the Corinthians, Paul does not mean than he has been more careful to operate with integrity among his churches than elsewhere, but he means that his integrity should be especially apparent to those in whom he has invested so much time. Included in this affirmation is the assurance that there is no bifurcation in his conduct, as if Paul wears a ministerial mask when he is on duty and takes it off when he is traveling between cities. In this context, the use of the first-person plural should probably be taken to refer primarily to Paul himself, without excluding that others may be in mind as well. These verses introduce Paul's defense of his change of plans (1:15–2:4), where the first-person singular dominates, and it is clear that it is Paul himself who is being accused of fickle behavior.

with integrity and godly sincerity. The NIV's "integrity" translates the Greek word *haplotēs*, which in this context refers more precisely to the simplicity of unmixed intentions (cf. 11:3; Eph. 6:5; Col. 3:22). Paul understands that accusations have been circulating in Corinth concerning his true intentions, and he is also aware that those sponsoring the discontent are driven by selfish motives (2:17; 4:2; 11:19). These two qualities, integrity and sincerity, summarize Paul's character and interactions with the Corinthians, and the apostle will reinforce these in specific contexts and with respect to specific allegations as the argument develops. The phrase "godly sincerity" may also be rendered "sincerity coming from God" (cf. NIV 1984; NLT).

relying not on worldly wisdom but on God's grace. The charge that Paul operates according to "worldly" wisdom is echoed again in 1:17; 5:16; and 10:2. Paul has in mind human judgments and plans that have a semblance of wisdom but from God's perspective are foolish. First Corinthians 1–4 contains extensive criticism of this worldly wisdom, particularly 1:20; 2:5–6, 13; and 3:19. In contrasting "worldly wisdom" with "God's grace," Paul expresses,

Paul: The Grace-Full Apostle

If word statistics are anything to go by, the apostle Paul was certainly the most grace-filled writer of the New Testament. Nearly two-thirds of the occurrences of the word "grace" (*charis*) in the New Testament are found in his letters (100 uses by Paul out of 155 occurrences). Second Corinthians, like all of Paul's Letters, begins and ends with "grace" (1:2; 13:14), and this can be taken as emblematic of Paul's entire apostolate. His calling was the result of God's grace (Rom. 1:5; Gal. 1:3), his labor was the product of God's grace (1 Cor. 3:10; 15:10), and his life was for the praise of God's grace (Eph. 1:6). The Corinthians too are recipients of God's grace (1 Cor. 1:4; 2 Cor. 9:14), and one could reasonably epitomize Paul's primary concern in this letter precisely as a matter of "grace": "As God's co-workers we urge you not to receive God's grace in vain" (2 Cor. 6:1). This context represents the most theologically weighty usage of Paul's "grace" vocabulary, which is more fully explained in Romans, Galatians, and Ephesians: God's unmerited favor bestowed on undeserving recipients. Paul's final wish-prayer for the Corinthians is that the grace of Christ, the love of God, and the fellowship of the Spirit continue working among them (13:14), and the contents of this letter represent the apostle's strenuous effort to help bring that about.

as elsewhere, the view that the totality of his life is the outworking of God's grace (Rom. 15:15; 1 Cor. 3:10; 15:10).

1:13 *For we do not write you anything you cannot read or understand.* Drawing an explicit corollary from 1:12 ("for"), Paul offers his written communication as a concrete example of his "integrity and godly sincerity" (1:12). In 1 Corinthians 2:1–5 Paul contrasts his spoken proclamation with worldly wisdom, and here he applies the same principle to his letters. Later in this letter (2 Cor. 10:10) we learn that some in Corinth regard Paul's letters to be "weighty and forceful," in contrast to his physical appearance and his speech (cf. 5:12). Paul also relates that some in Corinth are skeptical of his claim to be a divine spokesman (13:3). Paul counters that his preaching and instruction are not tainted by guile (4:2) or self-interest (2:17; 4:5) but are offered in sincerity (1:12; 2:17; 4:2; 6:11). Writing much later, the apostle Peter says that Paul's "letters contain some things that are hard to understand, which ignorant and unstable people distort" (2 Pet. 3:16); it is possible that Paul alludes here to some in Corinth who are intentionally distorting his letters.

1:14 *as you have understood us in part, you will come to understand fully.* In addition to confronting those who actively oppose him, Paul must also clarify certain misunderstandings. Verse 13 indicates that Paul's written communications have caused some confusion (see also 1 Cor. 5:9–11), and the most pressing clarifications relate to his evolving travel plans (2 Cor. 1:12–2:4) and his instructions concerning the sinning brother (2:5–11). The idea of incomplete knowledge flowering into full knowledge in the eschaton ("the day of the Lord Jesus") echoes 1 Corinthians 13:9–12.

you can boast of us just as we will boast of you in the day of the Lord Jesus. (See "Theological Insights" and "Teaching the Text," below.)

Theological Insights

"The day of the Lord" was a familiar theme among Israel's prophets, where it most commonly denoted a dark and ominous day of divine judgment (Isa. 2:12–21; Amos 5:18–20; Zech. 14:1–2) that would lead to Israel's vindication and renewal (Amos 9:11–15; Zech. 14:6–21). In 1:14 Paul reveals a theological and salvation-historical perspective of considerable consequence: the Lord of Israel's prophetic traditions is equated with "the [our] Lord Jesus" (the oldest and most reliable manuscripts read "our Lord Jesus"). This theological reorientation is foundational for Paul's mission (Gal. 1:15) and undergirds his theological discourse throughout his letters. It also contributes to a salvation-historical perspective that allows Paul to conclude that "no matter how many promises God has made, they are 'Yes' in Christ" (2 Cor. 1:20).

Teaching the Text

This introductory segment highlights at least three principles that deserve careful attention in teaching this passage: (1) the importance of a clear conscience, (2) the priority of grace, and (3) the proper place of boasting.

1. *The importance of a clear conscience.* A properly functioning conscience plays a vital role in the Christian life and in Paul's own moral deliberations. More than once the apostle appeals to the inner witness of his conscience as evidence of his trustworthiness (Rom. 9:1; 1 Cor. 4:4; 2 Cor. 1:12; 2 Tim. 1:3). A "good conscience" is essential for effective ministry (1 Tim. 1:5). The role of the conscience is to accuse or approve behavior (Rom. 2:15) with the ideal being the harmonious correspondence of action and belief, otherwise known as *integrity.*

2. *The priority of grace.* In 1:12 Paul contrast two manners of conduct, one relying on "worldly wisdom" and the other trusting in "God's grace." In dealing with the Corinthians, Paul must have been greatly tempted to take matters into his own hands and operate according to the wisdom of this age. Certainly many would have advised the apostle to continue his fruitful ministry in Troas rather than to cut it short in order to travel to Corinth to deal with this unruly and disobedient flock (see 2:12–13). Choosing to rely on God's grace, as opposed to worldly wisdom, reflects Paul's determination to do what is right rather than what is easy or expedient, knowing that God always provides the resources and stamina to those who entrust their path

to him. God's gracious provision, and his provision of grace, will never be depleted by his faithful servants.

3. *The proper place of boasting.* In 1 Corinthians Paul chides the Corinthians for "boasting about human leaders" (3:21) and taking pride in one man over another (4:6), yet here he affirms that some measure of pride in others can be appropriate, in certain circumstances. One of the chief differences between the boasting that is going on in 1 Corinthians and what Paul describes here is that the former issues from a spirit of rivalry and is causing dissension (1 Cor. 3:3–4). In Galatians Paul speaks approvingly of individuals taking pride in themselves "without comparing themselves to someone else" (6:4), and again it is carnal comparison that seems to be the root problem. The "boasting" that Paul speaks of in 2 Corinthians 1:14 refers to the appropriate affirmation that one believer expresses toward another regarding their faithful service.

Illustrating the Text

Some pride is good and healthy.

Quote: **C. S. Lewis.** Pride is the chief of the seven deadly sins and the original sin. Lewis says it well: "The essential vice, the utmost evil, is Pride. Unchastity, anger, greed, drunkenness, and all that, are mere flea bites in comparison."[2] Although we should diligently guard our lives against pride, there is also a form of pride that is healthy. Consider the following examples: The Marine motto: "The Few, the Proud, the Marines." The pride of a father with his newborn daughter. The pride of a nurse awarded their "pin" as they complete their RN degree.

There is a difference between proper and improper pride.

Story: A pastor told the story of a young lady in his congregation with a beautiful voice. One Sunday, after she sang a solo in church, the pastor remarked to her parents, "You must be so proud of her!" The parents were deeply offended at the suggestion that they would be "proud" of anything, even their own daughter. They did not understand the distinction between proper and improper pride.

Naked truth

Story: Erwin McManus tells of an interaction with his nine-year-old nephew. "After every sentence he kept saying *honest*, as if he felt a need to convince us." So McManus asked him, "Why do you keep saying *honest*?" His nephew replied, "It's just that I really want you to believe me. . . . Or maybe it's because of all the lies I've told all my life."[3] Developing a conscience that clearly distinguishes truth from lies is a nonnegotiable trait for those who follow Jesus. Encourage listeners to pay attention to what they say. Are they trying to convince people they are honest? If so, encourage them to live with integrity and honesty over time, and they won't have to try so hard to convince others.

2 Corinthians 1:15–2:4

Changing Plans, a Faithful God

Big Idea
Paul's decision to delay his promised visit was not from indecisiveness or impure motives but was made in the best interests of the Corinthians and is evidence of his, and God's, faithfulness toward them.

Key Themes
- Paul's change in his itinerary is evidence not of his fickleness but of his faithfulness.
- Paul's commitment to his spiritual children mirrors God's own faithfulness to his covenant promises.
- God proves his faithfulness through the sealing of the Spirit.
- Paul altered his travel plans out of concern for the Corinthians, not apathy toward them.

Understanding the Text

The Text in Context

Paul now takes up a very pressing matter of concern among the Corinthians, his changing travel plans. This has been interpreted by some in Corinth as evidence of Paul's lack of concern for them, or worse, his immature and "worldly" (1:17) perspective. Paul reassures them of both his and God's unwavering commitment to their welfare, and he explains that the true reason for his decision to change his plans was to spare them another painful visit. What the Corinthians have perceived as evidence of Paul's lack of concern for them is actually proof of his love for them.

Historical and Cultural Background

The historical circumstances that led to Paul's change of travel plans cannot be determined with absolute certainty, but the following sketch represents a plausible reconstruction of the events. In 1 Corinthians 16, written from Ephesus, Paul tells the Corinthians that he plans to journey through

Macedonia to Corinth, where he hopes to have a longer stay (16:5–6). This plan was abandoned, probably after Timothy returned to Ephesus from Corinth (1 Cor. 4:17; 16:10), reporting that intruders who were causing problems had arrived in Corinth. Paul decided he needed to return sooner than initially planned, and so he headed directly to Corinth from Ephesus. This visit, which Paul calls "painful" (2 Cor. 2:1), was unsuccessful, and Paul's authority and integrity were attacked (2:5–7). Upon leaving, Paul indicated that he would return to Corinth on his way to Macedonia and then head back to Corinth after strengthening the Macedonian believers. Paul later reconsidered this plan, reasoning that an early return would be too painful for everybody (1:23). Instead, he wrote a strongly worded letter through Titus (2:4), which had the desired effect of prompting repentance in the hearts of the Corinthians (2:6; 7:5–9). When Titus returned to Paul in Macedonia, he informed the apostle of the Corinthians' genuine contrition but also reported a new threat: rival missionaries had arrived in Corinth and were undermining Paul's message and ministry. This prompted Paul to send this letter ahead of him to Corinth in order to commend the Corinthians for the action against the offender while also addressing the claims of the rival missionaries (chaps. 10–13).

Interpretive Insights

1:15 *Because I was confident of this, I wanted to visit you first so that you might benefit twice.* Paul moves from the first-person plural ("we," 1:12–14), to the first-person singular ("I"), probably as a way of taking full responsibility for this matter. He assures the Corinthians that they have been at the center of his plans and concerns: "through you . . . to you . . . from you" (1:16; cf. LEB).[1] The NIV's "benefit twice" can be more literally rendered "a second grace," and employs the same term Paul used in 1:12 in referring to "God's grace." This expression reveals the extent to which Paul sees his ministry as the product of God's grace and himself as an instrument of that grace (cf. Rom. 1:11).

1:17 *Was I fickle . . . ? Or do I make my plans in a worldly manner . . . ?* The force of the accusation of fickleness may have been fueled by popular Stoicism, which was the most fashionable philosophy of Paul's day and attracted many followers and admirers. Arius Didymus (*Epit.* 11m), summarizing the Stoic teaching on the virtuous man, writes, "Nor do [the Stoics] assume that a man with good sense changes his mind, for changing one's mind belongs to false assent, on the grounds of erring through haste. Nor does he change his mind in any way, nor alter his opinion, nor is he confused." Allegations that Paul was operating in a worldly (or "fleshly") manner are confronted and dismissed by Paul several times in this letter (5:16; 10:2–3).

1:18–20 *our message to you is not "Yes" and "No." . . . no matter how many promises God has made, they are "Yes" in Christ.* Paul's strategy of defense against the charge of worldly duplicity and vacillation is not to reassure the Corinthians of his own trustworthiness but to remind them of God's. Paul aligns his mission in Corinth with God's mission in the world in order to imply certain correlations. Christ represents God's yes to his promises in that Christ is proof of God's faithfulness to his covenant with Abraham and Israel. As God was working to fulfill his promises to Israel in spite of their rebellion and in spite of what looked like his rejection of his promises, so too his apostle is committed to fulfilling his appointed task in Corinth in spite of what looks like his abandonment of this church. Hafemann aptly summarizes these verses by observing, "Because Paul's intention remained the same, his plans changed!"[2]

so through him the "Amen" is spoken by us. "Amen" is a Hebrew loan word meaning "firm, steady, faithful." In Paul's Letters it frequently occurs at the end of a doxology as a solemn affirmation of the theological pronouncement (e.g., Rom. 1:25; 11:36). The expression found a place in early Christian worship as a response to prayers and thanksgivings offered during worship (1 Cor. 14:16), much the way it functions in many churches today. Paul's "amen" in the present context refers not only to his verbal assent but to his life, ministry, and service as an embodied "amen" to God's plan of redemption.

1:21–22 *He anointed us, set his seal of ownership on us, and put his Spirit in our hearts as a deposit, guaranteeing what is to come.* Anointing and sealing are not two separate activities but two different images used to illustrate the decisive event, the gift of the Spirit (see the sidebar). Anointing was an important ritual in Israel's history and involved pouring oil on those consecrated to sacred service—priests, prophets, and kings.[3] The Greek word *arrabōn*, rendered "deposit" by the NIV, is drawn from the world of commerce, where

Roman Seals and the Gift of the Spirit

Seals were widely used in antiquity and performed a variety of functions in commerce and everyday life. On a letter or other written communication the seal acted as a signature ensuring the authenticity of the document. Parcels in transit were sometimes sealed to guarantee the contents had not been disturbed. The seal itself was made of metal or stone, etched with a distinct image, and was pressed into warm wax on the object being sealed. Seals became a work of fine craftsmanship in the Roman era and commonly bore the image of their owner. It is possible that Paul's reference to the believer being "sealed" contains an allusion to the divine image being embossed, so to speak, upon the believer through the Spirit. The Corinthians had already been instructed on being bearers of the divine image (1 Cor. 15:42–49), and Paul will take up the subject again in 2 Corinthians 3:18 and 4:4–6. Philo, Paul's contemporary in Alexandria, makes this same point in relation to God's creation of Adam: "He that was made according to the divine image was like . . . a seal" (*Planting* 18).

it denoted a partial payment in promise of full payment at a later time. The giving of the Spirit is called a "deposit," and the image implies that God has obligated himself to complete the transaction in the future. This same term is used in 5:5, where the future completion is described as mortality being "swallowed up by life" (5:4)—that is, our future bodily redemption at Christ's return (see further the comments on 5:5).

1:23 *I call God as my witness . . . it was in order to spare you that I did not return to Corinth.* Having dismissed the Corinthian interpretation of his actions (1:15–22), Paul now discloses the real reason for not returning as originally planned: to spare all parties a painful and potentially devastating confrontation. Paul invokes an unusually strong oath as a way of impressing upon the Corinthians the truthfulness of his testimony. In addition to the inner witness of his conscience (1:12), Paul now subpoenas God to confirm his account of his actions and motives.

2:1 *another painful visit.* See the comments on 2:5–11.

2:3–4 *I wrote as I did . . . out of great distress and anguish of heart and with many tears.* Paul not only needs to explain his change of travel plans; he also wants to clarify his motives and intentions in dispatching a strongly worded letter, which has not been preserved. He explains that it was not to inflict injury ("not to grieve you") but a demonstration of his love and genuine concern for them. He has earlier warned the Corinthians that he was prepared to come with a rod, although he prefers to come "in love and with a gentle spirit" (1 Cor. 4:21). Paul's decision to delay his visit is indicative of a pastoral heart that takes no pleasure in disciplining wayward children but stands ready to act in their best interest, even if this causes pain (2 Cor. 7:8–10).

Theological Insights

Prominent in discussions of Pauline theology are the contrasts the apostle draws between the old era and the new era, using antitheses such as law versus grace, faith versus works, flesh versus Spirit, Adam versus Christ, and the new covenant versus the old covenant. Yet equally important for understanding Paul's conception of the relationship between the old era and the new era is his *promise-fulfillment* schema. In Romans 15:8 Paul remarks that Christ confirms the promises made to the patriarchs, and here in 2 Corinthians 1:20 Paul broadens this to include "all the promises of God" (ESV). While allowing for an element of hyperbole, we can reasonably infer that Paul has in mind promises like Ezekiel's new heart (2 Cor. 3:3), Isaiah's suffering, sin-bearing servant (Rom. 4:25), Daniel's victorious son of man (1 Thess. 4:17), and of course the promise to Abraham that all the families of the earth would be blessed through him (Rom. 4:12–13). As heirs of these precious promises, believers today can affirm with Paul, "God is faithful" (2 Cor. 1:18).

Teaching the Text

Second Corinthians 1:15–2:4 provides an important opportunity to observe and reflect on Paul's pastoral strategy in handling misunderstandings and conflict in ministry. Broken people ministering to broken people in a broken world means that misconstruals and mix-ups will be par for the course. As we consider Paul's approach in this situation, and how to emphasize this theme in teaching, the following principles emerge.

1. *Guarding personal integrity.* The bedrock of Paul's defense of his actions to the Corinthians is his confidence that he has acted with complete sincerity and integrity (1:12–15). There is no flicker of doubt or pang in his conscience as he explains himself to his friends and detractors in Corinth. A leader who operates from pettiness or self-concern will inevitably expend a great deal of energy concealing their true motives and covering their tracks. Paul's candid exposition of the rationale behind his change of plans is possible only because he is confident that his actions have been entirely honorable. Integrity matters.

2. *Discerning how to confront.* Paul describes a difficult pastoral predicament in this passage. A severe crisis has demanded that Paul exercise his apostolic authority and confront the person(s) opposing him and undermining God's work in Corinth. Yet the apostle recognizes that a personal visit might result in a confrontation that would do more harm than good; the sparks that might fly could easily ignite a devastating conflagration. Ignoring the problem is certainly not an option, so Paul chooses a mediating path: he sends a letter through a trusted intermediary, Titus. This proves to be the better part of wisdom, as cooler heads prevail and Titus's mission is successful (2:5–11; 7:6–13). Discerning how to most effectively handle conflict is the product of experience, prayer, and seeking advice. No doubt Paul has made use of all three in negotiating a path through this dilemma.

3. *Aiming for restoration.* Although members of the Corinthian church have deeply grieved Paul, probably through some kind of personal attack (see the comments on 2:5–11), Paul refuses to be driven by anger or a carnal desire to settle the score: "It was in order to spare you that I did not return to Corinth. Not that we lord it over your faith, but we work with you for your joy" (1:23–24). Paul's purpose is redemptive, not punitive. Paul's strongly worded letter was motivated not by a personal vendetta but by a genuine concern for his wayward children, "to let you know the depth of my love for you" (2:4). Although we do not know the content of the letter, we know it brought about the repentance and restoration that Paul desired (2:5–11). We can be reasonably sure that, however forceful its wording, this letter also conveyed the depth of Paul's affection for his children, and in situations of conflict, this is absolutely crucial.

Illustrating the Text

Character matters.

Quote: **James Stalker.** The great Scottish preacher James Stalker said, "The most important part of the training of the twelve was one which was perhaps at the time little noticed, though it was producing splendid results—the silent and constant influence of character on them. It was this which made them into the men they became."[4] The character of a disciple in every era is the bedrock of strong leadership.

Even good intentions can be misunderstood.

Literature: ***Pride and Prejudice*, by Jane Austen.** In this novel Mr. Darcy illustrates how good intentions can be misunderstood. Because of his prideful demeanor and reserved character, everyone assumes the worst of him. Elizabeth Bennett develops a hatred for him and prejudice against him, even though his intentions are all honorable. But because of his pride and her prejudice, Elizabeth doesn't find out the true nature behind his actions for a long time. When Darcy proposes marriage, Elizabeth responds,

> From the very beginning—from the first moment, I may almost say—of my acquaintance with you, your manners, impressing me with the fullest belief of your arrogance, your conceit, and your selfish disdain of the feelings of others, were such as to form the groundwork of disapprobation on which succeeding events have built so immovable a dislike; and I had not known you a month before I felt that you were the last man in the world whom I could ever be prevailed on to marry.[5]

Eventually Elizabeth discovers that Darcy is in reality very generous, caring, and benevolent. And she does eventually accept his proposal of marriage, but only after a radical reappraisal of her initial impressions.

2 Corinthians 2:5–11

Forgiveness and Restoration

Big Idea

Discipline from the Christian community must be followed by forgiveness and love from the community, lest grief overwhelm the erring brother or sister and Satan exploit the situation for his purposes.

Key Themes

- It is the responsibility of the Christian community to discipline believers who sin.
- Forgiveness and a reaffirmation of love for the penitent brother or sister are crucial for full reconciliation.
- The sins of individual members affect the entire community.
- Satan is actively scheming against God's people and God's purposes in this world.

Understanding the Text

The Text in Context

Having explained his rationale for the strongly worded letter (2:3–4), Paul now turns to deal with the positive results of that letter—namely, the action taken by the community against the offending brother. Paul also sheds a little more light on why he refers to his previous visit as "painful" (2:1). He had experienced personal opposition from someone within the church in Corinth, and this confrontation was severe enough that Paul thought it wise to delay his promised return (1:15–24). This present section should be read in conjunction with 7:5–16, where Paul comments more extensively on the community's zeal to set the matter right.

Interpretive Insights

2:5 *If anyone has caused grief, he has not so much grieved me as he has grieved all of you.* Although the details of the offense and the offender remain obscure (see the sidebar), Paul's approach to the resolution of the difficulty

The Offense and the Sinner in 2:5–11 and 7:5–16

In chapters 2 and 7 Paul deals with a very serious matter involving persons and circumstances well known to both him and the Corinthians, but with such discretion that he leaves modern interpreters guessing as to the exact nature of the sin and the identity of the offender. The view of ancient writers (and recently capably defended by Garland)[a] is that Paul is referring to the matter of incest described in 1 Corinthians 5. This view is largely rejected today because the current matter is presented as a personal offense against an individual (7:12), and that individual is apparently Paul himself (note the first-person singular pronouns in 2:5, 10). It is also difficult to reconcile the punishment meted out to the incestuous man in 1 Corinthians 5:5 (delivered to Satan for the destruction of his flesh) with Paul's insistence on his restoration here. Barrett, who believes that chapters 10–13 constitute a portion of the "tearful letter" written prior to 2 Corinthians 1–7, argues that the offender was one of the false apostles mentioned in those chapters, perhaps their leader.[b] But would an outsider have submitted to disciplinary action by the church in Corinth? Thrall has argued that the offender was someone who had misappropriated funds from the collection.[c] However, it is doubtful that the evidence, fragmentary and vague as it is, permits such a precise delineation of the issue. Most commentators are content with a more general description of the problem based on the firm data of 2:5–11 and 7:5–16. The offense was not an issue of doctrine but a personal confrontation between Paul and someone in Corinth. Perhaps it was a power struggle, or perhaps this individual objected to Paul's teaching on some point (possibly disallowing visits to pagan temples; see 1 Cor. 8:8–13; 2 Cor. 6:14–7:1). In any event, the community rallied to Paul's side, the individual repented, and Paul now wants to put the matter behind him.

[a] Garland, *2 Corinthians*, 117–22.
[b] Barrett, *Second Epistle*, 7–8.
[c] Thrall, *2 Corinthians*, 1:68–69.

is rather clear. He is concerned to protect this individual from further shame and opprobrium, which is probably why he avoids mentioning the person's name. Paul's choice of the perfect tense ("*has* grieved," twice) may indicate the pain is still real for the apostle, yet he also wants the church to understand the corporate dimension of interpersonal conflict, lest they conclude, "This is just a matter between Paul and so and so." This painful incident has become a vivid illustration of Paul's earlier instruction regarding the nature of communal life in the body of Christ: "If one part suffers, every part suffers with it" (1 Cor. 12:26; cf. 2 Cor. 11:29).

2:6 *The punishment inflicted on him by the majority is sufficient.* Paul has learned from Titus that the discipline given by the community to the offender has had the desired effect, although he does not mention what that punishment was. The Greek phrase underlying the NIV's "the majority" might simply refer to the rest of the community, without implying a minority who dissented;

the same expression could possibly be interpreted that way in 2 Corinthians 4:15 and Philippians 1:14. However, the phrase more commonly refers to an actual majority (e.g., 1 Cor. 10:5; 15:6; 2 Cor. 9:2). The implication of this interpretation is that some in Corinth were not in agreement with the majority, who implemented punishment. This would help explain the situation we find in chapters 10–13, where Paul is dealing with a group of dissenters backing the "false apostles" (11:13).

2:7-8 *Now instead . . . forgive and comfort him . . . reaffirm your love for him.* In light of the effectiveness of the discipline and the repentance that it brought about, Paul now urges the community to forgive and comfort the wrongdoer. Forgiveness reflects an internal process in the heart of the forgiver, a determination not to allow past wrong to continue to rupture the relationship. Comfort, in this context, envisions an expression of that forgiveness directed toward the penitent; together they constitute a reaffirmation of love. Paul's urgent counsel is that both the internal disposition of the community members toward the sinner and their external treatment of this individual be changed in light of the response of genuine contrition.

2:10 *what I have forgiven—if there was anything to forgive.* Here and in 2:5 ("He has not so much grieved me . . .") Paul's use of the first person seems to indicate that the apostle himself was the person wronged by the actions of the offender. Later, in 7:12, Paul uses a singular form to refer to *an individual* who was wronged in this matter, which strengthens the likelihood that this inference is correct. It is instructive to note the very magnanimous posture Paul adopts in this matter. In insisting that the wrong to himself was minimal, Paul effectively deflects hostility away from the wrongdoer, preferring to absorb the injury himself.

2:11 *in order that Satan might not outwit us. For we are not unaware of his schemes.* Paul sees two harmful outcomes if a repentant sinner is not forgiven and embraced by the community. First, he may become "overwhelmed by excessive sorrow" (2:7); second, Satan may manipulate the situation to his advantage. It is likely (though not certain) that the two are connected: the evil one takes advantage of the sinner's state of unconsoled grief by intensifying feelings of isolation and rejection, which results in the individual abandoning the faith. Throughout 2 Corinthians Paul highlights Satan's pernicious cunning directed toward inflicting physical and spiritual harm. In 4:4 Satan blinds the minds of unbelievers; in 11:3 his deceptive work is compared to the serpent in the garden; in 11:14 he disguises himself as "an angel of light" in order to promulgate false teaching; in 12:7 Paul's painful physical ailment, the "thorn in my flesh," is perceived as an instrument of Satan. Paul elsewhere mentions the traps laid by the evil one (Eph. 4:27; 6:11; 1 Tim. 3:7; 2 Tim. 2:26), and one of Paul's concerns here is that the community be aware of the enemy's designs. The estrangement of a grieving sinner is a triumph for the evil one, and the first line of defense for the believing community is to recognize the spiritual battle that is raging beneath the surface.

Theological Insights

In the Old Testament Satan is depicted as "roaming throughout the earth" seeking to do injury and harm (Job 1:6–12). He is the one who opposes God's people and incites disobedience (1 Chron. 21:1) and who accuses the elect before God's throne (Zech. 3:1). The New Testament writers continue this picture of Satan as the opponent of God's people (Matt. 16:23; Mark 1:13; Luke 13:16; Rev. 12:9), and Paul's Letters in particular offer a vivid portrayal of his grim work. He tempts believers to sin (1 Cor. 7:5), ensnares the naive to do his work (1 Tim. 3:7; 2 Tim. 2:26), delights in harming believers (1 Cor. 5:5; 2 Cor. 12:7; Eph. 6:16), blinds the minds of the unbelieving (2 Cor. 4:4), masquerades as an angel of light (2 Cor. 11:14), and is even able to thwart Paul in his missionary work (1 Thess. 2:18). Yet Paul is equally clear that Christ has triumphed over the powers of darkness (Col. 2:15), that believers have been divinely armed and protected against Satan's devices (Eph. 6:10–17; 2 Thess. 3:3), and that God will ultimately "crush Satan under [the believers'] feet" (Rom. 16:20).

Teaching the Text

The central contribution of this passage relates to church discipline—its necessity, goal, and resolution. Although discipline is never pleasant, this passage reveals that appropriately applied discipline is part of a healthy, properly functioning church body. A teaching outline of this topic from this passage might look like this:

1. *The necessity of church discipline.* In the same way that parents who neglect the discipline of their children are considered poor parents, so too the church that refuses to exercise loving discipline of its members would be a neglectful church indeed. Verse 9 indicates that Paul considered it a measure of their obedience that the church in Corinth take disciplinary action in this matter. Although we are not told what the discipline entailed, elsewhere Paul counsels that unrepentant sinners and troublemakers be avoided (Rom. 16:17; 1 Cor. 5:9–11; Titus 3:10) or in severe cases excommunicated (1 Cor. 5:1–5; 1 Tim. 1:20). Because there is a genuine corporate dimension to sin (2 Cor. 2:5), failure to discipline willful sin will negatively impact the health and the witness of the church.

2. *The goal of church discipline.* One of the more interesting features of Paul's instructions on this matter is that the apostle is actually commanding

the believers in Corinth to terminate the disciplinary action and reinstate the repentant brother. Paul is concerned that discipline not be excessive or overbearing or degenerate into vindictiveness. Once the discipline has been positively received and true repentance has occurred, to continue to exercise disciplinary measures would cause unnecessary grief (2:7) and give Satan an opportunity to exploit the situation for his purposes. Reconciliation and restoration are the goals of church discipline, and a compassionate, Christ-honoring church will be eager, not reluctant, to restore a fallen brother or sister to fellowship.

3. *The resolution of church discipline.* Paul's teaching in this passage provides unique insight into what the resolution of church discipline should look like: forgiveness and comfort to the sinner. Our temptation might be to forgive such a person yet never intentionally reach out to them, or perhaps simply to continue on as if nothing has happened. While this may be the easy route, we run the risk of short-circuiting the process of full reconciliation if we don't extend our love to such a person in a tangible, heartfelt manner. The proper resolution of church discipline involves a hearty embracing of the sinner as a palpable expression of true forgiveness.

Illustrating the Text

A purposeful conversation can lead to healing broken relationships.

Story: A pastor was told by a member of the congregation that a senior in the congregation had quit coming to church because the senior felt the pastor was "mad at him" and therefore failed to acknowledge the death of the senior's spouse two years earlier. Immediately the pastor phoned the upset senior and apologized for the oversight; the two were reconciled. Three weeks later the senior passed away. At the funeral the pastor relayed the story to the congregation and challenged the audience to "keep short lists."

Allowing conflict to linger welcomes Satan's influence.

Scripture: Paul says that we are not unaware of the schemes of the devil. The church needs to wake up and stop running headlong into Satan's traps. Twice, Paul links Satan's activity with forgiveness issues: here, and again in Ephesians 4:26–27—"Do not let the sun go down while you are still angry, and do not give the devil a foothold."

Church discipline can turn an unrepentant sinner back to God.

Story: In a large church, a prominent member was discovered to be having an affair. The pastor had a frank conversation with the man, reminding him of the vows he had made to his wife and the responsibility he had to his children and telling him to end the affair immediately. The gentleman politely refused. The pastor then brought the situation to the attention of the elder board, and the elders exercised the first step of church discipline, sending a letter to the man informing him that until he repented of his adulterous behavior, he would not be allowed to receive the sacrament of communion. The man stopped attending services. Then the elders asked him to attend a meeting at which they would urge him to end the affair and be reconciled with his wife, or they were prepared to move toward excommunicating him from the church. Amazingly, the man went to the meeting. The elders said graciously but firmly that his behavior was destroying his family and was not pleasing to God. The gentleman confessed his sin to the elders and asked for mercy. He ended the affair that day and began the long journey of counseling and accountability with his wife. Five years later the man was elected as a deacon. Church discipline may seem parochial and outdated, but it is biblical and can be effective at turning an unrepentant sinner back toward God.

2 Corinthians 2:12–17

Led as Captives

Big Idea
Hardships experienced in the service of the gospel are one means through which God spreads the knowledge of his Son and his work in the world.

Key Themes
- Paul's suffering as an apostle serves to advance the gospel.
- For both believers and unbelievers, Paul's life and ministry are a reminder of their ultimate destiny.
- Paul's intentions in ministry are pure, and he conducts himself with complete authenticity before God and others.

Understanding the Text

The Text in Context

In 2:12–13 Paul returns to the topic of his canceled visit and changed travel plans, a theme that was interrupted by his instructions regarding forgiving the offender in 2:5–11. In this first major section of the letter (1:12–2:4) Paul has been explaining to the Corinthians that his sternly worded letter and his failure to visit them as originally planned should not be construed as indicating a lack of affection for them; just the opposite is true (1:23; 2:4). In 2:12–13 Paul offers further evidence of his love for his Corinthian family: he left a potentially fruitful ministry in Troas out of concern for their welfare. His recollection of the good news he received from Titus about the Corinthians (2:13) prompts an exclamation of thanksgiving (2:14), which is followed by an extended reflection (2:14–7:4) on the nature of his life and ministry as one of hope in the midst of despair, life revealed through death, and strength displayed through weakness. Paul returns to Titus and his travel itinerary in 7:5–7, picking up where he left off in 2:13.

Historical and Cultural Background

In 2:14–16 Paul alludes to one of the most noteworthy celebrations in antiquity, the Roman Triumph. Granted by vote of the senate, the triumphal procession was an elaborate parade through the heart of Rome designed to honor a victorious general and to give thanks to Jupiter, the chief deity of the Roman pantheon. The celebration could last several days, and all of Rome would turn out to view the spectacle. Josephus, who witnessed firsthand a triumphal procession, remarks, "It is impossible to describe the multitude of the shows as they deserve" (*J.W.* 7.5). Part of the parade involved displaying plunder taken from the foe, along with any leading officials of the enemy who survived (noblemen, princes, prominent military personnel), who were led before the chariot of the conquering general to be ridiculed and mocked by the crowds. In recounting the events of his reign Augustus boasts, "I waged wars on land and sea.... In my triumphs nine kings or children of kings were led before my chariot" (*Acts of Augustus* 1.4). The celebration climaxed with an offering to the gods and the execution of any eminent captives in the main forum of Rome.

Interpretive Insights

2:12 *when I went to Troas to preach the gospel of Christ.* According to Acts, Paul left Ephesus and began his journey to Greece (and Corinth) after a serious riot (Acts 20:1–2). Neither the Acts account nor Paul's description here indicates that he fled Ephesus out of fear or duress.[1] Rather, he embarked on a fresh ministry tour (Acts 20:1) and arrived in Troas with the express intention of evangelism: "to preach the gospel of Christ."

the Lord had opened a door for me. An "open door" is an image Paul uses to depict an opportunity for fruitful ministry (1 Cor. 16:9; Col. 4:3; cf. Acts 16:9). This door was opened by the Lord,[2] which underscores Paul's dilemma and the conflict he surely felt when he determined that he must abort this new work in Troas out of concern for his family in Corinth. This clause should probably be rendered concessively: "*Although* a door was opened for me by the Lord."[3]

2:13 *I still had no peace of mind.* Paul had sent Titus to Corinth with the strongly worded letter mentioned in 2:3–4 and made arrangements to rendezvous in Troas. When Titus did not arrive on schedule, Paul grew anxious concerning Titus's reception in Corinth and the effect of his letter, and so Paul decided he should press on toward Corinth through Macedonia and hopefully meet up with Titus en route. (On Titus and his later meeting with Paul, see the comments on 7:5–16.)

2:14 *But thanks be to God.* This exclamation of thanks interrupts the travelogue of 2:12–13 and initiates a profound theological excursus that extends as far as 7:4. The adversative "but" signals a new line of thought whose connection with the previous verses might be captured with the paraphrase, "Yet, in spite of these dire circumstances God showed himself faithful, as he always does." Paul's opening prayers and thanksgivings typically telegraph the main themes of the letter or the section that they introduce. Verses 14–17 reveal the following concerns: ministry through suffering and hardship (vv. 14–16a; see 4:7–18; 6:3–10; 7:5–13; 11:22–33; 12:9–10); Paul's sincerity and sufficiency as an apostle (vv. 16b, 17b; see 3:1–18; 4:1–2; 10:1–13:13); propriety in financial matters (v. 17a; see 8:1–9:15; 12:14–18), Paul's preaching (v. 17b; see 4:5; 10:10; 11:6; 13:3).

who always leads us as captives in Christ's triumphal procession. Formally, this relative clause is descriptive: Paul gives thanks to the God "who always leads us . . ." Its deeper semantic function, however, is causal, providing the grounds for Paul's thanksgiving: "Thanks be to God *because* he always leads us as captives." The rendering of the NIV, to be led *as captives*, is consistent with (1) the only known meaning of the underlying Greek verb (*thriambeuō*),[4] (2) the imagery of the Roman Triumph (see the "Historical and Cultural Background"), and (3) the larger theological perspective of these chapters as strength displayed through weakness. The only other New Testament use of the verb *thriambeuō* is found in Colossians 2:15, which speaks of God making a spectacle of the spiritual forces of evil by "triumphing over them" through the cross. In keeping with other Greek and Latin writers (Latin, *triumphare*), Paul uses this term to depict God's triumph over his foes, who are being led as captives before his chariot in triumphal procession. Paul makes a very similar statement in 1 Corinthians 4:9: "For it seems to me that God has put us apostles on display at the end of the procession, like those condemned to die in the arena." Although formerly an enemy of the cross (Gal. 1:13; 1 Tim. 1:13), Paul thanks God that precisely through his humiliation and suffering on behalf of Christ the gospel advances.

uses us to spread the aroma of the knowledge of him everywhere. This clause provides the second grounds for Paul's thanksgiving and continues the imagery of the Triumph through referencing the aroma that would have been present along the parade route. Incense and other aromatics were commonly used at religious and civic celebrations in antiquity. In recounting the triumphal procession of Aemilius Paullus, Plutarch relates that "every temple was open and filled with garlands and incense" (*Aem.* 32). Paul views his crushed and vanquished apostolic service as the means by which the fragrance of the crucified Christ is disseminated everywhere. This thought is echoed in 4:12: "So then, death is at work in us, but life is at work in you."

2:15-16 *aroma of Christ among those who are being saved and those who are perishing . . . To the one . . . death; to the other . . . life.* The perspective of the metaphor shifts as Paul notes the different responses the aroma of Christ provokes along the parade route. To the cheering crowds and the triumphing army, this was the sweet smell of victory. But to the captives destined for execution or slavery, this was the aroma of impending doom (cf. Phil. 1:28).

Peddling the Word

Although both Jesus and Paul affirmed the appropriateness of making one's living from the gospel (Luke 10:4–12; 1 Cor. 9:3–18), the early church had to establish strict rules for distinguishing sincere Christian teachers from those driven by greed. The Christian community represented by the *Didache*, written between AD 70 and 100, laid down the following guidelines concerning itinerant preachers ("apostles"): "And when the apostle leaves, he is to take nothing except bread until he finds his next night's lodging. But if he asks for money he is a false prophet" (11.6).

And who is equal to such a task? (See "Theological Insights" in the unit on 3:1–6.)

2:17 *we do not peddle the word of God for profit.* Paul contrasts himself and his associates with mere religious charlatans, who were motivated by greed rather than concern for others. The Greek word *kapēleuō* (NIV: "peddle for profit") was a pejorative term frequently used in accusations against sophists, the popular orators of Paul's day.

in Christ we speak before God with sincerity, as those sent from God. Each phrase in this segment modifies the main verb, "we speak," as Paul carefully delineates his modus operandi as a preacher. He explains that his proclamation is (1) in Christ, (2) in complete openness before God, (3) from sincere motives, and (4) the result of a divine commission. This is in contrast to those who "peddle the word of God for profit." Paul's spoken proclamation has been criticized by some of the Corinthians, and Paul has already spent a considerable amount of time defending himself on this matter (1 Cor. 1–4, summarized in 2:1–5). He will return to this issue more directly in 2 Corinthians 10:10.

Teaching the Text

This passage contains several important theological motifs, any one of which could be richly developed for teaching and preaching. The following three themes capture the primary theological emphases of 2:12–17.

1. *Suffering and weakness.* The primary message of this passage is that our suffering and weakness in the service of the gospel become the aroma of the crucified Christ to others—believers and unbelievers. By "the aroma of Christ" Paul may mean that the Christian's suffering echoes or retells the story of the suffering of Jesus and so serves to remind the world of the cross. This idea is stated explicitly in 4:10: "We always carry around in our body the death of Jesus." The message of the cross always provokes a response, either positive or negative. In 1 Corinthians 1:18 Paul says that his preaching of the cross "is foolishness to those who are perishing, but to us who are being saved it is the

power of God." In the present passage Paul notes that his cruciform suffering produces a sense of hope for believers ("life") but a sense of foreboding to unbelievers ("death"). Strength displayed through suffering and weakness is an important theme in 2 Corinthians (e.g., 4:7–12, 16–18; 6:3–10) and is brought to a climax in 12:10: "When I am weak, then I am strong."

2. *Financial integrity.* A second significant teaching point is the importance of the character of one who proclaims the gospel, particularly with respect to financial integrity (2:17). Paul contrasts his own conduct with that of "others" who use the gospel as a means for lining their own pockets. Paul is not categorically opposed to accepting money from those to whom he ministers (see Phil. 4:10–19; 2 Cor. 11:8), nor does he expect other Christian workers to serve without any remuneration. For example, he commands the congregations in Galatia to "share all good things" with those instructing them in the word (Gal. 6:6), and he instructs the believers in Ephesus to reward deserving elders with a double stipend (1 Tim. 5:17–18); both relate to monetary compensation. In fact, in 1 Corinthians 9 Paul flatly asserts that financial support from his congregations is his "right," but one that he foregoes. Paul's point in 2:17 is that gospel ministry should not be oriented toward personal benefit. It is an obligation ("as those sent from God") carried out with "sincerity" and divine accountability ("before God") and centered "in Christ."

3. *Divine guidance.* A final instructive issue relates to God's leading in the apostle's life and ministry. In 2:13 Paul notes that his decision to leave Troas was the result of a deep sense of unease concerning Titus (Greek, "no rest in my spirit"). This information helps fill out a biblical theology of God's leading in the Christian life. The book of Acts describes several significant incidents in Paul's travels where direction was supernaturally provided, usually through a visionary experience (Acts 16:9–10; 18:8–11; 27:21–24). The opening chapters of 2 Corinthians, on the other hand, reveal that Paul also (perhaps more frequently?) based his travel itinerary and ministry plans on his own (certainly prayer-filled) judgment concerning the circumstances he faced. His decision to abandon his plans to visit Corinth earlier (1:12–2:1) and his decision to leave the work in Troas are two notable examples.

Illustrating the Text

We can be the aroma of Christ.

Story: A pastor had the opportunity to invest for twenty years into the unchurched husband of one of his members. The pastor would visit him in the hospital, stop at his shop, and see him at sporting events. During a hospital visit the pastor told him, "I will always be your pastor even if you never come to church." Eventually this man and his family were at a wedding the pastor was conducting. Both the bride and groom were unbelievers, so the pastor preached the gospel. At 7:00 p.m. that Saturday, the man stood in the pastor's garage and shared that his life was a wreck and that he needed the Lord. What a beautiful thing, after twenty years of prayer and seed planting, to lead him to Christ. This man began attending the pastor's church every Sunday with his family. He was baptized and testified before the whole congregation on Christmas Eve how Jesus got ahold of him.

Pastors deserve a fair wage, not an opulent and obscene lifestyle.

Television: *Preachers of L.A.* This reality television series follows the lives of three bishops and three pastors, from their work within the church to their personal lives. The preachers are adherents of prosperity theology who profit handsomely from preaching the gospel. The Oxygen network has also produced *Preachers of Detroit* and *Preachers of Atlanta*.[5] There is a need for reasonable provision for pastors, but that does not mean an endorsement of excessive materialism.

Greed can sabotage effective ministry.

News: In 2010 the Reverend Kevin J. Gray was arrested for larceny. Gray was known to be humble and generous, and he was particularly recognized for helping immigrants in his parish. But a routine church audit revealed issues, and the investigation turned up "a secret double life of male escorts, strip bars and lavish spending on the finest restaurants, luxury hotels and expensive clothing, financed with money stolen from the parish."[6] When arrested, Gray admitted to having stolen about a million dollars. "Hidden sins" almost always become public. We should ask ourselves the question, If my sin is no longer secret, what will this cost the cause of Jesus?

Living "all in" for Christ is proved by one's handling of finances.

Church History: In 1744 John Wesley wrote, "[When I die,] if I leave behind me ten pounds . . . you and all mankind [may] bear witness against me, that I have lived and died a thief and a robber." Upon his death in 1791, his will mentioned only the coins to be found in his pockets and dresser drawers, since he had given away most of the money earned during his lifetime.[7]

2 Corinthians 3:1–6

The New Covenant

Big Idea

The transformative work of the Spirit in the lives of the Corinthians is proof for all to see of Paul's new covenant ministry, for which he has been divinely enabled.

Key Themes

- Paul has no need to commend himself or to be recommended by anyone; the changed lives of believers are proof of his apostleship.
- New covenant transformation is achieved not through obedience to an external written code but through the Spirit's work on the human heart.
- God makes his servants sufficient for the tasks to which he calls them.

Understanding the Text

The Text in Context

Paul's comments in 2:14–17, particularly his assertion that he and his co-workers have been "sent from God" (v. 17), prompt the apostle to reflect openly on the appropriateness of such self-commendation and to explain the basis of his confidence. Ultimately, Paul's confidence is grounded in his certainty of God's enabling call (3:4–6), and as proof of this calling he offers the Corinthians themselves; their changed lives are decisive evidence of his divine commission (3:1–3). Paul begins to elaborate more carefully the nature of his new covenant ministry in the hope that the Corinthians will begin to grasp the strength-in-weakness character of his apostolic service.

Interpretive Insights

3:1 *Are we beginning to commend ourselves again?* Proper commendation is an important issue between Paul and the Corinthians, and Paul's use of the Greek word for "commend," *synistēmi*, in 2 Corinthians accounts for nine of its sixteen occurrences in the New Testament (see the sidebar "Self-Commendation in 2 Corinthians" in the unit on 12:11–13). The rhetorical question that begins 3:1 implies that Paul is not inappropriately commending himself, which is made clear by the question that follows (see below). Although the topic of appropriate self-commendation arises naturally from 2:14–17,

A First-Century Letter of Recommendation

"Theon, to the most honored Tyrannus, very many greetings. Heraclides, the bearer of this letter, is my brother, wherefore I entreat you with all my power to take him under your protection. . . . You will do me the greatest favor if you let him win your approval. Before all else I pray that you may have health and the best of success, unharmed by the evil eye. Goodbye."

P.Oxy. 292 (*Sel. Pap.* 106), written about AD 25

---

it also appears that this is a sensitive issue for Paul, especially in light of the intruders of chapters 10–13, who are depicted as self-commending and arrogant (10:12–13; 11:18–19). The word "again" most likely recalls Paul's sincere effort to win the trust of the Corinthians in his earlier ministry among them.

Or do we need, like some people, letters of recommendation to you or from you? This second rhetorical question is phrased in Greek to expect a negative answer, "Of course not," which should probably be understood as applying to both questions in this verse. Neither is Paul commending himself, nor does he need to be commended by others. As is the case today, letters of recommendation were a standard feature of first-century society. They were used to introduce one party to another, usually for social advancement, and also by travelers, who often relied on local hospitality during their journeys. It is possible that the mention of letters of recommendation is an innocent reference to a common practice, with no polemical intent. However, the very real presence of outsiders who are challenging Paul's authority and threatening to undermine his work in Corinth (see chaps. 10–13) suggests that Paul is carefully contrasting himself with these rivals. Paul elsewhere refers to adversaries with the phrase "some people" (10:2; cf. 10:12; 11:21; 1 Cor. 4:18; 15:12; Gal. 1:7), and this verse is one link in a chain of references in these early chapters (2 Cor. 2:17; 4:2, 5; 5:12) aimed at exposing and subverting the arguments of his detractors before the direct assault begins in chapter 10.

3:2 *You yourselves are our letter.* The validity of Paul's apostolic ministry in Corinth was based not on letters from human authorities but on the reality of the changed lives of the Corinthians. At several points in his correspondence with the Corinthians, Paul is forced to defend himself, and the proof he offers of his apostolate is telling: he was commissioned by the Lord (1 Cor. 9:1; 15:7–9); he suffers for his spiritual children (2 Cor. 12:12–21); his evangelistic work was accompanied by "signs, wonders and miracles" (12:12); and his ministry produced fruit ("You are the seal of my apostleship in the Lord," 1 Cor. 9:2). In the present passage Paul again appeals to the undeniable reality of transformation, which, as he is about to explain, can be accomplished only by the Spirit.

written on our hearts, known and read by everybody. In this context "written on our hearts" refers to Paul's deep fatherly affection for his children. "Heart" is similarly used in 2:4; 6:11–12; and in 7:3, where Paul, probably referring back to this verse, says, "I have said before that you have such a place in our hearts that we would live or die with you" (see also 12:14–15; Phil. 2:4; 1 Thess. 2:17–20). "Known and read" relates primarily to the first clause in this verse, "You . . . are our letter," and affirms that the Corinthians themselves are a visible witness to the gospel (see also Rom. 1:9; 1 Thess. 1:7–9).

3:3 *a letter from Christ, the result of our ministry.* As the letter imagery continues, Paul notes that the author of the letter is Christ. The Greek expression underlying the NIV's "result of our ministry" may be interpreted to mean that Paul sees himself as the courier delivering the letter or as the *amanuensis* (scribe) to whom the letter was dictated. In any case, Paul's essential point is that Christ is the ultimate author of the new life the Corinthians are experiencing and that Paul and his co-workers play a mediatorial role. Paul made the same point in an earlier letter, using an agricultural image: "I planted the seed, Apollos watered it, but God has been making it grow" (1 Cor. 3:6).

written not with ink but with the Spirit of the living God, not on tablets of stone but on tablets of human hearts. Paul begins to argue more explicitly for the superiority of his own ministry and introduces two themes that he will elaborate as the argument unfolds in subsequent chapters: the work of the Spirit and the inwardness of new covenant transformation. "Tablets of stone" clearly echoes the Old Testament description of the law given to Moses on Mount Sinai (Exod. 24:12; 31:18; Deut. 9:10–11). Paul links and contrasts this image with an allusion to Ezekiel's promise that God would one day remove his people's "heart of stone" and replace it with a "heart of flesh" (Ezek. 11:19; 36:26). Paul's shrewd use of the letter analogy in 3:1–3 allows him to make the following points against rivals who require commendatory letters in order to validate their ministry: Paul's "letter" (ministry) is superior in that its author is Christ, not any human authority; it is written with the Spirit, not ink; it is interior (written on human hearts), not exterior; it is not merely words on a papyrus sheet but is incarnated by the Corinthians themselves (3:2–3).

3:4–5 *Such confidence we have through Christ before God. Not that we are competent in ourselves.* Paul returns to the confident assertions of 2:14–17 and directly answers the question posed in 2:16: "Who is equal to such a task?" Paul's point is that no one is equal to the task of new covenant ministry unless God makes them so.

3:6 *a new covenant.* The prophet Jeremiah foresaw the day when God would establish a new covenant with his people that would be unlike the first covenant; this new covenant would be written on the heart (Jer. 31:31–33). Similarly, Ezekiel announced a future "everlasting covenant" (Ezek. 16:60;

37:26), where God promises, "I will give you a new heart. . . . And I will put my Spirit in you" (36:26–27). Jesus inaugurated the new covenant during his final Passover meal with his followers (Matt. 26:28; see also 1 Cor. 11:25), and Paul was commissioned as its herald on the Damascus road.

the letter kills, but the Spirit gives life. In keeping with Jeremiah and Ezekiel, Paul's proclamation of the new covenant emphasizes interiority ("on tablets of human hearts," 3:3) and the enablement of the Spirit. As the following verses clarify, "the letter" is a metonym for the written code of the Mosaic era, or more precisely, for the attempt to fulfill the demands of the law without the enabling power of the Spirit. Paul offers an extensive commentary on the truth of this verse in Romans 7–8, where he explains that when the power of the Spirit replaces the inability of the written code (Rom. 7:6), the result is that the just requirements of the law are "fully met in us" (Rom. 8:3–4; see also Gal. 3:1–12). The "life" given by the Spirit entails both moral enablement (Rom. 8:5–11) and spiritual regeneration, a "new creation" (2 Cor. 5:17).

Theological Insights

"Who is sufficient for these things?" (2:16 ESV) is the prompt that Paul takes up in 3:1–6. The apostle is keenly aware of the magnitude of responsibility entrusted to him to be the "aroma of Christ" to the world (2:15) and a minister of a new covenant (3:6). Paul wants the Corinthians to understand that his boldness and confidence rest not in his own talents and ingenuity but in the knowledge that God has made him sufficient for his task (3:4–5). The crucial point to grasp is this: *God does not call the "qualified"; he qualifies those he calls.* Biblical history is replete with examples of inadequate men and women who were made adequate by God and used powerfully: Abraham, Sarah, Hannah, Moses, Gideon, Jeremiah, Peter, and Mary Magdalene, to name but a few.

Teaching the Text

In the teaching of 3:1–6, several prominent ideas require careful treatment, lest we misunderstand Paul's intent.

1. *Letters of recommendation.* Paul's insistence that he needs no letter of recommendation as far as the Corinthians are concerned should not be construed as a wholesale rejection of the practice. The New Testament contains positive references to such letters (Acts 18:27; 1 Cor. 16:3), and Paul's epistles regularly include commendatory sections (Rom. 16:1–2; 1 Cor. 16:15–18; Phil. 2:25–30). Both Philemon and 3 John fit comfortably within this literary genre. Paul's point is that as the Corinthians' spiritual father (1 Cor. 4:15; 2 Cor. 6:13), he needs no external validation of his apostolic credentials; the

changed lives of the Corinthians constitute a living letter of recommendation available for everyone to read.

2. *Sufficiency.* Paul's confidence that God has made him sufficient for the task to which he has been called should be heard as both an encouragement and an admonition for all engaged in the Lord's work—be it representing Christ in your community or preparing a sermon for Sunday. For those overwhelmed by the scope or size of their responsibilities, Paul offers the encouragement that "God has made us sufficient!" (see 3:4–6). For those tempted to think that their success is the result of their own effort and abilities, this passage contains the sobering reminder that we are not competent to consider anything as coming from ourselves (3:5).

3. *Letter versus Spirit.* The letter-Spirit antithesis of 3:6 can easily be misunderstood in terms of the contemporary idiom, "letter of the law versus spirit of the law," which refers to the strict interpretation of a code versus the true intent of the code. Another erroneous interpretation would be to see a hermeneutical principle being articulated in this antithesis: the literal, legalistic interpretation of Scripture versus the true spiritual interpretation given by the Spirit. The immediate context, as well as the larger context of Pauline theology, indicates that when Paul says, "The letter kills, but the Spirit gives life," he is contrasting the old era, where the command approached one from *without*, with the new covenant era, where obedience is prompted from the Spirit dwelling *within*. Apart from the enabling power of the Spirit, the law produced sin, guilt, and death. For new covenant believers, "the law of the Spirit who gives life has set you free from the law of sin and death" (Rom. 8:2).

4. *Spiritual fruit.* Paul is not afraid to set before the Corinthians proof of his apostolic commissioning: their changed lives. This is in keeping with a strong New Testament emphasis that true faith produces fruit (e.g., Matt. 5:15–20; Luke 6:43–44; James 2:18; Titus 2:11–12). In the present context Paul holds up his converts as evidence of his calling (2 Cor. 3:2–3), but elsewhere the concept is larger and includes growth in virtue (Gal. 5:22–23) and obedience (1 Pet. 4:2). By way of application, it would be appropriate to ask, what evidence can we present that we are fulfilling God's call on our lives? For Paul, the Corinthians were evidence "known and read by everyone" (3:2). Similarly, our lives of faithfulness should result in clear testimony of God's mercy and grace.

Illustrating the Text

Lodging one's confidence in God rather than self is a "win-win."

Musical: In a scene from the musical *The Sound of Music*, the young novice Maria, who has been sent by her abbey to be the governess of a large and unruly family, nervously contemplates the challenges that face her as she travels to her new assignment. Her reflection leads to a rousing, memorable song of self-reliance and determination that climaxes with the words, "I have confidence in confidence alone, besides which you see I have confidence in me!" Of course, one has to admire the plucky young Maria bravely attempting to boost her morale, yet one also has to wonder if her confidence might be better placed. One of the clearest teaching points of 2 Corinthians 3:1–6 is that Paul's confidence rests not in believing in himself but in believing in the God who called him: "Such confidence we have through Christ before God. Not that we are competent in ourselves to claim anything for ourselves, but our competence comes from God" (3:4–5). For a servant of Christ, proper confidence is not primarily a matter of having an optimistic, can-do approach to life's challenges, but it is based on believing that God makes us sufficient for the tasks to which he calls us.

Fruitful ministry is the finest credentialing.

Story: In contemporary society men and women typically prepare for ministry through a rigorous course of study, often in a seminary, which leads to a graduate degree, a diploma, and hopefully a position in ministry. For some seminary graduates it may be tempting to gaze at their elegantly framed credentials carefully positioned above the desk in their office and imagine that this piece of paper constitutes proof of their calling or provides validation of their ministerial expertise. One young seminary graduate, upon being asked by a pastoral interview committee how he had seen the Lord confirm his gifting for ministry, replied that he graduated first in his class and received an award from the seminary for his preaching ability. When later asked what ministries he was involved in while in seminary, the young man shifted in his seat uncomfortably and responded that he really didn't have any time to be involved in extracurricular activities. A week or so later when he was informed by the chairman of the search committee that he was not going to be offered the position, the chairman told him, "Friend, if ministering to others is 'extracurricular,' perhaps you weren't studying the right curriculum." The perspective of Paul in this passage is that confirmation of calling does not come from letters written by human authorities or—if we can extend the metaphor to the present day—from degrees granted by educational institutions; rather, it comes from the changed lives of those whom we serve: "You yourselves are our letter [of recommendation]" (3:2). Paul made the same point in an earlier epistle: "Am I not an apostle? . . . Are you not the result of my work in the Lord? . . . You are the seal of my apostleship in the Lord" (1 Cor. 9:1–2).

2 Corinthians 3:7–11

The Surpassing Glory of the Ministry of the Spirit

Big Idea
Although the Mosaic era of the law was divinely instituted, it has been surpassed in every way by the new covenant era of the Spirit.

Key Themes
- The law could not produce the righteousness it demanded. On the contrary, it led to condemnation.
- The glory that accompanied the old covenant was limited and transitory.
- The glory accompanying the ministry of the Spirit is limitless and permanent.

Understanding the Text

The Text in Context

The letter-Spirit antithesis of 3:6 raises the important question of the relationship between the old era and the new era and prompts Paul to contrast the Mosaic era of the law with the new covenant era of the Spirit. Although some scholars have argued that 3:7–18 is highly polemical, targeting opponents who glory in Moses and who have used the story of Moses's veiled glory (Exod. 34) against Paul, this hypothesis is unnecessary. Verses 7–18 follow quite naturally from Paul's reference to the new covenant and the contrast between the Spirit and the letter (the law) in 3:6.[1] Paul continues the defense of the strength-in-weakness character of his ministry by explaining the superiority of the ministry of the Spirit to that which it replaced (3:7–11). Paul will go on to explain that this superior covenant leads to boldness on the part of Paul and his fellow apostles (3:12–18) and requires complete integrity from those entrusted with such a responsibility (4:1–6).

Historical and Cultural Background

While Paul's critical assessment of the law and the Mosaic era in 3:7–11 is taken for granted by Christians today, it is important that we place these

From the Lesser to the Greater

Paul structures his argument in 3:7–11 around three *if-then* statements, which are arguments from the lesser to the greater. This was a common rhetorical device in both Jewish and Greco-Roman literature of Paul's day. This pattern of argumentation assumes that the "lesser" supposition is true and agreed on by the audience, which serves to validate the "greater" conclusion. The function of these three lesser-to-greater assertions is to emphasize the greater glory of the new covenant ministry of the Spirit by contrasting it with the inadequacies of the old era. The antitheses Paul employs to highlight the differences between the Mosaic covenant and the new covenant are death versus Spirit (= life; 3:7–8), condemnation versus acquittal (3:9–10), and provisional versus permanent (3:11).

sentiments in the context of first-century Jewish thought in order to perceive how subversive Paul sounded to his fellow Jews and to understand why they reacted so strongly to his message. For example, while Paul describes the law as an instrument of death (3:7), devout Jews of this era spoke of "the torah of life" (Eighteen Benedictions; Sir. 17:11; *2 Bar.* 45.1–2; *Pss. Sol.* 14.2). Far from believing that the law led to condemnation (2 Cor. 3:9), Jews of this period were taught that the law would "aid the quest for virtue and the perfecting of character" (*Let. Aris.* 144–45). In 3:7–11 Paul depicts the law as something transitory, whose limited glory is now completely eclipsed by the glory of the new covenant. Contrast this with the prayer from Qumran that blesses "the eternal commandments" (4Q369) and the words of *1 Enoch* that invoke a curse on any who would dare to alter "the eternal law" (*1 En.* 99.2). In a similar vein, Jewish thinkers of Paul's day believed that "the glory of God will never cease from his law" (*Liv. Pro.* 2.18) and that, while all else may perish, "the Law does not perish but remains in its glory" (*4 Ezra* 9.37). When Paul's perspective on the diminished glory and relevance of the law is compared with the convictions of his contemporaries, it is no wonder that Paul encountered such fierce resistance from his kinsmen, as happened in Corinth (Acts 18:12–14).

Interpretive Insights

3:7 *Now if the ministry that brought death.* The NIV rightly interprets the Greek conjunction *de* as explanatory, "now," not adversative ("but"). In these verses Paul unpacks the letter-Spirit antithesis of verse 6, particularly the idea that the new covenant produces life while the old covenant led to death. Paul offers a commentary on the expression "ministry of death" in Romans 7:5: "For when we were in the realm of the flesh, the sinful passions aroused by the law were at work in us, so that we bore fruit for death." The era of the law became a ministry of death and condemnation (2 Cor. 3:9) because without the indwelling, empowering Spirit the requirements of the law could not be fulfilled: "When the commandment came, sin sprang to life and I died" (Rom. 7:9).

engraved in letters on stone. This reiterates the thought of 3:3 ("not on tablets of stone") as a slighting reference to the Mosaic law, which commanded obedience from *without*, rather than impelling obedience from *within*.

came with glory. Paul is careful to affirm that the law did possess a measure of glory (this is reiterated in 3:9), yet Paul's argument is that the Mosaic dispensation is revealed as merely a flickering lamp when the floodlights of God's redemptive plan are turned on through the cross and the new covenant ministry of the Spirit. Again, this is entirely at odds with the perspective of Paul's fellow Jews, who described the law as "an eternal light" (*2 Bar.* 78.16) and "a lamp that will abide forever" (*LAB* 9.8).

so that the Israelites could not look steadily at the face of Moses. Paul alludes to Exodus 34:29–35, which describes Moses's radiant face after he met with the Lord to receive the stone tablets containing the Ten Commandments. The Exodus narrative says that Aaron and the people were "afraid to come near" Moses (Exod. 34:30), which Paul interprets to mean that the radiance of Moses's face caused them to turn away.

transitory though it was. A more accurate translation of the passive participle *katargoumenēn* would be "being abolished" or "being brought to an end." This is probably a divine passive, with God as the implied subject. Although the participle is modifying "glory," asserting that God was the agent causing the radiance of Moses's face to recede, the waning glory of Moses's face is taken by Paul to be symbolic of the divinely intended demise of the era of the law (Rom. 7:1–4; 10:4).

3:8–9 *will not the ministry of the Spirit be even more glorious? . . . the ministry that brings righteousness!* Paul contrasts the "ministry of death" not with "the ministry of life," as we might expect, but with "ministry of the Spirit." For Paul "life" is the defining feature of the Spirit (3:6), and so the two words become virtually interchangeable in some contexts (cf. Rom. 6:4; 7:6). In Romans Paul explains, "The Spirit is life for righteousness" (8:10, author's translation; cf. Rom. 8:2; Gal. 5:25). The regenerating work of the Spirit within enables obedience from the heart (2 Cor. 3:3), which makes the new covenant ministry of the Spirit far superior ("more glorious") to the written code engraved on tablets of stone.

3:10–11 *what was glorious has no glory now in comparison with the surpassing glory . . . how much greater is the glory of that which lasts!* Verses 9 and 10 contrast the glory of the new era and the old era in terms of scale and quality, while in verse 11 the contrast is that of duration: the law was a temporary measure, while the new covenant ministry of the Spirit is permanent.

Theological Insights

Paul's thoughts on the law are complex and need to be carefully interpreted in the contexts in which they are found. While in this passage Paul refers to the Mosaic era as the "ministry that brought death" (3:7), in Romans 7:12 he affirms that the law is "holy, righteous and good." In 2 Corinthians 3:9 he says the law has brought condemnation, yet in Philippians 3:6 he testifies that he is "faultless," in terms of "righteousness based on the law." How do we reconcile these statements? In Romans 7 Paul is describing the law from the vantage point of its origin and purpose, and so he can wholeheartedly affirm that it is "holy, righteous and good." Yet when speaking of its efficacy, what it has actually produced, he labels it "the law of sin and death" (Rom. 8:2). The problem is not the law but the inability of the unaided flesh to perform it. Similarly, Philippians 3:6 affirms not that Paul is sinless with respect to the law but that he is "faultless." That is, where the law has been broken he has performed the appropriate rituals of atonement. The purpose of the law, as Romans 7 and Galatians 3 explain, is to reveal our sin and lead us to Christ. In that sense, it is "holy, righteous and good" (Rom. 7:12) yet also "the ministry that brought condemnation" (2 Cor. 3:9).

Teaching the Text

Teaching this passage means coming to terms with some very heady and far-reaching theological issues. Foundational to understanding Paul's ministry of the Spirit—and, hence, this entire section of 2 Corinthians—is his understanding of the surpassing glory of the new covenant in salvation history and the righteousness that the new covenant offers.

1. *Surpassing glory.* The key term in 3:7–11 is "glory." This word occurs ten times in these five verses in both verbal and nominal forms. This motif will be developed further in 3:12–18 and 4:1–18. Paul's primary point here relates to the superior nature of the new covenant compared to the old. It is superior in its *effect* (the old produces death; the new, righteousness), its *mediation* (stone tablets vs. the Spirit), its *degree* (fading vs. surpassing), and its *duration* (provisional vs. permanent).

2. *Salvation history.* Crucial to apprehending Paul's teaching is adopting his perspective on the presence of the new era. Believers today are still in the era of the new covenant and the Spirit. The drama of redemption reached its climax in the cross and the resurrection, which revealed the law as merely preliminary to God's ultimate redeeming and transforming work (Gal. 3:23–4:6). Paul wants the Corinthians to understand that his work as an apostle, in spite of his suffering and hardship (2 Cor. 2:14–16; 4:7–18; 6:3–10), is part of God's new work in the world, his new covenant work of the Spirit. Further,

although this new work is dramatically different from the Mosaic era, the new covenant was foretold by Jeremiah and Ezekiel long ago and represents the continuation and consummation of God's redemptive plan for the world.

3. *Ethical and forensic righteousness.* One of the questions Paul does not answer in this passage is what sense we should ascribe to "righteousness" (*dikaiosynē*) in the expression "the ministry of righteousness" (3:9 ESV). The NIV renders the phrase, "the ministry that brings righteousness," which implies *ethical* righteousness—that is, moral growth toward Christlikeness. The NRSV translates the phrase, "the ministry of justification," which implies right standing—that is, a legal pronouncement of acquittal or vindication. Both senses of this word are attested elsewhere in Paul's Letters. The primary argument that "righteousness" should be understood forensically, indicating a legal standing, is that it is posed in antithesis to "condemnation." Acquittal seems like a very natural antithesis to condemnation. The best argument that the word has ethical connotations is that it is equivalent to "the ministry of the Spirit" (3:8). In Paul's Letters the Spirit is so commonly portrayed as the agent enabling right conduct and transformation (Rom. 8:1–17; 2 Cor. 3:18) that it is difficult to see "the Spirit" connected with "righteousness," as in 3:8–9, and not conclude that Paul has ethical renewal in mind. In this instance, it is not necessary to pit the ethical interpretation against the forensic as either-or alternatives. The context indicates that Paul intends a more comprehensive statement of new covenant righteousness that includes both moral renewal and right standing before God.

Illustrating the Text

The glory of Jesus cannot be contained.

Analogy: Think about a river at flood stage—it possesses almost unimaginable power. The people in towns along rivers who face a potential overflow stack sandbags and build earthen dikes, but the sheer volume of water often causes them to collapse or flows right over them. Trying to contain Jesus is like trying to hold back a river when the waters run high.

The gospel is the full light.

Visual Aid: Light a candle in the front of the room and have the room lights or stage lights turned off. The candle gives off light, a light for which we would be grateful in a dark place. Then turn the lights back on to show how the light of the candle is overwhelmed by the fuller and more glorious light. Paul argues that the Mosaic dispensation is merely a flickering lamp in comparison with the full light of God's redemptive plan that is revealed through the cross and the new covenant ministry of the Spirit.

2 Corinthians 3:12–18

New Covenant Transformation

Big Idea
Paul's bold declaration of the new covenant is fueled by the knowledge that the Spirit removes the veil of unbelief from all those who turn to Christ and transforms the new covenant community into the image of the Lord Jesus.

Key Themes
- The new covenant ministry of the Spirit enables Paul and his apostolic team to serve with boldness and confidence.
- Full apprehension of God's message is available only to those who have turned to Christ.
- Transformation into Christ's image comes by the Spirit.

Understanding the Text

The Text in Context

In 3:7–11 Paul explained the letter-Spirit antithesis of 3:6 and provided further grounds for the confidence he expressed in 3:4–5 regarding the superior glory of the new covenant ministry of the Spirit. In this section Paul returns explicitly to the theme of his confidence, using a more colorful term, *parrēsia* ("boldness," "confidence"), translated here by the NIV as, "we are . . . bold" (3:12). The motif of apostolic confidence is antiphonally connected in these chapters with the theme of suffering and hardship, so as to convey the idea of *confidence in spite of weakness*. The motif of confidence finds expression in 3:1 (no need for letters of recommendation); 3:4 ("such confidence"); 3:12 ("very bold"); 3:17 ("freedom"); 4:1, 16 ("we do not lose heart"); and the hardship catalog of 4:7–12 ("struck down, but not destroyed"). Paul also continues his reflection on Exodus 34:29–35 in this paragraph, focusing his attention on Moses's veil as a symbol of the veiled minds of his fellow Jews. In explaining that the veil is removed only by turning to Christ (2 Cor. 3:14–16), Paul introduces the motif of transformation, which will be brought to a climax in 5:17, "new creation."

Theodotus Inscription

The Theodotus inscription dates to the first century and was originally attached to a synagogue in Jerusalem. It emphasizes the function of the synagogue as a place for the reading and study of Torah. This setting forms part of the background to Paul's comments on the reading of Moses in his day, in 3:12–15. It reads, "Theodotus son of Vettenus, priest and synagogue ruler, son of a synagogue ruler, grandson of a synagogue ruler, built this synagogue for the reading of the Law and the teaching of the commandments, and the hostelry, rooms and baths, for the lodging of those who have need from abroad. It was established by his forefathers, the elders and Simonides."[a]

[a] *CIJ* 2.1404.

Historical and Cultural Background

The public reading of Scripture occupied an important place in Jewish community life in the first century. Unlike most Western societies today, with high literacy rates and an abundance of printed Scriptures, ancient Mediterranean societies were largely illiterate and very poor, and Jewish families did not possess private copies of Scripture to read. Jewish communities pooled their resources—often relying on wealthy benefactors among them—to build synagogues and acquire copies of their Scriptures on scrolls. Philo provides an illuminating picture of a synagogue service in Alexandria: "When the Jewish community gathers in the synagogue they sit according to their age in classes, the younger sitting under the elder, and listening with eager attention in becoming order. Then one, indeed, takes up the holy volume and reads it, and another of the men of greatest experience comes forward and explains what is not very intelligible, for a great many precepts are delivered in enigmatical modes of expression" (*Good Person* 12.81–83).

Interpretive Insights

3:12 *Therefore, since we have such a hope, we are very bold.* The conclusion Paul draws ("therefore") from the argument of 3:7–11, that the new covenant ministry of the Spirit has enduring glory ("such a hope"), is that he and his associates can operate with candor and openness. The word translated "very bold" by the NIV (*parrēsia*) could refer to frankness in speech, or more generally to candor and openness, or to an attitude of confidence or boldness. The following contrast with Moses, who veiled himself, together with the reference in 4:2 to renouncing "secret and shameful ways," suggests that Paul's boldness primarily relates to his sincere, open, "unveiled" proclamation and posture in ministry.

3:13 *We are not like Moses, who would put a veil over his face.* Paul returns to Exodus 34 and the story of Moses veiling his radiant face while among the people after being in the Lord's presence. In these early chapters of 2 Corinthians Paul contrasts himself and his co-workers ("we") with those who hawk the word of God (2:17), those who need letters of recommendation (3:1), those who are duplicitous and preach themselves (4:1–5), and those who boast in externals (5:12). Moses fits somewhat awkwardly in this collection, but Paul's intent is not to denigrate Moses, as the next clause will show, but to contrast his own new covenant freedom with the necessary constraint Moses had to show because of the Israelites' hardness of heart.

to prevent the Israelites from seeing the end of what was passing away. Here we encounter one of the most difficult phrases to interpret in the entire letter. Does Moses, in Paul's view, want to conceal from the Israelites the diminishing radiance of his visage (Barrett)? Does he desire that they not realize that the era of the law is destined to fade (Furnish)? Is he attempting to prevent the glory of the Lord mediated by him from destroying his stiff-necked people (Hafemann)?[1] Each of these proposals has difficulties. The former two attribute rather sinister motives to Moses, which Paul does not (see the comments on 3:14–15), while the third interpretation is extremely difficult to derive either from the Exodus narrative or from Paul's comments here. A simpler solution suggests itself.[2] Taking the verb *atenizō* (NIV: "seeing") in accordance with its normal meaning of "staring intently" at an object (as opposed to mental perception),[3] Paul is interpreting Moses's veiling as a means of keeping the people of Israel from becoming fixated on the transitory glory of his radiant face. The glory that was "passing away" refers to Moses's radiance (3:7) as well as to the era of the law that it symbolized (3:11).

3:14–15 *their minds were made dull, for to this day the same veil remains when the old covenant is read . . . a veil covers their hearts.* With the reference to the dull minds of the Israelites Paul clarifies the thought of 3:13: in spite of Moses's effort to keep the people of Israel from fixating on the transitory glory of the old covenant, their hardened minds resisted the truth, and now the veil covers their own heart. Paul reapplies the imagery of the veil, making it symbolic of his people's failure to perceive the temporary nature of the old covenant and to respond appropriately to its message, in particular its expectations of a suffering messiah.

3:16 *whenever anyone turns to the Lord, the veil is taken away.* Paul deftly rewords the Exodus narrative in order to make the application to his contemporaries explicit. Exodus 34:34 reads, "Whenever Moses entered before the Lord to speak to him, he removed the veil" (author's translation). Paul changes the subject of the verb from Moses to "anyone" (more literally, "he"); he replaces "enter" with "turn" (*epistrephō*), which introduces the idea of conversion (see Acts 9:35; 14:15; 1 Thess. 1:9); and he uses a divine passive, "the veil *is taken away*," indicating that God or Christ is responsible for lifting the veil from the hearts and minds of any who turn to him. In keeping with Paul's argument, "the Lord" would refer to Yahweh, as in the Exodus 34 narrative, but in light of Paul's shrewd reshaping of this story, it is likely the expression is intentionally allusive, so that it could also be heard as a reference to Christ.

3:17 *Now the Lord is the Spirit, and where the Spirit of the Lord is, there is freedom.* The consensus of recent scholarship understands this sentence as an explanation of the previous verse, applying it to the setting of his readers: "Now, this 'Lord' of the Exodus story means for us the Spirit."[4] The life-giving (3:6), new covenant Spirit (3:7–8) who brings righteousness (3:9) and unsurpassed glory (3:10–11) also brings "freedom" and transformation (3:17–18). Paul does not explain what type of freedom the Spirit brings, and it is possible that in not qualifying the expression he may intend it quite broadly. The immediate context, however, suggests that Paul may have in mind freedom from the written code of the old covenant (3:6–10, 14), freedom from death and condemnation (3:7–9), or freedom to approach the Lord with unveiled boldness (3:12–17). Verses 17 and 18 provide the grounds for the assertion of verse 12: we are very bold (v. 12) because the Spirit gives us freedom (v. 17) and is transforming us into God's image (v. 18).

3:18 *we all, who with unveiled faces contemplate the Lord's glory, are being transformed into his image with ever-increasing glory.* Paul began this section by contrasting himself and his co-workers with Moses (3:12–13), and Paul now completes his application of Exodus 34:29–35 by asserting that "we all" (= all believers) are exactly like Moses in that we can approach the Lord with an unveiled face, contemplate his glory (see "Teaching the Text," below), and experience glorious transformation. Grounding this audacious assessment is the statement in Exodus 34:34, "But whenever he [Moses] entered the LORD's presence to speak with him, he removed the veil until he came out." The "same image" (see ESV, LEB, NET, NRSV) refers to the image of the Lord as reflected in Christ. "Ever-increasing glory" involves the progressive renewal of the believer, along the lines of 4:16, "Inwardly we are being renewed day by day."

which comes from the Lord, who is the Spirit. Summarizing the prophetic message of inner renewal promised by Jeremiah and Ezekiel and heralded throughout this chapter, Paul once more reiterates his conviction that Ezekiel's life-giving Spirit (Ezek. 36:26; 37:14; 2 Cor. 3:3, 6) is currently effecting in believers the transformation promised by that prophet. "The Lord, who is the Spirit" recapitulates the thought of 3:17, as helpfully paraphrased by Harris: "This Lord (= Yahweh), who is (now experienced as) the Spirit."[5]

Theological Insights

Paul's critique of the law and the Mosaic dispensation in 3:1–18 is comprehensive and yet concise. He faults the law for approaching humanity *from without*, on tablets of stone, rather than *from within*, on the human heart (3:3). He faults it for producing *death*, rather than *life*, and for leading to *condemnation* rather than *righteousness* (3:7–9). He also finds fault with its transitory nature and its feeble and fading glory (3:9–11). In the end, rejecting Christ and the new covenant produces a thick veil that, in effect, covers the senses of the wearer so that they cannot perceive the light, even though it shines all around them (3:12–14). The solution that Paul sees in the new covenant is one that brings hope (3:12), boldness (3:12), freedom (3:17), and transformation (3:18). It offers these things because it offers Christ and the Spirit (3:14–18). This is in fulfillment of the Old Testament hope for a law that is written on the heart (Jer. 31:33), a Spirit that brings life from within (Ezek. 36:26), and people who shall "all . . . be righteous" (Isa. 60:21; see 2 Cor. 5:21).

Teaching the Text

The central theological truth of this passage relates to the process of conversion and what occurs when someone comes to faith in Christ. This can be summarized and clarified in the following teaching points.

1. *Apart from Christ our hearts and minds are darkened.* Using the people of Israel as a theological foil, Paul depicts the human condition apart from Christ as a state of darkened understanding. Although Paul's initial focus is the hardened minds and hearts of Israel, his careful rendering of Exodus 34:34 ("whenever *anyone* turns to the Lord," 3:16) is intended to bring out the larger anthropological dilemma that is so prominent in passages like Romans 2–3; Galatians 5; and especially 1 Corinthians 2:14: "The person without the Spirit does not accept the things that come from the Spirit of God but considers them foolishness, and cannot understand them because they are discerned only through the Spirit." In the verses that follow (2 Cor. 4:3–4), Paul will further explain that all those who are perishing remain "veiled" and blinded by "the god of this age."

2. *Turning to Christ brings true enlightenment.* The removal of the veil is a metaphor for conversion, turning to the Lord and embracing Christ (3:14–16). This initiates a process of enlightenment that encompasses both heart and mind. This enlightenment is not primarily an intellectual comprehension of facts about Jesus, although it may involve that. Rather, it is an apprehension of the divine purpose of Jesus's life, particularly his death and resurrection, and an acceptance of the significance of that story as the definitive narrative of God's redeeming work in this world.

3. Contemplating the Lord brings transformation. The moral transformation promised in 3:18 is the outcome of contemplating, or beholding as in a mirror, the glory of the Lord. The verb *katoptrizō* (NIV: "contemplate") connotes attentive, focused consideration of an object, though Paul does not take the time here to unpack this metaphor or to specify precisely what he expects this contemplation to look like for his readers. He explains clearly that transformation is initiated by faith, "turning to the Lord" (3:16), and effected by the Spirit (3:17–18). Although the verb entails an element of mental perception, Paul probably has more in mind than merely a cognitive process. Elsewhere Paul indicates that spiritual formation occurs through mental renewal (Rom. 12:2; Phil. 4:8–9), contemplating Scripture and apostolic teaching (1 Tim. 2:7; 3:16), enduring hardship (Rom. 5:3–4; 2 Cor. 1:8–9), and especially participating in Christian community: loving, serving, teaching, and admonishing one another (Gal. 6:2; Eph. 4:11–16; Col. 3:12–17; 1 Thess. 4:11; 5:18; etc.). If we were to calibrate this somewhat cryptic metaphor with Paul's teaching elsewhere regarding transformative growth, we might conclude that "contemplating the glory of the Lord" involves a life of faithful endurance, service, and prayer, one that is attentive to God's presence through his people and his Word.

Illustrating the Text

The power of the gospel transforms sinners into followers.

Biography: **George Müller.** The early life of George Müller (1805–98) is probably less well known than his later life, when he established orphanages in England. He is often thought of as the "man who got things from God," as he experienced many answers to prayer while opening and maintaining those orphanages. However, his story is far more complex than those dramatic accounts. Müller spent many of his early years living a sinful lifestyle, undeterred even by his mother's death. Invited one evening to a Christian meeting at a friend's house, he experienced something that he said he had been seeking his whole life. That was the beginning of Müller's freedom from the bondage of sin.

Biography: **John Newton.** This familiar story is, nevertheless, powerful. Though born into a godly home, Newton (1725–1807) sank to the lowest depths of sin. His life was spared over and over, but he always forgot the mercy of God. He became a slave trader and then, ironically, a slave himself, sold to a powerful black woman, who tossed him crusts under the table.

Later, Newton feared for his life during a terrible storm. Surrounded by "black, unfathomable despair,"[6] he sought enduring mercy and found it. "My prayer for mercy," he wrote, "was like the cry of the ravens, which yet the

Lord Jesus does not disdain to hear."[7] He went on to have a great Christian ministry, providing spiritual leadership for England; he wielded power for good in the best of ways and had influence on such great men as Wilberforce and Cowper. He wrote many great hymns, including "How Sweet the Name of Jesus Sounds," "Glorious Things of Thee Are Spoken," and "Amazing Grace."[8]

You Can't See It From There!

Story: A pastor met with a young man who was just three weeks away from his wedding day. This man was nervous and struggling with his decision. He was focusing on the challenges ahead, the sacrifices, and the responsibility of being married and maybe one day having a family. He said to the pastor, "I just don't know where I will get the strength and love I need to be a good husband and a good dad someday." The pastor looked at him and said, "You can't see it from here. You really can't understand until you enter in and become a husband and someday a dad. But when you are married, God grows your love, your servant heart, and your humility, and the Lord gives you what you don't have today—because you don't need it yet."

This is really true. Ask any parent if they knew how much they could love a child before their first son or daughter was born. They will tell you no. Some things can't be seen or fully understood until we cross into a new reality. Full understanding of God's message of love and grace can't be comprehended until a person becomes a follower of Jesus. When this happens, things begin to make sense and our understanding grows with each passing day of walking with the Savior.

2 Corinthians 4:1–6

New Covenant Service

Big Idea
Because Paul has been entrusted with such an important ministry, he serves with absolute integrity, pointing always to Jesus, not himself, yet recognizing that Satan has blinded many to the glory of Christ.

Key Themes
- Paul's response to the precious responsibility of becoming a herald of the new covenant is to serve with unflagging integrity.
- Satan is actively opposing the gospel, blinding people to its message.
- As a servant of Christ, Paul is a servant of Christ's body, his church.
- Conversion involves inner illumination of the heart, which reveals God's glory in Christ.

Understanding the Text

The Text in Context

In 4:1–6 Paul continues his apostolic defense (2:14–7:4) and concludes the argument that began in 3:7 regarding the superiority of the new covenant to the old. In 3:7–11 Paul made the assertion that the new covenant ministry of the Spirit is superior in every way to the old covenant ministry of the law. In the paragraphs that follow (3:12–18 and 4:1–6) Paul spells out two practical implications of this reality. First, in contrast to Moses, Paul serves with "unveiled" boldness, knowing that it is the Lord who removes the veil and transforms hearts (3:12–18). Second, in contrast to others, Paul serves with unwavering integrity, recognizing that the god of this age is actively opposing his work (4:1–6). This present section contains strong verbal and conceptual links to both 2:14–17 and 3:7–11 (see "Interpretive Insights," below), as Paul continues to distinguish his open and sincere heralding of the good news from the work of those whose motives are mixed or self-serving (compare 4:2 with 2:17 and 3:12–13).

Interpretive Insights

4:1 *Therefore, since through God's mercy we have this ministry, we do not lose heart.* "Therefore" is connected to both 3:7–11 and 3:18. In terms of 3:7–11, it draws out a second consequence of the superiority of the new covenant ministry of the Spirit. The first consequence is expressed in 3:12 and relates to Paul's demeanor in ministry: "Therefore . . . we are very bold." The second consequence is articulated in 4:1–2 and relates to Paul's character in ministry: "Therefore, we serve with unflagging integrity" (author's paraphrase). This "therefore" also issues from the lofty expression of new covenant transformation found in 3:18, which epitomizes the supremacy of the new era of the Spirit and provides fresh impetus for Paul to continue to reflect openly on his responsibility to fulfill his commission with utmost integrity (4:1–6). This commissioning (Acts 9:1–19) is regarded as evidence of God's "mercy." Paul often reflects on God's call as an act of mercy (Rom. 9:11–32; Eph. 2:4; 1 Tim. 1:13–16; Titus 3:5), which must have been a particularly poignant truth for him, as one who had persecuted Christians to their death (Acts 22:4), who had regarded Jesus as a fraud (2 Cor. 5:16), and whose pre-Christian life, according to his own testimony, was characterized by people pleasing, violence, and carnal ambition (Gal. 1:10–14; 1 Tim. 1:13). Paul is fully cognizant of the gravity and significance of the stewardship he has received as a minister of the new covenant, and this serves as a hedge against despondency or apathy ("Therefore . . . we do not lose heart") and an impetus toward principled integrity in his proclamation (2 Cor. 4:2). The Greek word rendered "lose heart" by the NIV is used elsewhere by Paul of growing weary in doing good (Gal. 6:9; 2 Thess. 3:13). In light of verse 2, that is probably the sense here.

The Noble Philosopher versus the Sophistic Pretender

Paul was not the only person who struggled to distance himself from less noble orators and religious counterfeits. The renaissance of sophistry during the first and second centuries led to large numbers of high-powered rhetoricians (sophists) who sought fame and fortune through wowing the crowds with their verbal wizardry. The philosopher Dio Chrysostom (ca. AD 40–120; Chrysostom means "golden mouthed") was a first-century orator of considerable fame and fortune. He was a younger contemporary of Paul, and he addressed the same issue that Paul does in 2 Corinthians 4:2 using similar language and imagery to express his concern:

But to find a man who in plain terms and without trickery speaks his mind with frankness, and neither for the sake of reputation nor for gain makes false pretensions, but out of good will and concern for his fellow-man stands ready, if need be, to submit to ridicule and to the disorder of the mob—to find such a man is not easy, but rather the good fortune of every great city, so great is the dearth of noble, independent souls and such is the abundance of flatterers, charlatans, and sophists. (*Or.* 32.11)

4:2 *Rather, we have renounced secret and shameful ways . . . On the contrary, by setting forth the truth plainly we commend ourselves to everyone's conscience in the sight of God.* The "secret and shameful ways" are defined by Paul as "deception" and distorting the word of God. As in 2:17–3:1, Paul's modus operandi is the clear and transparent proclamation of the truth, which commends itself to the inner witness of the conscience of his hearers. Paul is probably not refuting an accusation made against him of trickery and distortion but distinguishing himself and his co-workers from other itinerant philosophers and sophists (as in 2:17; 1 Cor. 2:1–5; 1 Thess. 2:3–6) who, on the surface, might have looked very similar: traveling through cities, discoursing on ethical themes, soliciting funds, gaining a following, and so on. Lucian (AD 120–80) uses the same terminology as Paul (*doloō*, "to distort, adulterate") in describing this brand of philosophic pretenders: "They sell their lessons as wine merchants . . . most of them adulterating, cheating, and giving false measure" (*Hermot.* 59).

4:3 *even if our gospel is veiled, it is veiled to those who are perishing.* Paul returns to the image of the veil (3:14–16) and connects it to the thought of 2:15 regarding "those who are perishing." Paul is anticipating the objection, If this new covenant ministry of the Spirit is attended with such glory (3:7–18), why is that glory not perceived by everyone? The veiled gospel is explained more fully as the work of "the god of this age" (4:4).

4:4 *The god of this age has blinded the minds of unbelievers.* Paul uses a variety of names and phrases to refer to Satan ("Belial," 6:15; "angel of light," 11:14; "ruler of the kingdom of the air," Eph. 2:2; "evil one," Eph. 6:16), but only here does he use the term "god." The expression "god of this age" is striking in that it betokens both power and limitation. Paul ascribes to Satan a kind of sovereignty, but one that is bounded by temporal restrictions: this present age. According to Paul this "present age" is evil (Gal. 1:4); it has its own false wisdom (1 Cor. 1:20; 2:6; 3:18), its own rulers (1 Cor. 2:8), and its own ephemeral perspectives (Rom. 12:2)—but it is passing (1 Cor. 7:31). The day is coming when every dominion and power will be in submission to God and even death itself destroyed (1 Cor. 15:23–28). Satan's power in the present age, however, is not unlimited or unchecked. Jesus has triumphed over the powers of darkness through the cross (Col. 2:15) and is enthroned at God's right hand "far above all rule and authority, power and dominion . . . not only in the present age but also in the one to come" (Eph. 1:21). Satan's power to blind is not greater than God's power to illumine (2 Cor. 4:6).

the glory of Christ, who is the image of God. In 3:18 Paul described the transformation of the believer into the "image" of the Lord, and here he identifies Christ as the representation of that image. According to Genesis, Adam was created in God's image (Gen. 1:26–27), and according to 1 Corinthians Christ is a type of second Adam, rectifying the failings of the first (1 Cor.

15:45–49). The transformation that Paul depicts in these chapters constitutes a renewal of the *imago dei*, a "new creation" in Christ (cf. 4:6; 5:17).

4:5 *For what we preach is not ourselves, but Jesus Christ as Lord, and ourselves as your servants for Jesus' sake.* The connection between this verse and what precedes ("for . . .") is not clear. Paul may be returning to the thought of 4:2 regarding his renunciation of trickery and manipulation and completing that thought by explaining that his motivation in ministry is not self-serving ("preaching ourselves") but Christ honoring. In his letters, Paul employs the whole gamut of household relations to depict his relationship to his congregations: father (1 Cor. 4:15), mother (1 Thess. 2:7; Gal. 4:19), infant (1 Thess. 2:7), and especially *brother* (some 130 times); but only here does he call himself a "slave" (NIV: "servant") to his congregation. Elsewhere Paul is Christ's or God's slave (e.g., Rom. 1:1; Titus 1:1). The scope of Paul's servitude, however, is carefully delineated: "for Jesus' sake." Paul does not envision the Corinthians as his "lord." Paul's perspective is that in the same way that Christ emptied himself and became a slave in his mission to God's people (Phil. 2:7–8), so too will Paul "spend and be spent" (2 Cor. 12:15 ESV) on behalf of his congregations. The slave of Christ is also the slave of Christ's church, his body (Eph. 2:21–22).

4:6 *For God, who said, "Let light shine out of darkness," made his light shine in our hearts.* Paul gives the reason ("for," "because"; Greek, *hoti*) why he proclaims Christ, not himself (4:5), with determined, unwavering integrity (4:1–2): God's new work of illumination in the human heart. As Paul searches for an analogy for the new covenant work of the Spirit in conversion, God's initial act of creation comes to mind, and so Paul alludes to Genesis 1:3, where God calls forth light from darkness. For Paul, conversion is a kind of "new creation" (5:17) in which veiled hearts (3:14) and blinded minds (4:4) are flooded with the light of God's love in Christ (Rom. 5:5).

to give us the light of the knowledge of God's glory displayed in the face of Christ. Paul's language in this passage closely parallels Luke's accounts of Paul's conversion in Acts 9; 22; and 26 and suggests that Paul's description here of a light that revealed the glory of God on the face of Christ betrays his own vivid recollection of the appearance of Christ to him on the road to Damascus.[1] In using the first-person plural ("our," "us") and removing the nonparadigmatic elements (an external light, a voice from heaven, blindness), Paul focuses on the universal and essential element of true conversion: God's illumination of the human heart.

Theological Insights

"Light from darkness" is typical conversion language (cf. Col. 1:12–13), and it is hardly surprising that, having described "turning to the Lord" as the removal of a veil (2 Cor. 3:16–18), Paul would soon invoke the imagery of light and darkness to describe conversion. Paul had a rich archive of material to draw on, particularly in the prophet Isaiah. This prophet depicts the messianic era as a time when light will shine on people walking in darkness (Isa. 9:1–2). He portrays the messianic servant as "a light to the nations" (51:4). Pointing to the day of a renewed Israel, Isaiah says, "Arise [and] shine, for your light has come, and the glory of the LORD rises upon you. . . . Nations will come to your light, and kings to the brightness of your dawn" (60:1, 3). For Paul, the light of a new creation and the glory promised by Isaiah are fulfilled in the new covenant whenever anyone turns to Christ (2 Cor. 3:16), experiences the power of the Spirit (3:18), and sees the light of God's glory on the face of Christ illuminating their heart (4:6).

Teaching the Text

The theme of 4:1–6 is enunciated in verse 1, and Paul expresses his determination to do nothing that will compromise the ministry with which he has been entrusted. The teaching points in this passage revolve around the responsibilities and realities of being a gospel herald.

1. *Principled conduct in ministry.* The first implication that Paul draws from the stewardship he has been given as a herald of the new covenant is that he will not "lose heart" or grow weary in discharging his duties (4:1). The Greek verb behind the NIV's "lose heart" (*enkakeō*) may refer to physical depletion (2 Cor. 4:16) or emotional, psychological discouragement (Eph. 3:13), but Paul uses it here and elsewhere (Gal. 6:9; 2 Thess. 3:13) of growing lax in one's conduct, failing to adhere to the highest principles of behavior in ministry. On the contrary, Paul insists that he has renounced any kind of trickery or deceit and that his sincerity should be evident to all (2 Cor. 4:2). The use of manipulative techniques and underhanded methods to accomplish ministry goals is rejected by Paul as unworthy of God's call.

2. *The reality of satanic opposition.* Paul understands that his calling to proclaim the good news of Christ's death and resurrection means opposition at every turn and on every level. Paul certainly has encountered his share of human resistance, but he also recognizes that he is involved in a spiritual battle of cosmic proportions (Eph. 6:12). Paul is aware that Satan plots the downfall of the believer (1 Cor. 7:5; 2 Cor. 2:11; 2 Tim. 2:26), and he also has experienced the evil one's interference in his own ministry (1 Thess. 2:18; 2 Cor. 12:7). Paul sees more than mere human stubbornness or an intellectual deficit behind the rejection of the good news. The hidden power of Satan is at work blinding individuals to the truth that Paul sets before them (Eph. 2:2).

3. *Preaching Christ, not ourselves.* In 1 Corinthians Paul explains that he has determined to preach nothing but "Christ and him crucified" among the Corinthians, and so he intentionally has eschewed eloquence and persuasive oratory (1 Cor. 2:1–4). Paul's reasoning is that he wants the Corinthians' faith to rest not "on human wisdom, but on God's power" (2:5). In contrast to the sophists and orators so common in this era, Paul is focused not on elevating himself and gaining a following and a reputation but on exalting Christ and advancing his kingdom. In reiterating here his resolve to shun trickery and shameful strategies and to preach Christ, not himself, Paul probably intends to contrast himself with orators and sophists, with whom the Corinthians are very familiar. Paul would heartily agrees with James Denny, who says, "No man can give the impression that he himself is clever, and that Christ is mighty to save."[2]

Illustrating the Text

Ministering to others is its own reward.

Story: One of the most effective discipleship strategies is to invite people to participate in a short-term mission trip. When Jesus's followers get outside their comfort zone and serve others in a new environment, it encourages them to develop more of an other-focused mentality. Encouraging followers to engage in some kind of short-term missions project at least once a year can change the culture of a church and help it become a church for the world. Have one or two people who have experienced life transformation on a mission trip share part of their story of how their faith and life have been impacted.

God initiates the transformation process.

Visual Aid: Introduce the idea of keeping a prayer card with the names of people in your sphere of influence who are not yet Christians. Encourage your listeners to pray daily for the veil to be lifted from the eyes of our lost family and friends. This is one of the most loving and effective things we can do to care for them. Tell of a personal encounter of a member of your community who came to Christ recently and highlight someone who prayed for that person to come to faith in Jesus.

Paul counted it a privilege to be awarded the title of "slave."

Story: A vicar, troubled by some of the decisions made by his diocese, wrote to his bishop to express his concerns. He began the letter, "Dear brother in Christ." Nearly the entire first page of the bishop's response was devoted to rebuking the young vicar for inappropriately addressing him as "brother," rather than by his ecclesial title. This contrasts sharply with Paul, who willingly took the designation of a member of the lowest social caste, a "slave" (4:5).

2 Corinthians 4:7–15

Jars of Clay

Big Idea
Paul's suffering for the gospel is the divinely intended means of mediating the crucified, life-giving Jesus to others, which emboldens Paul's faith in preaching and results in thanksgiving and glory to God.

Key Themes
- The glorious gospel is disseminated through frail humans to ensure that God is given due glory.
- Affliction comes as we proclaim Christ, but affliction does not mean destruction.
- Suffering for Christ reenacts the crucifixion and brings the renewal of resurrection life to both the sufferer and the Christian community.
- Our witness is emboldened by knowledge of the coming resurrection.

Understanding the Text

The Text in Context

In 3:7–4:6 Paul emphasized the glory of his apostolic ministry in service of the new covenant. Here in 4:7–15 he stresses the humiliation and suffering that also accompany that ministry. The interconnectedness of glory and suffering is an important theme in chapters 2–7, as Paul explains to the Corinthians that the hardship, deprivation, and opposition he faces do not discredit his ministry but allow fuller expression of God's redemptive purpose. Second Corinthians 4:7–15 concludes the argument of this section of the letter (2:14–4:15) by reiterating the message of its opening verses: through our suffering the aroma of the crucified Christ is revealed to those around us (2:14–16).

Interpretive Insights

4:7 *But we have this treasure in jars of clay.* The adversative "but" signals a perspective that contrasts with what precedes. Although the new covenant ministry of the Spirit is more glorious than the era of the old covenant (3:7–11), and effects glorious transformation (3:18) and glorious inner illumination (4:6), its glory is concealed by the frail earthen containers who administer it. Clay jars were used to store money and valuables and were sometimes buried to

Hardship Catalogs

Second Corinthians 4:7–12 constitutes the first of several "hardship catalogs" in this letter (see 6:3–10 and 11:23–33). Hardship catalogs were a standard feature of Stoic-Cynic exhortation, whereby the philosopher sought to exemplify fortitude, courage, and endurance in the noble cause of advancing wisdom and refuting folly. In form Paul's hardship catalogs bear remarkable similarities to the Stoic-Cynic tradition, as this excerpt from Plutarch's parody of the stoics reveals: "Confined, but not hindered, thrown down, but not constrained, tortured but not in pain, maimed, but not injured, pinned down, but not beaten, surrounded, but not defeated, enslaved, but not captive" (*Mor.* 1057E). In each case, the expected negative result is unexpectedly reversed, engendering respect and empathy for the one enduring such trials. Although similar in form and intent, the presuppositions undergirding Paul's use of hardship catalogs differed significantly from the presuppositions of the Stoics (see "Historical and Cultural Background" in the unit on 6:1–13).

protect one's wealth from robbers (cf. Matt. 13:44). "Treasure" is probably a comprehensive term referring to the privilege of being a new covenant herald (3:12–13; 4:1) as well as to the precious content and effect of that ministry (3:18; 4:6). The contrast with "jars of clay" (mortal humanity subject to death and decay, 4:16–5:5) includes both the value of the treasure compared to the container and the relative endurance of precious metals compared to the fragility of an earthen vessel.

to show that this all-surpassing power is from God and not from us. The power to save (3:14–16; 4:6), to transform (3:18), and to endure (4:8–12) is entirely God's work (cf. 3:5). Paul describes here God's primary modus operandi in human affairs: to intentionally choose the weak, lowly, and despised to accomplish his purposes so that he is not robbed of the glory due his name (1 Cor. 1:26–29).

4:8–9 *We are hard pressed on every side, but not crushed . . . struck down, but not destroyed.* Amplifying the clay jar symbolism of 4:7, Paul explains that his constant experience (Greek, *en panti*: "in everything," "at all times"; NIV: "on every side") in ministry is God's strength expressing itself in circumstances of weakness and affliction. The first element of each antithetical pair depicts a seemingly overwhelming hardship, while the second element emphasizes God's provision to endure. Paul's perspective is that his suffering—far from invalidating his apostolate—is decisive proof of God's call through a demonstration of divine power. To some in Corinth, strength and weakness are incompatible; for Paul they constitute the divine paradox and paradigm of true gospel ministry.

4:10–11 *We always carry around in our body the death of Jesus.* Verses 10 and 11 consist of two closely parallel statements that serve as a second amplification of verse 7, while also offering a profound theological interpretation of the hardships listed in verses 8–9. Paul interprets his suffering on behalf of Christ to be a continuation of Jesus's suffering and death, a kind of reenactment of the crucifixion. To "carry around" probably reflects the reality of Paul's itinerant lifestyle; Paul perceives his own (suffering) body to be the vehicle that portrays the crucified Jesus to the world (cf. Gal. 6:17).

so that the life of Jesus may also be revealed in our body . . . so that his life may also be revealed in our mortal body. Echoing 2:15–16, where the aroma of death is simultaneously the fragrance of life, Paul describes the result of his cross-shaped ministry as "life." As Christ's death led to the resurrection, so too Paul's embodiment of Christ's death leads to the manifestation of resurrection life. Paul's experience of inner strength in the midst of outer conflict (4:16–17), together with God's provision of endurance in spite of overwhelming circumstances (4:8–9), is evidence of the life of the resurrected Jesus pulsing through his "mortal body" (or "flesh"; Greek, *sarx*). The addition of "mortal" emphasizes the fragile, transitory nature of the human condition: "jars of clay" (4:7).

4:12 *So then, death is at work in us, but life is at work in you.* As Paul summarizes 4:8–11, he draws an important conclusion ("so then"): his suffering for the gospel does not hinder its effectiveness but increases its power. Suffering "for Jesus' sake" (4:11) produces life for the individual experiencing the affliction (4:10–11) as well as for the community that is the beneficiary of the suffering. It is through hardship that Paul brought the gospel to Corinth (1 Cor. 2:3), and it is Paul's suffering that authenticates his message by embodying its cruciform character. Paul's message was the cross preached; Paul's life was the cross lived.

4:13 *Since we have that same spirit of faith, we also believe and therefore speak.* The Greek text begins with a contrast, "but, since we have," indicating that the connection between these verses and what precedes is "although we suffer, yet we still speak boldly." Paul cites Psalm 116:10, where the psalmist describes God's rescuing him from harm even as "the cords of death" entangled him (116:3). It is possible that by "spirit" Paul means the Holy Spirit, the Spirit that produces such faith. Probably, however, "spirit" refers to the disposition or attitude of faith that endures in difficult circumstances (cf. the similar use of "spirit" in 1 Cor. 4:21; Gal. 6:1; Eph. 4:23). Paul's focus here is not on having the same divine Spirit but on having the same response of faith: bold proclamation.

4:14 *because we know that the one who raised the Lord Jesus from the dead will also raise us with Jesus and present us with you to himself.* Paul provides now a second reason for his courage in ministry by specifying the content of the faith expressed in 4:13, his belief in the coming resurrection. Later, Paul will explain to the Corinthians that although Jesus was "crucified in weakness, yet he lives by God's power" (13:4). Paul's conviction regarding the future resurrection put his present cruciform suffering in perspective and led to boldness; his eschatology informs his praxis. This resurrection hope extends to all believers, to the entire community of the crucified. The presentation (to God) envisioned here is not one of judgment, as in 5:10, but one of comfort and blessing (11:2; Eph. 5:27; Col. 1:22).

4:15 *All this is for your benefit, so that the grace that is reaching more and more people may cause thanksgiving to overflow to the glory of God.* Paul concludes by reiterating that "all this"—his suffering, his toil, his undaunted proclamation—is for their benefit: death in us, but life in you (4:12). More important, as the gospel of grace expands, so too does God's glory. Paul's thought has returned full circle from 4:7, reiterating again that it is the honor of God's name that is of ultimate consequence.

Theological Insights

The motif of dying and rising with Christ is one of the most important theological themes in Paul's Letters, and it constitutes the very heart of this passage. Paul sometimes describes dying and rising with Christ as the decisive event of the believer's past that initiates new life. The most important passages illustrating this are Romans 6:1–11; Galatians 2:19–21; 5:14–15; and 2 Corinthians 5:14–17. The memorable expression in Romans 6:8 captures this point well: "Now if we died with Christ, we believe that we will also live with him." At other times, however, dying with Christ is described by Paul not as the decisive event of the past but as the continuing experience of the present. In these passages, death is not something that initiates the believer's new life but something that defines the believer's new life. In addition to 2 Corinthians 4:7–14, other important passages illustrating this aspect are 2 Corinthians 1:3–9; 12:9; 13:4; Romans 8:17; and Philippians 3:8–11. From Paul's perspective, when a believer suffers for Jesus's sake, that person is reincarnating the suffering, crucified Jesus. Because Paul views his suffering through the lens of the cross, his hardships take on a cruciform character and gain meaning, purpose, and benefit. As the intense rays of affliction pass through the cruciform prism of the Christian life, those rays are refracted in such a way that, rather than scorching and killing, they produce and reveal life in its fullest form.

Teaching the Text

In this passage Paul puts our present frailty, suffering, and labor into perspective by reminding us of God's power and purpose. Through our weakness and mortality God's strength becomes visible and compelling. The teacher could stress this theme under the following headings:

1. *Human frailty and God's glory.* The first point Paul makes in this passage is that the frailty and weakness of the human condition is God's chosen mechanism to accomplish his purpose and bring glory to himself (4:7). This is an important theme in this letter (2:14; 3:5; 12:9) and, in Paul's view, is God's standard operating procedure. The apostle explained this in an earlier letter: "But God chose the foolish things of the world to shame the wise; God chose the weak things of the world to shame the strong. God chose the lowly things of this world and the despised things—and the things that are not—to nullify the things that are, so that no one may boast before him" (1 Cor. 1:27–29). In choosing to work through what is frail, weak, mortal, and subject to decay, God removes any doubt as to who should receive honor and glory.

2. *Suffering for Jesus and the suffering of Jesus.* Paul presents a theology of suffering in these verses that is both profound and perplexing at the same time. Paul's perspective on suffering *for* Jesus is that it extends the suffering *of* Jesus in the world. The apostle depicts his persecution-afflicted body as the locus of the "dying of Jesus" (4:10 NASB). Hence, he could tell the Galatians that the wounds on his body were the "marks of Jesus" (Gal. 6:17). To the church in Colossae Paul describes his suffering as filling up what is lacking in Christ's affliction (Col. 1:24). Paul's point is not that Christ's suffering was not perfectly sufficient for accomplishing full redemption but that the church is privileged to participate in those sufferings and so, in some real, tangible sense, complete that suffering (Phil. 1:29).

3. *Our present labor and our future resurrection.* Although Christians can sometimes become absorbed in unhealthy eschatological (end-time) speculation, often focusing on the date or timing of Christ's return, this should not lead us to minimize the importance of eschatology—what the Bible teaches about the end times—in the New Testament, and Paul's Letters in particular. In this passage Paul explains that his belief in the coming resurrection has the very practical effect of energizing his present ministry by galvanizing his determination to boldly proclaim the gospel. In fact, eschatology is almost always linked in Paul's Letters to very practical concerns, how-should-we-then-live issues. In 1 Thessalonians, for example, a correct understanding of future events tempers one's grief at the loss of a loved one (4:13–18) and leads to moral vigilance, love, and faith (5:4–10). In other words, eschatology is as much about how to live in the present as it is about what will happen in the future.

Illustrating the Text

We have treasures in jars of clay.

Metaphor: Philip Yancey tells the story of a bright, talented, and very funny friend named Carolyn, who suffers from cerebral palsy, as a powerful metaphor for the church as the body of Christ. He describes a chapel service for which Carolyn wrote a speech: "On the day of the chapel service Carolyn sat slumped in her wheelchair. At times her arms jerked uncontrollably, her head lolled to one side so that it almost touched her shoulder, and a stream of saliva sometimes ran down her blouse. Beside her stood Josee, who read the mature and graceful prose Carolyn had composed, centered around this Bible text: 'But we have this treasure in jars of clay to show that this all-surpassing power is from God and not from us.' For the first time, some students saw Carolyn as a complete human being, like themselves."

For Yancey, this provided a powerful metaphor: "The scene [Carolyn] described became for me a parable of transposition: a perfect mind locked inside a spastic, uncontrolled body, and vocal cords that fail at every second syllable. . . . We, the church, are an example of transposition taken to extreme. Sometimes, like Carolyn's body, we obscure rather than convey the message. But the church is the reason behind the entire human experiment, the reason that there are human beings in the first place: to let creatures other than God bear the image of God. He deemed it well worth the risk, and the humiliation."[1]

News: In 2010 an amateur treasure hunter in southwest England discovered a Roman-era pot containing over 52,000 Roman coins buried in a field. He came upon a few coins with his metal detector, and his initial discovery of twenty-one coins turned into a much larger find. The cracked and weathered food-storage pot was buried just over a foot underground. It may not have looked like much, but it contained untold riches in the form of stunning silver and bronze coins.[2]

Not all is as it seems.

Object Lesson: Present two ceramic pots on a table—one containing a potted flower and the second pot containing loose change. The teacher could ask the audience which pot has more value. Then pour out the change onto the table—you end up with a few dollars worth of coins. Next, smash the potted plant and reveal five $100 bills hidden in the dirt. The gospel is a hidden and exceptionally valuable treasure.

2 Corinthians 4:16–5:5

Fixing Our Eyes on the Unseen

Big Idea
In spite of the frailty of our present human condition and the hardships we face in this life, the believer experiences the power of God's renewal within and looks forward to the complete renewal of the eternal state, and so does not lose hope.

Key Themes
- In the midst of external affliction and eventual physical decay, believers experience the power of God's renewal within.
- Perspective on our present trials comes as we recognize that they are fleeting and inconsequential in comparison to the glorious eternity that awaits us.
- Our physical state in this life is temporary and characterized by groaning, as we look forward to a renewed and permanent glorified body that God will grant in the future.

Understanding the Text

The Text in Context

In 4:16 Paul draws a conclusion from the argument of 4:7–15, that his suffering advances the gospel: "Therefore we do not lose heart." Paul further grounds this conclusion with the assurance that even in the midst of suffering there is inner renewal (4:17–18), and even at the final physical demise of the body there is the promise of a glorious outer renewal (5:1–5). The twin foci of present, inner, spiritual renewal and future, outer, bodily renewal provide perspective and motivation for Paul to endure the hardships of his calling.

Interpretive Insights

4:16 *Therefore we do not lose heart.* Using the same expression as in 4:1, Paul again draws encouragement in the difficult circumstances of his ministry (4:7–15) from the reality of God's renewal within. In both contexts Paul juxtaposes inner renewal (cf. 3:18) and outer difficulties (cf. 4:2–5) in order to focus attention on the invisible reality of God's sustaining and transforming work within.

Though outwardly we are wasting away, yet inwardly we are being renewed day by day. This statement, together with 4:17–18, provides further rationale for why Paul does not lose hope: present renewal (4:16), future glory (4:17), and an eternal perspective (4:18). Paul refocuses the thought of verses 10 and 11, which describe his hardship as "being given over to death," and concentrates now on the inevitable deterioration of the visible mortal frame. This "outer person" (a more literal rendering of the Greek expression) is the clay jar of 4:7 and the mortal flesh of 4:11. The antithesis of "outer" and "inner" person was common in Greco-Roman thought, especially as a means of disparaging humanity's physical component as a worthless husk to be discarded at death. While recognizing that humanity's mortal frame was subject to decay and death, Paul also looked forward to a bodily resurrection and a transformed physicality (1 Cor. 15:35–54; 2 Cor. 5:1–5), which was very much at odds with Greek and Roman eschatology. The "inner person" that is being renewed is probably not an ontological reality (i.e., the immaterial soul) but the inner life of a person—their character, moral strength, and emotional-psychological constitution, which is growing into Christlikeness (Eph. 3:16–19). Paul is describing a process of external decline and internal revitalization that is both constant ("day by day") and simultaneous. In so doing, he puts flesh and blood on the image of an earthen vessel concealing a glorious treasure (2 Cor. 4:7).

4:17 *For our light and momentary troubles are achieving for us an eternal glory.* Verse 17 substantiates 16a ("we do not lose heart") by providing a second ground for persevering in ministry: present suffering results in incomparable glory that will be fully revealed in eternity (Col. 1:26–27; 3:4). The immeasurable, unending superiority of what awaits leads Paul to conclude that, when weighed on the scales of eternity, his present suffering is completely inconsequential (Rom. 8:18). This evaluation is all the more telling when we consider that Paul's hardships involved sacrificing his prestigious vocation; loss of reputation; persecution; slander; beatings; stonings; going without sufficient food, clothing, and sleep; shipwrecks; prison; and daily anxiety over his spiritual children (2 Cor. 4:7–12; 6:4–10; 11:22–29; Gal. 1:13–14). The "our," "we," and "us" in this passage refer to Paul and his companions, and by extension to other believers in similar circumstances.

4:18 *So we fix our eyes not on what is seen, but on what is unseen.* Verse 18 may be understood as a result of verse 17 (as the NIV here), or as the circumstances in which verse 17 takes place: our momentary affliction achieves glory *while we fix our gaze . . .*; or (more probably) causally: our momentary affliction achieves glory *because we fix our gaze . . .* Paul makes explicit that one's focus and perspective determine one's valuation of present affliction. Things that are seen are temporary: wealth, reputation, creaturely comforts, and sensual pleasures. Unseen things are eternal: faith, hope, love, endurance, humility, goodness, and so on. Living for what is unseen and hidden from mortal eyes leads to willing suffering and eternal rewards (4:17; 5:10).

5:1 *For we know that if the earthly tent we live in is destroyed, we have a building from God.* Paul's thought transitions naturally from hardships in ministry (4:7–15) to the inevitable ebbing of physical strength (4:16–18) to the final demise of physical life (5:1–5). Verses 1–5 amplify the temporary-versus-eternal theme of 4:18, while also augmenting the rationale for not losing heart of 4:16: even if our suffering leads to death, we have an enduring and transformed physical existence promised by God. If the clay jar image of 4:7 emphasized the fragility and low value of the container compared to its precious content, the image of a tent in this verse depicts our present physicality as temporary and easily dismantled compared to the eternal building that awaits (cf. Isa. 38:12; 2 Pet. 1:13–14). The present tense, "we have a building," should be interpreted not as indicating the *immediacy* of a renewed physicality upon death but as emphasizing the *certainty* of this transformed existence. Paul has already told the Corinthians that this coming transformation will occur at Christ's return (1 Cor. 15:50–54), and he is not retracting that teaching here.

5:2 *Meanwhile we groan, longing to be clothed instead with our heavenly dwelling.* The "meanwhile state" of embodiment produces an intense inner yearning prompted by the Spirit (5:5) for the consummation of salvation, the redemption of our bodies (see 5:4). This longing is a function of the already–not yet character of living between the cross and the resurrection. This groaning issues from both a deep desire for God's work to be completed

Nakedness in the First Century

As Paul contemplates the possibility of dying before Christ's return and thus experiencing the temporary separation of material (body) and immaterial (soul/spirit) components of personhood, he chooses a term with decidedly negative connotations for him as a Jew, "naked." Nakedness was distasteful to Jews for both theological and historical reasons. Theologically, it was associated with the sin of Adam and the shame that followed his transgression. Historically, Jews of the period considered nakedness to be one of the defining features of Greek culture and symbolic of Hellenistic cultural hegemony. During the Maccabean era (150–50 BC) the construction of a gymnasium in Jerusalem—where men exercised naked—prompted a violent reaction from the Jews (1 Macc. 1:10–14; 2 Macc. 4:7–20). The Jewish author of the book of *Jubilees*, writing during this era, exhorts his kinsmen, "Therefore it is commanded in the heavenly tablets by all who know the Law that they should cover their shame and not go about naked as do the Gentiles" (1.23).

and a frustration with mortal frailties and weaknesses. Yet it is essentially a longing of hope, not despair.

5:3–4 *we will not be found naked . . . clothed instead with our heavenly dwelling.* The Greek word translated "clothed" by the NIV in verses 2 and 4 is found only here in the New Testament. It is a double compound (*epi + en + dyō*) and refers to putting on a garment over another garment already being worn. It might be more accurately rendered "clothed over." This verb is intentionally chosen by Paul to express his desire to survive until Christ's return and so be able to put on his "spiritual body" (1 Cor. 15:44) over his present physical body. The alternative is to die before the return and be "naked" (2 Cor. 5:3) or "unclothed" (5:4)—that is, temporarily disembodied—during the period between death and the resurrection.

so that what is mortal may be swallowed up by life. This expression captures in almost poetic fashion what Romans 8:23 calls "our adoption to sonship, the redemption of our bodies." The consummation of salvation, from the perspective of individual anthropology, is not release from the shackles of physicality, as Paul's Greek and Roman contemporaries believed, but transformed and renewed physicality—mortality clothed with immortality (1 Cor. 15:54).

5:5 *Now the one who has fashioned us for this very purpose is God, who has given us the Spirit.* The most immediate antecedent to "for this very purpose" is the statement in 5:4 regarding the acquisition of the transformed, spiritual body at Christ's return. The descriptive clause "who has given us the Spirit" is connected to what precedes as its means. God has prepared us for this future renewal *by means of* the gift of the Spirit, given as guarantee. Paul has in mind the bestowal of the Spirit at conversion (1 Cor. 12:13; 2 Cor. 1:22; Eph. 1:13–14), whereby the initial, inner renewal is effected, and this initial renewal leads to inward longing for the completion of the work (Rom. 8:23).

a deposit, guaranteeing what is to come. As in 1:22 and Ephesians 1:14, Paul refers to the Spirit as a deposit by which God obligates himself to fulfill the transaction and complete the work he has begun (Phil. 1:6). In the parallel passage in Romans 8:23, Paul uses the image of the Spirit as the firstfruits, a foretaste of a much larger harvest to come: "the redemption of our bodies."

Theological Insights

The motif of transformation is an important theme in Paul's Letters and figures prominently in the argument of 2 Corinthians. Paul identifies two types of transformative events in the life of a believer subsequent to conversion. He speaks of a present, progressive, inner transformation as well as a future, instantaneous, outer transformation. The present transformation is gradual and relates to the moral and characterological development of the individual. It is sometimes depicted as mental renewal (Rom. 12:2), or the formation of Christ in the person (2 Cor. 3:18; 4:11–12; Gal. 4:19; Eph. 4:15), or more generally as in 2 Corinthians 4:16 of daily inner renewal. The future transformation will occur at the return of Christ (Phil. 3:20–21) and will take place "in the twinkling of an eye" (1 Cor. 15:52). This transformation will bring the physical, outer person into conformity with the already-regenerated inner person (Rom. 8:21–25; 2 Cor. 5:1–5). The motif of transformation is one manifestation of the already–not yet dialectic that we find throughout Paul's Letters, in which the power of the future is already operative in the present but will be consummated in the eschaton.

Teaching the Text

The primary teaching points of these paragraphs are crystallized in a series of antitheses that highlight the already–not yet character of the present state of God's redemptive work. These contrasts are intended to help us see the present in light of the future, which will bring perspective to the hardships of this life and prevent discouragement (4:16).

1. *Outer decay versus inner renewal.* Following his vivid depiction of his own distress and affliction in 4:7–12, Paul reflects on the inevitable toll that this has taken on his external frame. Paul's point, however, is not to bemoan the cussedness of life or the growing limitations of advancing years but to focus attention on the more important reality of inner renewal, which, in part, is being brought about by these very hardships (4:10–11).

2. *Light and momentary troubles versus unending glory.* Only when the difficulties of this life are seen from the vantage point of eternity can they be adequately assessed. Although Paul's difficulties were substantial, he regards them as "light and momentary" when compared to the weight and duration of the glory they achieve (4:17). Mortal creatures bounded by time and circumstance often fail to see beyond the ephemeral obstructions of personal trials to the "eternal glory" on the other side. Paul's reflection here is an attempt to help us elevate our gaze and see things in proper perspective.

3. *Seen versus unseen.* Paul articulates here the principle that undergirds these antitheses: there is an unseen reality that is more real, more important, and more permanent than the visible reality that daily confronts our senses. As material beings inhabiting a material world, we need material goods to survive—food, shelter, and the like. Yet hidden beneath and beyond the material is an unseen, invisible reality that is actually more crucial to survival than the visible entities that lie on the surface (Phil. 4:11–13; John 4:32–34). Striking a note of sober irony, Paul tells us he fixes his eyes on what cannot be seen, because only these things are of eternal significance.

4. *Temporary versus eternal.* The example that Paul lingers on, after observing that "what is seen is temporary, but what is unseen is eternal" (4:18), is our present physical state, which he likens to a tent that is quickly dismantled and packed away. He contrasts this with an eternal edifice not made by human hands, which the believer will receive when Christ returns. The proper perspective on our current embodied state is neither to despise it (as many in Paul's day did), nor to treasure it beyond all else (as many in our day do), but to recognize that it is destined to decay and die and so to long for the permanent spiritual body that awaits. Paul is not saying that our most significant longing should be for our eventual physical renewal. However, as we recognize the disintegration of our mortal frame, it is entirely appropriate to yearn for the bodily transformation that awaits. Equally important, Paul's palpable aversion to the prospect of a temporary separation of material and immaterial components of personhood underscores the intrinsic and eternal connection between body and soul as far as the human constitution is concerned.

Illustrating the Text

Paul's perspective on the present is animated by his conviction of the future.

Object Lesson: Ask the audience to take their cell phone and zoom in and out (in camera mode) while pointing the phone toward the stage. Have them observe how quickly the perspective can change. This is also true in life: our focus is often on our daily tasks, decisions, and problems, but by changing our view, believers can look at their daily issues through the lens of eternity. The truth is that most Christ-followers do not think nearly enough about the life to come. Paul did not live that way. I wonder if Paul was able to live so effectively in the present because he viewed his problems from the perspective of eternity. Wise Christ-followers will follow such wisdom.

We fix our eyes on the eternal, not the temporal prize.

Song: Madonna's famous "material girl in a material world" articulates the ephemeral perspectives and values that focus only on what is seen, with no appreciation of the deeper unseen realities.

Outwardly we are wasting away.

Statistic: According to the American Society for Aesthetic Plastic Surgery, cosmetic procedures experienced a 12-percent growth in the United States in 2013, with patients spending $12 billion annually.[1] Clearly, Americans place a high value on exterior appearance. Imagine if such resources were invested in kingdom causes that last for all eternity.

Our bodies are fragile and temporary—but our spirits are strong and eternal.

Metaphor: While camping in the Black Hills of South Dakota, a pastor and his wife were sleeping in a tiny two-person pup tent. A storm came up suddenly; one minute they were on their backs looking up at the tent's ceiling, and the next minute they were looking at the darkened sky as a strong gust of wind literally tore their tent in half. Our earthly bodies are extremely vulnerable, but our heavenly house can withstand any storm. Tell a story like this, about a time you saw how frail and temporary some things can be.

2 Corinthians 5:6–10

By Faith, Not Sight

Big Idea
Paul's aim is to be pleasing to the Lord, regardless of his circumstances, knowing that all believers will be held accountable for their actions and receive either reward or censure from the Lord.

Key Themes
- The believer can take courage from knowing that even if they die before Christ's return, they will be with the Lord.
- The believer's life is characterized by faith in what they cannot see.
- Regardless of circumstances, the believer should seek to please the Lord.
- The believer will receive reward or censure for their actions in this life.

Understanding the Text

The Text in Context

Second Corinthians 5:6–10 is tightly connected to the preceding section, 4:16–5:5, by spelling out the implications of focusing on the unseen reality of eternal glory (4:16–18) and the promise of an eternal bodily habitation at Christ's return (5:1–5). The primary conclusions Paul draws from these truths is that, inwardly, believers can be "confident" in God's provision for them (5:6–8) and, outwardly, their lives should reflect God's priorities in this world (5:9–10). This section also brings to a conclusion the argument begun in 4:7–12 regarding the connection between suffering and glory and transitions to the next stage of the apostolic defense, Paul's ministry of proclamation (5:11–6:13).

Historical and Cultural Background

Greeks and Romans entertained many conceptions of the afterlife. Because there was no canonical sacred text to teach "orthodox" doctrine on any point, denizens of the ancient world were faced with a wide variety of often contradictory notions on this subject. The writings of Homer popularized the dreary realm of Hades as the cheerless, eternal abode of mortals. Mystery religions and other popular literature envisioned Elysium (or the Elysian Fields) as the peaceful repose of legendary heroes, noble men and women, and those initiated into the mysteries. Epicureans taught that a person was nothing more than their physical body, so that when that body dies, there is nothing left. Funerary monuments reveal the primitive but enduring belief that the dead somehow continued to live on in the tomb. Tombs were frequently stocked with burnt food and utensils for the dead to use (a burnt item was a "dead" item and so could be used by the dead) and were sometimes constructed with openings for further provisions. Gravestones in Macedonia often depicted the deceased as a mythic Thracian Rider ascending to immortality. As diverse as these beliefs are—and many others could be cataloged—they were united in their denial of a bodily resurrection (cf. Acts 17:32; 1 Cor. 15). Moreover, since the denial of a postmortem physical rejuvenation was connected to a denigration of physicality, most Greeks and Romans would not have shared Paul's aversion to a temporary disembodied state (2 Cor. 5:2–4) nor felt as strongly as Paul his solace at being "at home with the Lord" during this period (5:6–8). Paul's readers, most of whom shared this common cultural heritage, were probably also puzzled at some of the concerns Paul expresses in 5:1–10.

Interpretive Insights

5:6 *Therefore we are always confident.* Paul begins to apply concretely the teaching in 5:1–5 related to personal eschatology (what happens to an individual when they die). The first point he makes is that a correct understanding of these issues should bring us encouragement. Paul makes a similar statement to the Thessalonians, who were distressed about the future of believers who had died before Christ's return: "I don't want you to be ignorant about those who have died . . . lest you grieve like those who have no hope" (1 Thess. 4:13, author's translation). In both contexts Paul stresses that a correct understanding of what happens next has a very practical benefit: confidence regarding one's personal destiny (2 Cor. 5:6) and comfort regarding other believers who have died (1 Thess. 4:13, 18).

at home in the body we are away from the Lord. Paul understands that in his current state "in the body" he is separated, in a sense, from the Lord (cf. 5:8). Paul is not deprecating his physicality but simply acknowledging that the immediacy of God's presence in the next life will bring about an intimacy and communion that cannot be fully achieved in this life. This sentiment is echoed in 1 Corinthians 13:12: "For now we see only a reflection as in a mirror; then we shall see face to face." Paul's hope is that he will remain until Christ returns and so bypass the intermediate "naked" state (2 Cor. 5:3–4) when his soul/spirit is temporarily separated from his body. However, he comforts himself with the knowledge that during this period he will be "at home" with the Lord, "which is better by far" (Phil. 1:23).

5:7 *For we live by faith, not by sight.* This verse clarifies the statement of 5:6 that to be "at home in the body" is to be "away from the Lord" by reiterating the "seen" versus "unseen" principle of 4:18. Because Christ is not now visible, the believer lives (or "walks") by faith in an unseen reality (Heb. 11:1). A reality that is unseen, however, is no less real than "visible forms" (a more literal rendering of the Greek word behind "sight"). Paul makes this same point in Romans 8:24: "But hope that is seen is no hope at all. Who hopes for what they already have?" The believer's present situation "away" from the immediate presence of the Lord necessitates a life of faith and hope and should express itself in loving obedience, a desire to please him (2 Cor. 5:9).

5:9 *So we make it our goal to please him.* The ultimate conclusion Paul draws from the dilemma of being "away from the Lord" while in the body is that our lives should be lived according to the unseen reality of our eternal home, to please the Lord whom we presently see only by faith, not by sight. Once again Paul's instruction on eschatology is eminently practical and aimed at ordering our present life in accordance with our truest home (Phil. 3:19). Throughout this section (5:1–10) Paul has employed a host of images and terms to depict the pilgrim-like status of the believer in this present life: a tent (5:1), walking (5:7), traveling ("away from," 5:6, 8, 9).[1] Paul himself traversed countless miles of Roman roads, mostly on foot, as he sought to fulfill his

One of the most prominent features of Corinth's civic landscape was its bema (Greek, *bēma*; "judgment seat," 5:10), the tribunal where judicial pronouncements were handed down by the governor and other civic magistrates. Corinth's bema was a large, raised platform centrally located in the main forum and was modeled after the tribunal in the main forum in Rome. It was originally covered in marble with elegantly carved molding. Its impressive remains are still visible today.

apostolic commission, and so it not surprising to see him depict the believer's present embodied condition as a tent, and the Christian life as a journey to a home yet unseen.

5:10 *For we must all appear before the judgment seat of Christ.* Grounding the implicit exhortation of 5:9 (live to please the Lord) is the sober reminder that "we all" will be held accountable for our actions in this life. The context, which focuses on what happens to the believer upon death, indicates that "we all" refers to the judgment of believers. However, Paul also speaks of the universal judgment of humanity (Rom. 2:3–11; 14:11–12), and it is not clear if there are two separate events in view. The passive form of the verb *phaneroō* (NIV: "appear") suggests more than merely an appearance in court; it connotes the idea of being revealed or exposed before a tribunal.[2] This is supported by the twofold use of the same verb in 5:11, and the parallel text in 1 Corinthians 4:5: "[The Lord] will expose the motives of the heart. At that time each will receive their praise from God." Paul's own public appearance before Gallio's tribunal in Corinth may be in the background as he writes these words (Acts 18:12–17).

so that each of us may receive what is due us. The reason for appearing before Christ's tribunal is to receive reward or censure for "things done while in the body." The singular pronoun "each" indicates that recompense is individually reckoned and that Paul has in mind personal accountability to God, as in Romans 14:12: "Each of us will give an account of himself to God" (ESV). As in 2 Corinthians 4:17, embodied existence is regarded as the forge of eternal glory, but here Paul adds the thought that the opposite is possible as well. The expression "whether good or bad" indicates that individual actions will be weighed, which is in keeping with Paul's comments in 1 Corinthians 3:14–15: "If what has been built survives, the builder will receive a reward. If it is burned up, the builder will suffer loss but yet will be saved." As in 1 Corinthians 3, Paul here is talking about due recompense, not about one's ultimate destiny. Paul gives us no information here on the timing of this future judgment, nor does he indicate the nature of the reward or censure. His focus is on accountability and recompense.

Teaching the Text

The primary teaching points of this passage, as noted in the "Interpretive Insights," relate to *confidence* and *accountability*. Because the believer will be "at home" with the Lord when they die, they needn't worry about dying before Christ returns; they can be confident of God's provision even during this disembodied intermediate state (5:6–9). This knowledge should lead the believer to aspire to please the Lord whatever the circumstances, especially in view of the fact that God will hold the Christian accountable for their actions in this life (5:10). In making these two points, Paul also explicitly provides instruction on two very relevant topics for Christians today: the connection between the body and the "soul" and the connection between faith and works.

1. *The connection between body and soul.* The argument of 5:1–10, and particularly verses 6–10, assumes that there are two essential components of personhood, the material and the immaterial. (Whether the immaterial should be further divided is not addressed in this passage.) The encouragement that Paul offers the believers in Corinth is grounded in the reality that to be "away from the body" is to be "at home with the Lord." Fundamental to Paul's argument is that there is an "I" (5:6, 8, 9, in the plural) that can be distinguished and separated from the body (see also 12:2–3; Phil. 1:22–25). Yet, while 5:6–10 highlights the composite nature of human constitution, 5:1–5 equally highlights that this is a composite unity: the material and immaterial components of personhood (body and "soul") belong together, and the prospect of their separation is not a pleasant one for Paul. Contemporary materialists, both secular and Christian, believe that a person is nothing more than a physical entity with a relational capacity, so that there is no immaterial component of personhood that survives death. If what Paul teaches here is correct, this position must be rejected.

2. *The connection between faith and works.* Paul teaches very clearly that a person is justified by faith (Rom. 3:28; 4:16; Eph. 2:8), not by works (Rom. 4:5; Eph. 2:9; 2 Tim. 1:9; Titus 3:5). This is consonant with other New Testament writers, and Jesus himself (John 5:24; 1 Pet. 1:5; Heb. 4:2–3). Yet Paul speaks equally clearly about judgment according to works, and the frequency of this topic in his letters indicates that he regarded it as of considerable importance (Rom. 2:3–11; 14:11–12; 1 Cor. 3:12–15; 4:5; Gal. 6:8–9; Eph. 6:8–9; Col. 3:24–25; 1 Tim. 6:18–19). Paul's vigorous championing of salvation by faith apart from works (Galatians) is sometimes misinterpreted to mean that Paul was opposed to good works (cf. Rom. 3:8; 6:1). Nothing could be further from the truth. Salvation by faith does not exclude reward for a life well lived, nor censure for a life poorly lived. The same Paul who wrote, "There is now no condemnation for those who are in Christ Jesus" (Rom. 8:1), also wrote, "The only thing that matters is faith *working* through love" (Gal. 5:6, author's translation).

Illustrating the Text

God invites his people to walk by faith, not by sight.

Scripture: The book of Deuteronomy opens with God telling his people that they had stayed in Horeb long enough (1:6). The nation had taken forty years to complete what could have been an eleven-day journey because they had walked by sight with a "wilderness mind-set." There is a temptation in every generation to retain a juvenile vision of what God can and will do. Instead, we must walk by faith, keeping the greater reality of God and his will always before us as we walk in obedience to him and live out the gospel in love.

Believing God will fulfill his promises results in far-reaching fruit.

Biography: **James Hudson Taylor.** Taylor, who is often referred to as the "father of modern missions," founded China Inland Mission (CIM). After spending time in the port city of Shanghai, Taylor became burdened for the millions of Chinese people who lived in the interior of the country, a vast area largely untouched by missionary activity. His early work in the interior was ended by a serious illness, and he had to return to England. He was troubled by the indifference there to the great numbers of people in China who hadn't heard the gospel. But even as he recruited missionaries and raised funds for a major mission outreach in China, he was beset with doubt, especially about the safety of the missionaries he was preparing to send unprotected into the interior of the immense country of China. It was on a brief retreat that God touched his heart: "There the Lord conquered my unbelief, and I surrendered myself to God for this service. I told him that all responsibility as to the issues and consequences must rest with him; that as his servant it was mine to obey and to follow him." It was that vision that launched CIM, and it was that principle, that God would provide, that guided Taylor through his long years of ministry and leadership. And despite many struggles (including the death of his wife and four of his children), Taylor led CIM in making great strides in ministry in China's interior and also inspired unnumbered thousands of Christians in the West to catch his vision to bring the gospel to people all over the world who haven't heard the name of Jesus Christ. Taylor's absolute trust in God was vindicated: CIM didn't solicit funds, but it continued to grow and prosper. Like Taylor, we too can walk by faith and not by sight.[3]

Every person must give an account to God.

History: In the wake of World War II and the state-sponsored execution of millions of Jews (and millions more non-Jews), the victorious Allies saw the need to bring key perpetrators of the atrocities to account for their actions. Many high-ranking military officers, as well as German leaders and professionals, were brought to justice before an international tribunal in Nuremburg, Germany, from 1945 to 1947. These trials showed the importance of accountability even for actions in a time of war and played a key role in developing an international court system. God has a completely just accounting of every person's life. No one ever ultimately gets away with injustice in God's economy.[4]

2 Corinthians 5:11–15

The Impelling Love of Christ

Big Idea
Paul's ministry is conducted in complete openness, is focused on the welfare of others, and is motivated by the example of the sacrificial love of Christ.

Key Themes
- Paul's proclamation of the gospel is carried out with sincerity and integrity and should be a cause of pride for the Corinthians.
- Paul's activities are driven by the glory of God and the welfare of Christ's people.
- Paul's deepest motivation for his labor issues from Christ's love as exemplified in his sacrificial death.
- In his death, Christ embodied the community as their representative and freed them from a life consumed with self.

Understanding the Text

The Text in Context

Continuing his apostolic defense, Paul turns to address his spoken proclamation, which has been heavily criticized by some in Corinth (10:10; 11:6; 13:3). This theme was highlighted as a topic of concern as Paul introduced this apologetic section ("in Christ we speak before God with sincerity," 2:17) and was alluded to in 4:2–5 and 4:13. Paul's concern here is to reiterate that he operates in an unconcealing and unselfish manner. Whatever deficiencies the Corinthians may perceive in his preaching, it is the sacrificial love of Christ that drives Paul's mission and proclamation.

Interpretive Insights

5:11 *Since, then, we know what it is to fear the Lord.* "Since, then," connects 5:11 with 5:10 as its consequence. The reality of a future evaluation at Christ's tribunal (5:10) elicits the appropriate response of "fear" within the apostle. This is not a paralyzing fear, for it motivates service on Paul's part. Nor is it a fear of condemnation (Rom. 8:1). Rather, it is a healthy, sober concern as a child of God (Rom. 8:16) to please the one who is "for us" (8:31), prompted by the knowledge that our actions in this life may be judged either "good or bad" (2 Cor. 5:10) and receive due recompense. In light of 5:10, "the Lord" here probably indicates Christ. Obedience motivated by the fear of Christ is also enjoined on believers in Ephesians 5:21 and 6:5.

we try to persuade others. What we are is plain to God, and I hope it is also plain to your conscience. In using the word *peithō* ("persuade") to describe his ministry, Paul has chosen a term with a rich and unmistakable background in Greek literature and culture. The term was synonymous with rhetoric and oratory, which were an essential part of the Greek and Roman educational system. In Paul's day, rhetoric was often associated with cunning methods and flowery eloquence, and Paul has already explained to the Corinthians that he repudiates all such manipulative techniques in his proclamation of the gospel (1 Cor. 2:1–5; 2 Cor. 4:2–5).[1] Recognizing the potential for confusion, Paul qualifies this reference to his verbal persuasion (as in 2:17 and 4:2) by emphasizing that his preaching is in full view of the God to whom he will one day give an account: "What we are is plain to God." Paul is also concerned that the Corinthians fully recognize his forthright behavior ("and I hope it is also plain to your conscience"), which is a prominent theme in 2 Corinthians (1:12–14; 4:2; 7:2; 12:16–18).

5:12 *those who take pride in what is seen rather than in what is in the heart.* One of Paul's main objectives in this letter is to confront and transform the superficial value system of his detractors and their sympathizers in Corinth (cf. 10:7). The immediate context suggests that "those who take pride in appearances" (a more literal rendering of the Greek expression) refers to those who criticize Paul's physical appearance as not measuring up to the standards of other orators and sophists so familiar in Corinth. When Paul later cites his

The Power of Persuasion

Dio Chrysostom was a younger contemporary of Paul, and in the following introduction to one of his invited orations in Tarsus he queries his audience as to why they seek out orators such as himself. As in 2 Corinthians 5:10–11, "persuasion" and the bema are closely connected:

> I wonder what on earth is your purpose, and what your expectation or desire, in seeking to have such persons as myself discourse for you. Do you think us to be sweet-voiced and more pleasant of utterance than the rest, so that, as if we were song-birds, you long to hear us make melody for you? Or do you believe that we possess a different power in word and thought alike, a power of *persuasion* that is keener and truly formidable, which you call rhetoric, a power that holds sway both in the market place and on the *bema*? (*Or.* 33.1)

opponents, this is precisely their criticism: "In person he is unimpressive and his speaking amounts to nothing" (10:10). Orators in Paul's day took great pride in their appearance,[2] and it would seem that some in Corinth were expecting Paul to operate in a similar fashion (see the comments on 12:8–10). "In the heart" refers to inner character as evidenced by, among other things, suffering for others (1:6; 4:7–11), purity of motives (1:12; 2:16; 4:2), and love (2:4; 6:6; 11:11).

5:13 *If we are "out of our mind," as some say, it is for God.* The NIV correctly identifies this verse as a citation of a complaint against Paul but incorrectly translates the first verb as a present tense. The verb is actually past tense (aorist) and should be rendered, "If we *were* 'out of our mind.'" Although the precise nature of the complaint is obscure, Paul's main point is clear enough; he is countering that his actions are not self-centered but are divinely mandated and other centered. Some believe the complaint behind the expression "out of our mind" is that Paul's zeal bordered on fanaticism. Others believe the charge was that his self-commendation was excessive, or that his wielding of authority was heavy handed. More common is the view that the accusation relates to Paul's past ecstatic experiences, glossolalia in particular. The difficulty with this interpretation is that the subject of ecstatic speech represents a very abrupt intrusion into the argument of 2 Corinthians. Moreover, from Paul's previous censure of the Corinthian enthusiasm for ecstatic expressions of spirituality (1 Cor. 12–14), it is surprising that the Corinthians would raise this objection. Another suggestion is that the Greek term translated "out of our mind" by the NIV can also refer to an orator whose delivery is somewhat disheveled.[3] Correspondingly, the Greek term behind the NIV's "in our right mind" could be used of a soundly delivered argument. This fits the context well and is in keeping with the only complaint of his opponents that Paul actually cites: "For some say, 'His letters are weighty and forceful, but in person he is unimpressive and his speaking amounts to nothing'" (10:10). This also explains the switch from the past tense to the present tense: "If we were, in our previous visit, rhetorically unimpressive, credit that to God; if we are presently, through our letters, cogent and lucid, that is for your benefit." Paul has already explained at length to the Corinthians (1 Cor. 1–4) that his refusal to preach with "eloquence" and "persuasive words" (1 Cor. 2:1–5) is divinely driven: "So that your faith might not rest on human wisdom, but on God's power" (2:5). Paul abbreviates that argument here ("it is for God"), reminding the Corinthians that his unadorned preaching is in keeping with his divine commission to proclaim nothing other than "Christ and him crucified" (1 Cor. 2:2).

5:14 *For Christ's love compels us.* The grounds Paul offers for dismissing the objection of 5:13 is that his fundamental motivation is not his own reputation, or honor, but "the love of Christ" (ESV). This expression is interpreted by the NIV to mean Christ's love for us (a subjective genitive), as opposed to our love for Christ (an objective genitive). Another possibility is that the expression denotes both (a plenary genitive). Most scholars agree with the NIV that it describes Christ's love for us, on the basis of the following clause, which supports this statement by offering Christ's sacrifice of love as an example. The word "impel" brings out more clearly than the NIV's "compels" the idea of motivation from within, and should be preferred.[4]

because we are convinced that one died for all, and therefore all died. The reason why Christ's love so moved Paul was rooted in his conviction concerning the significance of Christ's death. It was a death for "all," in which "all" died. As elsewhere in Paul's Letters (Rom. 5:19; 1 Cor. 15:22), the scope of the word "all" in this verse is difficult to determine. It is not likely that the two uses of "all" refer to two different groups (e.g., all humanity, and then all believers), because the second "all" is preceded by the definite article, which identifies it with the first.[5] Because verse 15 explicitly narrows the concept to "those who live" (= believers), it would appear that both "alls" in this verse refer to believers, and that there is an element of hyperbole in this formulation. This is supported by Romans 5:18–19, where "all" and "many" are used interchangeably by Paul in a very similar context discussing the beneficiaries of Christ's death. Also supporting this interpretation is the soteriological hyperbole in the verses that follow, where Paul depicts God reconciling "the world" to himself in 2 Corinthians 5:19 and then issues the appeal "be reconciled to God" in 5:20.

5:15 *that those who live should no longer live for themselves.* Verse 15 specifies the behavioral consequences of dying with Christ: living for Christ, not for self. As in 4:11, "those who live" are believers marked by identifying with the death of Jesus. Paul introduced these chapters as an elaboration of the phrase "life to life" (2:16 ESV), he proclaimed the Spirit as the giver of life (3:6), he explained how the "life of Jesus" is revealed in suffering (4:10–12), and he told the Corinthians that at Christ's return their mortality would be "swallowed up by life" (5:4). In this verse the believer's new life is characterized as a life purposefully devoted to the one who died and rose on their behalf. The intention of Christ's sacrifice of love was to create a community that follows in his steps. A Christ-directed life is the ethical imperative of dying and rising with him.

Theological Insights

In this passage Paul identifies his driving motive and his core value in his life and ministry, and both are articulated in terms of principles deeply rooted in the Hebrew Bible: the fear of the Lord and the priority of the internal over the external. In the Old Testament, the fear of the Lord is the reverence that all humanity should feel before God (Ps. 33:8; Eccles. 12:13). It is both the beginning and the essence of wisdom (Job 28:28; Ps. 111:10; Prov. 9:10) and is rooted in God's power (Jer. 5:22–24), his holiness (Exod. 3:5–6; Isa. 6:1–7), and his glory (Isa. 2:10). It leads to obedience to God's commands (Ps. 19:9; Eccles. 12:13), and in Paul's case, obedience to his call as the apostle to the gentiles. Similarly, Paul's insistence on the priority of what is "in the heart" (2 Cor. 5:12) issues from the important Old Testament principle of divine impartiality (Deut. 10:17). This quality is most poignantly expressed to Samuel: "But the LORD said to Samuel, 'Do not consider his appearance or his height, for I have rejected him. The LORD does not look at the things people look at. People look at the outward appearance, but the LORD looks at the heart'" (1 Sam. 16:7).

Teaching the Text

In this passage Paul explicitly reflects on his motive in ministry (fear and love), and the teacher will want to explain carefully how each can be an appropriate motivation. Similarly, "boasting" is not always regarded positively, so special care should be taken to explain this idea and to distinguish proper objects of boasting from improper.

1. *Motivation in ministry.* In this passage Paul candidly sets out what drives him in his life and ministry, and the two items he identifies might initially seem contradictory: fear (5:11) and love (5:14). That Paul would be driven by Christ's love is not surprising or problematic. Paul singles out love as the preeminent virtue (1 Cor. 13) and holds up Christ's willing sacrifice on behalf of sinners as the supreme example of love (Rom. 5:7–8). In Galatians 2:20 Paul says that it is Christ's love "for me," as exemplified in the cross, that propelled his mission to the gentiles. Fear, on the other hand, is considered by most to be only a negative, harmful emotion that inhibits rather than promotes human flourishing. While it is true that inappropriate fear, or fear grounded in pathology, is severely detrimental (Matt. 25:14–30; 1 John 4:18), it is also true that the "fear of the Lord/God" is always positively portrayed in biblical literature. "The fear of the LORD is the beginning of wisdom" (Prov. 9:10); it is the foundation of obedience (Deut. 31:12; 1 Sam. 12:14); it is the defining quality of a righteous person (Job 1:9; Ps. 22:23); it is "a fountain of life" (Prov. 14:27); it is the quality that the messianic servant of Isaiah "delights in" (Isa. 11:1–3); and so on. The kind of fear that these verses describe, and that Paul depicts in 2 Corinthians 5:11, issues from a confidence in God's goodness (Rom. 8:28) and reflects a value system ordered around God's priorities. To fear the Lord means to value his approval above all else. Its antithesis is "the fear of man" (Prov. 29:25; Luke 12:4; John 12:42–43).

2. *Boasting in the heart.* In 5:12 Paul identifies an important point of contention between him and the Corinthians, and in doing so he articulates a significant theme in Scripture: focusing on appearances versus focusing on the heart. Perhaps the most memorable expression of this biblical motif is

found in 1 Samuel 16:7, where God reminds his prophet, "People look at the outward appearance, but the LORD looks at the heart." In a few verses Paul will repudiate judging anyone according to "a worldly point of view" (2 Cor. 5:16), which is precisely the vantage point of the Corinthians with respect to Paul (10:10). For Paul, the priority of the internal over the external was fundamental and closely connected to his convictions regarding the supremacy of the new covenant to the old covenant (Rom. 2:28–29; 2 Cor. 3:3; Gal. 6:12–15).

3. *The sacrificial death of Jesus.* The centerpiece of this passage—and Paul's life—is the cross of Christ. It is Christ's sacrifice of love that both impels and transforms Paul. The apostle holds up the death of Jesus as that which frees us from serving ourselves and enables us to live our lives for the one who died and rose on our behalf. Paul presents Jesus's example of sacrificial love as the defining narrative for all believers; it grounds our motivation and effects our transformation.

Illustrating the Text

God does not judge by appearance, and neither should we.

Television: *The Voice.* In the popular television show *The Voice*, the judges have their backs to the contestant, requiring the judges to base their judgment solely on the quality of the contestant's voice. Thankfully, God does not render judgment based on externals either. God looks at the heart, not at appearance, and judges us according to the righteousness every believer receives from Christ.

The love of Christ compels us to be concerned about every injustice.

Story: Many people in the affluent West live in ignorance of the plight of poverty faced by millions around the world. Often confronting this reality firsthand changes a person's perspective on material wealth. For many, the question becomes, So what are we going to do about this? To be exposed to gaping human need and do nothing is to be an accomplice in the crime and to fail to reflect God's love for those whom he has created.

When fear meets its match

Scripture: Mark 4 records a scene when a dangerous storm is tossing the disciples' boat, and it is at the point of being swamped. Jesus was taking a nap on a cushion in the front of the boat. The disciples awaken Jesus, saying: "Teacher, don't you care if we drown?" (Mark 4:38). Jesus calmly commands the storm to stop, which caused the disciples to shift from fear of the storm to fear of Jesus. They respond, "Who is this? Even the wind and waves obey him!" (4:41). One sign of forward progress in discipleship is trading our fear of the "storm of life" for the fear of the Lord.

2 Corinthians 5:16–21

The Ministry of Reconciliation

Big Idea

In the atoning death of Christ, God has reconciled humanity to himself, freeing us from enslavement to a worldly value system and re-creating us in Christ. Paul's role as Christ's ambassador is to proclaim God's reconciling work to everyone.

Key Themes

- Because of our union with Christ in his death, believers no longer judge according to the value system of this world.
- All who put their faith in Christ are made new.
- God has reconciled humanity to himself by offering his Son as an atoning sacrifice in their place.
- Christ's atonement involved taking on our sin so that we can take on his righteousness.
- Paul's mission is to proclaim God's reconciling action in Christ to the world.

Understanding the Text

The Text in Context

Paul begins this section by drawing two conclusions from the statement in 5:15 that believers have died with Christ: (1) Christians no longer evaluate others from a worldly point of view (5:16), and (2) they have become new creations in Christ (5:17). Paul then specifies the means by which this transformation was effected: our reconciliation with God through Christ (5:18–21). Verses 16–21 continue Paul's apostolic defense by broadening the scope of the argument from the previous section, 5:11–15. In that discussion Paul responded to a complaint of the Corinthians that related (probably) to his intentionally unadorned preaching. Here Paul places that issue within the larger context of his role as an ambassador of Christ in the service of reconciliation. Paul's work of persuading others (5:11) is undertaken as part of his divinely commissioned task as a herald of God's reconciling work through Christ (5:18–21).

Interpretive Insights

5:16 *So from now on we regard no one from a worldly point of view.* The first conclusion Paul draws from the believer's identification with Christ in his death (5:15) relates to the way believers evaluate others. The plural pronoun "we" is in emphatic position, which may be intended to contrast with those mentioned in verses 12 and 13 who take pride in appearances and are attacking Paul. This "we" is inclusive or, more precisely, paradigmatic, in that it refers to Paul and his associates as well as all those who have died with Christ and no longer live for themselves (5:14–15). "From now on" does not refer objectively to the time of Jesus's death but refers to the time that this death was subjectively appropriated by the believer through faith. To regard someone from a "worldly" (or "fleshly") perspective refers to applying standards based in merely human, external values, be it status, ethnicity, wealth, talent, or appearances (cf. Phil. 3:1–8). In an earlier letter to Corinth, Paul characterized the Corinthians as "fleshly" and "infantile" in that they were operating according to "merely human standards" (1 Cor. 3:1–3, author's translation). A similar censure is probably implicit in this verse, particularly with reference to "those who take pride in what is seen rather than in what is in the heart" (2 Cor. 5:12).

Though we once regarded Christ in this way. In this parenthetical comment Paul concedes that his former evaluation of Christ was misguided and "according to the flesh" (rendered by the NIV as "in this way"). Although the first-person plural is used, foremost in Paul's mind is probably his own prior rejection of Jesus and violent persecution of Jesus's followers (1 Cor. 15:9; Gal. 1:13; 1 Tim. 1:13). Situated as it is in the context of an extended defense of his apostleship, this parenthetical observation was likely prompted by the thought that, as Paul once misunderstood the person and mission of Jesus, so too the Corinthians have now misunderstood the person and mission of Jesus's apostle.

5:17 *Therefore, if anyone is in Christ, the new creation has come.* The second conclusion Paul draws from 5:14–15 (dying with Christ) is that the person who is "in Christ" has experienced a profound inner revitalization. The traditional interpretation of the expression "new creation" understands it anthropologically, referring to the spiritual or ontological renewal of the person that occurs at regeneration.[1] This is a prominent theme of Pauline soteriology (e.g., Rom. 6:4; 1 Cor. 5:7; Eph. 2:15; 4:24; Col. 3:10; Titus 3:5). The 2011 revision of the NIV relegates this reading, "that person is a new creation," to the margin, preferring to render this clause "the new creation has come." The translators argue that Paul's thought in this verse is that "a new universe is in the works."[2] The traditional interpretation is surely correct. The motif of transformation, so prominent in the previous chapters, presents being "in Christ" as the sphere in which individual renewal takes place by God's Spirit (3:3, 6, 14–18; 5:5). In 4:6 Paul's allusion to Genesis 1 seems intended to depict conversion as a kind of creation *ex nihilo*: "The same God who said, 'Let light shine from darkness' made his light shine in our hearts" (author's translation). The prophetic traditions Paul explicitly relies on in chapter 3 are Jeremiah's and Ezekiel's promises of a radical anthropological renewal that would occur by God's Spirit (Ezek. 11:19; 36:26, alluded to in 2 Cor. 3:3) through the new covenant written on the heart (Jer. 31:31–33, alluded to in 2 Cor. 3:6). When read in light of these passages, together with Paul's affirmation that "the Spirit gives life" (2 Cor. 3:6) and his reference to our present inner renewal (4:16), there is little room for doubt that 5:17 also speaks of the inner renewal of the believer and should be understood as a continuation of the transformation motif.

The old has gone, the new is here! Paul explains his pronouncement that anyone in Christ is a new creation with a maxim-like statement that emphasizes the complete dissolution of the past and the arrival of something new. Paul alludes to a prominent motif in Isaiah whereby the prophet predicts that God's former act of deliverance at the Red Sea will be utterly eclipsed by God's future deliverance of Israel (42:9; 43:18–19; 48:3–6). Paul does not cite any text directly, nor can his meaning here be precisely defined by the Isaianic context. In the present context, the "old" that has passed probably refers to boasting in appearances (5:12), living for self (5:14–15), and looking at others from a worldly vantage point (5:16). The "new" present reality relates to the new covenant work of the Spirit (3:3–4:6). This involves the Spirit's transformation of the human heart (3:3, 18; 4:6), the granting of new life by

---

New Creation in First-Century Judaism

Although Paul introduced the expression "new creation" into Christian vocabulary in his letter to the Galatians (Gal. 6:15), the idea that conversion effected a new creation of the proselyte was already present in the Judaism of Paul's day. In the book *Joseph and Aseneth*, a Hellenistic romance of Diaspora Judaism, the patriarch Joseph offers a prayer for the beautiful Egyptian priestess Asenath (see Gen. 41:45) that she would convert from paganism to Judaism:

> You, O Lord, bless this virgin,
> make her new through your Spirit
> re-create her by your hidden hand
> give her new life through your
>   life . . .
> and number her with your people.
> (*Jos. Asen.* 8.9)

The imagery of this prayer—renewal through God's Spirit, re-creation, new life—strongly echoes the symbolism Paul uses in 2 Corinthians to describe conversion, and it seems reasonable to suppose that Paul's Jewish heritage influenced his depiction of conversion as "new creation."

the Spirit (3:6), the illumination of the mind by the Spirit (3:14–4:6), and the new reality of reconciliation with God (5:18–21).

5:18 *God, who reconciled us to himself through Christ and gave us the ministry of reconciliation.* Paul explains that "all this" (the work of Christ and its results detailed in 5:14–17) is from God, "who reconciled us to himself through Christ." This qualifying phrase summarizes the work of Christ described in the previous verses as God's means of reconciling the world. This will be reiterated in 5:19–21. Paul also transitions to his role in this story: someone entrusted with heralding God's reconciling work. The "us" in this verse refers primarily to Paul and his apostolic co-workers, and by application to other believers.

5:19 *God was reconciling the world to himself in Christ, not counting people's sins against them.* Paul reiterates the thought of 5:18, this time by describing reconciliation as the act of not reckoning sin—that is, removing the guilt and punishment of sin on the basis of Christ's atoning work ("in Christ" = "through Christ's sacrifice"). As elsewhere in Paul, God is the instigator in reconciliation (Col. 1:20–22), and Christ's death is the means of accomplishing reconciliation (Rom. 5:10; Eph. 2:16; Col. 1:20–22). The object of reconciliation is "the world," which is also designated by the pronouns "us" (2 Cor. 5:18) and "them" (5:19). In contrast to Colossians 1:20, where God's reconciling work includes the entire created order, in this context humanity is in view. Whether Paul intended reconciliation to be applied to all humanity or only believers is difficult to determine from this text, but in either case the reconciliation must be subjectively appropriated for reconciliation to be effective, hence the appeal to be reconciled in 5:20.

5:20 *We are therefore Christ's ambassadors.* The importance of these chapters as an apostolic defense is again made apparent as Paul marshals the preceding arguments to impress upon the Corinthians his divinely appointed status as an official emissary of Christ. An ambassador was due the same respect as the person he or she represented. To show disrespect to the ambassador was to show disrespect to the person who had sent the ambassador.[3] Paul summarizes his ambassadorial message with the words "Be reconciled to God."[4]

5:21 *God made him who had no sin to be sin for us, so that in him we might become the righteousness of God.* This verse stands as the most profound and yet also the most compact articulation of the atonement in Paul's Letters. In keeping with the Old Testament sacrificial system that foreshadowed Christ's sacrifice, the innocent one is made to bear the sin of the guilty ones. "Made . . . to be sin" does not mean that Christ became a sinner, but it means that he became the sin-bearer (Lev. 4). Although offensive to some modern readers, God the Father is portrayed as the one responsible for the sinless one becoming a sin offering (Rom. 4:25; 8:3; Gal. 3:13). God's purpose ("so that") in doing this was that believers ("we," inclusively) might be reckoned "righteous," just as Christ was reckoned "sin." While "becoming the righteousness of God" may be a forensic reckoning, Paul expects that this status will be increasingly actualized in the believer's conduct (Rom. 6; 8:1–17; Gal. 5:16–26).

Theological Insights

Although Paul never directly connects the righteous sufferer of Isaiah 52:13–53:12 with Jesus, it would appear that this passage informed Paul's depiction in 2 Corinthians 5:21 of Christ's atoning sacrifice (see table 1).

Isaiah's portrayal of a righteous servant who would bear the sins of many must have played an important role in Paul's understanding of Jesus's life and mission (cf. Rom. 4:25). In 2 Corinthians 5:21, Paul condenses nearly the entirety of Isaiah 53 into one simple, but profound, sentence: "God made him who had no sin to be sin for us, so that in him we might become the righteousness of God" (5:21).

Teaching the Text

Second Corinthians 5:14–21 is one of the richest passages in Paul's Letters in terms of understanding the apostle's theology and mission. Its main teaching points can be encapsulated under the following headings:

1. *Transformation*. Verses 16 and 17 express two results that follow from identifying with Christ in his death (5:14–15). These results encompass both *knowing* (5:16) and *being* (5:17)—how we think and who we are in Christ. In

Table 1. Comparing 2 Corinthians 5:21 and Isaiah 53

2 Corinthians 5:21	Isaiah 53
"God made him . . . to be sin"	He was "punished by God" (v. 4) "The Lord has laid on him the iniquity of us all" (v. 6) "It was the Lord's will to crush him" (v. 10) "The Lord makes his life an offering for sin" (v. 10)
"For us"	"He took up our pain and bore our suffering" (v. 4) "He was pierced for our transgressions, he was crushed for our iniquities" (v. 5) "He bore the sins of many" (v. 12)
"Who had no sin"	"Like a lamb" (v. 7) Free from "violence" or "deceit" (v. 9) A "righteous servant" (v. 11)
"So that in him we might become the righteousness of God"	He "brought us peace" (v. 5) He will make many to be accounted righteous (NIV: "will justify many," v. 11)

verse 16 Paul tells the Corinthians that their fundamental perspective should now change. Although they used to look at others from a worldly (or merely human) vantage point, they now look at others differently. Gone are the days when we live for ourselves (5:15) and evaluate others based on how they can benefit us. This new vantage point is possible because the believer is now a "new creation" in Christ (5:17). Those who have put their faith in Christ have experienced a profound inner renewal through God's Spirit in their hearts (2 Cor. 1:22; 3:3, 6, 18; 4:6). This renewal effects changes in values and behaviors, as believers—sometimes haltingly—grow to maturity in Christ (Eph. 4:15–16).

2. *Reconciliation.* In 2 Corinthians Paul describes his apostolic service as "the ministry of the Spirit" (3:8), "the ministry of righteousness" (3:9 ESV), and in 5:18 as "the ministry of reconciliation." While not quite interchangeable, these descriptors are tightly connected. When the lost are reconciled, they receive the Spirit, which enables righteousness. Paul portrays God's mission in the world as a reconciling endeavor, and he interprets his own mission as an extension of the reconciling work of Christ, as though God himself were issuing the appeal for reconciliation through him (5:20).

3. *Substitution.* In 2 Corinthians 5 Paul employs two different, but complementary, images to describe the atoning work of Christ: representation (5:14–15) and substitution (5:21). In 5:14 Paul notes that "one died for all, and therefore all died." A representative includes the community in his sacrifice, so that when he dies, they die. A substitute, however, dies in place of the community, so that when he dies, they are set free. In 5:21, the sin-bearer dies so that the community is cleansed and becomes "righteous." Although the idea of an innocent person receiving the punishment due a guilty person (substitution) runs counter to our modern ideals of justice, God's wrath demanded a sacrifice for sin that only he could offer: his perfect Son. As our substitute, Christ satisfied God's wrath and granted to us his status of "righteous." Our obligation, as Paul makes explicit in the next verse, is to not receive the grace of God in vain (6:1).

Illustrating the Text

Brand new

Object Lesson: Show pictures of a building that was repainted or had an exterior facelift. Explain that when Christ comes into our lives, the changes aren't merely cosmetic—he completely transforms us from the inside out. We don't need a facelift; we need a miracle.

Grace should be a catalyst toward transformation.

Literature: *Les Misérables,* **by Victor Hugo.** In Hugo's classic, Jean Valjean steals silver plates from the bishop, Monseigneur Bienvenu (chap. 12). Valjean is stopped by the police, and when they find him in possession of the silver, they bring him to the bishop's residence. Instead of pressing charges, the bishop demonstrates amazing grace to this thief, offering Valjean the silver candlesticks in addition to the silver plates that he stole. The law was in the bishop's favor, yet grace guides the bishop's actions. At the close of the chapter the bishop explains his actions to Valjean: "Don't forget, don't ever forget, that you promised me to use this silver to make an honest man of yourself. . . . Jean Valjean, my brother, you belong no longer to evil but to good. It is your soul that I am buying for you. I am taking it away from dark thoughts and from the spirit of perdition, and I am giving it to God."[5] The rest of the story beautifully demonstrates how Valjean embodies the grace shown to him by pursuing a life obedient to God in love toward others.

Love transforms.

Musical: In the musical *The Phantom of the Opera*, based on the book by Gaston Leroux, the phantom wears a mask to cover his hideously disfigured face. He resides in the basement of the opera house—in the dark, in the shadows. But a woman, Christine (a prototype of Christ), touches his heart. At the climax of the story, his mask is removed; he waits for her to scream in terror, but she does not. In tender compassion she kisses his scarred face. Her love begins the process of transformation.

Beautiful things

Lyrics: The song "Beautiful Things" by the music group Gungor proclaims that God makes beautiful things out of dust and chaos.

Touch of the master's hand

Song: The song "The Touch of the Master's Hand" is based on a poem by Myra Brooks Welch. It recounts the auctioning off of an old violin. At first, it only garners mild interest, but after a gray-haired violinist steps up and plays the instrument, its value skyrockets and it is sold for thousands of dollars. So too, the touch of Jesus's hand transforms things that seem worthless in the eyes of the world.

2 Corinthians 6:1–13

An Appeal for Reconciliation

Big Idea

Paul's appeal for reconciliation is strengthened by his proven character and his candid, authentic approach to the Corinthians.

Key Themes

- To refuse the opportunity to be reconciled to God is to forfeit God's grace.
- As a servant of the gospel, Paul endures all manner of hardship so that his ministry might not be discredited.
- A wide-open heart toward those in need of reconciliation is the posture of a wise Christian leader.

Understanding the Text

The Text in Context

Paul transitions now from a general summary of his ministry of reconciliation (5:11–21) to a specific and personal appeal to the Corinthians to be reconciled both to God (6:1–2) and to him (6:3–13). Paul's defense of his actions and his apostolate in chapters 1–5 has been preparing the ground for the appeals found in chapters 6–9 and the direct confrontation coming in chapters 10–13. These chapters still find Paul commending his integrity and selflessness to the Corinthians (e.g., 6:4–10; 11:23–33), but this recedes in comparison to chapters 1–5. The present passage contains a carefully constructed hardship catalog (6:3–10), which provides the basis for the appeals that immediately precede (6:1–2) and follow (6:11–13). Most of the hardships listed here are repeated in 11:23–33, where they will be more fully discussed. In the present section we will concentrate on comparing Paul's use of the very familiar hardship catalog with that of his Greco-Roman contemporaries.

Historical and Cultural Background

This passage contains the second of three "hardship catalogs" in 2 Corinthians. The two others are found in 4:7–12 and 11:23–33. The hardship catalog was a standard feature of Stoic and Cynic instruction in Paul's day (see the sidebar "Hardship Catalogs" in the unit on 4:7–15, as well as the sidebar "Paul and the Stoics Compared" in this unit). Through listing the adversities they endured in the service of humanity, these philosophers sought to demonstrate their superior virtue—in particular, their fortitude, self-sufficiency, and indifference to external circumstances. Like his Greco-Roman counterparts, Paul also used this rhetorical form to commend himself as a model to emulate (6:4), but he differs from the Stoics and Cynics in important ways. While Paul does offer himself as an example of fortitude and endurance, he also readily acknowledges his weakness and understands his suffering as a demonstration of his need for God's power (12:9–10). While the Stoics claimed to be "great, powerful, eminent and strong . . . because he [the Stoic] has possession of the strength which befalls such a man, being invincible and unconquerable,"[1] Paul's recognizes that his strength is entirely derivative (Col. 1:29; Phil. 4:13). Rather than boasting of his self-sufficiency, Paul makes it a point to tell his churches, "We are not sufficient to claim anything as coming from ourselves; our sufficiency is from God" (2 Cor. 3:5, author's translation).

Interpretive Insights

6:1 *As God's co-workers we urge you not to receive God's grace in vain.* Paul now applies the generic appeal of 5:20 to the Corinthian situation specifically. As Christ's ambassadors, with God making his appeal through them (5:20), Paul recognizes that he and his ministry team are "co-workers" with God (cf. 6:4; 1 Cor. 3:9).[2] Paul also recognizes the danger of not responding appropriately to God's grace, receiving it "in vain." Both surviving letters to Corinth include warnings in their concluding chapters regarding failing the test of authentic faith (1 Cor. 15:2; 2 Cor. 13:5), indicating that this was a genuine concern of Paul's with respect to some in Corinth. In the present context, "in vain" may refer to either apostasy from the faith (Gal. 3:4 with 5:5; 1 Thess. 3:5; 1 Tim. 4:1) or failure to experience the fullness of God's lavish grace because of unbelief or disobedience (2 Cor. 6:14–7:1).

6:2 *now is the time of God's favor, now is the day of salvation.* Paul grounds the appeal of 6:1 by citing a portion of Isaiah 49:8, the second of the four Servant Songs of Isaiah: "In the day of salvation I helped you." In the Isaianic context Yahweh is reminding his servant that he helped him in his time of need and promises his continual support. Paul sees this as analogous to God's gracious dealings with the Corinthians and cites this text to remind the Corinthians of God's mercy toward them and to motivate them not to spurn God's grace. "The day of salvation" refers to the era between Christ's resurrection and his return when the appeal for reconciliation (5:21)—the gospel—is being heralded by his ambassadors (5:20).

6:3 *We put no stumbling block in anyone's path, so that our ministry will not be discredited.* Paul articulates both his modus operandi in ministry and the motivation behind that method. Paul is keenly aware that his own personal conduct could adversely affect the reception of the gospel, even unintentionally. His change of travel plans seems to have been one such incident (1:12–2:4), and his determination to support himself through manual labor was another (12:13–18). Paul's careful, intentionally transparent handling of the collection for the poor in Jerusalem is an example of the effort he took to ensure that his conduct would be seen to be above reproach (8:20–21). Paul's concern is not simply his personal reputation but the advance of the gospel.

6:4–10 In this hardship catalog Paul seeks to commend the entire conduct of his ministry to the Corinthians. The content of the catalog can be organized as follows: character evidenced by enduring hardship (6:4–5), by exemplifying virtue (6:6), by fearless proclamation (6:7), by indifference to reputation (6:8), and by thriving in preposterous circumstances (6:9–10).

6:4–5 *in great endurance; in troubles, hardships . . . in beatings, imprisonments . . . sleepless nights and hunger.* "Exhibit A" in Paul's defense of his claim to be a commendable servant (6:4) is his willing endurance of hardship in the fulfillment of his calling. Paul's readers would have been familiar with this line of argument, as it was common among the Stoics. Musonius Rufus, one of Paul's Stoic contemporaries, taught that the wise man trained both body and soul "when we discipline ourselves to cold, heat, thirst, meager rations, hard beds . . . and patience under suffering."[3] This was especially commendable, Musonius argues, "when we know that we are suffering for some good purpose, either to help our friends or benefit our city."[4] Paul's judgment that sacrificial hardship strengthens character and promotes virtue (Rom. 3:3–5; 1 Cor. 9:24–27) was modeled by the apostle himself in his dealings with the Corinthians (see further the comments on 11:22–27).

6:6 *in purity, understanding, patience and kindness; in the Holy Spirit and in sincere love.* Not only the endurance of difficult external circumstances (6:4–5) but also the manifestation of Paul's inner life commended him to others and allowed him to claim with integrity that he put no stumbling block before others (6:3). "Purity" refers to Paul's sincere and unmixed intentions in serving others. The NIV's "understanding" renders the Greek word commonly translated "knowledge" (*gnōsis*). Occurring in a list of virtues, this word has connotations of "insight" and "wisdom" as opposed to intellectual knowledge of facts. "Patience and kindness" denote long-suffering and gentleness, particularly in situations of disagreement. It may seem out of place to mention the Holy Spirit in a list of virtues, but this simply attests to the apostle's awareness that these virtues are not his own achievement but are the product of the Spirit's work in his life (Gal. 5:22–23). These nouns are in the dative case, following the Greek preposition *en* ("in"), and indicate means: "by means of the Holy Spirit." The "sincere love" that Paul models denotes impartiality and lack of hypocrisy in affection and conduct.

6:7 *in truthful speech and in the power of God; with weapons of righteousness.* Paul focuses now on his verbal proclamation, which was under attack in Corinth (see 1 Cor. 2:1–5; 2 Cor. 10:10; 11:6). As in 1 Corinthians 2:5, Paul affirms that his proclamation has been accompanied by God's power, which is probably shorthand for the "signs and wonders and powers" (2 Cor. 12:12, author's translation) associated with Paul's evangelistic preaching (see also Rom. 15:19; 1 Cor. 2:4; Acts 19:11). "Weapons of righteousness in the right hand and in the left" envisions a battle-ready Roman soldier whose left hand carries a shield and whose right hand holds a gladius (a short thrusting sword) or a javelin. Paul's use of military imagery (cf. 10:3–5) is indicative of the reality that his apostolic work resembled a military campaign with both human (10:5) and spiritual (Eph. 6:10–20) adversaries.

6:8–10 *through glory and dishonor . . . having nothing, and yet possessing everything.* Verses 8–10 describe, using Harris's expression, "the vicissitudes of ministry"[5]—that is, the changing fortunes, volatile circumstances, and

Paul and the Stoics Compared

As this table illustrates, Paul and his Stoic contemporaries sometimes used similar patterns of argumentation when they made use of hardship catalogs to demonstrate their character. In this excerpt, Plutarch is actually poking fun at the Stoics by mimicking one of their stereotypical manners of expression.

2 Corinthians 4:8–9	Plutarch, *Moralia* 1057E	2 Corinthians 6:9–10
"Afflicted in every way, but not crushed;	"Confined, but not hindered,	"Unknown, yet well known;
perplexed, but not despairing;	thrown down, but not constrained,	dying, yet look! we live;
persecuted, but not abandoned;	tortured, but not in pain	punished, yet not killed;
thrown down, but not vanquished."	maimed, but not injured,	sorrowful, yet always rejoicing;
	pinned down, but not beaten,	poor, yet making many rich;
	surrounded, but not defeated,	having nothing yet possessing all things."
	enslaved, but not captive."	

Note: The translations in the table are the author's.

contradictory opinions concerning his apostolate and ministry that Paul faced throughout his life. Each antithesis finds numerous points of contact in Paul's Letters and Acts. For example, "through glory and dishonor" (v. 8) recalls Paul being worshiped (inappropriately) as a god in Lystra (Acts 14:8–12) and being imprisoned (wrongfully) in Philippi (Acts 16:16–24); "beaten, and yet not killed" (v. 9) reminds one of the numerous acts of mob violence Paul was subject to (e.g., Acts 13:50; 14:5, 19; 16:22–23); "sorrowful, yet always rejoicing" (v. 10) nicely summarizes Paul's letter to the Philippians, which contains a dozen or so references to joy yet was written from a prison cell. The final antithesis, "having nothing, and yet possessing everything" (v. 10), echoes a common Stoic argument aimed at demonstrating that what was truly necessary for happiness could never be taken from the noble sage. Seneca (4 BC–AD 65), for example, writes, "Alone and old, and seeing the enemy in possession of everything around me, I, nevertheless, declare that all my holdings are intact. . . . So far as my true possessions are concerned, they are with me and ever will be with me" (*Cons. sap.* 6.3). For the stalwart Stoic, what was truly necessary for contentment was fortitude, correct thinking, and indifference to outward circumstances. For Paul, true contentment was found in losing one's life for Christ and his kingdom (2 Cor. 12:15; Phil. 3:7–11).

6:11–13 *We have spoken freely to you . . . open wide your hearts also.* Paul concludes with a heartfelt appeal that is both conciliatory and affectionate. Paul stretches forth his hand as a father to his children (6:13) and pleads for their affection in return. Although Paul has wronged no one in Corinth, he is not above making the first move toward reconciliation, and with vulnerable candidness, he tenderly expresses his affection for his wayward children in Corinth.

Teaching the Text

This sobering passage contains important warnings and reminders for believers who are engaged in ministry and intent on spiritual growth. These teaching points could be organized under two headings, the first two points under "Reminders for Christian Leaders," and the second two under "Warnings for All Believers."

1. *The gravity of ministry.* In this passage Paul refers to himself as God's "co-worker" (6:1) and "servant" (6:4) and as a father to his Corinthian "children" (6:13). Paul understood that his calling as a pastor and missional evangelist necessitated a mind-set and a lifestyle that put his children's welfare above his own and his Master's interests above all else. Any other perspective would "discredit" the ministry (6:3). The long catalog of hardship that Paul

enumerates in this passage could not have been endured by someone who did not understand both the eternal significance of his work and his own role as a co-worker, servant, and father.

2. *The challenges of ministry.* Not many Christian leaders will be called to endure the kinds of difficulties that Paul describes here and in 11:23–33, but it is important for any who would aspire to lead God's people that they understand what this calling may entail: grueling labor, financial difficulties, and a low opinion in the eyes of many. To be sure, Paul's hardship catalogs do not provide the full picture of gospel ministry (in the previous chapter Paul refers to himself as an "ambassador"), but men and women heading into ministry need to bear in mind that their calling is not to middle-income suburbia but to service and sacrifice for God's kingdom.

3. *Receiving God's grace in vain.* The warning that opens this chapter (6:1) is capable of several interpretations, depending on one's larger view of perseverance and whether it is possible for a truly saved person to fall away from the faith (see the comments on 6:1, above). On any interpretation, however, the warning is grave and is intended to prevent God's grace from falling short of its divinely intended effects in a believer's life. God's purpose in dispensing his grace in our lives is not only for our own benefit but also that we might become a blessing to others. When God's grace in our life is truncated, not only do we ourselves suffer, but so do our family, our friends, our church, our community, and our society. It is no exaggeration to say that the world is a poorer place when God's grace in one person's life is quenched.

4. *Withholding affection.* Paul's final exhortation in this passage is an appeal to the Corinthians for reciprocal affection. Paul's words are full of pathos and emotion as he pleads with his "children" to open their hearts to him. Paul could make this appeal with integrity because he had sacrificed so much for his spiritual children, and so demonstrated his affection for them many times over. Mutual affection between pastor and flock is the ideal that Paul hopes to attain in Corinth, and it should be the goal of every local church today. The responsibility of the pastor is to love sacrificially; the responsibility of the congregation is to respond appropriately.

Illustrating the Text

The gospel contains "time-sensitive material."

Scripture: Paul articulates to the Corinthians the urgency of the gospel. God has extended his saving grace to the people of God, but it is grace for today. Isaiah 55:6 reminds us that we cannot wait to act on God's salvation: "Seek the Lord while he may be found; call on him while he is near." It is time to ratchet up the urgency in all of our evangelistic endeavors.

Spiritual parenting requires sacrifice, but it bears fruit that will last.

History: John Sergieff was a priest in Kronstadt, Russia, during the nineteenth century. Although other clergy lived a life of luxury, Father John had given up this lifestyle. Like the apostle Paul, he saw his ministry war wounds as a badge of authenticity. He took the church to the streets, where crime, prostitution, and alcoholism were rampant, and he looked for the roughest, most needy individuals he could find. Upon finding one of his "flock," he would hold their face and look directly in their eyes and say, "This way of life is beneath your dignity. You were created to house the glory of God." Father John was called "the pastor of all Russia," and wherever he went, revival, like transformation, followed him.[6]

Having the right disposition is paramount in Christian ministry.

Quote: **Stuart Briscoe.** On enduring hardship in ministry, Briscoe stated: "Christian leaders need the mind of a scholar, the heart of a child, and the skin of a rhinoceros."[7]

Spiritual formation is counter to a consumer mind-set.

Testimony: One of the greatest barriers to spiritual formation is a consumer mentality that permeates the church in the Western world. The trials, persecutions, and sufferings that Paul endured to advance the gospel are countercultural to our "What's in it for me?" mind-set. Churches that are making forward progress in multiplying disciples have confronted the consumer cancer and have given their members a vision of a preferred future that more closely lives out the Jesus mind-set and lifestyle. Have a church member share a testimony of a practical and sacrificial way they are seeking to live out their faith.

2 Corinthians 6:14–7:1

An Appeal for Purity

Big Idea
Separation from idolatry and impurity is a prerequisite for intimacy with a holy God.

Key Themes
- Believers should be morally distinct from unbelievers.
- Believers should separate themselves from activities and persons detrimental to their spiritual health.
- Full communion with God requires a determination to strive for moral purity.

Understanding the Text

The Text in Context

Although this passage appears to be an abrupt intrusion (note how 7:2 follows the line of thought in 6:13 so closely), its exhortation to moral purity could also be seen as a concrete example of what it means "not to receive God's grace in vain" (6:1). If this is correct, the generic appeal of 5:20 and 6:1–2 to be reconciled with God is now given specific content: continued dalliance with pagan temples must stop. On the other hand, Paul's Letters are known for their sudden digressions (cf. 2:14–7:2; Eph. 3:2–13), and 6:14–7:1 is no more difficult than these others. The apostolic defense of chapters 1–5 recedes as the tone and content of the remaining chapters become focused on exhortation and admonition.

Historical and Cultural Background

Although Paul's argument in 6:14–7:1 is made largely through imagery and symbolism (light, darkness; righteousness, wickedness; etc.), and he never explicitly identifies the precise matter he is concerned about, he provides us with plenty of clues to identify with reasonable confidence the issue he is addressing: the continued practice of frequenting pagan temples. Paul has already addressed this issue with the Corinthians on two other occasions. In 1 Corinthians 8:1–13 Paul takes to task "the strong" for dining in "an idol's temple" (8:10) and so destroying the faith of the weak. In 1 Corinthians 10:14–30 he extends this prohibition to knowingly consuming food, even in private venues, that has been previously sacrificed in a temple. However, separation from temple life was far more difficult for the first generations of believers than we moderns realize. Temples were an integral part of Greco-Roman society, quite apart from their religious functions. They were the locus of many family rituals (e.g., those marking puberty, marriage, death, harvest); private dinner parties were held in temples; local trade guilds and civic magistrates conducted business in the temples; civic festivals were hosted by the gods of the civic cults; and so on. Plutarch, writing of community-wide celebrations, observes, "It is not the abundance of wine or the roasting of meat that makes the joy of festivals, but the good hope and the belief that the god is present and graciously accepts what is offered" (*Mor.* 1102A). In a culture where religion and the social order were inextricably intertwined, the separation that Paul called for was a difficult and often dangerous task. It is no wonder that within a decade or so of this letter, Nero was executing Christians in Rome on the charge of misanthropy, antisocial behavior.[1]

Interpretive Insights

6:14 *Do not be yoked together with unbelievers.* The Greek word behind the NIV's "yoked" could be more literally rendered, "differently yoked" or "unevenly yoked." The verb expresses the idea of putting two animals of a different size, species, or temperament under one yoke, which would have disastrous results. This summary exhortation provides important information about the conduct coming under Paul's scrutiny: relational connections with unbelievers that would lead to a degrading of ethical conduct.

For what do righteousness and wickedness have in common? Paul supports the exhortation not to be unequally yoked with a series of five rhetorical questions, posed by means of antithetically paired elements meant to symbolize the Christian, on the one hand, and the negative behavior they were indulging in, on the other. Each question asks, essentially, in what ways the two elements are compatible and expects the answer, "None whatsoever!" The first two pairs (righteousness-wickedness, light-darkness) underscore the moral compromise involved in the conduct being censured. Righteousness and wickedness cannot cohabit, any more than can light and darkness; the presence of one necessarily excludes the other. Paul's point is that some believers in Corinth are engaging in activities that are inimical to their faith. As "children of light" (Eph. 5:8; 1 Thess. 5:5), believers cannot maintain fellowship with darkness.

6:15–16 *What harmony is there between Christ and Belial? . . . a believer . . . with an unbeliever? . . . the temple of God and idols?* The next three rhetorical questions highlight the religious character of the Corinthian offense and provide important information about the setting of that offense. Belial is one of the many names for Satan or an evil angelic prince in the Dead Sea

Scrolls and other Jewish sources from this period.[2] In Paul's view, the pagan world unwittingly worshiped demons when they sacrificed to idols in their temples (1 Cor. 10:20–21), so it is highly significant that his final antithesis relates this problem to "the temple of idols." Given Paul's previous reprimands related to dining in pagan temples (1 Cor. 8:1–13) and eating food sacrificed to idols (= demons; 10:14–30), we can be reasonably certain that Paul is addressing the same problem here: continued participation in temple activities or the religious life of the wider pagan culture. In affirming that believers and unbelievers have nothing in common, Paul is not referring to basic human needs (food, clothing, affection, etc.) or superficial common interests (the enjoyment of the arts, sports, a beautiful sunset, etc.) but to fundamental spiritual priorities and the resulting ethical commitments.

For we are the temple of the living God. The "we" is in emphatic position and is meant to clarify that the believing community is now the locus of God's presence—lest his readers think that Paul was referring to the Jerusalem temple in the previous clause. This verse also provides further grounds for the exhortation of 6:14. The expression "living God" is found frequently in the Old Testament (e.g., Deut. 5:26; 1 Sam. 17:26) and became an important polemical designation used by Jews to distinguish the true God from the lifeless idols of the gentiles,[3] which is how Paul is using it here. Both the individual (1 Cor. 3:16) and the community are the dwelling place of the holy God.

As God has said: "I will live with them and walk among them." As scriptural support for his claim that the Christian community is the true temple of the living God, Paul cites Leviticus 26:11–12, with slight modifications based on the parallel texts in Ezekiel 37:27 and perhaps Jeremiah 32:38. These texts contain the important covenant formula, "I will be their God, they will be my people," which Paul applies to believers. In essence, Paul is saying that these promises find their fulfillment in the new covenant community in Christ (see "Theological Insights," below).

6:17-18 *Therefore, "Come out from them and be separate, says the Lord. Touch no unclean thing."* The second appeal of this passage is grounded ("therefore") in the truths enunciated in 6:14–16, and particularly the affirmation that the Christian community is the true temple of God. Paul cites Isaiah 52:11, which addresses the Jewish community exiled in Babylon, specifically those carrying the articles used in worshiping the God of Israel. As Paul has already explained to the Corinthians, separation does not entail avoiding any and every contact with unbelievers (1 Cor. 5:9–10). Paul's point is that believers should avoid circumstances, activities, and individuals that may be morally and spiritually detrimental. The citation of Isaiah 52:11 is especially relevant to the Corinthians' situation and their continued association with pagan temple life (1 Cor. 8:1–13; 10:14–30). This is all the more so when we understand that feasts at pagan temples sometimes involved drunkenness, carousing, and promiscuity.

I will be a Father to you, and you will be my sons and daughters. The result of purity (6:17a) is acceptance by God and the experience of God's fatherly presence. Paul cites 2 Samuel 7:14, where God promises to establish David's throne and dynasty (7:11–13) and assures David that his descendant will be as God's own son. Paul adds, "and daughters," thus making explicit what later prophets already affirmed (Isa. 43:6; Jer. 31:9; Hosea 1:10), that all God's people are children of their heavenly father. The blessings of acceptance and adoption are made conditional on separation and purity, yet elsewhere Paul affirms that believers have already been accepted (Rom. 5:1–2; Eph. 2:18; 3:12) and adopted into God's family (Gal. 4:5; Eph. 1:5) and call on God as "Father" (Rom. 8:15; 1 Cor. 8:6; 2 Cor. 1:2; Eph. 4:6). The theological issue behind Paul's argument in these verses may be that separation from sin and a genuine concern for holiness demonstrate who God's children truly are. More probable, however, is that Paul is describing the increasingly intimate fellowship with God that accompanies growth in holiness.

7:1 *since we have these promises.* See "Theological Insights," below.

let us purify ourselves . . . perfecting holiness out of reverence for God. This summary exhortation may be understood as a call to perfect holiness, or as a call to complete consecration. Paul has already told the Corinthians that, in principle, no temptation is irresistible; God always provides a way of escape (1 Cor. 10:13). Yet Paul also makes it clear that he has not attained perfection (Phil. 3:12–13) and that the process of sanctification will not be complete until Christ's return (1 Thess. 3:13). It seems best to understand this verse as a call to "press on toward the goal to win the prize" (Phil. 3:14), rather than to see it as holding out the possibility of attaining perfect holiness in this life (cf. James 3:2; 1 John 1:8).

Theological Insights

In this passage Paul makes some remarkable claims concerning the Christian community, particularly with respect to his own Jewish heritage and Scriptures. For Jews of Paul's day, the temple was a visible reminder of God's presence with his people and his election of Israel. In keeping with the warnings of earlier prophets (Jer. 7; Mic. 3:9–12), Jesus (John 4:20–24), and other New Testament writers (Heb. 8:1–6; 1 Pet. 2:4–10), Paul marginalizes the significance of the Jerusalem temple by claiming that the new covenant community is now where God's presence dwells: "We are the temple of the living God" (2 Cor. 6:16). Paul also applies the promise concerning the sonship of the Davidic dynasty to the followers of Jesus (2 Cor. 6:18; cf. 2 Sam. 7:14). Paul's theological method is made explicit in 7:1, "We have these promises." Israel's promises belong to the new covenant community. This is a claim that certainly would have raised objections among Paul's Jewish contemporaries, as it still does today.

Teaching the Text

Paul's teaching on the importance of holiness can easily be misinterpreted or misunderstood. The following headings tease out key elements of this passage related to holiness and clarify elements that are sometimes misconstrued, even by informed readers of the New Testament.

1. *Intimacy*. Perhaps the most urgent point that Paul is making in this section is that personal holiness leads to intimacy with the Father. Paul marshals only a few of the many Old Testament texts that speak to this issue, and the primary verbs of 6:16–18 spell out clearly the results of faithful obedience: "I will live with them and walk among them. . . . I will receive you. . . . I will be a Father to you." At stake are intimacy and full communion with the Father, which is a message that echoes the teaching of Jesus: "Jesus replied, 'Anyone who loves me will obey my teaching. My Father will love them, and we will come to them and make our home with them'" (John 14:23). Paul is not saying that purity is a prerequisite for salvation or justification, but he is saying that true saving faith will lead to an increasing concern for holiness, which will lead to full intimacy with the Father. Paul has already told the Corinthians that their lack of attentiveness to such matters has led to death and illness in their community (1 Cor. 11:27–31), and his distress over the behavior of some will ultimately cause him to issue a grave challenge to the Corinthians: "Examine yourselves to see whether you are in the faith" (2 Cor. 13:5).

2. *Separation*. In this context, the primary means of attaining intimacy is to separate oneself from spiritual contaminants, be they relationships or activities. Separation is not the only crucial component of deep communion with the Father, but it is what Paul needs to address here. This passage is sometimes presented as if Paul's main concern were marriages between believers and unbelievers, which is not the case. On the other hand, I have also heard teachers and pastors insist that, since the issue Paul is addressing concerns frequenting pagan temples, this passage has nothing to do with marital relationships. This is also not quite correct. While the issue in Corinth relates to frequenting pagan temples, Paul intentionally frames his instruction quite broadly, by enunciating principles that relate to any spiritually detrimental relationship or activity (esp. 6:14–15). True, Paul is not talking about marriage between believers and unbelievers in this passage, but this is an appropriate application of the general principle he articulates.

3. *Motivation*. Paul employs a variety of motivational factors in exhorting believers to do what they ought to do. In the previous chapter Paul used the future judgment of believers at the bema seat of Christ as a rationale for pleasing God (5:9–10; cf. Rom. 14:1–12; 1 Cor. 3:12–15). In other contexts Paul uses eternal rewards as a stimulus toward good works (2 Tim. 4:7–8; Col. 3:23–24). Paul could also point out temporal, this-worldly benefits of

obedience as a proper motivation (Eph. 6:1–3). In this passage, however, Paul emphasizes the rich reward of present, relational communion with God as the by-product of faithfulness and purity. Paul holds out familial intimacy and the blessing of God's fatherly presence in our earthly pilgrimage as the very real reward for determinedly pursuing holiness, and this is something that believers today need to call to mind daily.

Illustrating the Text

The call of Jesus is a call to live distinctively Christ-centered lives.

Cultural Observation: No single religious group in the United States is more recognized for their commitment to live separately from the world than the Amish. Their plain, modest dress and commitment to live free from the electrical grid make their lifestyle countercultural to be sure. The Amish choose not to use conventional automobile travel. Their rationale is that car ownership breeds pride and fuels a fast-paced lifestyle that is to be resisted. Family is a high virtue in Amish culture. The value of the community supersedes the value of the individual. We may not understand the Amish resistance to the use of technology or emulate all facets of their approach to culture, but their commitment to be less worldly than others is a virtue that should not be mocked.

Maximum impact

Object Lesson: Hold up a large glass pitcher of water. Then place a few drops of red food coloring in the water and watch it transform the whole volume of water. Jesus's followers can change the chemistry of an office, a school, or a neighborhood when we live obediently and distinctively.

We belong.

Story: Max Lucado relates a story told by family therapist Paul Faulkner:

> A man set out to adopt a troubled teenage girl. One would question the father's logic. The girl was destructive, disobedient, and dishonest. One day she came home from school and ransacked the house looking for money. By the time he arrived, she was gone and the house was in shambles.
>
> Upon hearing of her actions, friends urged him not to finalize the adoption. "Let her go," they said. "After all, she's not really your daughter." His response was simply, "Yes, I know. But I told her she was."[4]

We too have been adopted, and we should return the Father's overwhelming love in an increasing pursuit of holiness and persistence in faithfulness.

2 Corinthians 7:2–4

An Appeal for Reciprocated Affection

Big Idea
Paul assures the Corinthians of his integrity and affection for them and appeals for them to return his affection by opening their hearts to him and his co-workers.

Key Themes
- Paul has acted with complete integrity toward the Corinthians.
- Paul's affection for the Corinthians remains undiminished.
- Paul's confidence in the Corinthians is firm.

Understanding the Text

The Text in Context

Paul finishes the thought that was interrupted by the appeal of 6:14–7:1, asking the Corinthians to return his affection and reassuring them of his own integrity and confidence in them. In this short paragraph Paul gathers up much of the preceding chapters in an abbreviated, allusive fashion (see "Interpretive Insights," below). This summative recapitulation will allow Paul, in 7:5–16, to pick up the line of thought he left dangling in 2:13, concerning his unease in Troas while he was awaiting news from Titus.

Interpretive Insights

7:2 *Make room for us in your hearts. We have wronged . . . corrupted . . . exploited no one.* Paul repeats the plea of 6:13 for reciprocated affection, this time offering a threefold defense of his personal integrity. Some have suggested that each of these assertions reflects a specific accusation against Paul of wrongdoing, for example, corrupting someone morally, or causing financial ruin through imposing Christian ethical standards in business practices or litigation (see 1 Cor. 6:1–11). More likely, however, the first two are general avowals of blamelessness, while the third reflects Paul's very real concern for transparency and probity in financial matters. The charge of financial exploitation will surface again in 12:17, which provides solid evidence that Paul is aware that some in Corinth may be harboring suspicions in this regard. Paul's insistence on his innocence probably alludes to his defense of his altered travel plans (1:12–19), his intentional differentiation from those who hawk the word of God (2:17) and preach themselves (4:5), and his willing endurance of hardship and injustice for the sake of the gospel (4:7–12; 6:3–10).

7:3 *I do not say this to condemn you.* Paul is aware that his thrice-repeated claim of innocence (7:2) might be construed as a backhanded indictment of the Corinthians, particularly by those who are chafing under his leadership. Not wanting to undermine the relational progress he has made with the Corinthians, nor to give any room for grumbling among his naysayers in Corinth, Paul clarifies the intent behind his avowals of innocence and grounds this explanation by reminding them, "You are in our hearts" (see, e.g., ESV, LEB, NET).

you have such a place in our hearts. Paul observes that he has already told the Corinthians that they are "in our hearts," which leads commentators to ask where precisely Paul has made this assurance. Most see the comment in 6:11 as the likely reference, but there Paul says only that he has opened his heart to the Corinthians, not that the Corinthians are in his heart. The reference to the Corinthians being in his heart is found in 3:2, where Paul explains that the Corinthians are a letter from Christ "written on our hearts." However, it is not necessary to isolate one or the other as the singular reference in Paul's mind. Paul is likely referring to the entire tenor of the previous chapters and numerous contexts where he emphasizes his deep affection for the Corinthians, including 2:1–4; 5:13–14; and 6:11–13.

that we would live or die with you. Although Paul has mentioned dying and rising earlier in this letter (1:8–9; 4:14; 5:14–17), the reference in this verse is not to the theological motif that is so important in Paul's Letters—dying and rising with Christ—but to the strong bond of affection he feels for the Corinthians. Paul echoes a proverbial expression of friendship found in numerous ancient writers.[1] The solidarity that Paul feels with his churches will be most poignantly expressed in 11:29: "Who is weak, and I do not feel weak? Who is led into sin, and I do not inwardly burn?" (cf. 1 Thess. 3:8).

7:4 *I have spoken to you with great frankness.* With this verse Paul looks back on the argument of the previous chapters and transitions into the next section (7:5–16), where he concludes the travelogue broken off at 2:13. Paul's "great frankness" (the same expression used to describe himself in 3:12–13 [NIV: "very bold"], in contrast to Moses) could be construed to include most of what precedes, including his opening words of comfort (1:3–7), his candid description of the crisis in Asia (1:8–11), his defense of his travel plans (1:12–2:4), his defense of his apostolate in chapters 3–6, his hardship catalogs (4:7–12; 6:3–10), and his call to purity (6:14–7:1). These chapters also include several vulnerable disclosures from Paul (e.g., 1:9; 3:2; 4:16; 6:12–13), rendering 2 Corinthians probably Paul's most personal letter. Paul's "frankness" also has in mind the letter he sent via Titus, which was written "out of great distress and anguish of heart and with many tears" (2:4; cf. 7:8).

I take great pride in you . . . my joy knows no bounds. As Paul prepares to return to the topic of his time in Macedonia in 7:5 (cf. 2:12–13), he echoes the joy and thanksgiving that his earlier discussion of this topic prompted (2:14), which will be fully clarified in 7:5–16. It is important to keep in mind, however, that Paul's pride and joy over the Corinthians does not extend to every aspect of their conduct (cf. 6:14–7:10) but relates primarily to their positive reception of Titus and their godly response to the sorrowful letter that Titus delivered from Paul (7:5–16). As chapters 8–9 and 10–13 will reveal, Paul has some serious issues to confront in this letter, including the Corinthians' failure to complete their promised collection for the poor in Jerusalem and the influence of "false apostles" (11:13) among them.

Teaching the Text

One element of this short section stands out in particular as worthy of reflection and emphasis in teaching: *Paul's heart as a pastor.* In 7:3 Paul observes that his affection for the Corinthians is such that "we would live or die with you." In this statement Paul reveals more clearly than anywhere else the affective, emotional connection that spiritual shepherds should feel toward their flock. Paul has invested not only time and energy in preaching the gospel to others but his very heart. Writing to Thessalonica, Paul says, "We loved you so much, we were delighted to share with you not only the gospel of God but our lives as well" (1 Thess. 2:8). Paul considers the Corinthians to be his children (1 Cor. 4:14; 2 Cor. 6:13), for whom he will gladly "spend and be spent" (12:15 ESV). Like a parent, Paul finds joy in his children's successes and pain in their failures, and he gives himself wholeheartedly, not begrudgingly, to their welfare. As Paul well knows, ministry involves relationships with broken and needy people, and that inevitably entails pain, misunderstandings, and sometimes unreciprocated affection. However, Paul also understands the joy that comes with patience, forbearance, and unrestrained devotion to the welfare of others, and Paul is able to express that joy in this passage: "In all our troubles my joy knows no bounds" (7:4).

Illustrating the Text

Lack of accessibility can compromise a pastor's connection with the flock.

Story: I was having lunch with a pastor of a small church. As we drove to his house, I noticed how remote it was from the town—through back roads and farming lanes. When I commented to him about this his response was, "Yes, that's intentional. It keeps my parishioners from bugging me." As our conversation continued, I learned that this pastor's concern was not to protect himself from burnout but to avoid being distracted by the needs of his flock. This pastor was also a scholar, and he did not want his pastoral work to interfere with his academic writing. Of course, every pastor has to make choices about how best to fulfill their calling, but if a pastor's heart isn't "to live or die" (2 Cor. 7:3) for their flock, perhaps his or her calling lies elsewhere.

Joy through caring for others

Ministry Connection: The apostle Paul found great joy in serving and caring for others. This attitude reflects the heart of Jesus and should be seen in the life of every Christian. Let the teaching of this passage be an opportunity to share about some of your church's ministries that provide care for others. Describe both the opportunities for service and also the joy that people find in serving others in these ways. You could include brief testimonies of those who do the caring and those who are cared for.

Self-sacrifice of a leader

Scripture: Highlight some of the ways the apostle Paul sacrificed as he gave leadership in the early church (see 2 Cor. 11). Then describe some of the ways your church lay leaders sacrifice as they serve your congregation. Many church members have no idea how faithfully and diligently their leaders serve Jesus and them. Finally, consider pausing during your message, inviting your board or coucil members to stand, and taking time to pray for them. Encourage your church members to pray regularly for those who have been called to leadership in your church.

2 Corinthians 7:5–16

Comfort, Repentance, and Reconciliation

Big Idea
Paul rejoices over Titus's report that the Corinthians responded with repentance to his strongly worded letter and were eager to make things right.

Key Themes
- God comforts the downcast.
- A godly rebuke may inflict pain, but this pain will work true repentance in sincere hearts.
- Genuine sorrow over sin leads to a flourishing life; insincere sorrow leads only to increased pain.

Understanding the Text

The Text in Context

In this segment Paul resumes the narrative of his travels (1:8–2:13) that was interrupted by the apostle's exclamation of thanksgiving in 2:14 and the digression in defense of his apostolate that followed (note how 7:5 follows seamlessly from 2:13). We discover here the reason for Paul's sudden outburst of thanksgiving: the mention of Titus in 2:13 called to mind the joyful news that Titus brought to Paul in Macedonia concerning the Corinthians' penitent response to his strongly written letter (2:3–4). This present section also sheds light on the content of the letter opening, which emphasized comfort in affliction (1:3–11). This same theme and terminology are taken up again here, indicating that the comforting news Paul had received from Titus was the dominant issue on Paul's mind as he began this lengthy missive. Paul now brings to a conclusion the first major portion of the letter, in which the apostle has defended his change of travel plans (1:12–2:4), addressed the matter of disciplining the offender (2:5–11), presented a lengthy and profound defense of his apostolate (2:14–7:4), and expressed his joy over the Corinthians' response to his letter. In the following chapters Paul will turn his attention to two serious issues that remain unresolved: the stalled collection for the poor (chaps. 8–9) and the presence of disruptive intruders (chaps. 10–13).

Interpretive Insights

7:5 *For when we came into Macedonia, we had no rest . . . conflicts on the outside, fears within.* After returning to Ephesus from his "painful visit" to Corinth (2:1), Paul had initially planned to return and assert his authority but decided instead to send a letter via Titus (1:15–2:4). Paul had made plans to meet Titus in Troas, but Titus's failure to arrive as scheduled forced Paul to abandon a fruitful ministry out of concern for the situation in Corinth (2:12–13). Paul crossed the Aegean into Macedonia, which was, apparently, their secondary rendezvous point, and he notes here that "our flesh [*sarx*]" (translated by the NIV simply as "we") had no rest. This probably refers to his entire person, as opposed to simply bodily exhaustion (cf. 2:13, "no rest in my spirit"; see KJV). We have no specific information on what Paul has in mind by "conflicts from the outside," although the long list of dangers encountered while traveling which Paul enumerates in 11:23–28 provides clues: dangers from shipwrecks, bandits, mobs, hunger, and so on. Paul's "fears within" must include anxiety over Titus and the situation in Corinth, in addition to concerns about personal safety (11:28).

7:6–7 *But God, who comforts the downcast, comforted us by the coming of Titus.* Relief came through the arrival of Titus, who reported on the success of his embassy to Corinth. Comfort in affliction has been a dominant theme in this letter (1:3–11; 2:2–3, 14–17; 4:7–12, 16–17; 6:3–10), and Paul

---

Titus: Paul's Trusted Co-worker

Titus was one of Paul's key ministry associates and was assigned tasks that required significant diplomacy and administrative know-how. We first hear of him in Galatians, where Paul tells how Titus accompanied him to Jerusalem and provided the Jerusalem leadership with a personal example of genuine faith in a gentile apart from circumcision (Gal. 2:1–4). Paul describes him as his true child "in our common faith" (Titus 1:4), which suggests that Paul played a decisive role in Titus's conversion (cf. 1 Cor. 4:15; Philem. 10). Titus was given the difficult task in Corinth of delivering Paul's letter of rebuke, while at the same time trying to effect reconciliation. He was also tasked with organizing the collection for the poor in Jerusalem (2 Cor. 8:6, 16), which was largely a matter of motivating the Corinthians to make good on their pledge (see chaps. 8–9). In view of Titus's success in Corinth, it is not surprising that Paul later entrusted to him the responsibility of organizing the new ministry in Crete (Titus 1:5). He was later summoned to meet Paul in Nicopolis (Titus 3:12), perhaps in preparation for ministry in Dalmatia (2 Tim. 4:10).

enunciates this theme here in the form of a theological principle: God comforts the downcast (cf. Isa. 40:1; 49:13; and 51:12, "I am the one who comforts you" [see CEB]).

but also by the comfort you had given him. Paul wisely affirms the Corinthians by relating Titus's report of his own encouragement from the Corinthians, as well as Titus's positive appraisal of their response to Paul's stern letter: "longing" (perhaps to be reconciled to Paul), "deep sorrow" (over the sin and resulting offense to Paul), "ardent concern" (or "zeal"—perhaps to set matters right).

7:8-9 *I see that my letter hurt you, but only for a little while.* Paul's strongly worded letter hit the intended target and produced the intended effect: repentance. Paul earlier described this letter as written out of "distress," "anguish," and "tears" (2:4), revealing that the letter was painful to both the writer and the recipients. Yet because Paul's dominant concern was the restoration and spiritual health of the congregation, he was not averse to causing pain, provided that the pain was ultimately beneficial. This course of action, however, was not taken eagerly by Paul, nor without some second thoughts: "I did regret it . . . yet now I am happy" (7:8b–9a). We are probably right to detect a measure of uncertainty on Paul's part as to the appropriateness of the letter, and also to infer that entrusting it to Titus involved a degree of courage and faith. Paul genuinely entertained the possibility that the letter might end up causing more harm (7:9) than good, which explains his immense comfort and joy at Titus's good report.

7:10 *Godly sorrow brings repentance that leads to salvation and leaves no regret.* Paul now elaborates what it means to become "sorrowful as God intended" (7:9) and defines two different kinds of sorrow: godly sorrow and worldly sorrow. The former results in "salvation," the latter in "death." It is possible that by "salvation" and "death" Paul is thinking only of one's final eschatological destiny. However, given the gnomic articulation of this truth in the form of general theological principles, it seems more likely that Paul's thought also includes the benefits or harm produced in this life by the two kinds of sorrow. Godly sorrow produces sincere contrition, together with deliberate action (see 7:11) to rectify the situation. Far from producing "regret," godly sorrow leads to peace in this life and eternal joy in the next life. "Worldly sorrow," on the other hand, regrets more the discovery of the sin than the sin itself and is closer to resentment than true repentance. This kind of sorrow cuts a destructive path through this life and finds only despair and death in the next life.

7:11 *See what this godly sorrow has produced in you: what earnestness . . . eagerness . . . indignation . . . alarm . . . longing . . . concern.* As proof of the theological axiom of 7:10, that godly sorrow produces positive spiritual benefits—even in this life—Paul enumerates seven specific manifestations of true repentance evidenced by the Corinthians in the present matter: "earnestness" (a diligent determination to set things right), "eagerness to clear yourselves," "indignation" (appropriate anger toward the offender), "alarm" (genuine distress at the offense to God and to Paul), "longing" (a deep desire for reconciliation with their founding apostle), "concern" (or "zeal": an energetic pursuit of justice), "readiness to see justice done" (or "vengeance": the meting out of punishment to the guilty [see 2:6]). Paul gauges the authenticity of the Corinthians' repentance by their actions (cf. Matt. 3:8; Acts 26:20) and concludes that they have proved themselves entirely "innocent." Although it is likely that a minority in Corinth bore more guilt than this statement publicly concedes—particularly in not dealing with the offense before being confronted by Paul—Paul's magnanimous pronouncement of innocence reflects his conviction that true repentance wipes the slate clean, and it is indicative of his determination to move forward in his relationship with the Corinthians.

7:12 *I wrote to you . . . neither on account of the one who did the wrong nor on account of the injured party.* What little can be known about the matter in dispute and the individuals involved has been laid out in the sidebar "The Offense and the Sinner in 2:5–11 and 7:5–16" in the unit on 2:5–11. The first-person pronouns in 2:5 and 2:11 indicate that the injured party was probably Paul. Referring to the painful letter of 2:4, Paul notes that its primary purpose was not to accuse the offender, or to vindicate himself,[1] but to provide an opportunity for the Corinthians to show their true colors and display their loyalty (NIV: "devoted") to Paul. This pastorally shrewd retrospective assessment allows Paul both to clarify his own intentions in sending the letter and also to affirm the Corinthians in their response.

7:13–15 *we were especially delighted to see how happy Titus was . . . you were all obedient, receiving him with fear and trembling.* Titus's report gives Paul another opportunity to encourage the Corinthians, by making them privy to Titus's positive assessment of them. This disclosure further strengthens rapport between Titus and the Corinthians and renders Titus's task of reinvigorating the collection that much easier. In biblical literature, "fear and trembling" depicts the appropriate response to a display of God's power, plan, or glory (Exod. 15:16; Deut. 2:25; Jer. 33:9; Dan. 6:26; Phil. 2:12). Thus, Paul depicts the Corinthian response to his apostolic censure in terms that underscore their fitting respect for Paul's apostolic delegate.

7:16 *I am glad I can have complete confidence in you.* This statement should probably be understood as restricted to matters related to Titus's embassy, particularly the manner in which the Corinthians dealt with the offender and their allegiance to Paul. We know from 6:14–7:1 that Paul had serious concerns regarding some in Corinth who were frequenting pagan temples, and chapters 10–13 will reveal even graver issues that Paul must confront.

Theological Insights

The emphasis in this passage on repentance is somewhat unique among Paul's Letters. In fact, Paul rarely speaks explicitly of "repentance." The terminology occurs only five times in his letters (Rom. 2:4; 2 Cor. 7:9, 10; 12:21; 2 Tim. 2:25), though it is implied in passages where Paul speaks of "turning" to the Lord (2 Cor. 3:16; Gal. 4:9; 1 Thess. 1:9). Here in 2 Corinthians 7, Paul speaks both of Christians repenting of their misjudgments and sin (7:9; cf. 12:21) and more broadly of "repentance that leads to salvation" (7:10; cf. Rom. 2:4). Repentance, of course, is deeply imbedded in the theology of the old covenant and is particularly prominent in the prophets Jeremiah and Ezekiel. The terminology commonly used in the Old Testament is *shub*, "to turn." Although the call to repentance in the Old Testament is most often directed toward Israel (1 Kings 8:47; Isa. 30:15; Jer. 8:6), it is also addressed to pagan nations (Jer. 18:7–8; Jonah 3:1–10) and to individuals (Job 42:6; Prov. 1:23; Ps. 51). From the perspective of the Old Testament, repentance is available even at the eleventh hour, when judgment is imminent (Jer. 18:8; Ezek. 18:30–32), and even after a lifetime of sin and rebellion (2 Chron. 33:10–13). This perspective is continued in the New Testament, as no one is excluded from the call to repentance (Acts 17:30), and confession and repentance are the sole condition for forgiveness (1 John 1:5–10).

Teaching the Text

This passage contains important and unique (in Paul's Letters) information on the process of confronting sin and the resultant repentance. Worth emphasizing in teaching this passage are Paul's own sense of comfort coming from the response of the Corinthians, his determination to confront the sin, and his description of what true repentance looks like.

1. *God comforts the downcast.* Second Corinthians 1–7 is home to some very grand designations of God. Through these descriptive appellations Paul connects the character and attributes of God to his work in and through the apostle. Paul describes God as the one who raises the dead (1:9), who triumphs over us in Christ (2:14), who makes us competent for service (3:5), who shines his light in our hearts (4:6), who gives us his Spirit as a deposit (5:5), and who reconciles the world to himself (5:18). To these lofty descriptions 7:6 adds the God "who comforts the downcast." As the opening verses of 2 Corinthians confirm (1:3–7), this letter—particularly chapters 1–7—was

written out of an overwhelming experience of God's comfort: "Our comfort abounds through Christ" (1:5). God's majesty is revealed not only in his work as Creator and Redeemer but also in his role as the one "who comforts us in all our troubles" (1:4).

2. *Confrontation takes courage.* The apostle Paul was certainly not one to retreat from a confrontation when there were kingdom issues at stake, as chapters 10–13 of this letter demonstrate. Yet the personal attack described in this passage and in 2:5–11 left Paul genuinely perplexed. At first he intended to return personally to Corinth, but later he changed his mind (1:12–2:4). Instead he sent a strongly worded letter, and then he admits to having second thoughts about this action as well (7:8). Inaction, however, was not an option. Even though Paul was not entirely certain how to proceed, he must have surmised that far graver consequences would result from doing nothing. Paul's willingness to confront sin rather than overlook it ultimately led to repentance and restoration. This serves as an important reminder to us that while we may not always have absolute clarity in how to deal with grievous sin in the body of Christ, failing to confront those involved will almost certainly bring more harm than good.

3. *True repentance bears fruit.* Perhaps the most instructive component of this passage is the distinction Paul makes between "godly sorrow" and "worldly sorrow" and his description of what godly sorrow looks like. The primary attribute of godly sorrow is that it expresses itself in taking responsibility for the offense and working energetically to rectify the matter (cf. Luke 3:8). Paul does not elaborate on "worldly sorrow," but we may infer that it is deficient both in acknowledging wrongdoing and in working to make things right. This response, according to Paul, leads only to "death" (7:10).

Illustrating the Text

What godly sorrow looks like.

Story: Teaching seminary students is both challenging and exhilarating. As a professor, I have the opportunity to interact with young men and women from all over the world who are preparing for ministry, and the task is genuinely rewarding. Occasionally, however, students take academic shortcuts in the coursework and decide to plagiarize a paper or cheat on a quiz. This is the challenging part. Several years ago I uncovered a cheating ring in one of my classes; three students, all involved in ministry, colluded together to misrepresent their quiz scores. The evidence I collected was decisive and irrefutable, but I always allow students to come clean on their own before confronting them with the evidence. I called the students into my office individually, and asked them about their quiz scores and if they had been honest, gently trying to coax them toward honesty. The first two students adamantly denied any wrongdoing, and even after seeing the evidence made excuses, and demonstrating more concern about the academic consequences than the deeper spiritual issue. The third student, on the other hand, needed little prompting. He broke down in tears almost before he sat down, and his remorse was both sincere and encouraging. The consequences he faced were quite different than the students who only begrudgingly admitted their offense. He ended up finishing the class respectably, and later thanked me for confronting him. This student demonstrated what Paul calls "godly sorrow"—sorrow that regrets the offense, not simply its discovery, and effects genuine repentance.

In times of loss and pain, God shows up and extends heavenly comfort.

Testimony: Have a church member, couple, or family share a story about how God drew near in clear and tangible ways as they walked through a time of pain, loss, and heartache. Let this story affirm that God truly does comfort the downcast. This can be live or prerecorded. You might want to have a time at the end of the service when people who are downcast and hurting can come forward for prayer and care from your church leaders.

Facing conflict can strengthen relationships.

Testimony: "Walking toward the mess" is a principle that helps foster a culture of candor with kindness. Tell a personal story of how a direct engagement in a conflict resulted in learning, growth, and especially the strengthening of the relationship. Paul was certainly no stranger to conflict and was willing to confront challenges head on.

2 Corinthians 8:1–7

The Generosity of the Macedonians

Big Idea

The sacrificial generosity of the churches in Macedonia is a model for other churches to emulate, both in giving themselves to others and in giving themselves to the Lord.

Key Themes

- The ability to give generously is evidence of God's grace working in our lives.
- Poverty and generosity are not mutually exclusive.
- Consecration to the Lord is the basis for service to others.

Understanding the Text

The Text in Context

As noted in the introduction, 2 Corinthians can be divided into three major sections, each with its own purpose and agenda. Chapters 1–7 constitute Paul's defense of his apostolate, his character, and specific actions that the Corinthians had misinterpreted (1:12–2:4). Chapters 8–9 represent Paul's attempt to reignite enthusiasm in Corinth for the collection for the poor in Jerusalem, which the Corinthians had already committed themselves to (1 Cor. 16:1–4; 2 Cor. 8:10–11) but had thus far failed to complete. Chapters 10–13 take up the challenge and claims of intruders in Corinth who oppose Paul and are attempting to drive a wedge between the apostle and this church. Paul's appeal to the Corinthians to keep their promise to contribute to the needs of the poor in Jerusalem could not reasonably precede his apostolic defense of chapters 1–7, where Paul addresses lingering hesitations on the part of some in Corinth and reestablishes the relational basis for this monetary appeal by accepting their repentance and affirming complete reconciliation (7:2–16). In this present section (8:1–7) Paul begins his appeal for the collection by holding up the example of the Macedonians, who have been generous even in their poverty. Paul hopes to use the Macedonians as a means of motivating the Corinthians to give generously as well.

Historical and Cultural Background

Chapters 8 and 9 provide a glimpse into a crucial poverty-relief effort that Paul undertook on behalf of the destitute believers in Jerusalem (Rom. 15:26), which he organized in tandem with his missionary work. The scope of this venture was quite significant by ancient standards, involving Christian assemblies all throughout the Aegean basin. The collection originated during Paul's famine-relief visit to Jerusalem (Acts 11:27–30), when the Jerusalem leadership urged Paul to "continue to remember the poor" (Gal. 2:10). What followed was a decade-long fund-raising campaign, with Paul actively promoting this endeavor in the churches he established in Asia Minor and Europe. The first explicit reference to the collection occurs in 1 Corinthians 16:1–4, though it is clear from this passage that both the Corinthian and the Galatian assemblies were already on board. In Romans 15:26 Paul confirms that the churches in Macedonia and Achaia are participating (which indicates that 2 Cor. 8–9 effectively persuaded the Corinthians), and in 2 Corinthians 8:19–20 we learn that Paul himself hopes to accompany the delegates from the gentile churches to deliver the relief aid to Jerusalem. According to Acts 20:4, as Paul sets out for Jerusalem he is accompanied by representatives from Derbe, Lystra, Berea, Thessalonica, and Ephesus. It is commonly assumed that these are the delegates chosen by the local churches to deliver the collection (cf. 1 Cor. 16:3; 2 Cor. 8:19, 23). Although 2 Corinthians 9:12–13 indicates that Paul expects that the collection will increase the bond of unity between the Jerusalem church and the expanding gentile movement, the primary motivation given for the collection, in both Paul's Letters and the book of Acts, is poverty relief: "I am on my way to Jerusalem . . . to make a contribution for the poor" (Rom. 15:25–26; cf. 2 Cor. 8:13–14; 9:12; Acts 24:17). While Paul is remembered today principally as an evangelist, missionary, and theologian, his work on behalf of the poor in Jerusalem warrants adding one more title to this list: relief worker.

Interpretive Insights

8:1 *the grace that God has given the Macedonian churches.* "Grace" (Greek, *charis*) is the dominant theme of 2 Corinthians 8 and 9, occurring fully ten times (in varying senses) in these two chapters. In this first occurrence of *charis*, Paul depicts the Macedonian generosity as a divinely bestowed gift, a spiritual disposition that has resulted in extraordinary liberality (8:2–3). This attitude of eager openhandedness is something "given" by God to the Macedonians and hence is attributed "neither to [Paul's] own successful ministry . . . nor to their own selfless action."[1] The Macedonian churches that Paul has in mind were probably located in Philippi, Thessalonica, and Berea, where Paul evangelized during his second missionary tour with Silas (Acts 15:36–17:15), joined by Timothy along the way (16:1–4).

8:2 *their extreme poverty welled up in rich generosity.* Paul now explicates what form this "grace" took, first in general terms (8:2) and then in more detail (8:3–5). The circumstances in which the Macedonian generosity budded and then blossomed are described as "a very severe trial" and "extreme poverty." The Greek expression underlying "severe trial" (*thlipsis*) commonly denotes suffering and persecution (2 Cor. 6:4; Col. 1:24), but it can also refer to other kinds of distress (1 Cor. 7:28; 2 Cor. 8:13). Persecution is likely the meaning here, as suggested by specific references to persecution in Paul's Letters to communities in Macedonia (1 Thess. 1:6–8; 2:14; Phil. 1:27–30). The beautiful paradox of the Macedonian gift is that a "severe trial" led to "overflowing joy," and "extreme poverty" resulted in "rich generosity." This is decisive proof that their offering was an act of divine grace on their behalf.

Poverty in the Greco-Roman World

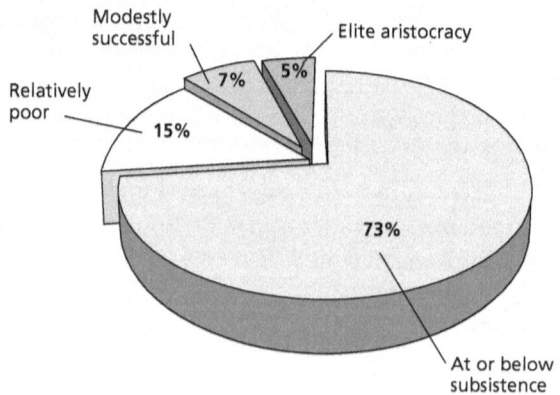

Paul's reference to the "extreme poverty" of the churches in Macedonia (8:2) needs to be understood in light of the fact that most people in the ancient world were very poor by modern standards. Unlike today, there was no middle class in antiquity, and the vast majority of property and capital resided in the hands of a very small portion of the population. Roughly 70 percent of the populace lived hand to mouth, surviving at or below a minimal subsistence level. The satirist Lucian depicts the unhappy lot of this large majority as follows: "Toiling and moiling from morning till night, doubled over their tasks, they merely eke out a bare existence" (*Fug.* 17). In light of the grinding poverty that characterized most of the Greco-Roman world, Paul's emphasis on the "extreme poverty" of the Macedonians brings to mind the expression "dirt poor," which would probably be an apt description of the communities responsible for this generous contribution.

8:3–4 *beyond their ability . . . on their own, they urgently pleaded with us for the privilege of sharing.* Having described the circumstances of their giving (dire poverty, 8:2) Paul now focuses on the manner of the giving. Paul prefaces his description with an oath-like expression of solemn testimony, emphasizing the absolute trustworthiness of his account (cf. Gal. 4:15; Col. 4:13). Paul emphasizes that their generosity was beyond any reasonable expectation, that it was free of external coercion, and that it was accompanied by determined insistence. The Macedonians recognized the "privilege" (*charis*) that sharing with others represented, and this was by no means their first act of giving. They partnered with Paul early in his missionary work (Phil. 1:5; 4:15), they sent him aid during his first visit to Corinth (2 Cor. 11:9), and later they sent Epaphroditus to supply Paul's needs while in prison (Phil. 2:25). There is a subtle note of irony in Paul's description of the Macedonians "clamoring to be allowed a share in the collection,"[2] while the Corinthians, who have committed themselves to the project earlier, are being needled by Paul to fulfill their promise.

8:5 *They gave themselves first of all to the Lord.* The expression "first of all" probably denotes priority (as opposed to temporal sequence) and can be rendered "most important." Paul recognizes that the wellspring of the Macedonian generosity is their consecration to the Lord, and in emphasizing this aspect of the Macedonian contribution Paul is tacitly urging the Corinthians to follow their example. In keeping with these spiritual priorities, the Macedonians also have devoted themselves to God's apostles and God's will ("by the will of God also to us"). While contributing to the poor in Jerusalem is entirely voluntary, Paul is not opposed to aligning proper spiritual priorities with following the leadership of God's servants, and thus fulfilling the will of God.

8:6 *So we urged Titus.* See the sidebar "Titus: Paul's Trusted Co-worker" in the unit on 7:5–16.

8:7 *But since you excel in everything . . . see that you also excel in this grace of giving.* Paul now gets to the point, offering an explicit but politely phrased directive: excel in the grace of generosity. This exhortation is grounded first by the example of the Macedonians in 8:2–5, which is intended by Paul to motivate the Corinthians out of a sense of rivalry, or perhaps honor, lest they be outdone by the impoverished Macedonians. The second ground for this request is Paul's appeal to their character—their faith, earnestness, love, and so on. Paul's persuasive technique is not so much flattery as a genuine attempt to help the Corinthians live consistently with the virtues the gospel has wrought in their lives. "Faith" may refer to trust in God and belief in the gospel (1 Cor. 2:5; 15:14; 2 Cor. 1:24; 10:15) or to the miracle-working faith that can "move mountains" (1 Cor. 13:2).

"Speech" and "knowledge" are similarly affirmed in 1 Corinthians 1:5, but in many contexts these attributes prized by the Corinthians are censured by Paul, where they connote intellectual arrogance (1 Cor. 8:1, 10; 2 Cor. 11:6) and an unhealthy devotion to oratory (1 Cor. 2:1–5; 2 Cor. 10:10). "Love" completes the list as the summative virtue. The object of this love is not defined, but since this love has been implanted in their hearts through Paul's proclamation of the gospel, it probably refers to the Corinthians' love of Christ and fellow believers.

Teaching the Text

In chapters 8–9 Paul will lay out crucial foundational principles related to giving and generosity. In this introductory paragraph, the teaching emphasis is on the nature of generosity as divine grace and the spiritual disposition and priorities of those who excel in this grace.

1. *The gift of generosity.* While Romans 12:8 speaks of the spiritual gift of philanthropy, in 2 Corinthians 8 and 9 Paul describes a Christian grace that he expects all believers to be committed to: generosity. Although Paul does not call generosity a "spiritual gift," as in his discussion of spiritual gifts in 1 Corinthians 12:1–11 and Romans 12:1–8, he is clear that this inner disposition is divinely given (2 Cor. 8:1). Paul wants the Corinthians to understand that generosity is an indication of spiritual maturity and a concrete expression of love (8:8). He calls it a "grace" (8:1, 6, 7), a "ministry" (9:12 ESV), and an act of "service" (9:1). He says that it is modeled on Christ's sacrificial example (8:9) and that it brings glory to God (8:19; 9:14). In Paul's view, generosity is a necessary consequence of faith in Christ (8:7).

2. *The riches of poverty.* Generosity and charitable giving are usually associated with those who are better off, giving to those who are worse off. The Macedonians, on the other hand, represent a situation where the poor and disadvantaged are giving to others who are in similar circumstances. The Macedonians have given out of their poverty, rather than out of their abundance, revealing the true riches of their spiritual state. They look to the needs of others rather than becoming fixated on, and crippled by, their own (legitimate) needs. Like the widow whose sacrificial generosity was praised by Jesus, in spite of the small amount of her gift (Mark 12:41–44), so too the Macedonians are praised by Paul, though we can safely assume their contribution is not as large as that of other, better-off communities. Poverty and generosity are not mutually exclusive states. External poverty may well cloak vast inner riches.

3. *The priority of consecration.* The churches in Macedonia prove to be exemplary in their attitude and approach toward sharing with others. They

give sacrificially, joyfully, and lavishly. They do not let their own difficult circumstances harden them toward the needs of others, but they respond with eagerness to the plight of their brothers and sisters in Jerusalem. Yet Paul's most important commendation of the Macedonians is found in his candid reflection on their spiritual priorities: "Most important, they consecrated themselves to the Lord" (8:5, author's translation). Paul describes a spiritual disposition among the Macedonian communities that seeks to order their priorities according to God's kingdom, not their own needs. Paul himself has been so impressed with their approach that he admits he was caught off guard: "And they exceeded our expectations" (8:5). A heart that is consecrated to the Lord will regularly exceed the expectations of others.

Illustrating the Text

Extreme poverty did not stop extreme generosity by the Macedonian churches.

Story: Gordon MacDonald, a longtime pastor and now chancellor of Denver Seminary, shares what God used in his life as a catalyst toward cheerful giving: Gordon and his wife were worshiping with a desperately poor church in West Africa. Every person coming to church brought something with them. Some brought chickens, others brought yams, and some others toted bags of eggs or bowls of cassava paste. Every Jesus-follower brought their "offering" to the altar with lots of dancing, clapping, and shouting at the offering time. People with far less than most of us gave far more, and they did it with a joyful heart! This experience led MacDonald on a journey toward understanding that our giving should not be merely to balance the church budget but is evidence of mature faith. God is the most generous Giver, and he calls his followers to be givers too.[3]

Deal or no deal?

Quote: **Andy Stanley.** Stanley invites followers to trust in God and give generously:

> There, at the center of Jesus' teaching, is a new deal for anyone who will follow him. The deal is simple. When you make God's kingdom your first priority, He promises to provide what you need to live. In other words Jesus is saying, "If you will be about My needs—taking care of the poor and making disciples—I will be about your needs." And just like you and me, Jesus' audiences lived in a world devoid of physical and financial certainty. Nevertheless, He promised that if they kept their end of the deal, He would—with certainty—meet their needs.[4]

We are most secure when we follow God's plan.

Generosity is not a function of income.

Article: Journalist David Crary reported in the *Huffington Post* in 2014 that despite a widening income gap, the wealthiest Americans are giving a smaller share of their income to charity. Meanwhile, poor and middle-income people are donating a larger share.[5] There may be a number of theories as to why this is true, but certainly the fact that wealth fosters (at least the illusion of) independence from others and God must be part of the reality.

The last cent

Scripture: In Mark 12:38–44, Jesus calls his disciples to observe the generous gift of a poor widow. Note that Jesus doesn't praise the widow as much as he calls his disciples to pay attention since the poor are often invisible. Jesus is teaching that a key question for his followers is not how much to give but how much to hold back. Jesus held nothing back, and neither did the generous widow. Invite listeners to reflect on what it would look like for them to give at a level similar to the generous widow.

2 Corinthians 8:8–15

Finish the Work!

Big Idea

Contributing financially to the needs of others represents a concrete expression of love and is grounded in the incarnational example of Jesus, who became poor to make others rich.

Key Themes

- Generosity is the by-product of sincere love and is defined by willingness and capacity, not by the amount given.
- Fulfilling our commitments should be a priority among God's people.
- The incarnation—Christ becoming poor for the sake of others—provides the model for believers to follow in terms of contributing financially to the needs of others.
- Believers should willingly assist in meeting the legitimate needs of other believers.

Understanding the Text

The Text in Context

In 8:8–15 Paul continues his appeal to the Corinthians to assist in the contribution for the poor in Jerusalem. Paul reminds them that this is a project that they have already committed themselves to, and so it is incumbent upon them to fulfill their obligations. Paul recognizes that his energetic pursuit of this topic might be misunderstood, so in this section he offers two important clarifications. First, he does not want his coaxing—however ardent—to be construed as an apostolic command; that would eliminate the blessing of a voluntary gift. Second, he wants to make clear that he is not trying to impoverish one group of believers and enrich another. Rather, he wants to make sure that those facing true deprivation experience relief, and so inculcate the value of reciprocal, mutual responsibility among his churches.

Interpretive Insights

8:8–10 *I am not commanding you.* The opening clause of 8:8 should be read in connection with the opening clause of 8:10 ("And here is my judgment about what is best") in order to grasp the important clarification that Paul is offering. He is not issuing an apostolic directive but giving his considered opinion. It is abundantly clear that Paul expects the Corinthians to do what is right and follow his advice. Yet for all his wheedling, coaxing, and urging, Paul recognizes that it is the better part of wisdom to refrain from issuing a direct command on this subject, lest the "gift" lose its voluntary character and become more like a tax. This approach is indicative of the extreme care Paul takes whenever money is involved, so as to preclude any hint of impropriety.

I want to test the sincerity of your love by comparing it with the earnestness of others. In Paul's eyes, the Macedonians have provided a new benchmark for charitable generosity. Their liberality, birthed out of poverty, has become the yardstick by which the apostle will measure the authenticity of the Corinthians' love. Paul may be interpreted as instigating a healthy competition between the churches in Achaia and Macedonia, or simply "encouraging friendly imitation,"[1] yet the important point remains that Paul expects genuine love to bear genuine fruit, and in this case that fruit is a monetary contribution to those in need.

For you know the grace of our Lord Jesus Christ. In order to illustrate the point that genuine love is measured by sacrificial generosity, Paul offers the quintessential example of this principle, the incarnation: "Though he was rich, yet for your sake he became poor" (8:9). The word "grace" in this context denotes Christ's "gracious deed" or "benefaction"[2] and might be better rendered "generosity."[3] The Greek sentence places "for your sake" in emphatic position, suggesting that Paul wants the Corinthians to apply this to their own situation and similarly act for the benefit of others. In referring to Christ's prior riches and voluntary impoverishment, Paul has in mind Christ's preincarnate glory, which was willingly laid aside when he took on human flesh, assumed the life of a Galilean peasant, suffered, bled, and died an ignominious death on a Roman cross (cf. Phil. 2:6–8). Paul probably has in mind the incarnation, as well as the death and resurrection of Jesus, as indicated by the purpose clause: "so that you through his poverty might become rich" (8:9). Paul adds the example of Jesus to the example of the Macedonians (8:1–7) in order to spur the Corinthians on to finish the work they had already begun.

8:11 *Now finish the work.* This statement represents the central exhortation of this passage, and indeed Paul's entire discussion of this subject in chapters 8 and 9. The exhortation is supported by two grounds, both emphasizing the importance of the Corinthians fulfilling their promises: (1) it is in their best interest to follow through on their commitment (8:10); (2) otherwise their supposed "eagerness" will be revealed as merely a hollow boast (8:11b).

according to your means. The final clause of 8:11 surfaces an important matter that Paul feels the need to dwell on. In 8:12–15 Paul unpacks, reiterates, clarifies, and illustrates this principle so that the Corinthians understand clearly that he is not expecting an equal contribution from everybody—rich and poor alike—nor does he intend this to be hardship for anyone.

8:12 *For if the willingness is there, the gift is acceptable according to what one has.* As Paul qualifies and explains "according to your means" (8:11), he puts the emphasis on the unseen, inward dimension of giving: a willing heart. Although Paul does not explicitly state to whom the gift is acceptable, 9:6–8 explains that God is the one who observes the disposition in which gifts are offered. From this important qualification, it follows that gifts given grudgingly would not be acceptable to God, however much they may impress others and genuinely benefit the recipients. This component of giving was anticipated and exemplified in the model of Jesus, who became poor to make others rich (8:9). The second qualification Paul offers is equally important: "according to what one has, not according to what one does not have." Gifts acceptable to God need not be large gifts, as the story of the widow praised by Jesus for her seemingly small contribution illustrates (Mark 12:41–44). In spite of the example of the Macedonians (8:1–6), Paul does not want those who are truly destitute to think that they are responsible to give what they do not have, nor does he want them to think that God (or his apostle) has no appreciation for their financial condition.

8:13-14 *Our desire is . . . that there might be equality.* Far from relieving one community through financially crippling another, Paul's desire is that there might be "equality." The expression Paul uses here (Greek, *isotēs*) need not be taken to mean strict economic parity. It frequently has the connotation of what is fair and equitable,[4] as Paul uses it in Colossians 4:1: "Masters, provide your slaves with what is right and *fair*." In the verses that follow Paul explains "equality" as ensuring that basic needs are met, which is his primary concern. What Paul envisions is that the network of Christian communities he established throughout the Mediterranean basin will form a mutually supporting association of churches, in which the "plenty" of one would make up the "need" of another (8:14).

8:15 *The one who gathered much did not have too much, and the one who gathered little did not have too little.* Paul finds an illustration of the

Aequitas ("Equality")

About the time Paul wrote 2 Corinthians, Rome began issuing coins bearing the image of the goddess Aequitas, "Equality." She is usually depicted holding a pair of scales, symbolizing fairness and equity, and also a cornucopia, symbolizing the abundance that comes when one does what is fair and equitable. The inscription on these coins typically reads *Aequitas Augusti*, "Augustan equality." It is quite possible that at least some coins of this type found their way into the collection for the poor in Jerusalem, which Paul tell us was aimed at producing "equality."

principle of fairness in distribution in the story of the Israelites, who daily gathered manna in the desert (Exod. 16:13–23). God ensured that each had what they needed, no matter how much manna a person gathered—too little or too much. The essential point that Paul is making, more implicitly than explicitly, is that it would be wrong for one person (or community) to have an excess of provisions, while another lacks what is essential for survival.

Theological Insights

Paul's instructions in 2 Corinthians 8 and 9 and in 1 Corinthians 16:1–4 regarding the contribution to the poor in Jerusalem are sometimes interpreted to refer directly to the modern practice of tithing, which is not accurate. The Old Testament practice of setting aside a tenth of one's income (agricultural products, livestock, profit from trade, etc.) for sacral purposes was not formally instituted in the New Testament, or the Pauline churches. However, there is ample evidence that the pooling of financial resources began very early among Jesus's followers. Paul instructs the Galatians that those being taught the word are to share "all good things" with those who teach them (Gal. 6:6). Similarly, the Romans are reminded to "contribute to the needs of the saints" (Rom. 12:13 ESV). By the time Paul wrote 1 Timothy (AD 61–63), the house churches in Ephesus had a registry of needy widows whom they supported financially (1 Tim. 5:1–16), and the teaching elders were afforded a double stipend (5:17). Clearly the Christian virtues of charity and generosity found expression in some kind of organized approach to contributing financially to the physical and spiritual needs of the community. So, while Paul's instructions to the Corinthians concerning the collection for the poor in Jerusalem are not explicitly addressing "tithing" in the early church, there are some important principles that we can relate to the modern setting: (1) giving should be *voluntary*, not a matter of compulsion (2 Cor. 8:8; 9:7); (2) giving should be *regular* and *orderly*: "On the first day of every week, each one of you should set aside a sum of money" (1 Cor. 16:2); (3) giving should be *proportionate* to one's income (1 Cor. 16:2; 2 Cor. 8:11); (4) giving should be *generous*, as defined by one's means (2 Cor. 9:6); (5) giving should be done *joyfully*, not grudgingly: "for God loves a cheerful giver" (9:7; cf. 9:5). As in all things, our model is Jesus, who became poor for our sake (8:9).

Teaching the Text

Paul continues to articulate his vision of generosity, and his advice in this section would be particularly valuable for teaching on stewardship.

1. *Fulfilling our commitments.* The fundamental imperative directed to the Corinthians in this passage is found in 8:11: "Now finish the work." Paul has earlier fended off an accusation of alleged fickleness on his part, that he was saying "yes" and "no" in the same breath (1:17–22), and Paul now is calling the Corinthians to adhere to the same principle he applies to himself: "Our message to you is not 'Yes' and 'No.' . . . But in him it has always been 'Yes'" (1:18–19). The principle behind Paul's admonition that the Corinthians make good on their promise corresponds to the emphasis in the Old Testament on fulfilling one's vows: "Whatever your lips utter you must be sure to do, because you made your vow freely to the Lord your God with your own mouth" (Deut. 23:23; cf. Prov. 20:25).

2. *Voluntary and eager giving.* Although Paul clearly wants the Corinthians to finish what they started and contribute to the collection for the poor in Jerusalem, he is equally clear that this should be an expression of love (8:8), and not an obligation fulfilled under duress. Paul does not specify an amount or suggest a percentage. There is no hint of a monetary target figure in his mind. He simply lays out the principles that giving to this special project should be voluntary and according to one's means. However, the exemplars that Paul offers to motivate the Corinthians—the Macedonians, who were poor but gave sacrificially, and Jesus, who was rich but made himself poor for others—are certainly aimed at producing generosity borne from a sense of gratitude and responsibility.

3. *Mutuality and reciprocity.* Although often overlooked when applying this passage to the modern setting, one of Paul's real concerns is that the members of the body of Christ care for each other and look out for each other. This applies on the individual level (one believer helping another believer: Rom. 12:10; Gal. 6:2; 1 Thess. 5:11) and on the community level (one community helping another community). Paul's vision, as articulated in 8:13–15, is larger than simply providing for those hard hit in Jerusalem. His desire is to inculcate the values of mutuality and reciprocity among his churches, so that a pattern is established whereby less fortunate churches (communities affected by some kind of crisis) are assisted by more stable churches. The expectation is that when fortunes are reversed, generosity will be reciprocated. In this way, Paul reasons, no one community will have too much while another has too little.

Illustrating the Text

The instinct to tithe preceded the law.

Scripture: Even before the law was given, we observe the patriarchs Abram (Gen. 14:20) and Jacob (28:22) tithing. It seems as though God has placed a seed of responsibility within us to want to express our devotion to God financially through a voluntary gift of love.

Good actions trump good intentions.

Story: There is a big difference between promise and performance. One congregation entered into a capital campaign where congregants made thirty-six-month pledges. In the previous capital campaigns 92 percent of the members fulfilled their pledges. The leadership team for the second campaign had confidence based on past performance that the congregation would fulfill the vows they had made to God and would fulfill their pledges. Sadly, only 78 percent of the pledges were fulfilled in the subsequent campaign. Twenty-two percent of the total never turned their good intentions into action. We must never confuse "willing" with "doing." Good intentions have never built churches, hospitals, or schools or provided food or shelter for those in need; only "good actions" have. The generous understand this and live it.

Wrong question

Personal Anecdote: One of the most common questions asked of pastors when it comes to the question of tithing is, Do I have to tithe on the net or gross? The question could be restated another way: What is the least amount I have to give to keep God from getting mad? John Ortberg says: "This is like going to your mom on Mother's Day and saying, "Mom, what's the least amount of money I can spend on your present without severing our relationship?"[5] God rejoices when we are aware of his goodness and provision and when we desire to give him our best as an act of love.

2 Corinthians 8:16–24

Money Matters

Big Idea

Financial matters should be entrusted only to individuals of proven character and should be handled in a way that ensures complete transparency and accountability.

Key Themes

- In dealing with other people's money it is important not only to act with integrity but to be seen to be acting with integrity.
- Contributing to the needs of others is done not only out of love for them but to bring glory to Christ.
- Character credentials are essential when money is involved.

Understanding the Text

The Text in Context

In 8:6 Paul began to detail the arrangements he was making to complete the collection, mentioning his urging of Titus to revisit Corinth. After clarifying his intentions concerning the collection in 8:8–15, Paul returns to the subject of plans for finishing the collection in 8:16 and introduces the rest of the ministry team that will accompany Titus. Paul is keen to emphasize to the Corinthians the measures he is taking to ensure that there is no hint of financial impropriety. This segment amounts to a brief letter of recommendation on behalf of the individuals responsible for gathering the funds in Corinth, emphasizing their qualifications and integrity.

Interpretive Insights

8:16–17 *God, who put into the heart of Titus the same concern I have for you.* Paul has been quite emphatic throughout this letter regarding his affection for the Corinthians: his suffering is for their comfort (1:3–7); the Corinthians are his "boast" before Christ (1:14) and his "joy" (2:1–3); they are a letter written on his heart (3:2); the apostle openly weeps on account of his love for them (2:4); he willingly accepts "death" so that "life" might accrue to the Corinthians (4:7–12; 6:3–10); he has "opened wide" his heart to them, not withholding any affection (6:11–12). This theme is brought to a crescendo in 7:3, where Paul candidly confesses, "You have such a place in our hearts that we would live or die with you." Paul's fundamental commendation of Titus in 8:16–17 is that he shares this "same concern" for the Corinthians. Paul wants to impress on the Corinthians that Titus undertook his mission not out of obligation, or merely out of obedience to his apostolic superior, but with "much enthusiasm and on his own initiative" (8:17). So, while Paul made the request of Titus to return to Corinth, God had already "put into the heart of Titus" (8:16) an affection for the Corinthians and an eagerness to see them thrive.

8:18–19 *the brother who is praised by all the churches for his service to the gospel . . . chosen by the churches.* In addition to Titus, Paul is sending two other delegates to oversee the handling of the donation from the house churches in Corinth.[1] Letters of recommendation—which is the function of this material—normally accompanied the person being recommended; it would be somewhat counterproductive to send the letter later. The first brother has a reputation among "all the churches," which should probably be taken as a hyperbole (cf. Rom. 15:13) for "widely known" among the Pauline assemblies. His renown is based "in the gospel" (author's translation), an expression that likely refers to proclamation and evangelism (2 Cor. 10:14; Rom. 1:9), as opposed to service and ministry more broadly. This brother was not only celebrated for his ministry, but he was also appointed by the churches to assist Paul in his administration of this monetary donation. Ministerial effectiveness and congregational endorsement, along with Paul's apostolic blessing, are this brother's validating credentials that Paul sets before the Corinthians.

The Anonymous Brothers

Neither the renowned brother of 8:18–19 nor the proven brother of 8:22 are named by Paul, and there has never been a completely satisfactory answer offered as to either their identity or why Paul does not mention their names directly. On the latter question, an explicit reference to their names is not really necessary. The two would have been present with Titus as the letter was read, with introductions already made. Since Paul was writing from Macedonia, it is likely (though not certain) that these brothers were associated with Macedonian assemblies Paul was visiting. Acts 20:4–5 mentions Sopater, Aristarchus, and Secundus as members of churches in Macedonia who were accompanying Paul to Jerusalem with the collection, and it is quite possible that these unnamed brothers were a part of this Macedonian contingent. While Paul does not mention their names, he does provide a significant amount of detail related to their reputation and personal qualifications. This observation is not incidental. From Paul's perspective, their names were not important, but their character was.

in order to honor the Lord himself and to show our eagerness to help. Although poverty relief is the motivation Paul most often associates with the collection for the poor in Jerusalem (Rom. 15:25–26; 2 Cor. 8:13–14; 9:12; Acts 24:17), that motivation cannot be isolated from the dominant concern in his life and ministry, to honor Christ (Phil. 1:20; Rom. 14:8; Gal. 2:20). Indeed, Paul's "eagerness to help" the poor in Jerusalem is probably a direct result of his desire "to honor the Lord himself."

8:20–21 *We want to avoid any criticism.* In these verses Paul enunciates the principle governing the extreme care he is taking with respect to the collection. His desire is to avoid any suspicion of financial impropriety by putting measures in place aimed at ensuring transparency and accountability. Paul's principled stand on financial matters, which included working "night and day" (2 Thess. 3:8) to support himself so that he could preach the gospel "free of charge" (1 Cor. 9:18), was a deeply personal value for the apostle, as his final words to the Ephesian elders attest: "I have not coveted anyone's silver or gold or clothing. You yourselves know that these hands of mine have supplied my own needs and the needs of my companions" (Acts 20:33–34).

this liberal gift. Throughout 2 Corinthians 8 and 9, Paul subtly—and sometimes not so subtly—presses the Corinthians to make their contribution to the collection for the poor in Jerusalem a generous one. He holds up the example of the impoverished Macedonians in order to stimulate the Corinthians' giving (8:1–7), and he will later warn the Corinthians that some Macedonians may accompany him, and so the Corinthian gift should be ready and generous lest they shame both themselves and Paul (9:1–5). The expression "liberal gift" indicates a lavish contribution[2] and (not so subtly) communicates Paul's expectation that the Corinthians will make a substantial donation to this charitable venture.

For we are taking pains to do what is right . . . also in the eyes of man. Here Paul further explains (note the explanatory "for" that begins 8:21) the rationale behind the procedures in place for this fund-raising campaign, which amount to complete transparency before everyone involved. When other people's money was at stake, it was not enough for Paul to be confident before the Lord of his own good intentions and the appropriate distribution of funds. Paul understood that others needed to be confident of this as well, and so he instituted measures to ensure openness and accountability. First, he assembled a team of individuals, rather than simply having Titus handle matters on his own. Second, he made sure each of the individuals were men of experience and of proven character. Third, this team did not consist simply of Paul's handpicked cronies, but included delegates selected and approved by "the churches." These measures were designed both to safeguard the collection from misuse and to avert criticism, by openly demonstrating to everyone intentional and determined accountability.

8:22 *we are sending with them our brother who has often proved to us in many ways that he is zealous.* Paul does not mention the matters in which this brother has proved his zeal, but it is reasonable to conjecture that he has been tested in terms of financial probity. It is important for Paul that candidates for leadership undergo scrutiny before their appointment (1 Tim. 3:10; 5:22) and be above reproach (1 Tim. 3:1–13; Titus 1:5–9), and their attitude toward money is particularly important (1 Tim. 3:6–8; 6:5, 10; Titus 1:7). Paul indicates that this brother has "great confidence" in the Corinthians, which may be the result of Titus's good report (7:6–16). In the ancient Mediterranean honor-shame culture, this kind of remark carries with it the oblique expectation that the Corinthians be found worthy of this confidence, which becomes more explicit in 8:24 and 9:3–4.

8:23 *As for Titus . . . as for our brothers.* In 8:23–24 Paul recapitulates the main point of 8:1–22 by reiterating the credentials of the individuals being dispatched to finish the collection of funds in Corinth (8:23) and issuing a direct appeal on the matter at hand (8:24). Paul stresses again the qualifications of these emissaries in order to impress on the Corinthians that this team has the full support of Paul and the other churches and is carrying out a mission that honors Christ. Specifically, Titus is named as an apostolic co-worker, and the unnamed brothers are identified as officially sponsored delegates of the Macedonian assemblies and additionally described as "an honor to Christ." In short, this embassy has the backing of the churches, the apostle, and Christ himself, which is a very effective segue to the concluding exhortation in 8:24.

8:24 *Therefore show these men the proof of your love.* For Paul (and other New Testament writers) virtue necessarily bears visible fruit. Paul thanked God for the Thessalonians' "work produced by faith" and for their "labor prompted by love" (1 Thess. 1:3). To the Galatians Paul warns, "The only thing that counts is faith working through love" (Gal. 5:6 NRSV). Similarly, Paul urges Titus to remind the Cretans that God's grace and Christ's sacrifice should create a people "eager to do what is good" (Titus 2:11–14; cf. Matt. 7:20; Luke 6:44; James 3:12).

Teaching the Text

In this passage Paul offers a wealth of sound advice on proper stewardship of the financial contributions of church members. The procedures Paul sets in place for the collection provide guidance in the contemporary setting for constructing wise policies that help ensure financial integrity. More important, the rationale for these procedures highlights a fundamental principle that should govern our policies on money matters today.

1. *The policies*. Perhaps the first policy to note is Paul's *team approach* to handling other people's money. The truth is, money has an immense power to corrupt, and in spite of the proven integrity of everyone involved, one can never tell what seeds of greed might suddenly sprout given the proper circumstances. Paul makes sure that multiple people are involved in order to decrease the likelihood of corruption. Moreover, the team Paul assembles is not handpicked by him but includes delegates chosen by other church bodies. Having *the wider approval of a larger church body* is a second safeguard against suspicion of corruption. Third, each of the individuals has a *proven record of ministry, service, and integrity*. The people involved have a reputation of faithfulness. They are not neophytes (cf. 1 Tim. 3:6). Finally, the team has *apostolic approval* as well; Paul himself commends each in their task. The approval of trusted, godly leadership is an important element in commissioning a team for ministry, be it gospel proclamation or fund-raising.

2. *The principle*. The fundamental principle governing the somewhat complex set of procedures involved in collecting this money from the Corinthians is articulated in 8:21: "We are taking pains to do what is right, not only in the eyes of the Lord but also in the eyes of man." Paul fully understands that people are justly concerned that their charitable giving is properly handled. Charlatans and con artists were just as common in Paul's day as in ours, and anything short of full disclosure and complete accountability before everyone involved would lead to murmurs and criticism (8:20). Although Paul is confident of his integrity before God, he takes extra measures so that his integrity will be clear to others as well.

Illustrating the Text

Personal integrity gives one credibility to call organizations to corporate integrity.

Manifesto: In 1979, Billy Graham took the lead in founding the Evangelical Council for Financial Accountability (ECFA). The "Modesto Manifesto 2" was birthed out of the same concerns Paul articulated in this passage.[3] The list of issues in the code of conduct in the manifesto is extensive, and the manifesto seeks to promote purity in life, transparency in finances, and propriety in conduct and appearance, all in service of the communication of the gospel.

Strict protocols in handling church finances protect everyone.

Story: Every church should follow strict operating rules regarding the finances of the church. Few things give Christ and his church more bad press than when a scandal involving church finances is made public. Upon further review, many of these affairs could have been avoided by simply following strict protocols with God's money. Many churches have written guidelines of how the offerings must be handled. These can include having a two-deacon minimum for transporting the offerings or giving no single deacon the complete combination to the church safe (two deacons in succession are needed to operate the safe lock). Share your protocols to assure people their offerings are being handled responsibly.

Work ethics

Article: One of the arenas where ethics are important is the workplace. The most common areas of misconduct according to the human resources website HRhero.com are misrepresenting time or hours worked; lying to a supervisor; lying to co-workers, customers, vendors, or the public; misuse of the employer's assets; and lying on reports or falsifying records.[4] The article further warns that one of the common violations is visiting website and social media on work time and property. Paul reminds us that followers need to live "above reproach" in ethical standards adhered to at work. Invite listeners to reflect on how they conduct themselves in the workplace. Do they seek to give their best and honor God in their work? Or, are they tempted to cut corners and do only what they must?

2 Corinthians 9:1-5

Giving Generously

Big Idea
Paul is dispatching a fund-raising team to Corinth to spare any embarrassment to himself and the Corinthians should their contribution not be ready when he arrives and also to avoid the appearance that their donation was not freely given.

Key Themes
- Good intentions sometimes need supportive intervention to help bring them to fruition.
- Contributing to the needs of others should be a voluntary act, not one born from coercion.

Understanding the Text

The Text in Context

Second Corinthians 9:1–5 is closely connected to 8:16–24 as an elaboration on Paul's rationale for sending "the brothers" (9:3; cf. 8:23) to assist the Corinthians in completing the collection. Although untranslated by the NIV, 9:1 begins with the word "for," indicating that Paul is offering further explanation for dispatching the brothers as an advance team to ensure everything is in order before he arrives. This, along with the fact that Paul refers to "the brothers" in 9:3 without any explanation, indicates that chapters 8 and 9 belong together and were not originally two separate letters.[1] Paul has assembled a team as a safeguard against any suspicion of misappropriation of funds (8:16–24), and he is sending them in advance for two primary reasons: first, to spare any embarrassment to both himself and the Corinthians should their contribution not be ready when he arrives (9:1–4); and second, to avoid feelings of compulsion or manipulation among the Corinthians should any Macedonians—who already completed their collection for the poor in Jerusalem—accompany Paul to Corinth (9:5).

Interpretive Insights

9:1 *There is no need for me to write to you about this service to the Lord's people.* As the following verses make clear, the thought behind Paul's vague "no need for me to write to you about" is something along the lines of "There's no need for me to *convince you* to join in [9:1], because you are already on board [9:2–3]." As noted above, 9:1 is tightly connected to what precedes by an (untranslated) explanatory "for" (cf. LEB, NET). However, this verse is also grammatically connected to 9:3 by the use of a Greek construction (*men . . . de*) sometimes translated, "on the one hand . . . on the other hand." The sense can be adequately grasped by rendering 9:1 and 9:3 in the following way: "While [*men*] you don't need me to convince you . . . still [*de*], I am sending the brothers to assist in collecting the funds." Paul politely affirms the Corinthians' good intentions, yet he recognizes that even the best intentions sometimes need external stimulus in order to become actualized in good deeds.

9:2 *For I know your eagerness to help, and I have been boasting about it to the Macedonians.* Paul balances his earlier reference to his own "eagerness to help" (8:19) by affirming the Corinthians' "eagerness to help" here. This verse locates Paul in Macedonia at the time this letter was written, which serves to connect these chapters with 1–7, which were composed just after Paul received good news from Titus, while in Macedonia (cf. 2:13; 7:5–6). The Macedonian churches would include communities in Philippi, Thessalonica, and Berea (Acts 16:1–17:15). Paul's boast to the Macedonians regarding Achaia (see the comments on 1:1) was (presumably) intended to stimulate their interest in the relief effort, which it did: "and your enthusiasm has stirred most of them to action" (9:2). In 8:1–8 we saw Paul boasting of the Macedonian involvement to stir up the Corinthians, and here we learn that Paul has been boasting of the Corinthian involvement to stir up the Macedonians. While this may appear to be "playing both ends against the middle," as the saying goes, there is no need to impute sinister motives to Paul. First, there is no secrecy on Paul's part—quite the contrary; he seems eager to let the Corinthians know he has been talking up their promised gift to the Macedonians. Second, there is no personal benefit to Paul involved. From Paul's openness regarding his tactics, it would appear that the apostle is instigating a healthy, friendly competition between the churches in these two regions for the benefit of the poor in Jerusalem.

9:3 *I am sending the brothers in order that our boasting about you in this matter should not prove hollow.* As noted above, this verse is grammatically connected to 9:1 in the following way: "While you don't need me to convince you . . . [9:1], still, I am sending the brothers . . . [9:3]." In Greek, 9:3–4 is one sentence, which specifies Paul's primary purpose for the sending of "the brothers" (see 8:16–24) and underscores Paul's genuine apprehension concerning the Corinthians' state of readiness. Paul's first purpose is initially stated negatively: "that our boasting about you . . . not prove hollow." This may not be simply a concern for his own personal reputation or to save face before the Macedonians but may also be a desire to foster healthy relations, brotherly affection, and mutual respect between the churches in these two provinces. The unity of the church was not only a theoretical doctrine for Paul (Eph. 4:1–6) but was expressed concretely through acts of love (2 Cor. 8:24). Restating this first purpose positively, Paul specifies the content of the boast he fears might be proved hollow: "that you may be ready" (9:3). To this Paul adds, "as I said you would be." Paul uses an imperfect tense in this phrase, probably iterative in sense, indicating a repeated action: "just as *I kept telling* them you would be."[2] Hence, Paul's choice of tense ratchets up the pressure on the Corinthians by reminding them of the frequency of his boast and increases the expectation that they prove themselves worthy of Paul's confident expectation.

9:4 *For if any Macedonians come with me and find you unprepared, we . . . would be ashamed.* Verse 4 amplifies verse 3 and states the result of possibly finding the Corinthians unprepared: shame for both Paul and the Corinthians. Paul expects that he will be escorted to Corinth by a contingent from the Macedonian churches. It was the normal procedure for travelers to journey in a sufficient company to ward off bandits. The Macedonians, who were poorer than the Corinthians (8:1–3), had already completed their collection (8:3), and it would be especially painful for everyone involved if the Corinthians were not ready. Paul words this clarification carefully and shrewdly, which the NIV rendering captures well: "We—not to say anything about you—would be ashamed." By mentioning himself first ("we"), Paul ostensibly concedes that the shame would primarily be his, referencing the Corinthians only as an apparent afterthought. It is likely, however, that both Paul and his readers understood that the shame would primarily fall on the Corinthians, and Paul's politically sensitive manner of expressing himself was not really intended to conceal that reality.

The final clause of this verse is difficult and capable of several interpretations. The crucial issue is the correct translation and meaning of the Greek word *hypostasis*, rendered somewhat freely by the NIV as "having been so confident." According to the interpretation suggested by the NIV's translation, Paul expresses his concern that his previous boasting would be revealed as naive and unwarranted (9:3), and this would cause considerable embarrassment. The alternative view is that the clause should be translated, "We would be ashamed in regard to *this project*."[3] This interpretation sees Paul's embarrassment related to the prospect of the Corinthians reneging on their pledge, which might jeopardize the entire enterprise. In favor of this view is the fact that this translation is more in keeping with the normal use of the Greek word. In favor of the NIV's rendering, which is by far the most common interpretation in English versions, is the immediate context, particularly 9:3.[4]

9:5 *Then it will be ready as a generous gift, not as one grudgingly given.* Paul adds a second reason for sending the advance team to make ready the promised donation: to avoid the impression that the gift was given under compulsion rather than voluntarily. Paul reasons that if the Corinthians begin pooling their funds only after he arrives with the delegates from the Macedonian assemblies, it would give the appearance that the Corinthians were not truly happy about contributing but did so under duress to placate Paul and save face before the Macedonians. Paul is contrasting two dispositions toward helping others: open-hearted generosity versus resentful compliance. In 9:1 Paul describes the collection as a "service" (Greek, *diakonia*) for the needy in Jerusalem, which reflects that this endeavor is an officially sponsored, organized, and administered ministry of the church. Here in 9:5 Paul twice refers to it as a "blessing," or "generous gift" (NIV; Greek, *eulogia*), which highlights the relational and gift character of this undertaking: one community giving graciously to another community.

Teaching the Text

This passage provides important insights into Paul's approach to "spur[ring] one another on toward love and good deeds" (Heb. 10:24). Specifically, Paul recognizes that good intentions sometimes need supportive intervention to help bring them to fruition. These verses detail Paul's proactive intervention to help the Corinthians keep their promise to be a blessing to the poor in Jerusalem. Although the particular issue Paul is dealing with here is voluntary giving, the larger principle would apply to many different kinds of situations where an individual's or community's noble aspirations were not matched by noble actions. In teaching this passage, it is not necessary to imply that Paul's precise methods need to be strictly applied in every fund-raising effort today. Rather, it would be wiser to emphasize the variety of means that Paul employed to help his flock "excel all the more" (1 Thess. 4:10, author's translation).

Perhaps the most obvious and direct manner of intervention offered by Paul is the dispatch of a team of co-workers to encourage the Corinthians to fulfill their promise and to assist them in gathering the collection. However, Paul employs more-subtle means of motivating the Corinthians as well. Although some may be uncomfortable with this approach, it is difficult to avoid the conclusion that Paul is fostering a healthy competition between the assemblies in Macedonia and Achaia. Paul understands that enthusiasm is contagious (9:2), and he uses the Corinthians' enthusiastic intention to stimulate the Macedonians, and the Macedonians' enthusiastic completion to stimulate the Corinthians. There is a difference, however, between competition among rivals for personal gain and competition between friends, family members, and comrades to benefit others. One can be very unhealthy and lead to ill will, while the other can actually strengthen ties of camaraderie and kinship through partnering together for the sake of others.

Paul not only motivates by means of friendly competition; he also candidly confronts the Corinthians with the prospect of losing face (both him and them), and he warns them not to let this happen. In describing the Corinthians' "eagerness to help" to the Macedonians, and then relating this boast to the Corinthians, Paul both affirms the noble intentions of the Corinthians and at the same time challenges them to live up to his high opinion of them. Paul holds up the preservation of honor as a value that is worth the monetary sacrifice that the Corinthians would make.

Finally, Paul makes it clear that charity should be voluntary, not compulsory, or it loses its gift character and becomes a levy imposed on "subjects" by "authorities." The disposition that accompanies a gift is as important as the gift itself, and this conviction is significant enough that Paul devotes much of the next section (9:6–15) to unpacking it.

Illustrating the Text

Enthusiasm can stir the church toward generous action.

Technology: Planes have an attitude indicator; it's an instrument that informs the pilot of the plane's orientation relative to the Earth's horizon. When the plane is climbing, the nose of the plane is pointing above the horizon. When the plane is diving, the nose is pointing below the horizon. To change the plane's altitude, pilots change the plane's attitude. Paul knew that enthusiasm has a catalytic effect on a congregation, much as the change in the plane's attitude changes the plane's direction.

Quote: **Samuel Taylor Coleridge.** "Histories . . . confirm by irrefragable evidence the aphorism of ancient wisdom, that nothing great was ever achieved without enthusiasm. For what is enthusiasm but the oblivion and swallowing up of self in an object dearer than self, or in an idea more vivid?"[5]

Positive peer pressure can result in beautiful outcomes.

Article: Brian Wilson of the Beach Boys relates how the Beatles were what really pushed his band to greatness: "It wasn't really a rivalry, though. I was jealous! I would get to hear their records before they came out and I was totally blown away by *Rubber Soul*. And *Sgt. Pepper's*—I was totally blown away by that. But it was inspirational, too. Then I did 'Good Vibrations' and *Smile*, and it was exciting. I got into it and really produced my head off."[6]

Enthusiasm is contagious, so why keep it quiet?

Video: Make a short video that simply depicts church members looking at the camera and telling, in one or two sentences, why they love to give and support the ministry of your church. What motivates them to give? What fruit have they seen in their own lives? Play this short video as part of your message.

2 Corinthians 9:6–15

Giving Cheerfully

Big Idea
Joyfully giving to God's work will open the doors of God's abundance and blessing.

Key Themes
- Giving to the collection should be done willingly and joyfully.
- God rewards the generous by both meeting their material needs and providing spiritual abundance.
- The contribution to the poor in Jerusalem will produce thankfulness to God on their part and will increase the bond of affection between the Jewish and gentile portions of the church.

Understanding the Text

The Text in Context

In 9:6–15 Paul amplifies the generous-versus-grudging antithesis of 9:5 by first warning of the perils of miserliness (9:6) and then enlarging in detail the benefits of generosity (9:8–15). Situated between the warning and the promise is a reiteration of the central exhortation of chapters 8–9: "Give what you have decided" (9:7). This section appropriately concludes Paul's fund-raising endeavor of chapters 8 and 9 by emphasizing the blessing that will result from a generous contribution. It will produce a material blessing for both the Corinthians (9:8, 10–11) and the poor in Jerusalem (9:12), as well as spiritual blessings for both (9:8–14).

Interpretive Insights

9:6 *Remember this.* Translated literally, this clause reads, "But this," which is helpfully rendered by the NET as, "My point is this." Paul is crystallizing the advice, encouragement, and admonitions of the entire preceding section concerning the collection for the poor (8:1–9:5) into a pithy agricultural aphorism that warns against stinginess.

Whoever sows sparingly will also reap sparingly, and whoever sows generously will also reap generously. Gnomic maxims relating to sowing and reaping are common in both Jewish and Greco-Roman writers and often emphasize the proportionate correlation between actions and results. In attempting to coax the Corinthians to make good on their word, Paul is not averse to motivating his readers by candidly laying out both the negative and the positive consequences of their deeds. Paul does not specify explicitly what the sparing and generous "reaping" involves. In Galatians 6:7–9, where similar imagery is used, the reaping is related to destruction or eternal life. However, nothing in the present context suggests this is Paul's thought here. Neither is it entirely convincing to focus exclusively on either material benefit/loss or spiritual benefit/loss. Verses 7–15 provide evidence that both are in view, as subsequent comments will clarify.

9:7 *give what you have decided in your heart . . . not reluctantly . . . for God loves a cheerful giver.* One final time Paul reiterates the central exhortation of chapters 8–9, which essentially amounts to "Keep your promise!" The grounds for this appeal begin with the warning of 9:6 and continue through a series of assurances in what follows: God will bless you (9:8–9); God will supply your needs (9:10–11); this generosity will increase the bonds of affection between Jews and gentiles (9:12–14). There is no hint that Paul has in mind a specific amount or percentage that each should contribute. Rather, Paul regards this decision as a matter of one's individual conscience ("what you have decided in your heart"). Paul's primary concern is to emphasize the appropriate manner of giving by highlighting three attitudinal qualities that he hopes will characterize all who contribute. Echoing Deuteronomy 15:10, which urges generosity to the poor "without a grudging heart," Paul first warns against a resentful disposition ("not reluctantly"), which may accompany outward generosity. Then, perhaps mindful of his own persuasive rhetoric in these chapters, he cautions against giving from a sense of coercion ("not . . . under compulsion"). Finally, and in antithesis to these dispositions, Paul reminds the Corinthians that joyful magnanimity ("cheerful") is the attitude that pleases God in the matter of giving to others.

9:8 *God is able to bless you abundantly, so that . . . having all that you need, you will abound in every good work.* Grounding the exhortation of 9:7, Paul reminds his readers that God is more than able to supply their needs so that their good work might abound all the more. Paul is describing God's blessing not as the reward for generosity but as the *basis* for generosity. Barrett observes, "The sense of the verse seems to be that if men are willing to give, God will always make it possible for them to give."[1] God's abundant blessing is not intended to produce ease, but it is intended to lead to "every good work."

9:9 *They have freely scattered their gifts to the poor; their righteousness endures forever.* Paul supports the promise of 9:8 through a citation of Psalm 112 (111 LXX), which describes the blessed state of the righteous, who are particularly characterized by generosity to the poor (112:5, 9). The verb behind

> **Demeter: Goddess of Abundant Harvests**
>
> With the writers of the Hebrew Bible, Paul takes for granted that there is one God who created the universe and generously supplies sun, rain, seed, and soil for an abundant harvest (Acts 14:15; 17:24; 1 Tim. 6:17; cf. Lev. 25:19; Isa. 55:10; Ps. 67:6). Yet in Corinth and throughout the Mediterranean world, other gods and goddesses were thought to bring agricultural bounty and fertility. Chief among these was Demeter, often pictured holding fruit, grain, a cornucopia, and other symbols of agricultural abundance. Her temple in Corinth was located on the north slope of the Acrocorinth. A well-preserved relief from this temple depicts the goddess holding poppy pods. Judging from the large number of inexpensive votive offerings excavated from the temple area, Demeter was particularly popular among the poor and the lower orders in Corinth.

the NIV's "freely scattered" is used of spreading seed or fertilizer in a field and suggests liberal abandon in distributing charity to the needy. In the context of the psalm, "righteousness endures forever" is a reference not to individual, forensic justification but to the enduring legacy of the righteous even beyond their generation ("They will be remembered forever. . . . Their horn will be lifted high in honor," Ps. 112:6, 9). This is probably uppermost in Paul's mind as well, but Paul's thought may also include divine remembrance of their faithfulness.

9:10 *Now he who supplies seed to the sower . . . will enlarge the harvest of your righteousness.* Paul now applies the teaching of Psalm 112 (cited in verse 9) to the Corinthians. The righteous are able to "freely scatter" their gifts (9:9) because God generously provides both seed and bread to distribute. Paul appeals to God's providential care of humanity as the basis for his particular care for his people. The future verbs ("[God] will supply . . . increase . . . enlarge") are logical futures indicating the certainty of God's action. The "harvest of your righteousness" should probably be understood as a harvest *produced by* righteousness. Paul does not specify what form this divinely enlarged harvest will take, which implies that it could be either spiritual or material blessings.

9:11 *so that you can be generous on every occasion.* Once again (see 9:8) Paul emphasizes that the purpose of God's abundant provision is to be a blessing to others. God's generosity to us contains both a model (see 8:9) and an exhortation: Go and do likewise! The final clause of 9:11 ("Your generosity will result in thanksgiving") is unpacked in 9:12–14, as Paul explains that the munificence of the gentile churches will be an occasion for great rejoicing and thanksgiving on the part of the recipients in Jerusalem.

9:12–14 *not only supplying the needs of the Lord's people.* Verses 12–14 articulate three outcomes that Paul anticipates will result from the collection for the poor in Jerusalem. First, as much of chapters 8 and 9 have emphasized, "the needs of the Lord's people" will be supplied (9:12a). Paul's primary concern in this endeavor is philanthropic, to relieve the poverty of the believers in Jerusalem, a point that Paul repeatedly emphasizes (see "Historical and Cultural Background" in the unit on 8:1–7). Yet Paul recognizes, second, that this will inevitably lead to the believers in Jerusalem glorifying God through their thanksgiving for this generous gift (9:12b–13). The final result is expressed in 9:14, as Paul describes an increasing bond of affection between Jews and gentiles. Hence, Paul envisions results that are practical (poverty relief), doxological (thanksgiving and glory to God), and ecclesial (unity between Jews and gentiles).

Because of the service by which you have proved yourselves, others will praise God. In Paul's estimation, the contribution to the poor in Jerusalem from the gentile churches would provide firm evidence to the Jerusalem church of the authenticity of the faith of their gentile brothers and sisters. The "others" (added by the NIV for the sake of grammar) who will praise God must refer to the believers in Jerusalem, who will be thanking God for this provision according to 9:12. The basis (and content) of the praise offered by the believers in Jerusalem is described as "for the obedience that accompanies your confession . . . and for your generosity" (9:13). The grammatical construction in Greek probably indicates (more precisely) obedience that is a product of faith. In Paul's view, true faith is faith that works (Gal. 5:6).

in their prayers for you their hearts will go out to you. Paul expects, with good reason, that the gift from the gentile churches will prompt prayers from the recipients and will increase their affection for the gentile brothers and sisters. As the New Testament elsewhere attests (Acts 15; Gal. 1–2), there was sometimes tension between Jewish believers in Jerusalem and the expanding gentile mission. There were debates concerning how "Jewish" the gentile believers needed to be, and even whether Jewish believers could share meals with gentile believers (Gal. 2:11–14). Although Paul's intention in sponsoring the collection is not primarily to win approval for his mission from the Jewish wing of the Jesus movement, he does recognize that this generous display of concern will prompt filial affection on the part of the Jerusalem church, which the NIV nicely renders as "their hearts will go out to you." The "surpassing grace" of God that will be evident in the successful completion of this endeavor involves not simply the monetary gift itself but also the gift of salvation to the gentiles and the authentic faith evidenced in this tangible fruit of generosity. This joyful prospect results in an emphatic exclamation of thanks from Paul, which serves as a fitting benediction to chapters 8 and 9: "Thanks be to God for his indescribable gift!" (9:15).

Theological Insights

The Old Testament system of tithing (see "Theological Insights" in the unit on 8:8–15) included gathering the third year's tithe to support "the Levite, the foreigner, the fatherless and the widow" (Deut. 26:12). Although Paul's collection for the poor has a similar orientation (helping the needy), it differs from the tithe described in Deuteronomy 26 in that it is completely voluntary, not legislated, and also in that Paul does not suggest any specific amount or percentage. The Old Testament also speaks frequently of "freewill offerings" (Lev. 7:12; 1 Chron. 29:6–7; Ps. 107:22; Ezra 2:68–69). These were voluntary, like the collection Paul is promoting, but were normally given to support the temple, not the poor and needy. Yet the Old Testament also attests to voluntary support of the needy (Deut. 15:7–8; Pss. 37:26; 112:9–10), which in the New Testament era was commonly called almsgiving (Matt. 6:2–4; Luke 11:41; Acts 9:36; 10:2). Paul's Letters provide evidence of an expectation that members of house churches contribute to the needs of those charged with teaching (Gal. 6:6; 1 Tim. 5:17). Like freewill offerings, the amount and form of the contribution is determined by the giver, yet like the tithe this money is used for sacral purposes, to support the ministry of the church.

Teaching the Text

As Paul concludes this fund-raising portion of his letter, he employs an extended agricultural image in order to emphasize to the Corinthians several fundamental principles of sowing and reaping. This agricultural imagery nicely encapsulates the main teaching points of this passage.

1. *Sow generously.* "Remember this," warns the apostle, "whoever sows sparingly will also reap sparingly, and whoever sows generously will also reap generously" (9:6). Paul has spent most of chapters 8 and 9 persuading and cajoling the Corinthians to make good on their promise to help the needy in Jerusalem, and his final persuasive tactic is to remind them that their actions have consequences. Sowing and reaping are as much a part of the divine order as of the natural order, and Paul wants the Corinthians to remember that they will be blessed in proportion to how they bless others. The truth that Paul is underscoring is echoed by the Old Testament Wisdom literature (Prov. 11:24; 22:9), the Prophets (Mal. 3:10), and Jesus himself: "Give, and it will be given to you. A good measure, pressed down, shaken together and running over, will be poured into your lap. For with the measure you use, it will be measured to you" (Luke 6:38).

2. *Sow determinedly.* Paul also takes the opportunity in this passage to help the Corinthians strengthen their resolve. He does not want the Corinthians to neglect the determination that each has made in their heart to contribute to this poverty-relief effort (9:7). His exhortation that each should follow through on their personal pledge is a reminder that procrastination breeds hesitation and doubt and can lead to broken promises.

3. *Sow joyfully.* Gifts given grudgingly or in a spirit of resentment may indeed contribute to the needs of others, but the giver will be robbed of the divinely intended satisfaction that comes from blessing others. The prerequisite for giving joyfully is not a full wallet but a full heart. This disposition is pleasing to God precisely because it delights in putting the needs of others first and so reflects Christ's own disposition toward humanity (5:14–15; 8:9; Phil. 2:5–8).

4. *Sow confidently.* Perhaps the most important point that Paul is making in 9:6–15 is that those who are determined to bless others will find that God is even more determined to bless them. The abundant blessing (9:8) and enlarged harvest (9:10) that Paul assures the Corinthians are God's provision to the openhanded may include both material and spiritual blessing and are intended to stimulate further good work (9:8) and generosity (9:11). In short, those who commit themselves to live as a blessing to others can be confident that God will provide both the means and the opportunity to do so.

Illustrating the Text

More is never enough.

Quote: **John Ruskin.** The gospel calls us to be givers, but we must fundamentally come to reject the myth that "more" is always better. One hundred years ago English critic and artist John Ruskin wrote: "There is no wealth but life—life, including all its powers of love, of joy, and of admiration. That country is richest which nourishes the greatest number of noble and happy human beings; that man is richest who, having perfected the functions of his own life to the utmost, has also the widest influence to help the lives of others."[2]

"Give to get to give" is a winning formula of reciprocity.

Testimony: A wealthy family had made a concerted effort to bless as many people and organizations as they could financially, but they just kept getting wealthier. At one point the wife expressed with genuine frustration: "Every time we give money away, we just seem to unexpectedly make more money!"

God blesses in proportion to our faith, not our finances.

Prop: In 2 Kings 4:1–7, the widow has a debt that is way too large for her to repay. She cries out to Elisha for help. He asks her what she has in her house. She reports that she has a little oil. Elisha then instructs her to go around to all her neighbors and ask for empty jars. And he tells her, "Don't ask for just a few." She obeys, pouring out oil into the empty jars until they are all full, and then the oil stops flowing. Elisha tells her to sell the oil and pay off her debt. Have many jars around the stage as you preach and tell this story. Ask your listeners how many jars they would have gotten.

2 Corinthians 10:1–6

Demolishing Strongholds

Big Idea
The spiritual arsenal at Paul's disposal in service of the gospel is sufficient to demolish any opposition, and the apostle is fully prepared to make use of this weaponry, if necessary, to advance Christ's work in Corinth.

Key Themes
- Paul has not conducted himself in a worldly manner, as some in Corinth allege.
- God has equipped his servants with powerful spiritual weaponry to advance his kingdom.
- Paul is willing to use the entire divine armory to bring about obedience to the gospel in Corinth.

Understanding the Text

The Text in Context

Chapters 10–13 represent the third and final movement of 2 Corinthians and constitute perhaps the most difficult literary-critical issue in the entire Pauline corpus. The abrupt and unsignaled change of tone—from warm entreaty in chapters 8–9 to harsh rebuke in 10–13—convinces many that these chapters address a different situation from the situation in the chapters that precede and that these chapters were appended to chapters 1–9 at some later point in the process of collecting and copying Paul's Letters. The most important proposals related to the composition of 2 Corinthians were surveyed and evaluated in the introduction, and that discussion need not be repeated here. In light of the difficulties attending to each theory, a cautious approach has been adopted in this commentary, whereby 2 Corinthians is understood as a composite unity. That is, 2 Corinthians appears to be a single communication from Paul addressing several distinct but interconnected matters of contention: Paul's apparent fickleness, as evidenced by his changing travel itinerary (1:1–2:13; 7:5–16), the legitimacy of his apostolate (2:14–7:4), the stalled collection (chaps. 8–9), and the influence of Jewish-Christian intruders (chaps. 10–13).

Chapters 10–13 divide naturally into three discrete segments. In 10:1–18 Paul defends himself against certain personal attacks leveled at him by the intruders related to his personal demeanor (10:1, 12) and conduct (10:3, 8). In 11:1–12:13, often called "the Fool's Speech," Paul engages in a tongue-in-cheek boasting competition with his adversaries to expose their folly. Finally, in 12:14–13:10 Paul prepares the Corinthians for his impending visit by warning them of the severity of their situation. The segment under consideration here, 10:1–6, both contains the thesis statement of chapters 10–13 (Paul does not live by "the standards of this world," 10:2) and discloses the aggressive approach Paul will take in establishing his thesis: the demolition of all argument and pretension that sets itself up in opposition to the gospel (10:4–5).

Interpretive Insights

10:1 *By the humility and gentleness of Christ, I appeal to you—I, Paul.* The Greek text places Paul's personal ascription first, and in a more emphatic form: "I, Paul, myself." This unusually strong language is probably not, as some have argued, an indicator of strong personal affection, nor is it used to distinguish Paul from his associates (perhaps Timothy, the cosender of this letter, 1:1). Rather, the emphatic placement and wording of this expression underscore the gravity of the issue at hand and may also bear connotations of authority (cf. Gal. 5:2; Eph. 3:1). "By the humility and gentleness of Christ" strengthens the urgency of the appeal (cf. Rom. 12:1; 15:30, 1 Cor. 1:10) by referencing the character of the earthly Christ.[1] The character of Christ as humble and gentle is evidenced both in his manner (Matt. 21:4–5; 27:14) and in his teaching (5:3–10).

who am "timid" when face to face with you, but "bold" toward you when away! Some translations place the words "timid" and "bold" in quotation marks, indicating (probably correctly) that Paul is citing, or at least alluding to, charges made against him by his opponents. The charge is that Paul is courageous only from a distance, through his letters, while in person he is feeble and cowardly. This accusation is more fully articulated (and discussed) at 10:10.

10:2 *I beg you that . . . I may not have to be as bold as I expect to be toward some people.* Resuming the appeal of 10:1, Paul finishes that thought by imploring the Corinthians not to force him to use his divinely given authority in a confrontational, disciplinary manner. In doing so he explicitly identifies two parties in the dispute that is threatening to unravel the work in Corinth: "you" (plural), meaning the Corinthian church as a whole, and "some people," meaning either the intruders specifically or the intruders together with their supporters among the Corinthians. This distinction helps us recognize that, while Paul is indirectly confronting the intruders in chapters 10–13, his direct appeal is to the Corinthian community as a whole; they are not fully estranged from Paul. Indeed, this exhortation assumes that it is within the power of the

> ## Roman Siege Warfare
>
> By the first century AD, the Roman military had developed an impressive array of sophisticated machinery for besieging a city and had virtually perfected the tactics of siege warfare. A siege typically began with a large circumvallation wall, which protected the attackers while cutting off the city from reinforcement and prohibiting flight. Siege towers protected soldiers digging under the defensive fortifications in order to collapse the city's wall. Massive battering rams—so called because the iron head was often shaped like a ram's head—hammered away at weak points in the wall. Catapults of various sizes hurled enormous boulders at the wall or smaller missiles and darts over the wall. The artillery piece known as the *tormenta* launched incendiary devices into the heart of the besieged city to create havoc, panic, and destruction. The goal was to breach the wall and capture the city. If the wall could not be breached, a siege ramp might be constructed under the cover of siege towers and artillery fire to allow the army to go over the wall. The remains of an impressive Roman siege ramp are still visible at the Jewish fortress of Masada, captured by the Romans in AD 73. Once the city was captured, the Roman army would usually demolish the defensive walls as a visual reminder of their domination, and also to prohibit any subsequent uprising. Corinth itself was besieged and ravaged by the Roman general Lucius Mummius in 146 BC. By Paul's day, the city walls had been rebuilt, but the defensive fortifications of the Acrocorinth, the fortress situated on a rocky butte immediately above the city, still lay in ruin, serving as a poignant reminder of a demolished stronghold (see 2 Cor. 10:4–5).

believing community as a whole to take action and resolve the situation, so that Paul will not have to come with a rod when he returns (13:1–3).

10:3 *For though we live in the world, we do not wage war as the world does.* In 10:2 Paul references those who allege that he and his ministerial associates operate "by the standards of this world." This allegation is phrased in such a way as to dismiss it as false. In 10:3–5 Paul grounds his rejection of this charge in the contrast between being in the world and being of the world. Paul's language is actually more vivid: "Although we walk *in the flesh*, we do not wage war *according to the flesh* [Greek, *kata sarka*]" (author's translation). Twice before in this letter, Paul has used this Greek expression, which the NIV renders, "in a worldly manner" (1:17) and "from a worldly point of view" (5:16). Whatever the precise issue behind the accusation—be it Paul's changing travel itinerary (1:12–24), his pastoral methods (11:7–9, 20–21), an alleged self-interest (3:1; 4:2–5:12), or avarice (2:17; 12:16–18)—Paul perceives it as a personal assault relating to values, practices, or goals that are selfish or this-worldly in orientation.

10:4 *The weapons we fight with . . . have divine power to demolish strongholds.* Perhaps because Paul himself feels under attack, he responds with combat imagery, depicting his evangelistic work as an extended military campaign against the citadels of unbelief and disobedience. His weaponry is not "of the world" (or "fleshly"), as his critics suppose, but derives credibility and effectiveness from God. In light of the governing warfare metaphor, Paul's terminology in 10:4–6 is likely intentionally shaped by the strategies of Roman siegecraft. If we were to situate Paul's language in this context, 10:4–6 could quite plausibly be rendered, "For our siege engines are not feeble, human weaponry, but divinely powerful for the demolition of any fortified encampment or bastion of argumentation. We destroy every raised battlement that resists the knowledge of God and take prisoner every scheming plan to bring it into submission to Christ. And we stand ready to avenge every treasonous act, once your subjection is complete."[2]

10:5 *We demolish arguments and every pretension that sets itself up against the knowledge of God, and we take captive every thought.* Paul now clarifies the "strongholds" he has in mind: intellectual conceptions that stand in opposition to the gospel. Paul's thought widens to include not only the machinations of his opponents in Corinth but other religious and philosophical ideologies with which he has contended as he has sought to advance "the knowledge of God." Paul's evangelistic work was always an active, sometimes combative, engagement with a world of ideas that stood opposed to the cross (1 Cor. 1:18–2:5). The expression translated "pretension" by the NIV is rendered "lofty opinion" by the ESV and "arrogant obstacle" by the NET. The common denominator of all of these is an emphasis on a haughty and conceited disposition. The issue is not simply faulty knowledge but the characterological defect of pride. Although the imagery of 10:3–6 may sound harsh, it was very common among moralists of Paul's day, particularly the Stoics and Cynics. Dio Chrysostom remarks that the wise man continually fights "a stubborn battle against lusts and opinions and all mankind" (*Or.* 77.38). Seneca, commenting on the moral development of the inner person, reasons, "Though earthworks rise to match the loftiest citadel, yet no siege engines can be devised that will shake the firm-fixed soul" (*Cons. sap.* 6.4).

10:6 *we will be ready to punish every act of disobedience, once your obedience is complete.* In 10:6 Paul brings the metaphor of siege warfare to its logical consummation. The siegeworks were laid in 10:4a; the stronghold, citadel, and ramparts were demolished in 10:4b–5a; the rebels were taken captive in 10:5b; and now the insurgents will be punished. Just as in a siege, the city must surrender or be taken before the instigators can be brought to justice, so Paul must defer disciplinary action until the community as a whole capitulates and reaffirms their loyalty to the gospel and their apostolic founder. In speaking of "your obedience," Paul addresses the Corinthian majority who are being called to openly declare their allegiance to Paul by rejecting the "disobedient" among them, be they the intruders or those who remain unrepentant of sin (13:2).

Theological Insights

Boldness and meekness are attributes not typically associated with each other, but in the pages of Scripture we often see them beautifully and powerfully combined in a single individual. Moses is said to have been the meekest of men (Num. 12:3), yet his courage in confronting Pharaoh, the most powerful man in the ancient world, can only be attributed to a divinely given boldness to carry out his task. Similarly, Jesus both modeled meekness (Matt. 11:29; 21:5) and enjoined his followers to pursue this virtue (5:5), yet he evinced no hesitation in boldly denouncing hypocrisy in high places when he encountered it, or confidently doing what was right, even when it was counter to accepted conventions. Paul appeals to Christ's "humility and gentleness" as he turns to confront the Corinthians (2 Cor. 10:1), yet he will spend most of the next three chapters aggressively contending with his detractors in Corinth, boldly—even caustically—exposing their arrogance and deceit. Paul is quite open about his posture of boldness toward the Corinthians (3:12; 7:4; 10:1), and he is well aware that this deportment may need to continue when he returns to the city (10:2). While the Lord's servant must strive to cultivate humility and to cherish meekness, this does not exclude bold leadership when the circumstances demand it, nor does it mean that the Lord's servant will not challenge, correct, discipline, and confront.

Teaching the Text

Every Christian leader will face those difficult situations where sin, disobedience, and destructive behavior need to be called out and confronted. For those in long-term ministry who are deeply involved in the lives of those they serve, this will be an unfortunate but regular responsibility of their calling. The situation in Corinth had reached a critical state, and chapters 10–13 were written, in part, in order to jolt the Corinthians to their senses and so, hopefully, to avoid the disciplinary confrontation Paul feared would take place on his next visit (10:2; 13:1–2). This present passage, 10:1–6, provides important guidance and insight on this topic, which could be appropriately titled, "Approaching Confrontation."

1. *Be reticent to wield disciplinary authority.* The first point to observe is that Paul actually does not want to have to use his divinely given authority to discipline and punish the recalcitrant. His preference is that they acknowledge the error of their ways and repent. In 10:2 he candidly tells the Corinthians

that he does not want to be forced to be "bold" when he arrives, and this sentiment is reiterated in subsequent chapters (12:19–21; 13:10). Paul has written the Corinthians letters, sent emissaries, and returned to Corinth personally. The combative and confrontational tone of chapters 10–13 is one last effort to bring about repentance, lest Paul have to return to Corinth and "take the gloves off," so to speak.

2. *Be willing to confront boldly when circumstances warrant.* While Paul certainly does not desire to punish his children—what parent does?—he recognizes that it is his divinely given responsibility to do everything he can to bring the Corinthians to maturity, and sometimes this involves discipline. Like any good parent (see 6:13; 12:14), Paul understands that the cost of ignoring destructive behavior is far greater than the difficulty involved in confronting it, and Paul is determined to consider the welfare of his flock above his own personal comfort.

3. *Be confident in the provisions for the battle.* Paul's willingness to confront his children in the face of disobedience is grounded in his parental affection (12:14–15), but his confidence in this task issues from the knowledge that God has provided him with all the spiritual arsenal necessary for the battle. Paul depicts his manner (10:3), his weaponry (10:4a), and his strength (10:4b) as spiritual and divinely infused, and so he is confident that the objective of this campaign (10:5) will be achieved, which is taking every thought captive to Christ.

Illustrating the Text

God has entrusted effective spiritual weapons to his followers.

Scenario: One of the most effective military strategies is a "flank attack." In military terms a flanking maneuver is when a portion of an attacking force is brought to bear behind the front lines of the enemy's position by approaching from the side. This tactic is useful due to the fact that a force's power and attention are usually concentrated in the front, where direct engagement is anticipated. A flank attack achieves its purpose because an enemy is most vulnerable behind the front lines. God has given us all the weapons we need to "flank" our enemy by demolishing strongholds.

Disciplined practice can help one to be effective in "taking captive every thought."

Scenario: A man who was in a substantial financial crisis for over a year described how he was on the verge of possibly losing his house and declaring bankruptcy. He shared that during that season he would wake up at night almost paralyzed with fear. He spoke of how this verse, "We take captive every thought to make it obedient to Christ" (10:5), was a lifesaver. Over time, and with great intentionality, he learned how to replace the fearful thoughts with faith thoughts, and he found freedom from the devil's schemes to make him feel shame and unworthiness. This verse works if we are willing to apply it deliberately. Suggest one or two Bible passages that can be memorized and recited during times of spiritual battle and struggle.

Changed thinking = changed behavior

Testimony: Twelve-step recovery groups are well versed in the reality that trying to stop an addiction by "behavior modification" does not produce long-term sobriety. Recovery groups instead pay close attention to patterns of thinking that need to be replaced with new, healthy patterns. Invite a person from your congregation to share their story of how changing their thinking has led to long-term sobriety or transformation. This would be a good week to include those who are struggling with addiction and ministries to them in your congregational prayer.

2 Corinthians 10:7–11

Authority to Build

Big Idea
Paul reminds the Corinthians that he and his apostolic team are genuine, divinely commissioned servants of Christ, and on his next visit he will answer his naysayers in both word and deed.

Key Themes
- Paul's authority is grounded in his apostolic calling.
- Paul's authority has been given to him in order to bring those under his care to maturity.
- Accusations that Paul wields authority only from a distance will be proved false on his next visit to Corinth.

Understanding the Text

The Text in Context

Second Corinthians 10:7–11 is tightly connected to 10:1–6, where Paul alludes to the charge among some in Corinth that he is "bold" when away but "timid" when face to face (10:1). This accusation is repeated in 10:10–11, where we hear Paul report another complaint current in Corinth: his speech and physical appearance are far from commendable. Both complaints are dismissed with a warning that when he returns to Corinth, the apostle will demonstrate powerful action corresponding to his powerful letters.

Interpretive Insights

10:7 *You are judging by appearances.* Support for this rendering (similarly, NET, NASB) comes from the larger exchange between Paul and the Corinthians, which can be accurately summarized as a critique of the Corinthians' superficial value system. They disdain his suffering (12:9–10); they cringe at his oratory (10:12; 11:6); they are embarrassed at his manual labor (11:7–10); and so on. This criticism is crystallized in 5:12 as boasting "in what is seen" (cf. Matt. 22:16). However, many versions (e.g., ESV, NRSV, NLT, NJB) and most commentaries regard the sense expressed by the reading in the margin of the NIV to be preferable: "Look at the obvious facts." This rendering makes slightly better sense in the immediate context

Who's Who in 2 Corinthians 10–13

In 2 Corinthians 10–13 Paul confronts the Corinthians concerning certain intruders who have gained influence in the community and are turning the church against their founding apostle. However, there are other players in this drama who are referenced in these chapters, and often it is unclear precisely whom Paul has in mind, even if to the original recipients of this letter their identities would have been quite obvious.

The primary group, addressed by Paul directly and frequently, is *the Corinthian community as a whole*. This group is behind the recurrent "you" (plural) in these chapters. For example, "I appeal to you" (10:1); "I promised you to one husband" (11:2); "How were you inferior" (12:13). Another group being confronted indirectly, but referred to explicitly, is *the intruders*. Clear references to this group are found in the sarcastic appellations of 11:12–15: false apostles, deceitful workers, servants of Satan. This group is also to be identified with the "boasters" of 11:16–23, who are exploiting the Corinthians (11:20) and who put forward their credentials as "Hebrews . . . Israelites . . . Abraham's descendants" (11:22). The intruders also have *their supporters* in Corinth, and this contingent may lie behind Paul's vague references to "some people" in 10:2, or those whom Paul warns in 11:16–21 not to take him as a fool. Paul also mentions a group of *unrepentant sinners* (12:21; 13:2), which might possibly harken back to situations confronted in 1 Corinthians (dining in pagan temples, 1 Cor. 8:1–9; 10:14–22; abuses at the Lord's Supper, 11:17–33). Although they are not involved directly in the disputes in Corinth, Paul also tangentially alludes to the *Jerusalem apostles, or other legitimate evangelists* in 2 Corinthians 10:15–16 ("work done by others," "someone else's territory").

Again, the individuals behind several of the explicit references are impossible to determine with certainty. For example, in 10:10 Paul directly quotes one group ("Some are saying . . . his speech is contemptible," author's translation), but is he citing the intruders and/or their supporters, or is this the same group behind the complaint against Paul's oratory addressed at length in 1 Corinthians 1–4? Similarly, the "super-apostles" of 11:5 may be Paul's sarcastic designation of the intruders. On the other hand, the expression might be better translated "eminent apostles" and hence be understood as Paul's own designation for the apostles in Jerusalem. These groups are more fully discussed in the commentary, with cautious identifications suggested where the referents are less certain.

(10:7–11), where Paul goes on to correct their "facts" regarding his ministry but doesn't overtly comment on their value system. More important, while the verb Paul uses can be understood as an indicative ("you are looking"), everywhere else that this form of the verb occurs in Paul's Letters it is an imperative: "Look!" In other words, we seem to be dealing with a Pauline idiom common in his moral exhortation. Moreover, the construction in this verse involves a different preposition from that in the alleged parallel text in 5:12, suggesting that Paul's meaning is slightly different as well. For these reasons, the translation in the margin of the NIV is preferred here. Paul is signaling that he is now going to be doing some serious fact-checking, correcting some of the misinformation that his opponents have been propagating in Corinth.

If anyone is confident that they belong to Christ . . . we belong to Christ just as much as they do. The main interpretive issue in 10:7 concerns the identity of the person or persons behind the vague references to "anyone" (10:7a) and "they" (10:7b; see the sidebar). The indefinite pronoun (Greek, *tis*) can represent a broad generalization with a very wide sphere of reference, "anyone at all" (cf. 5:17). On the other hand, it is sometimes used by Paul to denote a very specific group of people whom the apostle, for his own reasons, prefers not to name (e.g., 11:20–21). Since the individual or group referenced in this verse seems to be making a boast concerning themselves, that they belong to Christ, and since it is precisely the credential touting and boasting of the intruders that Paul will criticize at length in what follows (11:12–29), it seems likely that Paul has the intruders or their ringleader primarily in mind in here. The assertion "We belong to Christ just as much as they do" should probably be heard as a caustic retort to the claims of these rivals; the "we" includes Paul and his co-workers. By use of an intentional understatement (litotes), Paul is actually saying something closer to, "We belong to Christ all the more!" (cf. 11:22–23; Phil. 3:4). At issue is probably not whether Paul and his associates truly "belong" to Christ, in the sense of being believers, but whether he or his opponents are true, authoritative, commissioned servants of Christ (see 2 Cor. 10:14–16; 11:5–12, 23; 12:11–13).

10:8 *for building you up rather than tearing you down.* This verse establishes the grounds for the claim of 10:7, that Paul and his apostolic team are servants of Christ, through three distinct assertions: (1) he has been given authority from the Lord; (2) his apostolic commission is to build up the church; (3) as such he is confident of God's approval and vindication. In making these points Paul also raises three issues that will occupy his thoughts in confronting his rivals throughout these final chapters of 2 Corinthians: their authority (11:12–15), their boasting (11:16–29), and their destructive effect (11:20; 12:20–21). In essence, Paul is pointedly contrasting himself with his rivals by claiming that his own authority is legitimate, that whatever boasting he may do is appropriate, and that his purpose among them is beneficial.

10:10 *For some say, . . . "in person he is unimpressive and his speaking amounts to nothing."* This verse contains the only direct citation by Paul of his critics in Corinth (see the sidebar) and communicates two distinct but interrelated complaints against Paul: (1) he is bold, even intimidating (10:9), from a distance through his writing but timid in person (10:1); (2) his physical appearance and public speaking leave much to be desired. The first objection, already voiced in 10:1–2, is dismissed in 10:11 with the promise that when

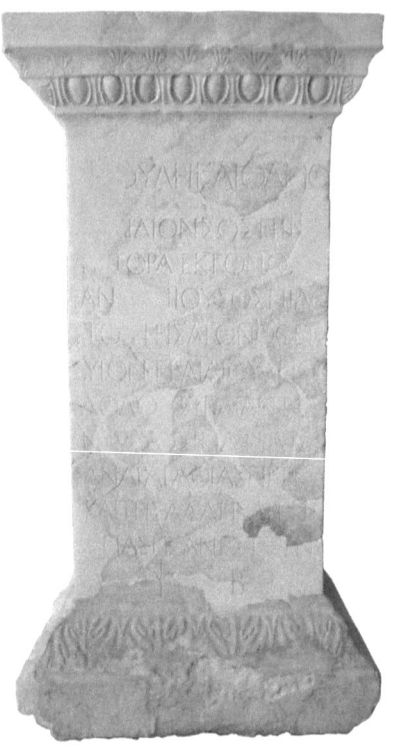

This monument from Roman Corinth (early second century AD) honors a notable Achaian orator and reads: "Because of his upright character and general excellence, the city council and the citizens set up this monument to honor Publius Aelius Sospinus, the orator."

he returns there will be no disjunction between his written persona and his personal presence. Paul will answer his critics in both word and deed.

The second objection is deeply rooted in cultural expectations of what an orator should be like. Training in rhetoric was one of the pillars of the Greco-Roman educational system, and the Corinthians had been fed a rich diet of oratory from birth. The Corinthians erected monuments to their favorite orators and placed a premium value on eloquence. Dio Chrysostom, an orator and younger contemporary of Paul, remarks that his listeners "are devoted to oratory . . . and tolerate speakers only who are very clever" (*Or.* 35.1). The complaint of Paul's poor oratory surfaces again in 11:6 ("I may indeed be untrained as a speaker, but I do have knowledge") and also in 13:3 ("since you are demanding proof that Christ is speaking through me"). Paul had responded to this complaint earlier, in 1 Corinthians 1–4, which is crystallized in 2:1–5: "When I came to you, I did not come with eloquence or human wisdom. . . . My message and my preaching were not with wise and persuasive words, but with a demonstration of the Spirit's power, so that your faith might not rest on human wisdom, but on God's power." In other words, Paul intentionally rejected the manipulative rhetorical strategies of so many of his contemporaries so that his hearers' faith would be focused not on the one preaching but on the one being preached, Jesus Christ.[1]

The complaint that Paul's physical appearance was "unimpressive" should probably also be understood in terms of the Corinthians comparing Paul with the winsome, finely attired orators and sophists they were so used to. Orators of Paul's day prided themselves on their appearance and went to great lengths to impress their audiences with their dress, hairstyle, and grooming. Epictetus, the Stoic philosopher and contemporary of Paul, describes a young orator from Corinth who was "elaborately dressed . . . and whose attire in general was highly embellished" (*Diatr.* 3.1.1, 14). This budding rhetorician, sporting a lavish hairstyle and bedecked in jewelry, plucked out all his body hair to enhance his physical appearance (*Diatr.* 3.1.27–35). In comparison to these high-powered, smooth-talking showmen, Paul, the leatherworker (see the comments on 11:7), was a sorry figure indeed.

Teaching the Text

As Paul begins to take up specific complaints circulating among the Corinthians, his first order of business is to reestablish his authority and to explicitly delineate the character of that authority. In 10:7–11 Paul provides insights regarding the origin, purpose, and manifestation of the authority entrusted to him in his apostolic commission.

1. *The origin of Paul's authority.* The primary assertion of 10:7–11 is that Paul is a legitimately commissioned servant of Christ (10:7) and has received authority from the Lord to fulfill his task (10:8). Paul has derived his authority not from any human agency or institution (cf. Gal. 1:11–12) but from his personal commission from the Lord (cf. 1 Cor. 9:1–2; 15:3–8). Although Paul's authority as an apostle is somewhat unique, his use of the inclusive "we" in these verses indicates that Paul includes his co-workers among those who also possess legitimate authority as officially recognized and consecrated ministers of the gospel. The Pastoral Epistles (1–2 Timothy, Titus) provide the theological basis for this derivative, yet fully legitimate, extension of authority to publicly recognized, consecrated servants of the gospel (1 Tim. 4:12; 2 Tim. 1:6; 2:2).

2. *The purpose of Paul's authority.* Although Paul understands that his job description as an apostle of Christ necessarily involves the destruction of strongholds of opposition (10:3–6), his primary mission is to build up the church (10:8) and to "present everyone fully mature in Christ" (Col. 1:28). The authority entrusted to Paul is not for his own personal benefit, honor, or prestige but is meant for the benefit of others (2 Cor. 12:15).

3. *The manifestation of Paul's authority.* The Corinthians and Paul are at odds over many issues, but preeminent among them is how a divinely commissioned servant should look and sound. The Corinthians expect an impressive appearance and powerful oratory. Paul insists that his authority and worth should not be measured by such externals as an appealing stage presence and winsome rhetoric. Rather, Paul contends that his apostolic authority will be manifest in his courage to confront opposition, his consistency in word and deed, and his determination to build up the body of Christ.

Illustrating the Text

Don't judge by the standards of the crowd.

Object Lesson: Invite a person from outside your community to dress up as a homeless person (or as someone really out of fashion) and have them sit in a rather conspicuous location for the worship service. At some point during the service, have them share a prayer or testimony or other element of the service. Follow up by reflecting on how easy it is to judge people by their exterior appearance rather than their heart.

Strong roots are important.

Pop Culture: Some of the magazines that push our culture's agenda are *Vanity Fair*, *Vogue*, *GQ*, *Muscle & Fitness*, and *Cosmopolitan*. It is unlikely that magazines like *Self-Control Digest*, *Lifelong Monogamy*, *Selfless Living*, or *Popular Morality* would make it to the checkout counter. Our culture is obsessed with the "leaves" of the tree, but God wants to develop our roots. Paul's exterior appearance was unimpressive, but his message and his life were rooted in the character of Christ. If you have the capacity to do so (possibly using some high school or college students from your church) you could make up magazine covers for some of these "magazines you will never see" and show them while you talk about them.

The heart of the matter

Scripture: In 1 Samuel 16:7, God reminds Samuel that his criteria for selecting a king have little to do with external features. And God evaluates his followers in the same way he evaluates a king: God looks at the heart. Is he finding yours praiseworthy?

It's not about me.

Testimony: Paul insists that his gifts and authority are for the purpose of building up the body of Christ. Invite one or two people to share their testimony of how God is using their spiritual gifts to build up the body of Christ. Let this be an opportunity to encourage other people in the church to find their place in ministry and service. This would be a good opportunity to encourage people to participate in a class about finding spiritual gifts.

2 Corinthians 10:12-18

Boasting in the Lord

Big Idea

As the founding apostle of the church in Corinth, Paul is not reaching beyond his legitimate ministerial jurisdiction in attempting to strengthen the believers in Corinth and expand the gospel through them.

Key Themes

- Comparing oneself to others without an objective criterion of assessment is a foolish endeavor that leads to foolish boasting.
- Paul is within his rights to cultivate and expand the field of ministry God has assigned to him; it is the intruders who are encroaching on his territory, not vice versa.
- Legitimate boasting focuses on what God has accomplished, not on what we may vainly perceive to be our accomplishments.

Understanding the Text

The Text in Context

In 10:12–18 Paul continues the assault on his rivals that began at the outset of this chapter. His goal is to counter their criticism of him and undermine their influence in Corinth, so that he can continue to nurture this conflicted community and eventually expand the gospel beyond Corinth with their help (10:15–16). In 10:1–6 Paul refuted the charge that he operates according to worldly standards. In 10:7–11 he contests the accusation that he is bold only from a distance, through his letters, while in person his appearance is shabby and his speech uninspiring. In the present passage Paul focuses on his opponents' boasting—which will continue to occupy his attention in chapters 11 and 12—and their intrusion and disruption of his labor in Corinth. Paul is keen to remind the Corinthians that it was he and his apostolic team who first preached the gospel in Corinth, and it is his rivals who have encroached on his legitimate sphere of ministry. Paul's line of thought in 10:12–18 can be summarized thus: We do not boast improperly (10:12–13), nor are we reaching beyond our divinely allocated field of ministry (10:14–15). Rather, we desire to advance the gospel in you and beyond you (10:16), for all boasting should be in the Lord, and true commendation should be from him (10:17–18).

Interpretive Insights

10:12 *We do not dare to classify or compare ourselves with some who commend themselves.* Verse 12 begins with a conjunction (Greek, *gar*) that is untranslated by the NIV but indicates some kind of explanatory connection between these verses and those that precede: "*You see*, we do not dare . . ." captures the transition nicely.[1] The accusations in 10:10–11 of lack of assertiveness, poor personal appearance, and dismal oratory—that is, his lack of qualities essential for a successful sophist—prompt Paul to contrast himself and his colleagues with those who compare themselves with others and then commend themselves (see the sidebar). The unique constellation of criticisms and contentions identified by Paul in 10:7–18 almost certainly indicates the presence of sophistic values among Paul's detractors and/or opponents. According to one first-century observer, "crowds of wretched Sophists" could be seen in the environs of Corinth,[2] so we should not be surprised that the perspectives and ideals of sophistry gained traction in this cosmopolitan city. What is less clear is if Paul is confronting the influence of this larger cultural phenomenon known as the Second Sophistic,[3] or if Paul's opponents themselves have adopted some of these attitudes and behaviors. The close connection in 11:5–6 between the "super-apostles" (the intruders) and Paul's defense of his speaking ability render the second alternative very likely. Be that as it may, Paul regards as utter folly any self-comparison or self-evaluation that uses oneself as the criterion for judgment ("They measure themselves by themselves," 10:12).

10:13–14 *We, however, will not boast beyond proper limits.* With the emphatic "we, however," Paul clearly contrasts himself and his co-workers

---

Sophists and the Art of Comparison

The art of comparison was a standard feature of rhetorical technique and was particularly common in sophistic oratory. It is defined by Quintilian, the preeminent teacher of rhetoric in the first century, as the determination of "which of two characters are the better or worse" (*Inst.* 2.4.21). Plutarch, a younger contemporary of Paul, characterizes the sophists of his day by their excessive use of comparison to win an audience and attract a clientele: "For this it is not like friendship, but sophistry, to seek for glory in other men's fault, and to make a fair show among the spectators" (*Adul. amic.* 71). Lucian, writing from the second century, sarcastically relates the standard pitch of a sophist attempting to recruit a student: "Do not expect to see something that you can compare with So-and-so, or So-and-so. . . . Indeed, you will find that I drown them all out as effectively as trumpets drown out flutes" (*Rhet. praec.* 13). As this citation illustrates, equally characteristic of sophistry according to writers of the period is boasting, self-commendation, and arrogance, which Paul addresses in 10:13–16.

with the previously mentioned group of those who commend themselves improperly. Boasting "beyond proper limits" probably includes the foolish self-commendation of 10:12, which lacks any objective standard of evaluation, as well as the improper boasting of 10:14–16, which lays claim to work accomplished by others. Rather than boasting improperly, without reasonable justification and criteria as some do, Paul offers a legitimate basis for his boast concerning the Corinthians. God himself has allotted to his ministry team this field of ministry. The aorist tense ("God . . . *assigned* to us," 10:13) may allude to Paul's calling as an apostle to the gentiles (Acts 9:15–16; Rom. 15:15–16),[4] though the plural ("to us") counts against this. Alternatively, the simple fact that Paul's team reached Corinth first with the gospel may be the decisive proof in Paul's mind that God has sovereignly assigned Corinth to Paul's allocated sphere of ministry. This interpretation is supported by 10:14: "We are not going too far in our boasting . . . for we did get as far as you with the gospel of Christ." The Greek term translated "boasting" throughout this passage does not necessarily connote active verbal boasting to others, as the English word does. It also denotes "taking pride" in something or someone. Paul's "boasting" in the Corinthians, in the present context, probably involves taking pride in them and in what God has accomplished (see 10:17–18).

10:15–16 *Neither do we go beyond our limits by boasting of work done by others.* Echoing the assertion of 10:14, this verse more clearly alludes to a group of those who are indeed exceeding their legitimate scope of ministry ("limits") and encroaching on Paul's allotted field. As subsequent chapters will reveal, this is a group of "false apostles" (11:13) with no legitimate field of ministry, though in the present context Paul is only establishing the principle of rightful fields of labor. The issue is not that the intruders are actually boasting that they have founded the church in Corinth, but they are attempting to build on Paul's foundation as if they had a part in laying it.

Our hope is that . . . our sphere of activity among you will greatly expand. Verses 15b–16 form a natural unit of thought that expresses Paul's chief aim (the growth of the Corinthians, v. 15b) and his overriding purpose (the expansion of the gospel into unreached regions, v. 16). Paul's hope to extend the gospel beyond Corinth is predicated on two important contingencies: the maturing of the Corinthians' faith ("as your faith continues to grow") and their active participation in this endeavor ("our sphere of activity, with your help, will greatly expand," author's translation). This second contingency, the assistance of the Corinthians, is based on interpreting the Greek expression *en hymin* as "by/through you," in the sense of "through your assistance," as opposed to the NIV's "among you." Two considerations support this interpretation: (1) it is better suited to what immediately follows in verse 16, where Paul describes his desire to expand the gospel beyond Corinth; (2) it is consistent with Paul's missional strategy, to use sending churches to finance his evangelistic work in other regions (Phil. 4:15; Rom. 15:23–24; 1 Cor. 16:6). The connection between these two contingencies is also significant. It is as (because) their faith matures that Paul expects to be able to count on their material and spiritual support in his pioneer evangelistic efforts. Paul reiterates at the close of verse 16 that his calling is to unreached peoples, as he notes that he does not want to boast "about work already done in someone else's territory." In Romans 15:20 Paul articulates this missional burden in very clear terms: "It has always been my ambition to preach the gospel where Christ was not known, so that I would not be building on someone else's foundation."

10:17 *Let the one who boasts boast in the Lord.* Paul now offers the only legitimate basis and object of boasting, "the Lord," and so reveals the boasting of his rivals as counterfeit. This maxim is taken from Jeremiah 9:23 (LXX) and is also cited in 1 Corinthians 1:31, where it is introduced by the citation formula "as it is written." In both instances Paul modifies the Old Testament text by substituting "[boasting] in the Lord" for "[boasting] in this, that he understands and knows me, that I am the Lord" (Jer. 9:24 ESV). Paul's abbreviated citation allows him to represent the gist of the prophetic oracle in a concise manner and to apply the truism more broadly. In both the Old Testament context (certainly) and 1 Corinthians (most probably), "the Lord" refers to God the Father, and there is no compelling reason to read it differently here, as referring to Christ. The larger context suggests that "boasting in the Lord" means, for Paul, extolling not only God's character but also his work in this world, which he graciously allows us to participate in.

10:18 *For it is not the one who commends himself who is approved.* Paul returns to the topic that began this section, self-commendation, and provides the decisive argument against the self-commendation of his rivals. Their approval of themselves is both irrelevant and illegitimate, because the only approval that matters comes from God. Verses 17 and 18 are foundational for chapters 12 and 13 in that they provide the orientation for the "foolish boasting" that follows. Paul has established what constitutes legitimate boasting and what should be rejected as disreputable, self-serving boasting. The irony of what follows is Paul's tongue-in-cheek strategy of "foolish boasting" that glorifies God.

Theological Insights

Proper commendation is an important theme in 2 Corinthians. Paul has already pointedly disavowed self-commendation on two occasions earlier in the letter (3:1; 5:12), which alerts us to a matter that the apostle feels he needs to clarify with the Corinthians. In 10:12 we discover that others, probably the opponents whom Paul takes to task in chapters 10–13, are "comparing themselves with themselves" and then "commending themselves." Paul calls this "unwise," but he appears to do just this in 4:2, "We commend ourselves to everyone's conscience," and again in 6:4, "We commend ourselves in every way." However, in these passages Paul qualifies his version of self-commendation by defining it as renouncing deception (4:2), as being under God's scrutiny (4:2), and as sacrificial service on behalf of others (6:4–10). In other words, Paul's self-commendation consists of offering proof of his integrity, sincerity, and selfless labor on behalf of the Corinthians; he is not comparing himself to others and boasting. Paul can "commend [himself] to everyone's conscience" (4:2) and then immediately claim that he does not "proclaim himself" (cf. 4:5) because his goal is to serve others, not to exploit and manipulate others. Near the end of the book Paul chides the Corinthians that they ought to have commended him (12:11) rather than preferring the pretensions of the false apostles (11:12–13). This motif climaxes and is crystallized in the sober dictum of 10:18: "For it is not the one who commends himself who is approved, but the one whom the Lord commends."

Teaching the Text

In 10:12–18 Paul introduces a topic that will occupy much of his attention in the chapters that follow: boasting. Paul is confronting a group of encroaching missionaries who claim to have authority to lead the Corinthians (cf. 11:21–22) but are actually leading them astray (11:12–15). They may be boasting in their credentials as "Abraham's descendants" (11:22) and "servants of Christ" (11:23), but Paul sees through their ruse and intends to expose their boasting as mere swagger and conceit. His target in this section is proper boasting, and he carefully delineates his boundaries. As boasting is a major topic of these chapters, it will be important to properly define this concept in teaching this material.

1. *Proper boasting does not boast in oneself.* You should not boast in yourself, especially when your standard of evaluation is your own inflated ego and your aim is to commend yourself in comparison to others, as was the case with the intruders in this passage. Our tendency is to magnify our strengths, ignore our weaknesses, and then compare ourselves favorably to others. The result is an evaluation completely out of proportion to reality. Paul's clearest formulation of this problem is found in Galatians: "If anyone thinks they are something when they are not, they deceive themselves. Each one should test their own actions. Then they can take pride in themselves alone, without comparing themselves to someone else" (6:3–4).

2. *Proper boasting does not boast in work done by others.* Taking credit for someone else's work can take many forms. In 10:12–18 it involves rivals usurping the authority of Paul by building on his foundation in such a way

that they undermine his labor, his authority, and even the gospel. Paul is not opposed to others ministering to his flock, as 1 Corinthians makes abundantly clear: "I planted the seed, Apollos watered it, but God has been making it grow" (3:6). Nor is his territorialism a matter of petty envy or a desire for control. The intruders are actually harming the cause of Christ and dismantling what Paul has built by preaching a "different Jesus" and a "different gospel" (2 Cor. 11:4; cf. NLT).

3. *Proper boasting boasts only in God and what he has accomplished.* Paul does allow "boasting" within certain limits and for specific reasons. Proper boasting is self-effacing, Christ honoring, and Christ focused. It correctly attributes any success to the one who truly is responsible: "So neither the one who plants nor the one who waters is anything, but only God, who makes things grow" (1 Cor. 3:7). Paul's "boasting in the Lord" is probably closer to what we would refer to as praising or magnifying the Lord. This kind of boasting is rooted in the knowledge that we are not sufficient "to claim anything as coming from us, but our sufficiency is from God" (2 Cor. 3:5 ESV).

Illustrating the Text

An occasional snapshot does not paint a picture of real life or real people.

Modern Culture: On many social media sites people place snapshots of their life. They capture fun, happy, exciting, adventurous, and meaningful experiences and share them with their "friends." The problem is, most people don't take a picture of when they take out the trash, sit and work at their desk, mindlessly watch TV, or have countless other mundane daily experiences (not to mention preserving and proclaiming their failures). The end result is an impression that our lives are more dynamic and exciting than they really are. Others look at our highlights and feel their lives do not measure up. Comparing yourself to others is usually a bad idea, which is why Paul reminds us that the only commendation that really matters is the commendation that comes from the Lord (10:18).

Boasting beyond proper limits can leave you looking like a GOAT.

Sports: American sprinter Maurice Green, anticipating running in the 2004 Olympic Games in Athens, was so confident of his ability that he had the acronym GOAT, "Greatest of All Time," tattooed on his shoulder. Naturally, the world media took an interest in this boast and spent a fair amount of time talking about this audacious claim in the run-up to his signature event, the one-hundred meters. When he crossed the finish line in third place, the letters GOAT quickly took on a new meaning to the press, becoming synonymous with ego and arrogance.[5]

2 Corinthians 11:1–6

Divinely Jealous

Big Idea
The "gospel" preached by the intruders amounts to preaching a different Jesus and is threatening to lead the community away from their sincere devotion to Christ.

Key Themes
- Jealousy (properly understood) in service of the preservation of the gospel can be an honorable and appropriate disposition.
- Not everyone who proclaims "Christ" is actually serving and proclaiming the authentic apostolic message of the crucified and resurrected Jesus.
- Paul's perceived deficiency in oratory does not in any way discredit him as a divinely approved herald of the gospel.

Understanding the Text

The Text in Context

Second Corinthians 11:1–6 introduces what is often called the "Fool's Speech" (11:1–12:13), in accordance with Paul's frequent references to the foolishness of the strategy of argumentation that he adopts in this section (11:1, 16, 19, 21, 23; 12:1, 6, 11). Having criticized his opponents' self-commendation and boasting in 10:12–18, Paul now engages in a tongue-in-cheek boasting competition with his rivals, fighting folly with folly, so to speak. Paul's ironic posture in this argumentative maneuver is apparent throughout (e.g., "I have made a fool of myself, but you drove me to it," 12:11), as is his sarcastic tone (e.g., "You even put up with anyone who enslaves you!" 11:20). Paul's ultimate aim is to expose the intruders as charlatans and reclaim the respect of the Corinthians, while also inverting the Corinthian value system. What the Corinthians call weakness, Paul calls strength (12:10), and this represents the ironic climax of this section.

The present passage, 11:1–6, articulates the thesis of the "Fool's Speech"—namely, that the message of the intruders is both a distortion of the gospel (11:1–4) and a misrepresentation of Paul (11:5–6). Each section that follows supports this thesis by offering various proofs of its validity, with 12:11–13 serving as a conclusion of the argument and a recapitulation of the thesis.

Interpretive Insights

11:1 *I hope you will put up with me in a little foolishness.* Paul announces here the ironic intent of this section, the "Fool's Speech" (11:1–12:13). Having just defined proper boasting as boasting in the Lord, and true commendation as coming only from the Lord (10:18), it is entirely unexpected that Paul would proceed to enumerate his own credentials and experiences in order to laud himself and denigrate his opponents. Yet, Paul has been so undermined by his opposition, and so poorly defended by the Corinthians (12:11), that he is compelled to set the record straight. Paul's strategy is to candidly present his résumé to the Corinthians, while inserting comments throughout to the effect that this tactic is beneath him, and even worldly (11:18). This approach allows him to censure obliquely the self-commendation of his rivals, while also reestablishing his character and ministry as one clearly commended by the Lord.

11:2 *I am jealous for you with a godly jealousy.* The Greek expression behind the NIV's "godly jealousy" might denote a holy or upright jealousy (an attributive genitive), or a jealousy that comes from God (a genitive of source), or perhaps a jealousy that is God's own jealousy (a possessive genitive). Paul is saying more than that his jealousy is appropriate (as the NIV implies); he is claiming that his jealousy corresponds to God's own fervent, protective passion for his people and his own holy name: "Do not worship any other god, for the Lord, whose name is Jealous, is a jealous God" (Exod. 34:14). For Paul, jealousy can be either a noble quality (1 Cor. 14:1; 2 Cor. 7:7) or a vice (Rom. 13:13; 1 Cor. 13:4), depending on its object and motivation: "It is fine to be jealous, provided the purpose is good" (Gal. 4:18, author's translation). See "Theological Insights," below.

I promised you to one husband, to Christ. In 11:2b–4 Paul justifies his jealousy on behalf of the Corinthians by portraying himself as a father who has betrothed his daughter to a suitor, only to discover that she is being wooed by someone else and her affections are being swayed. Both Jewish and Roman marriage customs could involve a lengthy betrothal period, and it was the father's responsibility to safeguard the purity of his daughter until the formal consummation of the marriage. In the wider social context, presenting the bride as a "pure virgin" was not only a moral issue and a matter of familial honor; it was also a financial matter. If the bride were found to be defiled, the marriage could be aborted and the dowry forfeited.

11:3 *as Eve was deceived by the serpent's cunning.* Paul assumes a basic familiarity with the Genesis account of Eve's deception and draws several very pointed parallels (some explicit, some implicit) to the situation in Corinth. The intruders are analogous to the serpent in the garden, who was "more crafty than any of the wild animals" (Gen. 3:1; cf. Matt. 10:16). The serpent deceived

Eve (Gen. 3:13; 1 Tim. 2:14) and led her to reject the clear instructions that the Lord had given her and Adam (Gen. 3:4–5). This deception was partly intellectual, the planting of falsehoods in her mind. Paul knows that "the god of this age" blinds the minds of unbelievers (4:4), so he warns the Corinthians of his fear: "Your minds may somehow be led astray" (11:3). The Corinthians are in danger of losing "their sincerity and their purity, which is in Christ" (a more literal translation of 11:3b). This language both develops the betrothal imagery of 11:2 and alludes to the loss of innocence and purity in the garden of Eden. Most important, the intruders are identified with the serpent, which Paul and other Jewish writers of this era regard as a manifestation of Satan (see 11:13–15; Rev. 12:9; *Life of Adam and Eve* 33.3).

11:4 *For if someone comes to you and preaches a Jesus other than the Jesus we preached . . . a different spirit . . . a different gospel.* This verse has invited much speculation as to the character of this "other" Jesus, the nature of this "different spirit," and the content of this divergent "gospel."[1] Some interpreters see Judaizers, as in Galatians, who require torah observance of some kind in addition to faith in Christ (see 11:22). Others believe Paul refers to Jewish-Christian pneumatics who downplay Jesus's suffering and emphasize his miracle working, along with their own manifestations of spiritual power. The difficulty with these proposals is that Paul never identifies any deficiencies in the content of the intruders' proclamation, nor does he correct their Christology. From what Paul says in 2 Corinthians 10–13, it is not their doctrine he objects to but their arrogance, their boasting, their abusive manner, their criticism of his apostolate, and their encroachment on his field of ministry. It is entirely possible that the primary heresy of the intruders was a matter not of doctrine but of demeanor. Paul understood that the medium and the message are inseparable. So, to proclaim a humble, self-sacrificing Savior in an arrogant, bombastic, self-serving manner constitutes a distortion of the message itself. The self-absorbed and self-promoting character of the messenger both garbles the message and misrepresents the Savior.

you put up with it easily enough. Paul uses the same Greek word here as in 11:1, where he entreats the Corinthians to "*put up with* me in a little foolishness." In essence, Paul is (somewhat sarcastically) saying, "Since you put up with the folly of these intruders, certainly you can put up with a little of mine."

11:5 *I do not think I am in the least inferior to those "super-apostles."* Paul is probably saying more than that he is not inferior to his rivals. Through this understatement for rhetorical effect (litotes) Paul is actually affirming his superiority to these newcomers. Although some have suggested that "super-apostles" refers to the Jerusalem apostles, it is unlikely that Paul would abruptly mention them here, interrupting the flow of thought. The designation occurs again in 12:11, where it certainly refers to the intruders. The expression represents

> **Wisdom and Eloquence**
>
> From as early as Isocrates (an influential Greek rhetorician, 436–330 BC), who taught that "the power to speak well is the surest index of sound understanding" (*Nic.* 7), to the famous second-century orator Aelius Aristides, who claimed that "the title 'wise' and the ability to speak well are attributes of the same man" (*Plat.* 391), wisdom and eloquence were deemed inseparable. Stoicism, the most popular philosophy in the New Testament era, was particularly vocal on this point, as Arius Didymus relates: "They [the Stoics] say that only the wise man is a good prophet, poet, and orator" (*Epit.* 5b12). Seneca, perhaps the most important representative of Stoicism in Paul's day, reasoned, "What is he [the listener] to think of their souls, when their speech is sent into the charge in utter disorder?" (*Ep.* 40.12). Not only was oratory valued at a premium in Greco-Roman society (see the comments on 10:10), but rhetorical prowess was considered an accurate gauge of one's knowledge, wisdom, and character: "As character is, such is the speech. The reverse is also true" (Aelius Aristides, *Plat.* 392).

Paul's own derisive appellation of his opponents, cynically reflective of their own high opinion of themselves. The NIV communicates this ironic intent by placing the phrase in quotation marks.

11:6 *I may indeed be untrained as a speaker, but I do have knowledge.* Once again Paul explicitly raises the issue of his oratory as a matter of contention between him and the Corinthians (10:10). Paul concedes he is not a professionally trained and polished rhetorician, but he insists that he is competent and knowledgeable. The intruding missionaries had rhetorical expertise that Paul lacked, and his detractors in Corinth (perhaps incited by the intruders) were making much of Paul's deficiency. Paul's predicament is significantly illuminated by considering the larger cultural perspective, especially among the educated elite, concerning the connection between the ability to speak well and the ability to live well and think well (see the sidebar). The open criticism of Paul's skill in public address was not simply a matter of quibbling over trivialities; it was a deliberate attack on his character and credibility that forced the apostle to engage in a much wider campaign to reestablish both.

Theological Insights

In contemporary usage, "jealousy" has a decidedly negative connotation. It denotes selfishness, rage, envy, and the like and is considered a negative character quality. The biblical notion of jealousy is more complex and nuanced. In the Old Testament, God himself is frequently called a "jealous God" (Exod. 34:14; Deut. 4:24; Josh. 24:19), in that he is justly concerned for the covenant faithfulness of Israel, both for the sake of his holy name

(Num. 25:11) and for the benefit of his people. Human jealousy is most often morally blameworthy in Scripture, in that it is self-centered (Gen. 30:1; Ps. 106:16–18) and concerned with personal benefit, often at the expense of others (Gen. 37:11; Acts 17:5). In Paul's Letters it is frequently found in vice catalogs (Rom. 13:13; 2 Cor. 12:20; Gal. 5:20). On the other hand, human jealousy can also be morally praiseworthy in the Bible, when it is concerned for the benefit of another, or when the jealousy is aroused to preserve a necessarily exclusive relationship.[2] For example, the jealousy of a husband or wife is deemed appropriate if infidelity is involved (Num. 5:11–18), and Paul applauds the Corinthians for being jealous for his honor (2 Cor. 7:7, 11). This positive sense of jealousy usually utilizes the same terminology as the negative counterpart, but it is commonly translated with "zeal" or "zealous" by modern translations, especially when the "jealousy" is religious in nature (1 Kings 19:10; Rom. 10:2; John 2:17).

Teaching the Text

Paul's reference to his divine jealousy (11:2) on behalf of the Corinthians signals the depths of Paul's emotional response when the welfare of his spiritual children is at stake. The expression "righteous indignation" is not often heard today—and when it is used, it is usually pejorative—but it is an apt description of Paul's response to the situation he is facing in Corinth and could serve as a heading for all of chapters 10–13. Paul is certainly angry, but his anger is not selfishly oriented. He recognizes the perilous cliff this community is blindly approaching, and he knows that his tone must be appropriate to the looming calamity. Righteous indignation is not righteous if its motivation is mixed or impure. Paul identifies four critical facts that the Corinthians have missed and that justify and substantiate his righteous indignation in this letter. In order to properly interpret this passage, the causes of Paul's "jealousy" and resulting anger need to be carefully examined.

1. *The Corinthians have been deceived.* The interlopers, through cunning and ruse, have misled the Corinthians and are destroying the foundation that Paul and others have laid (11:3; cf. 1 Cor. 3:5–9).

2. *The Corinthians are being turned away from true discipleship to Christ.* The deception perpetrated on the Corinthians is not an inconsequential error but one that threatens to stifle their growth by leading them away from the source of their life and hope, Christ (11:3–4).

3. *The intruders have distorted the gospel.* Be it outright doctrinal error or a demeanor and persona that contradicts the gospel, the intruders are peddling a truncated message that does not correspond to the apostolic message proclaimed by Paul and others (11:4).

4. *The intruders are intentionally undermining Paul's influence and credibility in Corinth*. The rival missionaries are bent on separating Paul and the Corinthians, and their tools are criticism and slander (11:5–6). Paul understands their attack on his credibility not so much as a personal assault but as assailing the good news he is commissioned to preach to the gentiles. Paul's righteous indignation in chapters 10–13 is a reflection of God's own jealousy on behalf of his covenant people and echoes the prophets of old in their attempt to turn Israel from her folly.

Illustrating the Text

Godly jealousy can preserve a marriage.

Story: Pastor and author Timothy Keller tells the moving story about how his wife, Kathy, got his attention to prioritize their family. Timothy had promised her that it would take three years of long hours to establish their new church in New York, but then things would slow down.

> But the three-year mark came and went, and Kathy asked me, as we agreed, to cut back on my work hours. "Just a couple more months, I said. "I have this and that commitment that I have to see through. . . ." I kept saying that. . . .
>
> One day I came home from work. It was a nice day outside and I notice that the door to our apartment's balcony was open. Just as I was taking off my jacket I heard a smashing noise coming from the balcony. In another couple of seconds I heard another one. I walked out onto the balcony and to my surprise saw Kathy sitting on the floor. She had a hammer, and next to her was a stack of our wedding china. On the ground were the shards of two smashed saucers.
>
> "What are you doing?" I asked.
>
> She looked up and said, "You aren't listening to me. You don't realize that if you keep working these hours you are going to destroy this family. . . . You aren't seeing how serious this is. This is what you are doing," and she brought the hammer down on a third saucer.[3]

Kathy's carefully calculated demonstration got Timothy's attention and led to an important conversation. He admitted: "I was addicted to the level of productivity I had achieved. I had to do something. She saw me listening for the first time and we hugged."[4] Jealousy for the welfare of one's family is a godly jealousy.

God has a jealous love for his own.

Lyrics: **"How He Loves," by John Mark McMillan.** The song "How He Loves," by singer and songwriter John Mark McMillan and performed by The David

Crowder Band, has a vivid description of the holy jealousy of God: "He is jealous for me, loves like a hurricane, I am a tree."[5]

The church has been promised to Christ and should take care to remain his faithful bride.

Literature: *War and Peace*, by Leo Tolstoy. In this epic novel tracing the lives of five aristocratic families in nineteenth-century Russia, young Natasha Rostova charms the jaded Andrei Bolkonsky and accepts his proposal of marriage. However, at his father's insistence, Andrei agrees to postpone the marriage for a year. While he is away, another man, Anatole Kuragin, woos Natasha and asks her to run off with him. She agrees and breaks off her engagement with Andrei, only to find out that Anatole is already secretly married and therefore never intended to legally wed her. Andrei refuses to take her back, leaving Natasha shamed and disgraced by her broken engagement. As a father figure to the Corinthians, Paul says he has betrothed them to Christ, but now he finds that other suitors have begun to woo the bride. Paul wants to end this seduction before it goes too far and the Corinthians are disgraced by abandoning their intended husband.

Satan is a deceiver.

Television: *The X-Files*. In the seventh-season episode "Signs and Wonders," when a series of deaths occur due to snake bites, suspicion falls on the pastor of an intolerant, snake-handling church. However, it turns out that the real criminal is the man masquerading as the pastor of another church in town, the tolerant, mainstream church. After a final confrontation with Agent Mulder, this imposter takes the form of a snake and slithers away, to turn up again later at another congregation, as their new pastor with "an open and modern way of looking at God." Mulder says of him, "People think the devil has horns and a tail. They're not used to looking for some kindly man who tells you what you want to hear." Paul communicates to the Corinthians that Satan can come in many deceptive forms, even as an angel of light. God's people need to be alert to the subtle, seductive lies of false teachers that can undermine the truth of the gospel.[6]

2 Corinthians 11:7–15

True and False Apostles

Big Idea

Paul's principled determination to support himself through manual labor or the assistance of other communities while he was establishing the church in Corinth is evidence of his love for the Corinthians and distinguishes his authentic apostolate from the false apostolate of the intruders.

Key Themes

- In proclaiming the gospel in Corinth, Paul relied on his own manual labor or the help of other churches to finance his work, rather than burdening those he was evangelizing.
- Proclaiming the gospel "free of charge" was evidence of Paul's love for the Corinthians, not a rejection of their friendship, as some have interpreted his refusal of support.
- The intruding missionaries have taken money from the Corinthians and are resentful of Paul's selfless approach.
- The jealousy of the intruders is proof that they are false apostles who stand under condemnation.

Understanding the Text

The Text in Context

In the first movement of the "Fool's Speech," Paul addressed the charge of his poor oratory (11:1–6). Paul now raises a second criticism leveled against him in Corinth: his refusal to accept the patronage of the Corinthians. Paul's determination to engage in manual labor ("lowering" himself, 11:7) and to accept help from other Christian communities rather than from the Corinthians (11:8–9) has offended some in Corinth. They have interpreted Paul's actions as a rejection of their friendship (11:11). Paul, on the other hand, insists that his motivation for this approach has nothing to do with lack of affection for the Corinthians. Rather, it issues from Paul's unique apostolic calling (11:10; 1 Cor. 9) and is a means whereby he demonstrates the authentic character of his ministry and distinguishes himself from hucksters masquerading as servants of the gospel (11:12–15).

Interpretive Insights

11:7 *Was it a sin for me to lower myself . . . ?* The rhetorical question expects the answer "no" and introduces a new charge that Paul must address. Two questions arise: (1) What does Paul mean by "lowering" himself? (2) Is this Paul's own terminology and assessment, or is he echoing his detractors, who are scornful of Paul's willingness to "lower" himself? In relation to the first question, both the immediate context and the larger context of Paul's ministry point to Paul's determination to support himself through plying his trade as a leatherworker as the manner in which Paul "lowered" himself. This makes the best sense of Paul's assertion that this "lowering" meant he could preach the gospel "free of charge" (11:7b). It is also supported by the following verses, where Paul explains that the issue at hand was how his needs were supplied so that he did not "burden" the Corinthians (11:8–9). Further, it corresponds to what we know of Paul's missionary strategy from elsewhere in his letters and Acts. According to Acts, Paul set up shop in Corinth with Priscilla and Aquila because they were leatherworkers like him (18:1–3). In 1 Corinthians 9 Paul tells the Corinthians that although he has a right to be supported by them, he prefers to work so that he can offer the gospel "free of charge" (9:18). In his final words to the Ephesians the apostle affirms that "these hands of mine have supplied my own needs and the needs of my companions" (Acts 20:34; see further the comments on 11:27). It would appear that some Corinthians, probably those of the upper social orders, were embarrassed by Paul's manual labor, and this was being exploited by the intruders. In sarcastically asking if he committed a "sin" in choosing to support himself, Paul is belittling the value system that would so depreciate the motive behind his sacrificial ministry of the gospel as to be offended by it.

The second question, whether Paul is echoing his detractors when he speaks of "lowering" himself, is more difficult to answer. Hock has argued that as a highly educated rabbi from a family of substantial means, Paul himself regarded manual labor as beneath him, and so the apostle refers to it here as "lowering" himself.[1] On the other hand, Paul frequently cites teachings or positions he does not endorse, in order to correct them (1 Cor. 6:12–13; 7:1; 8:1; 10:23; 2 Cor. 10:10; 11:5).

11:8–10 *I robbed other churches by receiving support from them . . . the brothers who came from Macedonia supplied what I needed.* Paul "robbed" other churches in the sense that he used their resources—with their permission—to finance his work in Corinth. The practice of the early church was for Christian communities to provide traveling funds and provisions for itinerant evangelists and prophets to help them on their journey to the next locale (Acts 15:3; Rom. 15:24; Titus 3:13; 3 John 6; *Did.* 12–13). Paul expected such material assistance from the Corinthians (1 Cor. 16:6, 11; 2 Cor. 1:16). This practice was derived from the ancient (unwritten) code of hospitality. In the present context, however, Paul is referring to more than provisions for travel. The Philippian church took it upon themselves to assist Paul financially (Phil. 1:5; 2:25; 4:14–19), which may be what Paul has in mind here. Harris plausibly conjectures that "the brothers from Macedonia" may have sent their gift through Timothy and Silas, who joined Paul in Corinth from Macedonia (Acts 18:5).[2] It was at this point, Luke tells us, that Paul was able to leave the leatherworker's stall and "devoted himself exclusively to preaching" (18:5).

I have kept myself from being a burden to you in any way . . . nobody in the regions of Achaia will stop this boasting of mine. A guiding principle of Paul's evangelistic work was not to accept support from the community in which he was actively preaching the gospel (1 Cor. 9:1–23). However, as noted above, Paul would accept assistance from other, established churches, as an expression of their "partnership in the gospel" (Phil. 1:5; cf. 4:10–19). The apostle affirms that this has been true in Corinth and supports this affirmation with a solemn vow: "as surely as the truth of Christ is in me" (11:10). Paul's rationale for this practice is articulated in various places throughout his letters, but especially here and in 1 Corinthians 9. First, and most important, Paul does not want to financially "burden" those he is currently evangelizing (11:9). Given the bleak economic reality of the first century (see the sidebar "Poverty in the Greco-Roman World" in the unit on 8:1–7), this measure ensured that Paul's presence in a locale would not create further hardship on an already hard-pressed community. Second, taking money from new converts might prove to be "a hindrance to the gospel of Christ" (1 Cor. 9:12 NET), in that motives might be suspect (2 Cor. 12:16–18; Acts 20:33–34), especially with the abundance of charlatans eager to prey on the gullible (2 Cor. 2:17). Third—and not often acknowledged—Paul obviously derives a deep sense of satisfaction and personal pride from supplying his own needs, which he is quite emphatic about, both here and in 1 Corinthians 9. In both passages Paul explicitly acknowledges that this practice is cause for "boasting," which he is very concerned to preserve. In 1 Corinthians 9:15 Paul says that he "would rather die" than allow anyone to deprive him of this boast and that his reward for preaching the gospel is precisely that he offers it "free of charge" (1 Cor. 9:18). "Boast" in this context denotes not active "bragging" but the basis for pride, or the deep sense of satisfaction Paul derives from not burdening others. Fourth, Paul is keen to distinguish himself from the intruders (and any others), who expect or acquiesce to receiving monetary support from the Corinthians (see the comments on 11:12–15). Fifth, Paul sees his sacrificial labor as a concrete demonstration of his love for those he is evangelizing (11:11; 12:15). Finally, although Paul understands that ministers of the gospel have a legitimate right to be supported by the communities they serve (1 Cor.

9:1–12; 2 Thess. 3:7–10), Paul's strategy allows him to model a work ethic that emphasizes supplying one's own necessities and helping others in need (2 Thess. 3:6–12; Acts 20:33–35; Eph. 4:28).

11:11 *Why? Because I do not love you? God knows I do!* Paul's rhetorical question exposes the Corinthians' interpretation of his refusal to accept support from them. To the Corinthians, this is tantamount to a rejection of their friendship; it is evidence of Paul's lack of affection for them. Paul's principled stand on not accepting money from a community he is currently evangelizing violates certain cultural conventions related to giving and receiving material support, and the Corinthians have taken offense. Paul is eager to correct their misinterpretation of his stance, and so he reaffirms his love for them and calls God as a witness of his truthfulness. Paul's concern to set the record straight on this matter is seen in his frequent references to his affection for the Corinthians throughout this letter: 1:14; 3:2; 6:6, 11–12; 7:3; 12:15. The cultural background to this issue is important enough to require specific elaboration in the "Additional Insights" section following this unit.

11:12 *in order to cut the ground from under those who want an opportunity to be considered equal with us.* Paul's determination to continue his practice of self-support has the added benefit, in terms of the situation in Corinth, that it undermines the intruding missionaries' desire that the Corinthians consider them "equal" to authentic gospel heralds, like Paul and his co-workers. Given the true identity of these intruders (11:13–15), Paul is especially keen that they be exposed, not elevated, in the eyes of the Corinthians. Paul does not define the content of their boast or how precisely his refusal of financial support discredits their claims, which has led to substantial speculation among commentators.[3] We can, however, reasonably conclude at least this much: it clearly distinguished him in character from the intruders in that it revealed his altruism, selflessness, and personal sacrifice, while eliminating any hint of avarice and greed. Paul's approach to his churches was that of a father laboring selflessly on behalf of his children (12:14–15; cf. 6:13; 1 Cor. 4:14–15; 1 Thess. 2:9–12).

11:13 *false apostles, deceitful workers, masquerading as apostles of Christ.* In 11:13–15 Paul finally lays all his cards on the table and reveals his full assessment of the intruders: they tout counterfeit credentials ("apostles"), engage in counterfeit activities ("deceitful workers"), and serve a counterfeit master ("masquerading" as servants of Christ while actually serving Satan; 11:14–15). We should not suppose that the opposition in Corinth knowingly infiltrated the Corinthian church as servants of Satan. Paul is describing the effect of their mission, not their intent. Yet the strength of Paul's invective and the gravity of these accusations indicate that more is involved than merely a territorial dispute.[4] Especially illuminating in this regard is 1 Corinthians

3:1–16. In this passage, the prospect of other apostolic emissaries ministering in Corinth is treated rather nonchalantly by Paul: "So then, no more boasting about human leaders! All things are yours, whether Paul or Apollos or Cephas or the world or life or death or the present or the future—all are yours" (3:21–22). What concerns Paul, however, is the quality of the work that is done: "I laid a foundation as a wise builder, and someone else is building on it. But each one should build with care. For no one can lay any foundation other than the one already laid, which is Jesus Christ. . . . Their work will be shown for what it is, because the Day will bring it to light" (1 Cor. 3:10–13). The work of these false apostles is already becoming evident, as enumerated in 2 Corinthians 12:20: "discord, jealousy, fits of rage, selfish ambition, slander, gossip, arrogance and disorder."

11:14–15 *Satan himself masquerades as an angel of light . . . Their end will be what their actions deserve.* Several Jewish works of this era depict Satan as one who can assume various forms to accomplish his evil intent,[5] but the closest parallel to this text is from the *Life of Adam and Eve*, where Satan transforms himself into "the brightness of Angels" to deceive Eve a second time (9.1). Paul's point is that as Satan deceives and tricks (2 Cor. 2:11; 4:4), so too do his servants. The verdict Paul pronounces on the false apostles corresponds with the principle of final judgment enunciated in 5:10: "For all of us must appear before the judgment seat of Christ, for each of us to be repaid for what we have done" (author's translation).

Theological Insights

Paul's invective in 2 Corinthians 10–13 reveals the presence of a new threat in Corinth, but it is a very old problem as far as God's people are concerned: false teachers who distort God's word and exploit God's people for their own selfish ends. Religious charlatans of this kind were a constant problem throughout Israel's history. The warnings against false prophets in Deuteronomy 13:1–4 and 18:21–22 foreshadow a long line of counterfeits who would lead God's people astray. Frequently they were motivated by pleasing the crowd (Jer. 28:8–9) or the current ruler (1 Kings 22:13–14). Greed, not truth, dictated the content of their oracles (Neh. 6:12–13; Jer. 6:13–14; Mic. 3:11), and their lives mirrored the base practices of the surrounding nations (Isa. 28:7; Jer. 23:10–11; Mic. 2:11). Their legacy continued into the New Testament era. Jesus warns against the presence of false prophets (Matt. 24:10–11), as do Peter (2 Pet. 2:1) and John (1 John 4:1). Similarly, Paul's Letters frequently warn against false teachers who are infiltrating the Christian assemblies (Gal. 1:6–9; 2 Thess. 2:1–2; Col. 2:8; 1 Tim. 6:3–5). False teachers and false prophets are a very real threat to the contemporary church as well. Christians always need to be prayerful, discerning, and firmly grounded in Scripture to guard against false teaching. In addition, we can ask some very simple questions of those purporting to be Christ's emissaries: Does their teaching conform to the gospel (2 Thess. 2:15; Gal. 1:8)? Is their teaching beneficial to the body of Christ (1 Cor. 14:3)? Or is their teaching financially motivated (1 Tim. 6:3–5)? A desire for financial gain is the most consistent characteristic of false teachers, both in Paul's day and in ours.

Teaching the Text

In this passage Paul assumes his readers are familiar with his earlier instructions in 1 Corinthians 9, where he lays out in fuller detail his thoughts on supporting Christian workers and his rationale for his own approach. It would be easy to read 2 Corinthians 11:7–15 as a mandate that all Christian workers should support themselves as "tentmakers" rather than accepting support from the community they are serving, but this would be to misread Paul. First Corinthians 9 is particularly illuminating on this point. In this chapter Paul spends most of his time defending his right to be supported, and in so doing he appeals to the example of the other apostles (9:5a), the example of Jesus's own brothers (9:5b), to the Old Testament (9:8–10), to current practice in the Jerusalem temple (9:13), and to the teaching of Jesus (9:14). Paul's practice, by his own admission, is somewhat idiosyncratic (9:6) but is undertaken as a precaution against any possible hindrance to the gospel (9:12). It is also important to note that as a church in a local community becomes established and grows, Paul expects that local believers will contribute materially to those laboring in teaching and leading, as Galatians 6:6 and 1 Timothy 5:17–18 make explicit.

Yet, while Paul does not intend his specific approach to be adopted universally as a standard policy for Christian workers, we would be wrong to ignore the two clear principles articulated by Paul that appear to be determinative of his practice as far as ministry finances are concerned: (1) to cause no hindrance to the gospel (1 Cor. 9:12) and (2) not to burden those to whom he was preaching (2 Cor. 11:7–9). The second tenet, not to be a burden, seems to be a specific application of the general principle, to cause no hindrance for the gospel. Laying aside personal rights for the sake of the cause of Christ is one indicator of Christian maturity and should be held up as a universally applicable principle of conduct for believers. It also follows that, in many contexts, refusing the support of the Christian community would actually hinder the gospel, in that the Christian workers would be obliged to labor at supporting themselves (and their dependents), rather than devoting themselves to full-time gospel ministry. In seeking to apply these principles today, Christian workers need to be guided by the Spirit, the full counsel of Scripture, and the larger Christian community in order to determine the wisest procedures for their particular setting.

Illustrating the Text

Some ministers follow Paul's example today.

Story: The pastor of a medium-sized, growing congregation in the Midwest has a full-time job as a mailman. He has worked out an agreement with the congregation that he will make sure Sunday services are planned and preached as long as the parishioners take care of everything else. He frequently tells them, "I'm no different from you. Nobody gets a free ride; everyone has to volunteer somewhere to make this work." The pastor was emulating Paul.

Fast-growing church-planting movements use tent-making leaders.

Informational: David Garrison, executive director of Global Gates and former vice president for global strategy for the International Mission Board, writes, "Church Planting Movements are driven by lay leaders." These lay leaders are typically bivocational and come from the harvest—that is, the people group being reached. In other words, if the people being reached are hearing impaired, so too are the lay leaders; if the people are former addicts, so are the lay leaders. If the world is to be reached with the gospel, bivocational lay leaders must become normative in every country, in every denomination.[6]

Additional Insights

Paul, Patronage, and the Corinthians

Patronage and benefaction were foundational to the social and economic system of the Greco-Roman world. In a society where the vast majority of property and wealth were possessed by a small minority of the populace, and where most people lived at or below the poverty level (see the sidebar "Poverty in the Greco-Roman World" in the unit on 8:1–7), the survival of the impoverished majority depended on the generosity of the wealthy elite. The patron-client system involved a mutually beneficial exchange of goods and services between people of unequal social and economic status. Upper-class patrons assisted lower-class clients materially, providing income, food, and so on, in exchange for support in the political sphere, honor in the public arena, and a great variety of other services. Some clients would simply accompany their patron to and from his daily activities as a means of enhancing his status. Both patrons and clients were ranked according to social position. To be the client of a Roman senator brought more honor and advantage than to be the client of a provincial magistrate. Similarly, a patron desired clients of higher social rank to enhance his or her status. A client might have several patrons, and a patron would have as many clients as he or she could reasonably support. Many patrons were themselves clients of someone more highly ranked on the social scale. The wealthy were also expected to bestow largesse on the cities, communities, and provinces where they lived by funding public works: theaters, libraries, civic structures, and the like. A patron's liberality to a community, civic group, or religious association is commonly called "benefaction."

The generosity of a patron always entailed an obligation on the part of the client, as Martial, a first-century satirist, observes: "Whoever gives much, wants much in return" (*Epig.* 5.59). Hence, the client became beholden to the patron, and the common depiction of clients in the literature of the period is that of groveling, flattering "yes men" at the beck and call of their patron. Publilius Syrus, a first-century BC writer of maxims, expresses the unfortunate reality of becoming a client: "To accept a benefaction is to sell one's freedom" (*Sent.* 61). Moreover, in the politics of patronage there was something of a social obligation to accept patronage if it was proffered. To refuse patronage of a social superior was to risk offending a potentially powerful individual in the community. Such an act might be construed as communicating that the patron was unworthy in the eyes of the client.

Based on Paul's assessment of the predicament he is in with the Corinthians, it would appear that his decision to support himself through plying his trade as a leatherworker rather than accepting the support of the Corinthians has offended some of the Corinthians and is being interpreted as a rejection of their friendship. When Paul asks, "Is it because I don't love you that I am lowering myself by working with my hands and not accepting your help?" (11:7–11, summarized), he divulges the Corinthians' perspective on his refusal of their assistance: it was a rejection of their friendship and affection.[1] Paul's willingness to accept occasional help from other churches but not from the community he is currently working in might be due to his concern to avoid any hint of a patron-client relationship that might hinder his freedom. It is possible that Paul perceives that the Corinthian offer of material assistance might have such patron-client strings attached, while the help that the distant Macedonians have offered entails no such obligation. In this scenario, it would be the members of the upper social strata who were offended at Paul's renunciation of material support.

It is true that Paul accepted hospitality from the Corinthians, in the form of both a place to stay and travel assistance (Rom. 16:23; 1 Cor. 16:6; 2 Cor. 1:16), but this was part of the normal conventions of hospitality that were universally accepted in antiquity. Even the supply of provisions for the next day's travel was considered proper etiquette for an honorable host.[2] It is possible that some of the Corinthians knew of Paul's relationship with Phoebe in nearby Cenchreae, whom he refers to as his "patron" in Romans 16:1–2 (ESV). If Phoebe's assistance was given to Paul while he was ministering in the environs of Corinth, this might be construed as a violation of Paul's policy. However, we do not know if Phoebe was merely his host, and so he is applying the term "patron" somewhat broadly, or if she provided him with assistance in travel, or if she sent help to him while he was working in another area.

Paul's determination to support himself through manual labor and not to accept help from the Corinthians obviously offended some in Corinth. Paul has taken a position that runs against the grain of social convention and the scruples of the elite, though he has done so for honorable reasons (see the comments on 11:8–10). In striving to live as an example of hard work, to model the sacrificial love of Christ, and to proclaim the gospel on his own terms, with no patron-client constraints, Paul has chosen a somewhat unconventional approach.[3] This may have bothered some, but it only underscores Paul's central commitment to the unhindered, undiluted proclamation of the gospel: "I do all things for the sake of the gospel" (1 Cor. 9:23, author's translation).

2 Corinthians 11:16–21a

Playing the Fool

Big Idea
With heavy sarcasm, Paul promises to out-boast the boasting intruders, since the Corinthians seem to be so taken with these charlatans.

Key Themes
- Boasting in the manner of the opponents is unseemly and not pleasing to the Lord.
- Although the Corinthians imagine themselves shrewd and discerning, their willingness to tolerate the abusive manner of the false apostles proves precisely the opposite.

Understanding the Text

The Text in Context

As Paul prepares (reluctantly) to engage in his most explicit campaign of comparison and self-elevation (11:22b–12:13), he pauses to offer one final rationale and remonstrance for such folly. He candidly admits that this is not the Lord speaking but a "fool" who must fight folly with folly in order to bring to their senses those who have been beguiled by a band of apostolic pretenders. These six verses serve as a preamble to the risky parading of credentials that follows, as Paul feels compelled to qualify this braggadocio as only begrudgingly given, and "worldly" (cf. 11:18) by any standard of Christian maturity.

Interpretive Insights

11:16–18 *I repeat: Let no one take me for a fool . . . I am not talking as the Lord would . . . boasting in the way the world does.* Paul echoes ("I repeat") the ironic plea of 11:1, to be granted the freedom of some foolish boasting ("Tolerate me just as you would a fool"), but in a sterner tone. He warns the Corinthians that he is utterly serious, while admitting that he is about to don the guise of a fool. Paul's acute discomfort at having to enumerate his credentials for the purpose of bolstering his standing and denigrating his rivals leads him to explicitly announce his wily intent, so that there is no misunderstanding. Further, he qualifies this entire maneuver as a fool's charade (11:16), not entirely in keeping with the Lord's example

(11:17), and utterly worldly (11:18). This serves to protect Paul's character while indicting the character of his rivals, who engage in such practices unapologetically.

11:19 *You gladly put up with fools since you are so wise!* The sarcasm so obvious in these words serves to focus attention on the glaring contradiction between the Corinthians' self-perception and their practice. The Corinthians pride themselves on their wisdom, and Paul has addressed their inflated corporate ego in this regard extensively in 1 Corinthians 1–4. Paul's evaluation is that "not many of you were wise by human standards" (1 Cor. 1:26), and he warns them not to deceive themselves about being "wise by the standards of this age" (3:18). In language and tone similar to 2 Corinthians 11:19, Paul ironically disparages the Corinthians' pretension to wisdom: "We are fools for Christ, but you are so wise in Christ!" (1 Cor. 4:10). The characterological defect of intellectual pride has left the Corinthians blind to the conceit of the intruders and vulnerable to their propaganda. Paul's acidic humor and mocking posture are probably intended to jolt them back to reality by forcing them to reconsider their evaluation of him, the intruders, and even themselves.

11:20 *you even put up with anyone who enslaves you or exploits you or takes advantage of you or puts on airs or slaps you in the face.* Paul provides important information about the intruders in this verse, even if exaggerated somewhat by his ire. The five operative verbs describe Paul's perception of the opposing missionaries, but the accusations focus not on their doctrine but on their demeanor. (1) To "enslave" probably indicates the domineering and bullying manner in which the opponents use their self-arrogated authority. (2) To "exploit"—literally, "devour"—denotes consuming greedily, and the context suggests financial exploitation (cf. Mark 12:40; Luke 15:30 ESV). (3) To "take advantage of" perhaps also denotes financial exploitation, but it may also suggest trickery in a more general sense (cf. 12:16–18). (4) To "put on airs" refers to the arrogant, self-exalting behavior of the opponents. (5) To "slap in the face"—not literally, as some take it, but metaphorically—is a vivid depiction of the abusive, heavy-handed tactics of the intruders.

It would appear that the opposing missionaries have adopted the method and strategies of certain religious and philosophical propagandists of the day, in particular the sophists. Dio Chrysostom describes a scene in nearby Isthmia where "crowds of wretched sophists [hang] around Poseidon's temple shouting, reviling, fighting with one another" (*Or.* 8.9). Philo refers to the sophists as "lovers of disputations" (*QG* 3.27) who "raise themselves up to heaven in pride and arrogance" (*Migr.* 172) and who are constantly "stirring up a quarrelsome confusion, which tends to the adulteration of the truth" (*Agr.* 159). In seeking to convince others of their point of view, Philo relates that they would "never cease struggling against them with every kind of weapon, till they compel them to succumb, or else utterly destroy them" (*Worse* 33). In fact, the intruders embody the antithesis to what Paul has taught and modeled before the Corinthians (1 Cor. 13; 2 Cor. 10:1; 12:15–16a).

11:21a *To my shame I admit that we were too weak for that!* Continuing the sarcastic tone, Paul ironically concedes that he and his team were too "weak" to exploit the Corinthians. As 10:10 made clear, Paul is aware that his opponents are accusing him of being "weak" (rendered "unimpressive" in 10:10), and he is using a verbal form of the same word group here. Hence, "weak" should probably be in quotation marks in this verse as well (cf. 10:1), since Paul seems to be intentionally alluding to this same denunciation. "Weakness" vocabulary will play an important role in 2 Corinthians 11–13, where it occurs thirteen times. Paul's ultimate strategy will be to concede weakness, while redefining it (12:10).

Teaching the Text

This passage serves as an important reminder that the church needs to always be on guard against leaders who are bullying and self-centered, rather than meek and Christ-centered. From Paul's description of these opponents, it may sound incredible that any group of Christians would follow their "leadership." Sadly, however, history is full of examples of Christian flocks who were fleeced and ultimately butchered by the very shepherds charged with their care. In teaching this passage, it might be profitable to emphasize the characteristics of the false teachers in question (boasting, exploitive, abusive), as they represent the antithesis of godly leadership.

1. *Boasting*. Arrogance is perhaps the most un-Christian quality that a leader can model, precisely because it is so un-Christlike. Paul's opponents were guilty of boasting (11:18) and "putting on airs" (11:20), both verbal and attitudinal arrogance. Christian leaders not only should reject this more crass expression of arrogance; they also need to be wary of more subtle ways of boasting: telling self-serving stories about oneself, reminding others of one's accomplishments or credentials, and so on.

2. *Exploitive*. Financial exploitation is another characteristic of the false apostles, and Paul is particularly keen to distinguish himself from them on this score (11:7–11) and to model financial integrity (8:18–21; 12:14–18).

3. *Abusive*. The leadership style of the intruders is bullying and coercive, and from Paul's description in 11:20 the Corinthians are not being shepherded but are being manhandled. Paul is not at all opposed to firm, decisive leadership, but when leadership becomes pushy and manipulative, there is good reason to ask whom the leaders are serving—Christ or themselves.

Illustrating the Text

Believers should be vigilant against those who would exploit the church.

Television: ***Grimm.*** In this show where many of the characters (the Wesen) can morph into animal-like personas, a "wolf" (Blutbad) is pastoring a church of "sheep." In the episode "The Good Shepherd," Reverend Calvin calls himself a reformed Blutbad, but as the detectives investigate the apparent theft of church funds by the treasurer, it becomes clear that this wolf in sheep's clothing was not reformed at all but was duping the church in order to steal from them and lay the blame on one of their members.[1] Jesus's warning to be on guard for wolves in sheep's clothing extends to those in ministry who dress up their message in familiar words but really intend to exploit or abuse God's sheep. A true shepherd should emulate the good Shepherd.

Healthy skepticism is wise in considering doomsday prophets.

Story: The late Harold Camping, of Family Radio, convinced thousands of followers that "Jesus would return on May 21, 2011, to usher in the end of the world." Three days after that failed to occur, Camping reversed his prophesy, saying it must be October 21. Many listeners were crestfallen, especially those who took money out of their college or retirement accounts to get the word out. Camping would later apologize for his "incorrect and sinful" predictions. What makes people like Camping dangerous is the crowd of people putting their faith and trust in a false prophet.[2]

The Scriptures warn against the dangers of false prophets.

Scripture: John warns repeatedly in his epistles to beware of false prophets: "Do not believe every spirit, but test the spirits to see whether they are from God" (1 John 4:1). Similarly, the apostle Paul instructs the Thessalonians to test prophecies, hold on to the good, and reject every form of evil (1 Thess. 5:19–22).

2 Corinthians 11:21b–29

Apostolic Credentials

Big Idea
Through his suffering for the sake of the gospel, Paul proves his character, his love for the Corinthians, and his superiority to his opponents.

Key Themes
- Paul's Jewish credentials are equal to those of his rivals.
- Paul's service to Christ far exceeds that of his rivals.
- Paul's commitment to the gospel has entailed enduring mortal dangers, grueling labor, and much psychological anguish.

Understanding the Text

The Text in Context

Paul announced his intent to engage in a little foolishness in 11:1, which he immediately justified in 11:2–4 through the image of a betrayed betrothal: the Corinthians have been seduced by a rogue, and Paul, like a protective father, is justly concerned. He began his self-defense/comparison with the "super-apostles" in reference to his oratory (11:5–6) and then took up his philosophy of self-support (11:7–15), again comparing himself directly to his opponents and proving to be more honorable. Paul has been building momentum to his most audacious series of boasts, where he details his hardships (11:21b–29), his weakness (11:30–33), and his visionary experiences (12:1–10). In the present passage, focusing on his hardships, Paul first establishes that he is equal to his opponents in terms of lineage (11:22), and then he goes on to demonstrate that he is superior to them in his service to Christ because of the numerous and extreme adversities he has endured (11:23–29). Beginning with a general statement that his hardships outnumber those of his opponents (11:23), Paul then specifically enumerates (1) his frequent near-death experiences (11:24–25), (2) his many dangers from travel (11:26), (3) his grueling manual labor (11:27), and (4) his extreme pastoral anxiety (11:28–29).

Interpretive Insights

11:21b *I am speaking as a fool.* As an orientation to what follows, Paul reiterates again (cf. 11:16–17, 23; 12:1, 11) that such boasting is beneath his dignity and "foolish" (see the comments on 11:16–18). The boasting of his rivals has forced him to do something that runs counter to every fiber of his being, but the apostle recognizes that he needs to set the record straight. Paul's continued insistence that this self-adulation is actually knavish serves to raise him above his opponents while indicting their character.

11:22 *Are they Hebrews? . . . Israelites? . . . Abraham's descendants? So am I.* This verse confirms that Paul's opponents are Jewish, probably of Palestinian origin. The intruders must have placed heavy emphasis on their Jewish pedigree or their connections to Jerusalem and the Jewish heartland, perhaps deliberately drawing attention to Paul's Diaspora roots (Acts 21:39; 22:3). Paul's primary point is clear: his Jewish credentials are as impeccable as his opponents'. It seems probable that, in this context, "Hebrew," "Israelite," and "seed of Abraham" are roughly synonymous, being piled up for rhetorical effect. Some, however, argue for subtle distinctions between each (see table 1).

11:23 *Are they servants of Christ? . . . I am more.* With his religious heritage and ethnic lineage established (11:22), Paul now takes up a more important issue, which will occupy the remainder of this section: his labor on behalf of Christ. The opponents are claiming that they are "servants of Christ," which Paul has labeled a "masquerade" (11:13–14). As proof of his character

Table 1. "Hebrews," "Israelites," "Abraham's Descendants"

	Hebrew	**Israelite**	**Abraham's Descendant**
Matera	Racial purity, speaking Hebrew (Aramaic)	Member of God's chosen people	Partaker of the covenant made with Abraham
Barrett	Pure-blooded Jew	Socially and religiously Jewish	Jewish, from a theological point of view
Harris	Linguistically and culturally Jewish	Citizen of the commonwealth of Israel	Heir of God's promises to Abraham
Lambrecht	Racially Jewish	Religiously Jewish	A theological affirmation, heir of the promises
Furnish	Ethnic descent, of Hebrew stock	Partaker of Israel's heritage and traditions	Identical to "Israelite"
Thrall	Fully Jewish, in birth and ancestry	Member of God's holy people	Heir of the promise to Abraham

Note: See Matera, *2 Corinthians*, 259–70; Barrett, *Second Epistle*, 293–95; Harris, *Second Epistle*, 794–96; Lambrecht, *2 Corinthians*, 190; Furnish, *2 Corinthians*, 514–15; Thrall, *2 Corinthians*, 2:723–30.

Forty Lashes Minus One

The rabbis of the Mishnaic period (AD 10–220) offered detailed commentary on the Deuteronomic prescription of flogging, employing the same expression as Paul in 2 Corinthians 11:24, "forty stripes less one" (*m. Makkot* 3:10). The Mishnah describes which infractions merit flogging, how to determine the precise number of lashes, and also the manner in which the flogging should be carried out:

> How do they flog him? One ties his two hands on either side of a pillar, and the minister of the community grabs his clothing—if it is torn, it is torn, and if it is ripped to pieces, it is ripped to pieces—until he bares his chest. A stone is set down behind him, on which the minister of the community stands. And a strap of cowhide is in his hand, doubled and redoubled, with two straps that rise and fall [fastened] to it. . . . And he who hits him hits with one hand, with all his might. (*m. Makkot* 3:12–13)

and superior service, Paul recounts a sampling of his hardships in 11:24–29, introducing this enumeration in general terms here, under the headings of work, prison, flogging, and exposure to death. To each of these is attached an adverbial qualifier indicating abundance. Hardship catalogs like this were used by Stoics to demonstrate their honor and fortitude (see the sidebar "Paul and the Stoics Compared" in the unit on 6:1–13) and would have been familiar to the Corinthians.

11:24-25 *forty lashes minus one . . . beaten with rods . . . pelted with stones . . . shipwrecked.* Paul begins by relating near-death experiences, many of which can be correlated with material in the book of Acts. "Forty lashes minus one" refers to the punishment mandated by Deuteronomy 25:2–3 and is evidence of Paul's evangelistic work within the jurisdiction of the synagogue. To be "beaten with rods," on the other hand, was a characteristically Roman method of punishing a malefactor, as Paul and Silas experienced in Philippi (Acts 16:22–23). Stoning was commonly an act of mob violence, as rocks were immediately available if the crowd became suddenly inflamed (Acts 14:19; cf. John 8:59; 10:31; Acts 7:57–58). Acts records only one shipwreck involving Paul, which occurred after this letter was written; this underscores the selective nature of Luke's accounts. Yet Paul made numerous voyages by sea prior to writing this letter, and his reference to three shipwrecks is not at all implausible. Travel by sea was notoriously dangerous, as the literary and inscriptional remains amply attest.[1] Lucian, for example, speaks of "crowds" of mariners in the temples telling of "waves, tempests, headlands, strandings, masts carried away, rudders broken," and the like (*Merc. cond.* 1). So commonplace were stories of maritime peril that Plutarch remarks, "As for me, I would be amazed to see a skipper live to old age."[2]

11:26 *I have been constantly on the move. I have been in danger.* From life-threatening incidents (11:25), Paul moves to the more routine harrowing experiences of an itinerant evangelist, many of which concern the hazards of travel in antiquity. "Constantly on the move" serves as a kind of heading introducing this topic, and the underlying Greek verb emphasizes journeying by foot, which would have constituted most of Paul's travels. This should bring to mind heat, dust, sweat, mud, inclement weather, and exhaustion. Various groupings for this list have been proposed,[3] but it might be simplest to classify them as dangers from people ("bandits," "fellow Jews," "Gentiles," "false believers") and dangers from places ("rivers," "city," "country," "sea"). Banditry was a perennial problem in antiquity, which is why Epictetus, a first-century philosopher, recommends always traveling in groups (*Diatr.* 4.1.191). Each locale mentioned by Paul ("city," "country") offered its own set of risks, particularly as accommodation at inns was sought only as a last resort. First-century guesthouses were known for bedbugs, brawling, rough characters, and swindling proprietors. Josephus (*Ant.* 12.276) includes the innkeeper in his list of dishonorable trades (along with prostitutes and slaves) because of their reputation for scamming patrons. Acts records numerous difficulties connected with Paul's work in the cities he evangelized, including beatings (14:19–23), imprisonment (16:16–24), and mob violence (17:5–6). Although some of these events occurred after the writing of 2 Corinthians, they are illustrative of the kind of incidents Paul has in mind. Acts also records a variety of harassment from fellow Jews (Acts 13:50; 14:1–7), which are echoed in Paul's Letters (1 Thess. 2:14–16; Phil. 3:18). We have no specific information on "false believers" who represented a personal, physical threat to Paul (cf. Gal. 2:4), as their inclusion on this list implies, though there is no reason to doubt Paul's depiction.

11:27 *I have labored and toiled . . . gone without sleep.* As in 11:26, the first phrase ("labored and toiled") serves as a heading for what follows. Paul uses this expression on two other occasions, where it indisputably refers to his manual labor, working "night and day" not to burden those he is evangelizing (1 Thess. 2:9; 2 Thess. 3:8). In light of this, it is probable that the expression means the same thing here. On this reading, this verse describes not Paul's labor in ministry generally but the reality of a bivocational evangelist who works with his own hands to supply his needs. In fact, each of the phrases that follow can be quite plausibly connected to the conditions typically associated with peasant artisans, manual laborers, and shopkeepers: poorly clad, laboring till the wee hours of the morning to make ends meet, frequently lacking the basic necessities of food and comfortable accommodation.

11:28–29 *Besides everything else, I face daily the pressure of my concern for all the churches.* Having described the external and visible side of his hardships in 11:23–27, Paul now focuses on the internal and unseen dimension of his suffering: his pastoral concern—even anxiety—for the spiritual welfare of his churches. Paul has already told the Corinthians that they have such a place in his heart that "we would live or die with you" (7:3; cf. 3:2), and the present verses provide commentary on that earlier expression of love. Paul affirms his complete sympathetic affection, so that he feels their "weakness" and "burns" over their sin. He describes this inner pressure as "daily" and extending to "all" his churches. Paul is like a parent who longs to see his children thrive, rejoicing in their triumphs and weeping in their tragedy; Paul's pastoral, fatherly heart is bound to his spiritual children.

Equally striking is how discordant this perspective would appear to Paul's philosophical contemporaries, particularly Stoics and Cynics, who taught that the whole point of adversity was to leave the noble sage impervious to sorrow, fear, and distress. According to Dio Chrysostom, Diogenes (whose legendary home was in Corinth) represented the ideal all should emulate: "Disclosing no weakness, even though he must endure the lash ... he holds his hardships as mere trifles" (*Or.* 8.15–16). Epictetus, another Stoic contemporary of Paul, puts it this way: "Men, if you heed me, wherever you may be, whatever you may be doing, you will feel no pain, no anger, no compulsion, no hindrance, but will pass your lives in tranquility" (*Diatr.* 4.1.91). While Paul's hardship catalogs have much in common with the Stoics, the underlying value system is quite different (see the sidebars "Hardship Catalogs" in the unit on 4:7–15 and "Paul and the Stoics Compared" in the unit on 6:1–13). Paul's transparency and vulnerability reveal an emotionally engaged pastor, not an aloof, unmoved Stoic.

Theological Insights

Although God's call on a person's life does not necessarily entail danger, it certainly meant that for Paul, and this placed him in strong continuity with his Old Testament predecessors. Even though Abraham was ultimately blessed by God, his call involved leaving his home and embarking on a long and hazardous journey, with many twists and turns. Moses, Joshua, the judges, David, and other leaders of Israel often experienced severe hardships and life-threatening ordeals as a result of following God's call on their lives. The prophets in particular faced extremely dangerous situations as they confronted idolatry, obstinacy, and treachery among the people. Jeremiah was mocked (Jer. 26:1–6; 36:20–26), beaten (20:2), imprisoned (37:16), thrown in a pit and left to die (38:1–13), and starved (52:6), and finally he died in exile in Egypt (43:1–7). Paul's hardship catalog in 2 Corinthians 11:22–29 represents his curriculum vitae to the church in Corinth, but it does not enumerate accomplishments. Rather, it demonstrates Paul's cruciform way of life and his commitment to follow God's call no matter the cost.

Teaching the Text

1. *Measuring success.* What does success look like? How does one measure effectiveness in ministry? Paul's opponents, together with their sympathizers in Corinth, have measured the apostle by their own standards and found him wanting. They are unimpressed with his preaching (10:10; 11:5), they ridicule his principled stand on supporting himself through manual labor (11:7–11), and they regard him as their "inferior" (11:5; 12:11). In response, Paul does not recount how many people he has led to Christ, or how many churches he has established, or how many countries he has preached in. Rather, he recounts how much he has suffered for Christ. Hardship and suffering are not normally viewed as decisive evidence that one is faithfully fulfilling Christ's calling on their life, but Paul's perspective is different, and his argument provides an opportunity for the contemporary teacher to reflect seriously on how we measure success and how suffering factors into this assessment. In Paul's view, his credibility as a gospel herald is authenticated not by the number of his converts but by the number of his hardships. To be sure, this is not the whole of his thoughts on this matter, but we can say this much with certainty: Paul does not regard the adversity he has encountered as evidence that God is not with him or that his ministry is not aligned with God's will and plan. In fact, judging from this passage, Paul seems to view his hardships as badges of honor demonstrating his faithfulness. This sentiment is most boldly expressed in Galatians 6:17: "So, let no one cause me trouble, for I bear on my body the wounds of Jesus" (author's translation).

2. *The emotional cost of leadership.* A second issue that would be valuable for the contemporary teacher to emphasize comes to the foreground in 11:28–29: investing in others involves emotional toil, as the discipler necessarily feels the pain of the sin and the distress of missteps taken by the one being discipled. For Paul, fulfilling Christ's call on his life means not only external physical hardship; it also entails internal psychological anguish. In 11:28–29 Paul speaks of "pressure," "concern," "weakness," and "burning," and to this list we could add many other terms: tears (2 Cor. 2:4), anger (Gal. 3:1), disappointment (1 Cor. 11:17), and so on. Again, this is not the complete story—certainly Paul has experienced joy as well (2 Cor. 7:4; Phil. 4:4)—but it serves as an important reminder that a healthy, effective ministry will involve both joys and heartbreaks.

3. *Paul's call to suffer.* Finally, it might be worthwhile to place Paul's hardship catalogs in the context of Paul's conversion narrative, as told by Luke in Acts 9:1–31. Saul (Paul) has made a name for himself as a violent persecutor of Christians, so much so that when Ananias is told by the Lord to go to Saul and restore his vision, Ananias objects out of fear for his own safety (9:11–14). God's response to Ananias is both ominous and sobering. The Lord dismisses

Ananias's objection with a firm "Go!" and then tells him that Saul is the Lord's chosen instrument to proclaim his name among Jews, gentiles, and the kings of the gentiles (9:15). The Lord concludes by casting this foreboding destiny over the former persecutor of Christians: "I will show him how much he must suffer for my name" (9:16). One senses that this destiny is connected to Paul's violence, as a just recompense. Its fulfillment is amply attested throughout Paul's Letters, and by his hardship catalogs in particular.

Illustrating the Text

Reformation pastors chose persecution rather than compromise.

Church History: Bishops Hugh Latimer and Nicholas Ridley were sixteenth-century preachers and teachers in England. When Mary I became queen, one of her first actions was to bring England back to the Roman Catholic Church. She had Latimer and Ridley arrested and held at the Tower of London. When the men were examined by the Catholic authorities, Ridley said that he could not honor the pope since the pope was seeking his own glory and not the glory of God. Neither of the men could accept the Catholic Mass as a sacrifice of Christ. Latimer told the commissioners that Christ made one sacrifice. The officials ordered their execution. The men were tied back to back at the stake. As flames arose, Latimer said to the bishop, "Be of good comfort, Mr. Ridley, and play the man! We shall this day light such a candle by God's grace, in England, as I trust shall never be put out."[4] These men, and many other Reformers, were committed to follow God's call, no matter what the cost.

Infectious joy can see us through the hardships of a life lived for God.

Church History: Dietrich Bonhoeffer, the German theologian and pastor, was one of the limited number of Christian Germans who vocally opposed Hitler and his push to establish world dominance. Bonhoeffer played a vital role in providing intelligence to the coup leaders attempting Hitler's assassination. Bonhoeffer was arrested and eventually taken to Flossenbürg concentration camp, where he would be hanged. One of the English officers with Bonhoeffer testified that he had never met a man who was so full of joy and expressed his gratitude for the most seemingly insignificant blessings. His last words were a message to George Bell of England: "This is the end, for me the beginning of life."[5]

2 Corinthians 11:30–33

Boasting in Weakness

Big Idea
The inglorious spectacle of Paul's flight from Damascus provides a counterbalance to his previous boasts of fortitude and illustrates the principle of apostolic weakness.

Key Theme
- Hardships that reveal Paul's weakness and his need for God's power are more significant to Paul than hardships that reveal his fortitude and endurance.

Understanding the Text

The Text in Context

Second Corinthians 11:30–33 constitutes an important bridge section in the "Fool's Speech" (11:1–12:13), as Paul transitions from boasting in his hardships (11:21b–29) to boasting in his weakness (12:1–10). In 11:29 Paul mentioned feeling "weak" when one of his brothers or sisters was led into sin, which provides a natural segue to the more crucial topic of weakness in Christ, which will be fully developed in 12:1–10. This present passage provides an ironic climax to the hardship catalog that precedes it, while also introducing the theme of argument that follows in 12:1–10, weakness as strength.

Historical and Cultural Background

The incident described in this passage is recounted by Luke in Acts 9:23–25 and is significant for reconstructing a chronology of Paul's early ministry, as King Aretas IV (2 Cor. 11:32) died in AD 40. This establishes the latest possible date for Paul's flight from Damascus.[1] The Nabatean Kingdom arose from various nomadic groups in the deserts of Arabia and at the time of Paul's conversion may have controlled Damascus (see the comments on 11:32). After his conversion on the road to Damascus, Paul began vigorously preaching Jesus in the synagogues of Damascus, "proving that Jesus is the Messiah" (Acts 9:22). According to Acts 9:23, it was "after many days" that the Jews in Damascus plotted to kill Paul. This important temporal marker probably suggests an interlude, which Galatians 1:17 tells us involved an unspecified time in Arabia,[2] after which Paul returned to Damascus. The only significant difference between the account in Acts and the account by Paul here is that Luke tells us that the Jews in Damascus were behind the plot that forced Paul's clandestine escape, while Paul mentions only the involvement of the ethnarch (NIV: "governor," 2 Cor. 11:32) of King Aretas. As the arrest and execution of Jesus involved a collusion between Jewish and Roman authorities, it would appear that the Jews of Damascus enlisted the help of the ethnarch, who may have already been concerned about reports of Paul's activities in the Nabatean communities of Arabia. This reconstruction renders it unlikely that Paul's time in Arabia was dedicated to meditation and reflection, as is popularly assumed. It seems to have been a period of active ministry, which roused the ire of King Aretas IV, who then tried to arrest Paul. Both Acts 9:26 and Galatians 1:18 have Paul leaving Damascus for Jerusalem.

Interpretive Insights

11:30 *If I must boast, I will boast of the things that show my weakness.* Verses 30–33 function as the ironic climax of the hardship catalog that began in verse 23. Once again forswearing boasting (in the sense of carnal gloating), Paul turns the traditional hardship catalog upside down by "boasting" in his inglorious flight from Damascus. Not unlike today, fleeing danger was considered the mark of cowardice by the ancients. Heracles/Hercules figured prominently in popular folklore as the model of bravery in the face of danger and hardship. Philosophers held up Socrates as the ideal, who refused the chance to escape certain death when it was offered. According to Philo (*Flight* 3–5), Paul's Jewish contemporary in Alexandria, there were only three possible reasons for flight: hatred, fear, or shame.[3] Writing from Rome, Horace defines the true sage as one whom "neither poverty, nor death, nor chains can frighten" (*Sat.* 2.7.83–85). Paul, on the other hand, interprets his suffering and weakness christologically, as the revelation of God's power, an idea he hints at here and explains more completely in the following chapters (cf. 12:10; 13:3–4).

11:31 *The God and Father of the Lord Jesus . . . knows that I am not lying.* Paul's solemn assurance of truthfulness at this juncture seems slightly out of place and has been interpreted in two different ways. Some believe that it signals the ironic intent of what follows: the story of Paul's flight from Damascus is offered as an intentional, tongue-in-cheek affront to the Corinthian value system.[4] However, the oath formula "I am not lying" is used by Paul on three other occasions (Rom. 9:1; Gal. 1:20; 1 Tim. 2:7), where it communicates a sober asseveration, not parody. Others interpret it as signaling the gravity of what follows. Barrett captures the intent by paraphrasing, "Do you doubt

> ### Strength and Weakness: A Corinthian Perspective
>
> "For God has appointed strength over weakness," wrote Dio Chrysostom (*Or.* 3.62). This perspective, of course, makes perfect sense and would have been accepted without question in Corinth, a city whose culture, history, and economy were bound up with athleticism and the celebration of strength over weakness. Since Corinth was the proud host of the Isthmian Games, a Panhellenic athletic competition, the figure of the victorious athlete stood at the center of Corinth's civic pride. Statues of mighty victors crowned with a pine or celery wreath graced many of the temples in Corinth; mosaics of sprinters, boxers, and wrestlers adorned the homes of the wealthy; city coinage displayed wreaths and other athletic achievements. Unlike in other cities, the highest civic office and crowning achievement of one's political career in Corinth was not election to the duumvirate (the chief magistrates of a city) but selection as the *agōnothetēs*, the president of the games. The Corinthians worshiped the goddess Victoria (Victory) in her sanctuary in Corinth and depended on the biennial influx of festival tourism to enrich their treasuries and expand their city's acclaim. Heracles too was venerated in Corinth, and his mythology contributed significantly to the cultural-ideological landscape of the region. Five of his famous labors were performed in the Peloponnese. He was considered the epitome of courage, ingenuity, and brute strength. Paul's strategy of boasting in weakness and his claim that weakness is strength (12:10) are more than mere rhetorical bravado; they are sharply and polemically countercultural. Paul's mission is to invert the Corinthians' superficial value system and to help them finally understand that "the foolishness of God is wiser than human wisdom, and the weakness of God is stronger than human strength" (1 Cor. 1:25).

either the depth of the humiliation I have experienced or my willingness to accept it?"[5]

11:32 *the governor under King Aretas had the city of the Damascenes guarded in order to arrest me.* As suggested above (see "Historical and Cultural Background"), it is possible that Paul's evangelistic work in the Nabatean communities of Arabia (Gal. 1:17) attracted the attention of Aretas IV, who was happy to assist the synagogue leaders in Damascus in their attempt to detain Paul. According to Acts 9:23, the Jews in Damascus were planning to kill Paul. The NIV's "governor" could be more literally rendered, "ethnarch." If Damascus was indeed under Nabatean rule at the time of Paul's conversion, "governor" may be the best English equivalent for the individual appointed by Aretas to maintain order in the city. On the other hand, the Greek word more commonly refers to the head of an ethnic community, and if Damascus was not directly controlled by Aretas at this time, the "ethnarch" would refer to the leader of the Nabatean community in Damascus appointed by Aretas.

11:33 *I was lowered in a basket from a window in the wall and slipped through his hands.* Paul emphasizes the inglorious manner of the escape, rather than its daring. Some commentators,[6] following Judge,[7] understand

Paul to be intentionally parodying a Roman military honor, in which the first officer over the wall of a besieged city is awarded the *corona muralis*, "wall crown." On this reading, Paul would be wryly portraying his escape as the antithesis of strength and bravery by intentionally contrasting it with this military achievement. As clever as this suggestion is, there is little in the context to suggest that this was Paul's intent, or that the Corinthians would have understood him this way.[8] This interpretation is correct to recognize, however, that Paul's climax to this hardship catalog is not a great feat of bravery but an illustration of his weakness and need for God's rescue.

Teaching the Text

"Let the one who boasts boast in the Lord." This sober dictum of Jeremiah 9:24 is cited by Paul in both his letters to the Corinthians (1 Cor. 1:31; 2 Cor. 10:17) and expresses the theological principle undergirding this passage and the entirety of the "Fool's Speech" (11:1–12:13). Paul knows that there is "nothing to be gained" in boasting (12:1), because even our most storied achievements are rubbish before a holy, righteous, omnipotent God (Phil. 3:4–11). Paul understands that it is Christ who enables him to overcome adversity (2 Cor. 12:9; Phil. 4:13), so he counterbalances the catalog of adversities detailed in 2 Corinthians 11:21–29 with the ignominious spectacle of his escape from Damascus. In essence, rather than citing Jeremiah 9:24 again, he illustrates the principle with a scene from his own missionary experience. In teaching and applying this text, it would be appropriate to emphasize not only that we are needy and weak, and that God is our rescuer, but also the value of imitating Paul by being willing to share stories of our own weakness in order to illustrate God's power. Through this self-effacing manner of ascribing greatness to God we effectively crack the clay jar of our human frailty and feeble pride so that the "surpassing power" can be fully revealed (2 Cor. 4:7).

Illustrating the Text

A narrow escape can become a lasting testimony.

History: Before the Thirteenth Amendment, many slaves went to extreme lengths to secure their freedom. Henry "Box" Brown wedged himself into a crate with a few biscuits and water to hold him for the twenty-seven-hour trip by wagon and ship to freedom in Philadelphia. Box Brown would become a magician, and one of his acts was to restuff himself into the original crate that earned his freedom.[9] Although Paul did not reenact his escape from Damascus, he too made use of this event as part of his ongoing career. Paul recognized that we are all in need of God's rescue, to God's glory.

We are more than what we do.

Applying the Text: It is a common modern fantasy that if we can get to the "right" place in life, we will be satisfied. We work overtime to pursue an elusive promotion, we build networks designed to help us get ahead, and we pack our calendars with activities—much of this effort is focused on making our lives better "someday." But achievement isn't the road to satisfaction, and we shouldn't mortgage our lives and sacrifice our souls in its pursuit. Paul seems to break out of this mold by exploiting his weakness as his badge of honor. As pastor M. Craig Barnes says in his book *Yearning*, "In truth, doing does not determine being; rather being determines doing. It is only after we have a firm understanding of who we are that we know what to do with life."[10]

2 Corinthians 12:1–10

Weakness as Strength

Big Idea
Hardship, suffering, and weakness convey God's grace and are the means by which God's power is most vividly displayed.

Key Themes
- Although ecstatic spiritual experiences are divinely intended means of grace, they are no substitute for character, faithfulness, and daily obedience.
- Paul's painful physical infirmity (his "thorn in the flesh") and his daily hardships in ministry have been God's tools for cultivating humility in Paul and for keeping his apostle dependent on divine strength.
- God answers our prayer in accordance with his will and our good, but that answer is not always an affirmative response to our request.
- God's strength is more perfectly manifest in human weakness, rather than strength, triumph, and glory, because only then is there no question as to who is responsible for the results.

Understanding the Text

The Text in Context

In 12:1–10 Paul continues his defense against the character assault of his rivals. In the previous section, 11:30–33, Paul climaxes his hardship catalog by "boasting" of his weakness, illustrated by his ignominious flight from Damascus. Boasting in weakness is held up by Paul as the antidote to the kind of foolish boasting his rivals are doing (11:30), which the apostle, to his own embarrassment (11:18, 21), has been compelled to mimic. Paul remains committed to boasting in weakness, and now provides another example: a painful infirmity that resulted from a remarkable rapture to "the third heaven" (12:2). The ironic connection between 11:30–33 and 12:1–10 is crisply articulated by Harris: "First, an embarrassing descent to escape the hands of men, then an exhilarating ascent into the presence of God."[1] The present section, then, functions to bolster Paul's credibility before the Corinthians—particularly those deceived by the intruders—by relating a divinely granted mystical experience of profound magnitude. Yet, more important, it also functions as a critique of Paul's opponents and their value system, which despises human frailty as incompatible with God's purpose and plan.

Interpretive Insights

12:1 *I must go on boasting. Although there is nothing to be gained.* Boasting in this manner runs contrary to Paul's character and sense of decorum (cf. 11:1, 17, 23), but he feels compelled to address one more matter, his revelatory experiences. This may have been prompted by Paul's opponents having boasted in their own ecstatic experiences and denigrated Paul for his comparative lack. In Paul's view, character is more important than flashy spiritual experience, as he has already explained: "If I speak with tongues of men or of angels . . . If I have the gift of prophecy . . . if I have a faith that can move mountains, but do not have love, I am nothing" (1 Cor. 13:1–2). In his letter to the Colossians Paul openly mocks as arrogant and unspiritual the person who "goes into great detail about [alleged visions] they have seen" (Col. 2:17–18). The extreme reluctance with which Paul engages in this "madness" (2 Cor. 11:23; cf. ESV, NLT, NRSV) serves to indict the character of those who participate in such practices lightly, as well as those who admire them.

visions and revelations from the Lord. As the book of Acts reveals, Paul was the recipient of numerous revelatory experiences (Acts 9:3–19; 16:9–10; 18:8–11; 22:17–22; 23:11; 27:21–24), although Paul himself never recounts any of these in his letters. Even his momentous encounter with the risen Jesus on the Damascus road is only alluded to (1 Cor. 9:1; 2 Cor. 4:6), never explicitly discussed in his writings. Some have argued that the plural, "visions and revelations," indicates that Paul may have intended to relate several experiences but reconsidered after recounting this particularly significant event. Alternatively, "visions and revelations" may simply denote a class or category of experiences Paul wishes to address.[2] Although a "vision" (*optasia*) and a "revelation" (*apokalypsis*) are technically distinguishable, it seems preferable to see the expression as a hendiadys, in which two terms are used to express one idea: divinely granted ecstatic experiences.[3]

12:2-4 *I know a man in Christ.* In recounting this remarkable rapture to the heavenly realm, Paul attributes it to "a man in Christ" (= a believer), abruptly speaking in the third person of an experience he later tells us was his own (12:7). A variety of explanations have been proposed for this unusual locution. Some regard this as merely the literary convention of Jewish apocalypses of this era, which regularly attribute their revelation and heavenly ascent to someone else, usually a venerated figure from Israel's past (e.g., Adam, Enoch, Baruch, Moses).[4] Others conjecture that the grandeur of the vision and the magnificence of the experience affected Paul so profoundly that he could not bring himself, "the least of the apostles" (1 Cor. 15:9), "the foremost of sinners" (1 Tim. 1:15 RSV), to speak of it in the first person.[5] Matera argues that Paul's use of the third person is indicative of "the very nature of the vision, where Paul experienced a certain distance from himself."[6] Finally, and not exclusive of any of these, it is often observed that speaking in the third person deflects attention away from Paul himself, lest the apostle appear to violate his previous renunciation of boasting (11:30).[7] The intentionally generic "man in Christ" focuses attention on Christ as the crucial figure, not on the merits or piety of the individual.

who fourteen years ago was caught up to the third heaven. If 2 Corinthians was written around AD 55, then "fourteen years ago" would place this event during Paul's time in Cilicia (Tarsus; Gal. 1:21; Acts 9:30) or in Antioch (Acts 11:25–26). It does not correlate with Paul's Damascus road encounter with Christ or any other visionary experience recorded in Acts. Ascending into the heavenly realms was characteristic of Jewish apocalypses, where the visionary is given insight into the workings of the cosmos and God's plan for Israel. In this literature the number of heavens ranges from one to ten, with seven being the most common.[8] The Greek verb behind the NIV's "caught up" usually denotes a sudden, forcible action; the passive construction implies God was the agent performing the action (cf. 1 Thess. 4:17). The overall impression is that this incident was unexpected and traumatic from Paul's perspective, and entirely God's initiative.

Whether it was in the body or out of the body I do not know—God knows. Twice Paul asserts that he does not know the precise mode of this rapture, and twice Paul assures his reader that God does know. He is certain that he was transported to the heavenly realm, but less certain if both the physical and immaterial components of his personhood participated, or if "he" (Paul identifies himself with his immaterial component) was temporarily separated from his body. Why he repeats this qualification is unclear, but we can conclude that the experience was so overwhelmingly real to Paul that he could not discern the precise nature of this altered state of being; his normal bodily senses seemed, for all he could tell, to be operative.

And I know that this man . . . was caught up to paradise. Paul is not describing a two-staged rapture, first to the third heaven (12:2) and then to paradise (12:3–4). Rather, we have two descriptions of the same event. Paul was transported to the third (and highest) heaven, which he alternately refers to as "paradise" (cf. Luke 23:43; Rev. 2:7). The closest parallel comes from the roughly contemporary Jewish pseudepigraphal work the *Apocalypse of Moses*, where the archangel Michael instructs other angels regarding Adam, "Take him up into Paradise, to the third heaven" (37.5).

and heard inexpressible things, things that no one is permitted to tell. Paul gives no indication of what he saw, be it the risen Jesus, the throne of God, or angelic hosts. Instead, he focuses on what he heard: unutterable utterances (retaining the Greek wordplay). The sense of "inexpressible" is probably "too wonderful" or "too profound," as opposed to "impermissible," which is communicated in the clause that follows. Particularly striking is that Paul returns from his heavenly ascent with absolutely nothing to reveal. This is quite at odds with the numerous Jewish ascent texts from this era, where the seer returns with specific information gained from the apocalyptic revelation.

12:6 *I would not be a fool, because I would be speaking the truth.* Paul now reveals explicitly that "the man in Christ" (12:2) is Paul himself. His use of the third person puts hypothetical distance between himself and this "man in Christ," so that Paul is not formally boasting of his own achievements. Yet Paul qualifies this cautiously narrated tale by observing that its veracity means that he would not be rendered a "fool" were he to straightforwardly relate it in the first person. Paul's caution is further justified by his concern that "no one will think more of me than is warranted by what I do or say." Paul understands that religious charlatans, like the intruders, use grandiose spiritual claims as a substitute for character (see the comments on 12:1), and his implicit appeal is "consider their life and conduct, not their unsubstantiated boasts."

12:7 *I was given a thorn in my flesh, a messenger of Satan, to torment me.* Because the "surpassingly great revelations" could potentially lead to arrogance or a sense of superiority, God (the implied actor of the passive verb "was given") graciously provides an antidote: "a thorn in my flesh." Speculation abounds regarding the nature of this affliction. The specification "in my flesh" suggests a bodily condition, which finds support in Galatians 4:13, so that suggestions such as Paul's opposition, sensual temptation, or recurring guilt over past sin (e.g., persecuting Christians) can be safely set aside. Many physical maladies have been proposed (headaches, depression, vision problems, epilepsy, etc.), though none are more than conjectures. The ailment was painful ("a thorn . . . to torment me"); it weakened the apostle (12:9–10) and became a chronic burden that likely made his work, travel, and ministry difficult, yet without completely incapacitating him. It is probable that the Corinthians knew what this ailment was, and also that some may have disparaged Paul because of it (cf. 10:10). Providing the backstory to his condition may reduce some of this criticism and create empathy, if not respect, in Corinth. Significantly, Paul perceives that God's provision for his spiritual welfare was, at the same time, a means of satanic attack (see also the comments in "Teaching the Text," below).

12:8–10 *Three times I pleaded with the Lord.* As the final clause of 12:9 reveals, the "Lord" whom Paul is addressing is Christ. It would appear that while Satan's use of the affliction ("to torment me," 12:7) is obvious to Paul, Christ's intention is not, so that Paul prays for release. Some suggest that "three times" may indicate fervency and frequency ("again and again"), as opposed to three specific occasions. On the other hand, Paul uses different terminology to express frequency and urgency in prayer (Rom. 1:9; 1 Thess. 1:3–4; 2 Tim. 1:3), and also when speaking of an indeterminate number (Rom. 1:13; 2 Cor. 13:1; 1 Thess. 2:18). The usage here seems closer to 2 Corinthians 11:25, "Three times I was beaten with rods, . . . three times I was shipwrecked," suggesting three specific occasions, perhaps when the ailment became acute.

But he said to me, "My grace is sufficient for you, for my power is made perfect in weakness." Christ's reply comes in the form of a spiritual maxim of profound magnitude: his abundant grace will sustain Paul (Phil. 4:13), because power is made perfect (or complete) in weakness. Although it is counterintuitive, human frailty reveals God's power more perfectly and potently than human strength, talent, or intelligence, because the latter may tend to obscure the true origin of the strength, and human pride is prone to take credit for success even when it belongs elsewhere.

I will boast all the more gladly about my weaknesses . . . when I am weak, then I am strong. Paul takes great comfort in Christ's words and resolves to apply this spiritual lesson broadly to the suffering, hardship, and persecution he has endured on Christ's behalf (cf. 6:4–10). Although the Corinthians have disparaged Paul because of his difficulties and his bodily affliction, Paul comes to understand that it is precisely through these that the presence and power of the crucified Christ are more perfectly mediated to the world.

Theological Insights

Although visions and revelations are attested throughout Scripture, the particular manner of the revelation described here is unusual: a physical or spiritual ascent into the heavenly realms. The clearest Old Testament antecedent is Ezekiel, whom the Spirit of the Lord "lifted up between earth and heaven" (8:3) to show him visions of the exiles (8:12–15; 11:24), the temple (8:3; 11:1; 43:1–5), and the valley of the dry bones (37:1–2). As with Paul's experience, Ezekiel seems to equivocate between descriptions of being lifted physically and visionary revelations. Isaiah's vision of the Lord in his heavenly temple (Isa. 6:1–13) might be closer to the actual content of Paul's vision, but there is no reference in Isaiah to a physical or spiritual ascent. The seer of Revelation tells us of "a door standing open in heaven" (4:1), which he enters "in the Spirit" (4:2), and he is shown mysteries concerning God's plan. As noted above, the striking difference between these heavenly ascents and the one Paul describes here is that Paul relates nothing of the content of what he saw. The purpose of this heavenly ascent seems to have more to do with Paul himself than with God's mission for Paul or God's plan for human history.

Teaching the Text

This passage offers the contemporary teacher the opportunity to address and correct two very widespread misinterpretations of the biblical teaching on health and prayer.

1. *Infirmity is not incompatible with impact.* Is it God's will for you to be healthy, vigorous, and unhindered by physical infirmities? There are some voices in the Christian community who would answer this question with an unqualified, "Yes!" According to this contingent, illness can be banished by faith. "Name it and claim it," as the saying goes. While it is certainly true that good health is a blessing from God, it is also true that pain and difficulty can be God's chosen instruments to accomplish his purposes in this world. In the incident Paul describes in 2 Corinthians 12, the apostle's physical ailment is God's preventative cure for an even more debilitating spiritual malady: pride. God understands that the lofty heights of the third heaven could engender a lofty attitude of superiority. Paul's "thorn in the flesh" is God's prescription for a deadly disease of the soul, as even the apostle himself acknowledges (12:7). More important, however, God reveals to Paul the crucial lesson that human weakness, frailty, suffering, and illness can actually be the means by which God brings even greater glory to himself. This principle is expressed generically in 1 Corinthians 1:27–29: "God chose the foolish things . . . the weak things . . . the lowly things . . . and the despised things—and the things that are not—to nullify the things that are, so that no one may boast before him." In 2 Corinthians 12:1–10, Paul illustrates this principle personally.

2. *Prayer is not always answered affirmatively.* Another widely held belief promulgated by the "Word of Faith" movement is that true prayer, prayer that is offered in faith, is always answered affirmatively. According to one popular exponent of this perspective, to qualify your petition with "if it be your will" is to utter "faith-destroying words," which nullify the prayer. Once again, there is an element of truth in this. Certainly we are encouraged to pray boldly in faith (Matt. 21:22) and told not to doubt (James 1:6–7; 5:14). On the other hand, Jesus himself qualifies his prayer in Gethsemane with, "Yet not as I will, but as you will" (Matt. 26:39), and it would seem that the apostle Paul, in 2 Corinthians 12:1–10 is providing a very personal illustration of this principle. What we can be sure of is that God wants his children to bring their needs before him and to do so with persistence and faith. We can also be absolutely certain that God hears all of our prayers. For those who are committed to God's kingdom purposes in this world, God's gentle "no" will be reckoned as an opportunity to receive God's abundant supply of grace (12:9) in grateful anticipation of seeing God's purposes accomplished through even better means.

Illustrating the Text

It may take time to see fruit.

Object Lesson: During your message, take a seed and plant it in a pot. Add fertilizer and water. Stand over the pot and tell the audience that you are waiting for something to happen. Explain how frustrated you are that no plant seems to be appearing. Tell the audience, "I guess this didn't work." Carry the pot toward your audience and share that God's work in us may often be like farming: it may take time and require patience and persistence to perceive the fruit that comes from our suffering. And the same applies to our prayers: in prayer we plant seeds and trust that God will bring the growth. Sometimes even our best efforts do not guarantee that the seed will produce a plant.

No formulas

Quote: **Philip Yancey.** If we think critically about the miracles of Jesus, we must conclude that Jesus did little to solve the problem of pain while he walked the earth. Blindness, leprosy, birth defects, and hunger remained largely unsolved. "The miracles He did perform," writes Philip Yancey, "breaking as they did the chains of sickness and death, give me a glimpse of what the world was meant to be and instill hope that one day God will right its wrongs."[9] Paul's thorn in the flesh was a daily reminder to Paul that as yet, the world is not as it was meant to be.

Even in hardship, weakness, and loss, gratitude cannot be contained.

Church History: **Martin Rinkart.** Rinkart (1586–1649) was a German pastor, composer, and poet. He pastored in the city of Eilenburg during the Thirty Years' War. The city was racked by pestilence in 1637. But Rinkart carried out his ministry nonetheless, conducting burial services for 4,480 victims of the epidemic, one of which was his own wife. Despite all of the grief and loss Rinkart had experienced, and even in the face of continued great suffering, he penned a prayer that became his great hymn, "Now Thank We All Our God."[10]

2 Corinthians 12:11–13

Not the Least Inferior

Big Idea
Paul's miraculous deeds and his sacrificial labor among the Corinthians demonstrate that he is in no way inferior to the intruders.

Key Themes
- Paul is more than equal to the rival "super-apostles."
- Paul's miraculous works further demonstrate his apostolic status.
- The Corinthians do not occupy a lesser place in Paul's affection than do other churches.

Understanding the Text

The Text in Context

In a final summation of the "Fool's Speech" (11:1–12:13), Paul leads by expressing (again) his chagrin at being forced to defend himself through boasting. He then reiterates his equality with the "super-apostles" (12:11), his affection for the Corinthians (12:13a), and his principled stand on refusing their financial support (12:13b). Along the way, Paul also manages to add one final boast in support of his apostolic credentials: the performance of "signs, wonders and miracles" (12:12).

Interpretive Insights

12:11 *I have made a fool of myself, but you drove me to it.* Conceding that he has compromised his principles by defending himself so vigorously against his critics in Corinth, Paul lays the blame on the Corinthians, who ought to have taken up Paul's cause against the intruders from outside the community and his detractors from within the community. Paul reiterates that he is in no way inferior to the "super-apostles" (see 11:5), even though he is "nothing." It is possible that Paul is echoing a criticism of his opponents, "Paul is nothing!" (see 10:10), but it is equally likely that this is an expression of self-deprecation, as in 1 Corinthians 3:7: "So neither the one who plants nor the one who waters is anything, but only God, who makes things grow" (cf. 1 Cor. 15:9–10).

Self-Commendation in 2 Corinthians

Proper commendation is clearly a contentious issue between Paul and the Corinthians. Nine of the sixteen New Testament occurrences of the Greek verb for "commend" (*synistēmi*) are found in 2 Corinthians. Paul is sensitive about commending himself "again" to the Corinthians (3:1; 5:12), having already proved his character among them. Yet Paul understands that there is both proper and improper self-commendation. Proper self-commendation is nonverbal and is accomplished through (1) sincerity and truthfulness (4:2); (2) enduring hardship for the benefit of others (6:4); and (3) doing what is necessary to right wrongs (7:11). Improper self-commendation relies on the credentials of others (3:1; 10:15), is fixated on externals rather than on "what is in the heart" (5:12), and is aimed at self-promotion (10:12). These folks preach themselves, not Christ (4:5), verbally commending themselves to all who will listen (10:18). Paul also understands that ultimate commendation comes from the Lord, not from oneself or others (10:18), which is why he so persistently points out the folly of his own self-commendation in his speech of defense (11:1, 23; 12:11). Paul realizes that he has sullied himself in commending himself to the Corinthians. His final censure, "I ought to have been commended by you" (12:11), brings to a climax this important motif in 2 Corinthians, with a note of remorse and indignation.

12:12 *I persevered in demonstrating among you the marks of a true apostle.* Paul supports his claim that he is in no way inferior to the so-called "super-apostles" (12:11) by reminding the Corinthians of both *the fact* of the miraculous works he has performed among them and *the manner* in which these deeds have been carried out: "with great perseverance" (NET). This expression is also found in the earlier hardship catalog (6:4; cf. 1:6) and communicates a setting of difficulty that has required endurance and patience on Paul's part. Genuine apostolic labor is a labor of love, and Paul is keen to remind the Corinthians of the *character* of a true apostle (cf. 1:12; 4:2; 12:18) as well as the *works* of a true apostle. The emphasis in this verse, however, falls on the assertion that miraculous works are characteristic of an authentic apostle. This does not mean that only apostles can be used by God to perform miracles. In 1 Corinthians 12:28–30, Paul allows that others, besides apostles, may possess gifts of healing, prophecy, and miracles. Nor does this text indicate that the performance of signs and wonders is sufficient in itself to validate someone as an authentic messenger of God. In Matthew 24:24 Jesus warns that false christs and false prophets will attempt to deceive others by precisely this means.

signs, wonders and miracles. Although the account in Acts 18 of Paul's initial ministry in Corinth records no supernatural deeds, elsewhere Acts chronicles numerous miraculous events that attended Paul's evangelistic work (Acts 13:8–11; 14:8–10; 19:11–12; 20:9–10; 28:7–9). The three terms Paul uses here need not be sharply distinguished; the phrase denotes all manner of supernatural works performed in advancing the gospel. Paul makes a similar statement in Romans, where Christ and the Spirit are specifically designated as the empowering agents: "I will not venture to speak of anything except what Christ has accomplished through me in leading the Gentiles to obey God by what I have said and done—by the power of signs and wonders, through the power of the Spirit of God" (Rom. 15:18–19; cf. 1 Cor. 2:4; 1 Thess. 1:5). The expression "signs and wonders" is particularly prominent in describing God's rescue of Israel from Egyptian bondage (Exod. 7:3; Deut. 4:34; 26:8; Neh. 9:10; Ps. 135:9; Jer. 32:20), and it became something of a set phrase to describe God's miraculous intervention on behalf of his people (Dan. 4:2; 6:27; Sir. 36:6; Wis. 8:8; John 4:48; Acts 2:19, 22; 5:12; 15:12; Heb. 2:4).

12:13 *How were you inferior to the other churches, except that I was never a burden to you? Forgive me this wrong!* Paul finishes his "Fool's Speech" with a sarcastic rhetorical question that, again, reflects a crucial disagreement between him and the Corinthians. Paul's refusal to accept Corinthian support, to "burden" them, is perceived as a slight by some in Corinth. Perhaps they regarded it as a rejection of their offer of friendship (see the comments on 11:11). Or perhaps, as Barrett suggests, the Corinthians felt that Paul's disavowal of their offer of monetary support "seemed to stamp them as less responsible and trustworthy than, say, the Macedonian churches."[1] Either way, Paul insists that his treatment of the Corinthians has been entirely honorable, as expressed in his final, ironic, and exasperated plea for forgiveness.

Teaching the Text

As Paul concludes his defense against the accusations of the intruders and their supporters in Corinth, his summation brings to light the responsibilities of a congregation in such circumstances, as well as the responsibility of leadership, as modeled by Paul in his ministry in Corinth. In teaching this passage, the following points could be profitably emphasized as a means of summarizing Paul's perspective on this topic.

1. *The responsibility of a congregation.* Paul's opening remarks to the Corinthians in 12:11 crystallize the issue as the apostle sees it: "I ought to have been commended by you." The teaching point from this verse, and much of 11:1–12:13, is that a Christian community is responsible to commend and defend godly leadership. Paul's record of hard work, selfless labor, and genuine affection for the Corinthians is clear. Some of the Corinthians have been beguiled by the opposing missionaries, and their betrayal of their founding apostle has forced Paul to do what they should be doing themselves: supporting him before his detractors.

2. *The responsibility of godly leadership.* Paul's comments also reiterate the grounds for his expectation that the Corinthians should have rallied to his defense, and highlight the primary responsibility of leadership: to persevere in exercising one's gifts (12:12) and to serve one's flock sacrificially (12:13). Emphasized here is Paul's exercise of miraculous gifts and his renunciation of monetary support.

3. *The perspective of godly leadership.* Although Paul is strongly defending his apostolic status, he is under no delusions of his own self-importance: "I am nothing" (12:11). Paul understands that it is God's power and God's grace that work through him, not his own talent and ability. The perspective of godly leadership concisely articulated in 12:11 is more fully enunciated in 1 Corinthians 3:5: "What, after all, is Apollos? And what is Paul? Only servants, through whom you came to believe."

Illustrating the Text

Brokenness can be a blessing.

Quote: **Leading with a Limp, by Dan Allender.** Author and psychologist Dan Allender reminds leaders that being open and honest about our failures and deficiencies is good leadership.

> I won't be so naive as to say the long, dark valley of leadership can be avoided simply by learning to name your failures. In fact, new and, at times, more difficult challenges will arise simply because you begin admitting your status as the organization head sinner, *and* the normal challenges will remain whether you confess your flaws or try to hide them. But realize that most leaders invest too much capital obscuring their need for grace, which not only keeps their staff at arm's length but also subverts their trust and steals energy and creativity they could otherwise devote to the inevitable crises that continue to arise. And, perhaps even more dangerous, hiding failure prevents leaders from asking for and receiving the grace they most desperately need to live well, not to mention lead well.[2]

Paul did not deny his weaknesses; he readily admitted them. The sacrifice and humility of God's servants lay a foundation for future ministry.

Story: Philip Yancey reflects on his visit to Yanghwajin Foreign Missionary Cemetery in South Korea. Plaques have been added to tell the stories of various missionaries buried there, recounting many hardships, including the loss of family members. "Yet the fruit of their work lives on, in schools, libraries, hospitals, and church buildings dotting the landscape of modern South Korea." Like Paul, these missionaries were willing to suffer losses for the kingdom, but their work was not in vain. Today, 30 percent of South Koreans identify themselves as Christian.[3]

A disciple is willing to sacrifice to follow.

Church History: Pastor and writer David Platt calls the comfortable Western church to consider the cost of being a follower of Jesus. "Fishing for men," he writes, "would become central for them—and costly to them":

> Peter preached the gospel to thousands at Pentecost and to throngs thereafter, and because he would not shut up, . . . tradition says he was crucified upside down. Similar tradition tells us that Andrew was crucified while preaching the gospel in Greece, Judas (not Iscariot) was clubbed to death for ministering near modern-day Turkey, Thomas was speared through his side while making disciples in India, James was beheaded, Philip was stoned, and Matthew was burned at the stake, all for preaching the gospel. As a result of being disciples of Jesus, every one of these men literally gave their lives to making disciples of Jesus.[4]

These apostles and so many who have come after them have recognized that following Jesus is costly. Paul's mark of authenticity was his suffering as much as his miracles. Challenge the congregation to consider if they are so marked.

2 Corinthians 12:14–21

Ready or Not, Here I Come

Big Idea

Paul prepares the Corinthians for his third visit, vowing that he will continue his practice of not accepting their financial support and warning that this visit may be difficult for everyone if he finds those Corinthians who have sinned still unrepentant.

Key Themes

- Paul's policy of not accepting monetary aid from the Corinthians is grounded in his conviction that, like parents for their children, he desires to live sacrificially for them.
- Neither Paul nor any of his associates have taken advantage of the Corinthians financially.
- Paul's lengthy apologetic in the previous chapters is less a personal defense than a forthright, candid exposition of the facts aimed at bringing the Corinthians to repentance.

Understanding the Text

The Text in Context

In this concluding section of the body of the letter (12:14–13:10), Paul begins to prepare the ground for his impending visit to Corinth (12:14, 21; 13:1). Here in 12:14–21 he reiterates his resolve to provide for his own needs (12:14) and explains that this issues from his desire to live sacrificially for them (12:14–15), in the hopes that their affection for him will increase (12:15b). Paul also addresses two lingering objections: the possible accusation that some of his associates might have taken advantage of the Corinthians (12:16–18) and the concern that his lengthy apologetic in chapters 11–12 might be misinterpreted as a petty diatribe of self-vindication (12:19–21).

Interpretive Insights

12:14-15 *Now I am ready to visit you for the third time.* The Greek construction behind the NIV's "now" is stronger than a mere logical connector or temporal marker. In this context it connotes nearly a warning: "Look, now . . ." Paul's tone in 12:14–13:10 is grave and is moving toward an explicit warning (13:5–10). By referring to his impending "third" visit, Paul indicates that his founding visit (Acts 18) was his first visit and his "painful visit" was his second (2 Cor. 2:1).

what I want is not your possessions but you. The fact that Paul brings up the matter of financial support yet again (1 Cor. 9:1–18; 2 Cor. 11:7–11; 12:13) underscores the significance of this issue between him and the Corinthians. Paul reiterates his determination not to burden the Corinthians, and then he enunciates one of the guiding principles behind this resolve: his desire to be a benefit to his flock, not to benefit from them. His aspiration is not for their material goods but for their very hearts and souls. Earlier in this letter Paul referenced those peddling the word of God for profit (2:17) and exploiting and taking advantage of the Corinthians (11:20), and this suggests that 12:14b may be another reference to the abusive greed of the intruders, who desire to enrich themselves with the Corinthians' "possessions."

children should not have to save up for their parents, but parents for their children. Paul elaborates his desire to gain their souls, not their possessions, by the analogy of parents, who accumulate wealth for their children, not vice versa. Paul has chosen the most common and universally recognizable image of loving generosity: fathers and mothers who daily sacrifice their own comfort for the benefit of their children. So too, Paul's desire is to live sacrificially for his spiritual children. More than this, however, he expresses his eagerness ("most gladly") to "spend and be spent" (ESV) for the welfare of the Corinthians. The two words Paul uses are cognates, with the latter signifying fully exhausting one's resources for another. But this is not "reckless generosity," as the expression goes. Rather, it is a careful, calculated, and joyful recognition that daily dying for others is nothing more than following Jesus and is the call of every believer.

If I love you more, will you love me less? Paul now adds a second reason for not accepting the Corinthians' offer of financial assistance, expressed as a rhetorical question. The obvious answer is "No, we will not love you less." However, this figure of speech, a litotes, represents a deliberate understatement for rhetorical effect. Hence, what Paul is communicating with this rhetorical question is actually closer to this: "I am refusing to take your money because *as I demonstrate my love for you, your love for me will only increase.*"

12:16–17 *Yet, crafty fellow that I am, I caught you by trickery!* Verses 17–18 function as support for the claim that Paul has not (12:16) and will

Images of an Apostle in 1–2 Corinthians

Paul employs a diverse array of images to illustrate his relationship to the Corinthians. He is a farmer working God's field (1 Cor. 3:6; 9:10–11), a servant/minister fulfilling his responsibility (1 Cor. 3:5; 2 Cor. 3:6), a laborer (1 Cor. 3:9; 2 Cor. 6:1), an administrator (1 Cor. 4:2; 9:17), a builder (1 Cor. 3:10), an ambassador (2 Cor. 5:20), a soldier (2 Cor. 10:4–6), and a brother (2 Cor. 1:8 and throughout 1–2 Corinthians). Yet Paul's most important image to depict his pastoral and apostolic relationship to the Corinthians is that of a *father*. He begat the Corinthians through the gospel (1 Cor. 4:14–15) and provides for his children a paradigm of conduct to emulate (4:15–16). He admonishes (1 Cor. 4:14) and disciplines his children (4:21), and he speaks tenderly to them with fatherly affection (2 Cor. 6:11–13). He is fiercely protective of them (2 Cor. 11:2) and, like any loving parent, is willing to sacrifice all he has for them (12:14–15). The problem Paul faces in Corinth is the Corinthians' own arrested development. They are children—even infants—who refuse to grow up. Like a mother or wet nurse, Paul has fed them milk as newborns, and although they should be ready for solid food, their spiritual development has stagnated, and they refuse to be weaned from the "milk" of the elementary principles of the faith (1 Cor. 3:1–2).

---

not (12:14) be a burden, by dismissing a possible objection to this claim, that he has exploited them indirectly, through his emissaries. It is quite possible that Paul is echoing an actual complaint leveled against him, perhaps at the instigation of his rivals. The Greek verb behind the NIV's "exploit" (12:17–18) frequently denotes financial exploitation (cf. 7:2), as here. The charge, summarily dismissed by Paul, is that the collection that Titus has been tasked with organizing is really a confidence scheme aimed at enriching Paul and his associates.

12:18 *I urged Titus to go to you and I sent our brother with him.* This previous mission of Titus was referred to in 8:6, where Paul noted that Titus "had earlier made a beginning" with the collection. We have no information on the identity of the unnamed brother. If 2 Corinthians represents a single communication from Paul, as argued in the introduction, this brother cannot be one of the two unnamed brothers mentioned in 8:16–9:5, as that mission lies in the future from the perspective of the letter; the mission mentioned here has already taken place, as demanded by the past-tense verbs. Paul is quite confident that no evidence of graft could be marshaled against him or his delegates. His rhetorical questions expect answers confirming their integrity, and he evinces no concern over circumstances or events that require explanation.

Did we not walk in the same footsteps by the same Spirit? The NIV reorganizes this final clause, inverting the major elements. A more literal translation would be, "Did we not walk in the same spirit? In the same footsteps?" The NIV is also virtually alone among modern versions in seeing a reference to the divine Spirit in this verse.¹ Most translations and commentators understand "in the same spirit" to be indicating a common manner of conduct (ESV, RSV, NET, KJV, NLT, NIV 1984). The use of "walk" to indicate ethical conduct is a common idiom in Paul (e.g., Rom. 4:12; 6:4; 14:15; 2 Cor. 5:7; 1 Thess. 2:12). This interpretation is strongly supported by the explanatory clause that follows: "Did we not walk in the same footsteps?" On this reading, "spirit" should be related to expressions like "a spirit of gentleness" (1 Cor. 4:21 ESV; cf. Gal. 6:1), indicating a particular disposition or approach. Both Paul and his associates have dealt with the Corinthians in the same spirit of honesty and integrity.

12:19 *Have you been thinking all along that we have been defending ourselves to you?* Verses 19–21 represent a short aside in which Paul explains and clarifies his defensive posture in the previous verses (12:16–18) and chapters (chaps. 10–12). He returns to the topic of his impending visit in 13:1. Paul concedes that, to all appearances, he seems to be defending himself while at the same time denying that this is his primary intent. Rather, the Corinthians should recognize his forceful rhetoric as a frank exposition of the facts (12:19b) in order to strengthen them (12:19c). Moreover, all he says and does, Paul reminds them, is "in the sight of God as those in Christ." Openness before God and others has been a regular emphasis in the earlier chapters of this letter (1:12–13; 2:17; 3:2, 12–13; 4:2; 5:11; 6:11; 7:11) and is appropriately reiterated as Paul finishes his appeal.

12:20–21 *For I am afraid that when I come I may not find you as I want you to be.* Amplifying the thought of 12:19, that his hard-hitting rhetoric is for their benefit, Paul explains that he fears that their spiritual state might not be what it should be, which would lead to a difficult visit for everyone (cf. 2:1–4). Specifically, Paul fears that vice and discord will be rampant in the community (12:20) and that he will be humbled and grieved over unrepentant sinners (12:21).

discord, jealousy, fits of rage, selfish ambition . . . impurity, sexual sin and debauchery. The vices of 12:20b would find particular expression in the communal life of the church, while the vices of 12:21b are connected to sensuality; many have already surfaced in the Corinthian correspondence. "Discord" (*eris*) was reported to Paul by Chloe's messengers (1 Cor. 1:11), and both "jealousy" (*zēlos*) and "discord" are revealed in the factionalism of those who say "I follow Paul" or "I follow Apollos" (1 Cor. 3:3–4). The opponents addressed in chapters 10–12 of this letter represent the supreme example of "selfish ambition, slander, gossip, and arrogance." In 1 Corinthians Paul strenuously rebukes their inflated, puffed-up opinions (4:6, 18–19; 5:2; 8:1) and their boasting (1:31; 3:21; 4:7; 5:6), reminding them that love is never proud (13:4). Similarly, the "disorder" rife within the Corinthian assemblies is hardly surprising given Paul's estimation of their celebration of the Eucharist, with its divisions and schisms (1 Cor. 11:17–22). In Corinth, the central act of worship of the church has become a mechanism for separating the "haves" from the "have-nots."[2] The impenitent sensuality mentioned at the close of 12:21 might possibly refer to the incestuous relationship of 1 Corinthians 5:1–5 or more generally to various kinds of promiscuity that continue to plague the church (see the comments on 6:14–7:1).

I am afraid that when I come again my God will humble me before you. With most commentators, "again" should probably be taken with "humble" rather than "come," as the NIV has it.[3] Some believe the verb "humble" should be translated as "humiliate." The reference would then recall the confrontation with an unnamed member of the church that occurred during Paul's previous "painful visit" (1:23–2:11), and Paul's fear would be that this experience might be somehow repeated. This is quite possible, but the final clause, where Paul anticipates being grieved over sin, suggests that Paul has in mind not a loss of honor but the humbling disappointment of finding his children unfruitful, unprepared, and unrepentant.

Theological Insights

Although the prophets of the Old Testament were frequently endowed with stunning visions of the future, the bulk of their prophetic ministry was focused on their present situation. They rebuked the idolatry, vice, and apathy of the people of Israel, and these lengthy, searing critiques were punctuated by moments of visionary oracles—whether woeful or hopeful. In 2 Corinthians 10–12 Paul dons the prophetic mantle and censures the folly and rebellion of his wayward children in Corinth. Although Paul's rhetoric may seem harsh to our ears, he stands in a long line of prophetic heralds whose task, as God tells Jeremiah, is "to uproot and tear down, to destroy and overthrow, to build and to plant" (Jer. 1:10).

Teaching the Text

The primary teaching points of 12:14–21 can be handily summarized under a heading provided by Paul himself: "Everything we do . . . is for your strengthening" (12:19). Although in the context of 12:14–21 the principles enumerated below relate primarily to the obligations of pastoral leadership to their flock, they also represent the ideals of Christian maturity that all believers should aspire to model.

1. *Live sacrificially.* The first and most important point Paul makes is that he regards his life as a sacrifice for others (12:14–15; cf. Rom. 12:1; Phil.

2:17; 2 Tim. 4:6). Like a parent who would gladly give everything to see his children thrive, Paul is willing to "spend everything and spend myself as well" (2 Cor. 12:15, author's translation). This perspective not only governs his determination to support himself, rather than relying on the Corinthians; it also governs his choice to return to this troubled community and set things right. Paul could have remained in Troas, where he had an "open door" for ministry (2:12), but his parental concern for his children in Corinth and how they have received Titus and the strongly worded letter compel him to close that door, at least for the moment, and continue on to a potentially difficult confrontation in Corinth.

2. *Love generously*. Paul has every reason to turn his back on the Corinthians, to cut them loose and spare himself further abuse. And he certainly has a right to accept their support for his work among them, his traveling expenses, and so on. Paul, however, deems it necessary in Corinth to forge on and forgo any remuneration, as a concrete expression of his love for them (12:15). Paul reasons that this would cause their affection for him to grow, thus allowing his influence to expand, and with that, the gospel.

3. *Walk blamelessly*. The insinuations and accusations swirling around Paul in Corinth have been leveled against many ministers of the gospel over the centuries. Sadly, allegations of misappropriation of funds sometimes turn out to be true. Other times, however, the charges cannot be proved, yet an aura of suspicion remains. Paul's strongest defense against the whispers in Corinth is his character. His integrity, and that of his co-workers, has been amply demonstrated before the Corinthians (12:16–18). Paul's confidence in dismissing the rumors circulated by his opponents has been earned by his daily determination to live honestly and uprightly before all. This kind of defense cannot be feigned, and it cannot be refuted.

4. *Admonish candidly*. Perhaps the most difficult duty a pastor has toward their flock, or a Christian toward a fellow Christian, is to confront them concerning sin. Paul has done quite a lot of confronting, admonishing, and rebuking in 2 Corinthians, and all of it has been "in the sight of God as those in Christ" (12:19). This has been Paul's consistent posture in this letter (see 1:12, 23; 2:17; 4:2). Paul's conscience is clear before God that his candid admonition does not spring from vindictiveness or wounded pride. His sole concern is for their "strengthening" (12:19).

Illustrating the Text

The Christian life is a life given away for others.

Quote: *The Cost of Discipleship*, by Dietrich Bonhoeffer. Bonhoeffer was a German Lutheran pastor and scholar before and during World War II. He recognized the rise of the Nazi party and its ideology as totally counter to the gospel of Christ, and he committed to staying in Germany despite the danger he would face. He was imprisoned by the Nazis for his resistance, and he was executed at Flossenbürg concentration camp on April 9, 1945, just two weeks before its liberation. He famously wrote, "When Christ calls a man, he bids him come and die."[4] He not only wrote about costly discipleship; he also lived it.

Sacrifice for others is a testimony of genuine faith.

Testimony: A young mother overheard that the mother of another player on their kids' soccer team was on a waiting list for a kidney transplant. Though neither woman really knew the other, the Spirit prompted the mom with two good kidneys to get tested. She was a near perfect match for the other woman, so she proceeded with surgery to donate her kidney. Her example showed her kids what Jesus-followers do in putting the good of others above their own comfort and security. Paul was just as willing to make sacrifices for his churches, treating them as he would family members, even as though they were his own children.

2 Corinthians 13:1–4

Be Warned

Big Idea
Paul issues a stern warning that he will be firm in punishing any wrongdoers when he returns, just as Christ has shown himself powerful through his resurrection.

Key Themes
- Those who have continued to sin and cause trouble in the community will face judgment when Paul returns.
- Judgment will be firm but conducted according to proper protocols for establishing guilt or innocence.
- Just as Christ's weakness was turned to strength through God's power, so God will turn Paul's weakness into strength to enable him to execute judgment in Corinth.

Understanding the Text

The Text in Context

Paul returns to the topic of his impending visit (cf. 12:14). After just expressing his fear that he might find vice and discord rampant in the community (12:20–21), he now stresses that any such behavior will be judged. This serves to make explicit what was somewhat cryptically articulated in 12:20 with the words "When I come . . . you may not find me as you want me to be." In chapter 13, the opening verses (13:1–4) provide a final warning to the Corinthians to change their ways or face "a rod of discipline" (1 Cor. 4:21).

Interpretive Insights

13:1 *This will be my third visit to you.* Paul mentions the number of his visits not simply as a matter of clarifying the historical record but to add gravity to the warning that follows. The first visit was his founding visit, and the second was the painful visit described in 1:23–2:11.

Every matter must be established by the testimony of two or three witnesses. Paul cites Deuteronomy 19:15 somewhat abruptly, without clearly indicating its connection to the immediate context. The intent of the Deuteronomic regulation was to ensure due process and prevent conviction of an innocent person on the basis of a single "malicious witness" (Deut. 19:16). Before rendering their verdict, the priests and judges are called to make a "thorough investigation" (Deut. 19:17–18) to verify that the witness was not a "false witness" (19:19). Who, or what, are the "two or three witnesses" that Paul has in mind here? Most commentaries argue that these witnesses should be correlated with Paul's visits to Corinth, with the impending third visit becoming the final necessary "witness." The primary support for this interpretation is the direct mention of Paul's third and then second visit in the immediately preceding and following clauses, respectively (13:1a, 2a). On this reading, Paul intentionally mentions the number of his visits in order to establish the legal grounds for his impending judgment. This view, however, is open to serious objections. It is difficult to imagine how Paul's founding visit, which was concerned with evangelism and establishing a Christian community, could be reasonably construed as a "witness" against the Corinthians. Moreover, in every other instance where this Deuteronomic rule is cited in the New Testament, including by Paul, the reference is to personal witnesses producing evidence in a matter (Matt. 18:16; John 8:17; 1 Tim. 5:19). More important, this interpretation seems quite at odds with the spirit and intent of Deuteronomy 19:15–21, which was intended as a safeguard against a rash or corrupt verdict by insisting on multiple attestation of guilt. If the majority interpretation is correct, Paul becomes the judge, the jury, and the chief witness for the prosecution! For these reasons, I find this interpretation unconvincing. A more plausible interpretation takes the statement at face value: on his next visit, Paul intends to carefully consider accusations, weigh evidence, and render a judgment. We need not suppose that Paul has in mind establishing a formal tribunal when he arrives in Corinth, but he will be following accepted procedures to ensure that there is no miscarriage of justice. Although the apostle will be "unsparing" (13:2) in judging offenders, his insistence on "two or three witnesses" assures the community that there will also be due process.

13:2 *On my return I will not spare those who sinned earlier or any of the others.* After the painful confrontation that occurred on his second visit to Corinth (see 2:1–7), Paul warned the Corinthians (upon departure?) that his next visit would not be pleasant if he did not see substantial change in their conduct and disposition. The perfect tense of the verb *prolegō* (NIV: "I already gave you a warning") indicates that this warning is still in effect, and it is now explicitly reiterated. Paul already has exercised considerable leniency in not returning to Corinth when he originally intended (1:23–2:2). However, leniency unchecked becomes indulgence, which would then be construed as a license for sin. "Those who sinned earlier" repeats the same expression of 12:21, where "impurity, sexual sin and debauchery" are mentioned. "Any of the others" may have in mind a specific group (those who supported the intruders, those who contributed to the divisions and strife, those who had committed egregious transgression in the intervening months) or, more broadly, the rest of the community. Paul may be concerned to give notice to those who, by their inactivity and apathy, have contributed to the declining state of affairs in Corinth.[1]

13:3 *since you are demanding proof that Christ is speaking through me.* Paul's judgment of sinners on his return to Corinth (13:2) will constitute proof that Christ is indeed speaking through him. Paul handily summarizes the two central, and interrelated, objections concerning him and his ministry among the Corinthians: his unimpressive oratory and apostolic legitimacy. Paul's unsophisticated—and intentionally so—rhetoric has long been a complaint in Corinth. He dealt with it at length in 1 Corinthians 1–4, but he was unable to silence his critics. In 2 Corinthians 10:10 he directly cites his detractors: "For some say, 'His letters are weighty and forceful, but . . . his speaking amounts to nothing.'" He also alludes to this complaint in 11:6: "I may indeed be untrained as a speaker, but I do have knowledge." Paul's poor oratory (by Corinthian standards), his determination to work with his hands to support himself (see 11:7), and the hardships and persecution he regularly experienced in fulfilling his calling (11:16–12:10) have caused some in Corinth to question his apostolic credentials. They have judged Paul too "weak" to be Christ's representative. In response, Paul's argument in 2 Corinthians has been aimed at redefining weakness and strength: "That is why, for Christ's sake, I delight in weaknesses, in insults, in hardships, in persecutions, in difficulties. For when I am weak, then I am strong" (12:10). Paul will make one final attempt to bring this point home to the Corinthians, this time by correlating Christ's "weakness" and "power" with his own ministry and dealings with the Corinthians.

He is not weak in dealing with you, but is powerful among you. Paul alludes again to the accusation of his opponents already cited in 10:10: "Some say . . . his physical presence is weak."[2] There may be a hint of sarcasm or dismissiveness in Paul's tone. Mindful of the Corinthians' unfavorable comparison of him vis-à-vis "the philosophers of this age" (1 Cor. 1:20) or Apollos (1 Cor. 3:4–5; 4:6) or the intruders (2 Cor. 11:12–24), Paul implicitly contrasts his own alleged weakness with Christ's power, in order to strengthen the symmetry of the analogy he is about to draw between Christ's weakness and strength and his own weakness and strength.

13:4 *crucified in weakness . . . Likewise, we are weak in him, yet by God's power we will live with him in our dealing with you.* Paul now explains the weakness-strength motif of 13:3 and draws a parallel between Christ's suffering and his own. The essence of Paul's thought is this: in the same way that Christ appeared weak on the cross yet was vindicated by God, so too this apostle may appear weak on account of his suffering and hardships (see 12:10), yet he will be fully vindicated by God's power when he returns and sets matters right in Corinth. Paul sees his own hardships through the lens of the cross, and so he reckons that his suffering for Christ is tantamount to "carrying around in our body the death of Jesus" (4:10 NET). In the same way that Christ's "weakness" was actually a potent demonstration of his willing obedience to his calling, even to death on a cross (Phil. 2:8), so too Paul's weaknesses, insults, hardships, persecutions, and difficulties are the means by which God manifests his power: "For when I am weak, then I am strong" (2 Cor. 12:10). In this context, the future verb "we will live with him" refers not to the resurrection but to his Christ-enabled ministry among the Corinthians, as the qualifying expression "in our dealing with you" makes clear.

Theological Insights

Although Paul categorically sets aside the old covenant as utterly surpassed by the new covenant (3:4–18), he continues to treasure the Old Testament Scripture as a reliable source of doctrine, wisdom, and insight. In fact, Paul directly cites the Old Testament nearly 130 times, and this number dramatically increases when we factor in the many allusions to the Old Testament in his letters. In 13:1 Paul cites Deuteronomy 19:15 in order to establish a legal precedent for his manner of dealing with disputed issues during this impending visit, demonstrating the apostle's continued reliance on the books of Moses to inform and guide him in practical matters. Elsewhere in 2 Corinthians Paul has cited the Old Testament to explain his own boldness and his people's continued hard-heartedness (3:12–18), to explain his faith in spite of suffering (4:13), to illuminate the newness of life in Christ (5:17), to censure the Corinthians' lingering dalliance with pagan temples (6:16–18), to encourage generosity (8:15; 9:9), and as a guide to proper and improper boasting (10:17), among others. This illustrates the importance of the Old Testament for Paul and gives substance to his later reminder to Timothy: "All Scripture is God-breathed and is useful for teaching, rebuking, correcting and training in righteousness" (2 Tim. 3:16).

Teaching the Text

Second Corinthians 13:1–4 represents one of the most sobering passages in this letter. Paul's tone is solemn, even stern, and his words have been carefully chosen. The topic is Paul's judgment of sin on his next visit. Without laying out detailed plans and procedures, the apostle clearly indicates that he has given forethought to the process and protocols of judging sin and implementing discipline. Paul may not provide us with procedural details with regard to disciplinary action, but we can identify five very important principles that undergird Paul's approach in such matters. These principles would be particularly useful to underscore when teaching on the matter of church discipline.

1. *Patience.* It would not be accurate to say that Paul is reluctant to punish sin, but it would certainly be true to say that Paul does not rush to judgment, nor does he mete out punishment without giving ample opportunity for repentance. Paul emphasizes here that this will be his third visit to the Corinthians, and the clear implication is that his patience has run out. He has already intentionally delayed an earlier visit in order to spare the Corinthians (1:23), and then he sent Titus with a stern letter to allow further opportunity to repent. Paul's patience is evidence of his fatherly affection for his children (6:13).

2. *Due Process.* The only procedures that are explicitly stated here relate to ensuring that anyone accused of sin will receive due process: "Every matter must be established by the testimony of two or three witnesses" (13:1). Paul is aware that convicting someone of sin without clear proof—even if the person is actually guilty—would foster animus and undermine his credibility. Paul's commitment to due process should probably include his repeated warning of impending judgment (13:2).

3. *Scope.* It may seem rather obvious to point this out, but the scope of Paul's judgment is limited to persistent and flagrant *sin* (12:21; 13:2). Paul is not out to settle personal vendettas, nor is he dealing with issues of genuine disagreement. Pastoral leaders involved in discipline need to consider carefully whether the matter involves cultural taboos, personal disagreements, or actual sinful activity.

4. *Unsparing.* Paul's resolve not to spare anyone is not a threat that he will be merciless (one possible connotation of the English word "unsparing") but a promise that there will be impartiality and complete accountability. No one can rely on connections, wealth, or status to avoid discipline. Corruption based on status is indicative of the Roman court system, and Paul is taking pains to assure the Corinthians that in the church, matters will be handled differently.

5. *Through the power that God supplies in Christ.* Paul's final words in 13:4 emphasize the ultimate source and authority for the disciplinary activity that he intends to undertake. God's power will enable Paul to manifest Christ's presence in the matter of judging sin. In himself, Paul may be "weak," but through God's enablement he will deal boldly and firmly with those Corinthians who have continued in sin.

Illustrating the Text

Carefully administered church discipline can produce positive results.

Testimonial: Church discipline has always been a part of what it means to be a body committed to each other and the teaching of Scripture. "Discipline is not a hammer for crushing a wayward brother or sister. It's a redemptive intervention that calls people to turn back to the Lord, who loves them." Administering discipline is a gut check for the elders and pastors to live a circumspect life. One church's protocol is "to meet and talk . . . one elder, one pastor and the person who is struggling." This strategy has often been well received by the one being confronted in love. However, church discipline should be administered regardless of the outcome. God honors the prayerful, careful administering of loving church discipline.[3]

Is church discipline out?

Survey: Chuck Lawless, professor of evangelism and missions and dean of graduate students at Southeastern Seminary, conducted a survey that included attitudes about church discipline. His research has shown that most churches talk very little about church discipline, and he lists several reasons he has found for the reluctance. Among the twelve he details are the following: "The church is afraid to open 'Pandora's Box,'" "They don't want to appear judgmental," and "Their Christianity is individualistic and privatized."[4] Let's be honest; who wants their church to appear judgmental? Church discipline may have been one of the three keys to the kingdom for the Reformers, but it's not likely to become fashionable in Western Christianity anytime soon.

Tardy church discipline seldom works.

Quote: **Ken Sande.** "Unfortunately most churches don't employ formal discipline until offenses are so terrible, relationships so shattered, and patterns so engrained, that the chances of restoring someone are very small."[5] What Sande is driving at is the reality that many churches have an unbiblically high tolerance for obvious sin. Such a tolerance breeds ineffective church discipline: too little, too late. For church discipline to be effective, leaders must be willing to address biblical infractions earlier in the process, thereby increasing the odds of getting a believer back on track.

2 Corinthians 13:5–10

Test Yourselves!

Big Idea
Paul's ultimate hope is for the complete spiritual restoration of those in Corinth who are estranged from him or living in sin. The first step in this process is serious self-examination.

Key Themes
- Self-scrutiny is an important component of discipleship.
- Paul's chief desire is for the Corinthians' restoration and spiritual growth, regardless of whether they change their opinion of him.
- Paul's purpose in writing so strongly to the Corinthians is to avoid a painful confrontation on his return to Corinth.

Understanding the Text

The Text in Context

In 13:5–10 Paul brings the argument of chapters 10–13 to a conclusion and in the process reiterates both his main purpose in these final chapters and the central thrust of 2 Corinthians as a whole. In regard to his primary objective in chapters 10–13, Paul's hope and prayer is for the restoration of those in Corinth who have been deceived by the intruders and those who have not repented of previous sin (13:9b). With respect to the letter as a whole, Paul has been trying to correct and reprove the Corinthians from a distance so that he will not have to exercise his disciplinary authority when he arrives in person (13:10). Paul ends this letter on a note of genuine concern for the Corinthians' spiritual state and a reiteration of his own integrity and commitment to his wayward flock in Corinth.

Interpretive Insights

13:5 *Examine yourselves . . . test yourselves.* Paul's point is made emphatic both by the repetition of the command and by the word order. In Greek, the pronoun is placed first, in emphatic position, which could legitimately be rendered, "Examine *yourselves*, not me." Although Paul has been on the defensive for most of the last three chapters, he now reverses course completely and presses the Corinthians to do some serious soul-searching with respect to their own spiritual state. Paul challenges them to discern if they are truly "in the faith"—a broad expression that the immediate context can unpack: *having a living and vital connection to Christ* ("Christ Jesus is in you," 13:5b), and *walking in obedience to the truth* (doing "what is right," 13:7; walking in "the truth," 13:8). The expression "Christ Jesus is in you" should probably be understood in reference to the individual believer, as opposed to the community ("Christ Jesus is *among* you"), as the idea involves testing the genuineness of personal faith (see 2 Cor. 4:6; Rom. 8:9–10; Gal. 4:19; Eph. 3:19; Col. 1:27).[1]

unless . . . you fail the test. The rhetorical question, "Do you not realize that Christ Jesus is in you?" expects an affirmative answer, but the qualification that immediately follows, "unless you fail the test," puts that assumption in doubt. It is certainly true that the Corinthians are "the seal" of Paul's apostleship (1 Cor. 9:2) and that the majority in the Corinthian assembly possess genuine faith (2 Cor. 3:2–3). However, it is also true that dissension, sin, rebellion, and false teaching are rife in this community. In light of this, it seems best to take this qualifying clause at face value, as Paul's recognition that some of those listening to his letter being read will not be able to pass the test of self-scrutiny. Paul illustrated this principle earlier, in 1 Corinthians, with reference to Israel in the desert: "They were all baptized into Moses. . . . They all ate the same spiritual food. . . . Nevertheless, God was not pleased with most of them; their bodies were scattered in the wilderness" (10:2–5). In Paul's mind, the assembled church is composed of those who have God's approval and those who do not: "For there must in fact be divisions among you, so that those of you who are approved may be evident" (1 Cor. 11:19 NET). The Greek word for "approved" in 1 Corinthians 11:19 is the same word found in this passage, which suggests that both passages are communicating the same principle: not all who associate with the Christian community have genuine faith. The question of how Paul would expect those who lack genuine faith to discern this truth by self-examination is not clear. Paul's primary intention is to jolt the community in Corinth into sober soul-searching.

13:6 *I trust that you will discover.* Two issues confront us in this short verse. First, does "I trust that you will discover . . ." convey an expectation that is confident of fulfillment ("Of course you will discover that we are approved") or a wish that is uncertain of fulfillment ("I certainly hope you come to the conclusion that we are approved")? The extremely tense environment of the immediately preceding chapters, which finds Paul pulling out all the stops to defend his apostolate before the Corinthians, seems to support the latter. On the other hand, while the previous clause (13:5c) appears to admit that some in Corinth might not pass the test of authentic faith, the verse as a whole suggests that Paul expects most will discover that

"Christ Jesus is in [them]" (13:5b). As Paul is confident that the community as a whole will pass the test, so too he is confident that they will find him approved as well.

we have not failed the test. The second issue involves the meaning of Paul "failing the test" as far as the Corinthians are concerned. Does failing the test have to do with the legitimacy of his apostolate? The larger context of 2 Corinthians supports this interpretation. Does failure involve proving to have inauthentic faith? Verse 5 supports this interpretation. Or does failing the test refer to Paul's ability to follow through on his threats to punish wrongdoers? Verse 3 might be understood as support for this interpretation. On the whole, the first and second options seem to have a stronger textual basis than the third option.

13:7 *we pray to God that you will not do anything wrong—not so that people will see that we have stood the test.* Paul qualifies the thought of 13:6 in order to correct any who might get the impression that he is overly concerned with his own vindication. Reiterating the thought of 12:19 ("Everything we do . . . is for your strengthening"), Paul emphasizes that his primary concern is that the Corinthians flourish in their faith and in their conduct, even if he remains unvindicated in the eyes of some. Ultimately, Paul's prayer is that this stumbling and erring flock may "do what is right," regardless of his own reputation or standing. Paul's concern for their conduct is deliberately posed in the broadest possible terms, to do "what is right," so as to encompass the entire gamut of ethical and spiritual issues that this community is facing, and will face. Uppermost in Paul's mind, however, must be the critical issues addressed in the last three chapters: the deception of the intruders (11:1–4, 13–14), the devaluation of Paul's apostolate (11:16–12:13), and the persistence of all manner of vice and sin (12:20–21).

13:8–9 *For we cannot do anything against the truth . . . We are glad whenever we are weak but you are strong.* Paul explains his seeming indifference to the hypothetical situation posed in 13:7b, that some might perceive that he has failed, by placing it in the widest possible field of reference: his commitment to "the truth." It is possible that "truth" here is Pauline shorthand for the gospel specifically (Gal. 2:5; Eph. 1:13; Col. 1:5), but Paul's point is unaffected either way. The apostle affirms that his life and ministry stand or fall at the bar of truth. If the cause of truth is advanced, though he himself appears discredited, that is all that matters. Paul knows that at the judgment seat of Christ he will receive his just reward (2 Cor. 5:10) and any perceived failings in this life will be rightly assessed. If Paul's suffering (4:7–12; 6:3–10), or his manual labor (11:7–11), or his poor oratory (10:10) is deemed "weakness" by the Corinthians, yet results in their growth and "strength," Paul has fulfilled his calling, and in that he is satisfied.

our prayer is that you may be fully restored. This clause is better translated, "This, indeed, is our prayer: your restoration" (author's translation). Verse 9b should be punctuated as a separate sentence, following the ESV, NET, and NLT, and regarded as the summative thesis of 2 Corinthians 10–13, and also of the letter as a whole, as the following verse confirms: "This is why we write to you . . ." (cf. 13:10). This call to restoration encapsulates the plea for reconciliation in chapters 1–7, the appeal for the Corinthians to make good on their pledge to the collection in chapters 8–9, and the bold challenge of the last three chapters for Paul's children to reject the claims and pretensions of the intruding missionaries and repent of their carnality. The Greek word behind "restoration" occurs only here in the New Testament and is not widely attested elsewhere. Some translations render it in terms of growth and maturity: "We pray that you will become mature" (NLT; cf. GNT, NASB, NRSV). The verbal form is found in Mark 1:19, where it describes repairing torn fishing nets and, particularly noteworthy, in Galatians 6:1, where it refers to restoring a brother or sister who sins. The context of 2 Corinthians suggests that "restoration" is the intended sense here, which is the first step toward maturity. This appeal to restoration need not indicate that the entire community is alienated from Paul or trapped in carnality. However, Paul recognizes that there are divisions, disorder, and sin in the community that affect the spiritual health of the collective body (12:20–21). Some are actively contributing to the ill health of the body by engaging in sinful behavior, while others are passively contributing through apathy and toleration. The blanket appeal to communal restoration represents a call to the entire community to take ownership of the issues addressed in this wide-ranging letter and to respond by actively confronting sin and punishing wrongdoers.

13:10 *This is why I write these things . . . that when I come I may not have to be harsh.* Paul now reiterates one of the primary purposes of this, at points, strongly worded letter: to avoid a discipline process that would be painful for everyone. As Garland puts it, "He writes sharply, so that he will not have to act sharply."[2] "This is why" refers both to what precedes and to what follows: Paul prays for the restoration of the Corinthians (13:9b) so that he will not have to exercise his authority in a punitive manner when he returns (13:10b). What does Paul have in mind by "these things"? Some believe Paul is referring to the material of chapters 10–13, where his tone is confrontational. For those who regard chapters 10–13 as a separate letter, this position is almost inevitable.[3] Others, however, note the placement of this purpose statement just prior to Paul's farewell and conclude that it is intended to summarize the primary purpose of the letter as a whole.[4] This position is slightly preferable, although it should be acknowledged that the principal reasons for disciplinary action are addressed in chapters 10–13.

Paul concludes the body of this letter by echoing the letter opening, which emphasized Paul's apostolic authority and the origin of Paul's apostolate in Christ and "the will of God" (1:1). Paul repeats the words of 10:8, reasserting that the purpose of the authority given to him by the Lord is for building up, not tearing down. However, the possibility of "tearing down" the Corinthians through the execution of discipline remains real, and Paul's plea is that the Corinthians do everything necessary to avoid this eventuality.

Theological Insights

Paul's appeal to the Corinthians to examine themselves echoes numerous passages in the Old Testament where the prophets and psalmists urge the people of Israel to honestly examine their conduct and return to the Lord with their whole heart. The author of Lamentations makes this poignant appeal: "Let us examine our ways and test them, and let us return to the LORD. Let us lift up our hearts and our hands to God in heaven, and say: 'We have sinned and rebelled and you have not forgiven'" (Lam. 3:40–42). The plea of the penitent sinner in Psalm 51 reflects the contrition that Paul desires to be manifest in the hearts of the Corinthians: "Have mercy on me. . . . Wash away all my iniquity and cleanse me. . . . Create in me a pure heart, O God" (Ps. 51:1, 2, 10). According to the superscription of this psalm, it represents David's confession after being confronted by the prophet Nathan concerning his adultery with Bathsheba. In a very real sense, chapters 10–12 of 2 Corinthians represent an analogous confrontation of the Corinthians by Paul. Paul's desire is that those Corinthians who are still unrepentant would come to their senses, acknowledge their sin, and be restored, as was David.

Teaching the Text

In 13:5–10 we find a call to honest self-evaluation, with the ultimate goal being the restoration of a right relationship with God, the community, and the Lord's apostle. In this passage Paul emphasizes the posture of penitence as well as the self-denying perspective of a true apostle, one who is more concerned with the advance of the truth than with his own reputation. These points could be useful for both teaching and personal reflection.

1. *The posture of penitence: self-scrutiny.* Paul's strong adjuration that the Corinthians should examine themselves comes at the end of a lengthy emotional discourse that confronts false teachers, disloyalty, and sinful behavior. It is a sincere call to sober soul-searching, with the ultimate goal of spiritual restoration and interpersonal reconciliation. This admonition is not unprecedented. Paul advises that everyone should "examine themselves"

before eating the bread and drinking the cup (1 Cor. 11:28). He also encourages believers to "test their own actions" without comparing themselves to others (Gal. 6:4). Numerous passages also imply that Paul applies this principle to himself (1 Cor. 4:4; Phil. 3:12). Focused introspection in the service of repentance and personal insight should be distinguished from unhealthy, obsessive navel-gazing. The former leads to restoration and growth; the latter leads to condemnation and paralysis. Although Paul offers no specifics in this passage as to what this self-scrutiny should look like, the larger context of Paul's Letters suggests that the involvement of other brothers and sisters in Christ could provide perspective, as well as serve as a safeguard against unhealthy brooding (Gal. 6:1–2; 2 Cor. 2:7; 1 Thess. 5:11; Col. 3:16).

2. *The perspective of a leader: magnanimity.* Magnanimity is a virtue that is undervalued in our society, and one that many people today probably could not even define. One dictionary defines "magnanimity" as "being free from petty vindictiveness."[5] It is a virtue rooted in a deeply secure identity and a big-picture perspective. Those who harbor insecurities need vindication, validation, and the approval of others. Those whose focus is on their own kingdom, not the true kingdom, will never be able to endure personal insult for the larger good. Paul's perspective in this passage is genuinely magnanimous. He is secure enough in his identity in Christ to value the advance of truth more than personal exoneration. Paul is willing to look like a failure (13:7), if it means his flock succeeds. From Paul's cruciform perspective, his "weakness" for the Corinthians' "strength" (13:9) is an exchange he will gladly make. It was the exchange that Jesus made on the cross (13:4), and Christ's apostle is determined to follow in his steps.

Illustrating the Text

Practicing secrecy

Applying the Text: One of the better strategies to grow in our discipleship is doing good deeds under cover. The more we intentionally bless others without drawing attention to ourselves, the more we begin to break the bondage associated with addiction to approval. There is something joyfully liberating in practicing our piety in secret (see Matt. 6:1–4). When we get to the point of truly enjoying the reward of the Father, we are gaining ground on being citizens of the kingdom. Challenge those present to engage in at least one act of Christian service in the coming week that can be done in secret and be kept in secret. Ask them to evaluate themselves and see if they find it difficult to keep from telling others what they did.

Testimony: I remember being in a very tense meeting at our church, where the lead pastor was being heavily criticized for failing to initiate certain activities related to our building program. As an elder, I happened to know that these items had nothing to do with him but were the responsibility of someone else, who was also sitting in the room. Rather than putting this individual on the spot, and legitimately relieving his own pressure, the pastor simply accepted the responsibility and moved the meeting forward. This pastor had a bigger, kingdom perspective and didn't need to be vindicated. He didn't mind being judged as failing (13:7b) if it would contribute to the well-being of the church.

Alexander at his greatest

History: After Alexander the Great had conquered Greece, Asia Minor, Egypt, and Persia, he met the formidable opponent King Porus at the Battle of Hydaspes. Alexander would execute a brilliant military flanking strategy to defeat Porus and his massive army of chariots and elephants. The ancient historian Plutarch wrote of the aftermath of the battle, "When Porus was taken prisoner, and Alexander asked him how he expected to be used, he answered, 'As a king.' . . . Alexander, accordingly, not only suffered him to govern his own kingdom as satrap under himself, but gave him also additional territory of various independent tribes whom he subdued."[6] The scene is famously depicted by French painter Mignard Pierre in his work *Magnanimity of Alexander the Great*. Encouraging Jesus-followers that being more magnanimous than a conquering king should be a hallmark of aggressive discipleship.

2 Corinthians 13:11–14

Finally, Brothers and Sisters . . .

Big Idea
Paul concludes the letter by subtly reemphasizing key elements of concern, and he finishes with a strongly trinitarian blessing.

Key Themes
- Full restoration will lead to the full presence of the God of love and peace.
- Familial affection should characterize the relationship among believers.
- Growth and sanctification are the work of the Triune God—Father, Son, and Spirit.

Understanding the Text

The Text in Context

Paul concludes this letter in a manner typical of his letter closings: a series of exhortations (13:11a), a peace benediction (13:11b), mutual greetings (13:12–13), and a grace benediction (13:14).[1] Also typical is the way this letter closing echoes prominent themes of the body of the letter, particularly the appeal to restoration (13:11a) and harmony (13:11b–12). The strongly trinitarian form of the final blessing is not characteristic of Paul's letter closings and serves to underscore the role of the entire Godhead in bringing about the restoration that Paul is calling for in 2 Corinthians.

Interpretive Insights

13:11 *Finally, brothers and sisters, rejoice!* The exhortation section of the letter closing is composed of five independent imperatives. While there is no obvious semantic connection between these exhortations, they do concisely encapsulate important elements of the letter. The first command, to "rejoice," is a theme that is especially prominent in chapters 1–7, where "joy" and "rejoice" occur eleven times—more than in any other letter, apart from Philippians. In the opening chapter Paul tells the Corinthians that his labor is for their joy (1:24) and that the Corinthians themselves are the cause of his own rejoicing (2:3). Paul characterizes his life as "sorrowful, yet always rejoicing" (6:10), which is illustrated by the mission of Titus. The good news of the Corinthians' warm reception of Titus has turned Paul's sorrow into rejoicing (7:7, 9, 13, 16) and caused him to "overflow" with joy (7:4 ESV).

Strive for full restoration, encourage one another. The translation and meaning of the next two exhortations are disputed. The first verb is sometimes understood in a passive sense: "be restored" (LEB; cf. NASB). However, it makes more sense to translate the Greek verb with a middle voice, as in the NIV, in that Paul expects the Corinthians to be actively striving toward restoration (cf. 13:9). The restoration of the Corinthians to spiritual health represents, perhaps, the most important theme of this letter, which has also prominently emphasized reconciliation (5:18–6:2). In a similar vein, Paul began this letter with the theme of encouragement or "comfort" (see 1:3–7, utilizing the same Greek word as here), and it is fitting that this theme is reemphasized as he concludes (see also 2:7–8; 5:20; 6:1; 7:4–7, 13).

be of one mind, live in peace. The call to unity and peace suitably concludes these letters to Corinth, a community racked with divisions, conflict, and disorder. Paul provides a complete commentary on the expression "be of one mind" in Philippians 2:2–11, where it describes mutual love, humility, and sacrificial service, as exemplified by Christ. Paul is appealing not for unanimity in all matters of opinion but for solidarity in values, perspective, and mission.

And the God of love and peace will be with you. The most natural way to understand the connection between the five preceding imperatives and the final promise of God's presence is condition to consequence: the full presence of the God of peace and love is contingent upon walking in joy, seeking restoration, pursuing peace, and so forth.[2] This interpretation does not entail the notion that God's presence is utterly dependent on our fulfilling these commands. It merely affirms that growth in holiness leads to a fuller experience of God's love and peace. On the other hand, some interpret this promise not as the consequence of fulfilling the preceding exhortations but simply as a reminder of God's enabling support as the Corinthians strive to actualize these commands.[3]

13:12-13 *Greet one another with a holy kiss.* The adjective "holy" distinguishes the Christian kiss from romantic kissing, and perhaps also from the kind of kiss offered by an inferior to flatter his or her superior (see the sidebar). In this context Paul is addressing "brothers and sisters" (13:11), which indicates that this kiss is an expression of familial affection and the bonds of spiritual kinship (see Rom. 16:16; 1 Cor. 16:20; 1 Thess. 5:26; 1 Pet. 5:14). Given the diverse social makeup of the Corinthian assembly, this greeting would have the effect of undermining deeply ingrained Roman scruples related to class and rank, while also reinforcing the community's identity as a family.

Kissing in the Ancient Mediterranean World

Social conventions in the ancient Mediterranean relating to kissing differ significantly from conventions in contemporary North America. Kisses of greeting and farewell were exchanged between friends and family members (Apuleius, *Metam.* 4.1; Seneca, *Dial.* 4.24.1; Epictetus, *Diatr.* 2.22.13; Acts 20:37). Social inferiors (slaves, clients) kissed their superiors on the hand (Epictetus, *Diatr.* 1.19.24; Martial, *Epig.* 11.98), and superiors would bestow kisses on their select favorites (Suetonius, *Tib.* 10.2). Kisses sometimes accompanied reconciliation after a dispute (Petronius, *Sat.* 109) and were also exchanged between members of a religious fraternity or civic association (Lucian, *Alex.* 41.41). Paul's instructions on greeting with a holy kiss are best understood in the context of familial affection, as brothers and sisters in Christ.

All God's people here send their greetings. The NIV adds the word "here," which would imply that this greeting is from those with Paul (cf. Col. 4:10–14), or from the believers in Macedonia where Paul is writing. Alternatively, Paul could be sending greetings from the worldwide community, along the lines of Romans 16:16: "All the churches of Christ send greetings."

13:14 *May the grace of the Lord Jesus Christ, and the love of God, and the fellowship of the Holy Spirit be with you all.* Paul's final words to the Corinthians are noteworthy both as a witness to Paul's incipient trinitarian theology (cf. Rom. 8:9–11; 1 Cor. 12:4–6; Gal. 4:4–6) and also because of the explicit reference to the Spirit. Paul regularly mentions God and Jesus in his epistolary farewells (e.g., Rom. 16:27; 1 Cor. 16:24; Gal. 6:18; Philem. 25), but only here does he refer to the work of the Spirit. In light of the lingering mistrust, wavering loyalty, and widespread dissension that Paul addresses in this letter, it is certainly fitting that Paul appeals to the fellowship and unity produced by the Spirit as he closes.[4] Further, this blessing is pronounced on "all" of the Corinthians, even those he has had to reprimand in this letter.[5]

Theological Insights

Second Corinthians is home to some of Paul's most profound theological reflection—the glory of the new covenant, new creation in Christ, strength in weakness, to name just a few. Undergirding and connecting these themes is the Spirit, though 2 Corinthians is rarely given the attention it deserves in constructing a Pauline theology of the Spirit.[6] Quite unlike 1 Corinthians, which highlights the more "flashy" expressions of the Spirit corporately experienced (tongues, prophecy, revelation, and the like), 2 Corinthians focuses on the broader salvation-historical framework of the Spirit and the transformative work of the Spirit in the individual and the community. In 2 Corinthians 1:22 and 5:5 the Spirit is described as a down payment, the promise of a future fulfillment. The emphasis is on the "not yet" of salvation; what believers experience now is only a small portion of what God has planned. Second Corinthians 3:1–6, on the other hand, depicts the Spirit as the fulfillment of an ancient promise. Weaving together imagery from Ezekiel and Jeremiah, Paul portrays the Spirit as the solution to the anthropological dilemma so powerfully dramatized by these prophets (Jer. 13:23; 17:9; Ezek. 16:3; 20:16) and the fulfillment of God's promise of a new heart, a new spirit (Ezek. 36:26–27), and a new covenant (Jer. 31:31–34). This salvation-historical perspective is deepened in the argument that follows, as Paul contrasts the old covenant with the new covenant and identifies the Spirit as the much greater glory of the new covenant (2 Cor. 3:7–11). The center of Paul's pneumatology is concisely expressed in 3:6: "The Spirit gives life." Like Ezekiel before him ("I will put my Spirit in you and you will live," Ezek. 37:14), Paul portrays the chief significance of the eschatological Spirit as its ability to produce life (Rom. 8:2, 6, 10; Gal. 5:25). Indeed, so complete is the Spirit-life equation in Paul's thinking that he can contrast the "ministry of death" not, as one might expect, with the ministry of life but with the "ministry of the Spirit" (2 Cor. 3:7–8). In this connection, "Spirit" and "life" become virtually interchangeable for Paul (cf. Rom. 6:4, "newness of life"; 7:6, "newness of the Spirit," NASB). In 2 Corinthians, the life that the Spirit produces relates to both the individual and the community. On the individual level, it renders the believer a "new creation" (5:17) and leads to progressive characterological transformation (3:18). On the corporate level, the Spirit produces "fellowship" (13:14), or *koinōnia*. The Corinthians were in need of spiritual renewal on the individual level and the corporate level, and both, says Paul, are produced by the Spirit.

Teaching the Text

Paul's concluding comments to the Corinthians not only recapitulate central themes of the letter; they also point the way forward for the Corinthians by reminding this divided and beleaguered community of concrete steps for restoring the spiritual health of the church. The imperatives of 13:11–12 can be summarized under the heading "Mending Discord."

1. *Remember to rejoice.* Joy is a powerful antidote to bitterness, rivalry, and other spiritual contagions that threaten the health of a community. Joyful hearts tend to be thankful hearts, and thankful hearts are more resistant to gossip and factiousness. Read against the backdrop of the conflict in Corinth, Paul's call to "rejoice" is a call for the Corinthians to regain perspective and to immunize their corporate body against dissension.

2. *Work to set things right.* The NIV's "strive for full restoration" (13:11) represents only one Greek word, but it captures well the intent of this expression.

Full and complete restoration requires effort, "striving" to set things right. The previous chapters mention repentance (12:21), self-scrutiny (13:5), and doing what is right (13:7), among other things. For the Corinthians, full restoration will be achieved not by passively waiting and watching but by actively striving to bring it about.

3. *Encourage others.* Paul's "one another" statements constitute his vision for communal life in the body of Christ. Believers are to "love one another" (Rom. 13:8), "accept one another" (Rom. 15:7), "carry each other's burdens" (Gal. 6:2), "teach . . . one another" (Col. 3:16), and "encourage one another" (2 Cor. 13:11; 1 Thess. 5:11). Mutual encouragement strengthens relational bonds, rendering them less susceptible to being severed by stress and discord.

4. *Strive for harmony.* The by-products of spiritual health and maturity are unity and peace. Paul's commands to "be of one mind" and to "live in peace" represent the highest ideal of the Christian community. This does not necessarily entail the absence of all disagreement but reflects a perspective that is properly focused on kingdom issues, in spite of differing opinions.

5. *Demonstrate familial affection.* In asking the believers in Corinth to "greet one another with a holy kiss" (13:12), Paul, in effect, is commanding them to regard each other as family members and to demonstrate genuine familial affection. A warm greeting—be it an outstretched hand, a friendly embrace, or a "holy kiss"—fosters community and represents a visible demonstration of spiritual kinship.

Illustrating the Text

We are called to encourage one another, not tear one another down.

Quote: **Ray Ortlund.** The call of the New Testament is to live horizontally what we believe vertically. Paul calls the Corinthians to encourage one another, but there are a number of other things that he does not call them to do. Pastor Ray Ortlund lists some of these "one anothers" that are not found in the New Testament: "Sanctify one another, humble one another, scrutinize one another, pressure one another, embarrass one another, corner one another, interrupt one another, defeat one another, sacrifice one another, shame one another, judge one another, run one another's lives, confess one another's sins, intensify one another's sufferings, point out one another's failings."[7] Ultimately, Jesus summarizes the proper attitude with one simple idea: "Love one another" (John 13:34; cf. Rom. 13:8).

Learning to rejoice and give thanks in all circumstances proves effective.

Literature: *The Hiding Place,* **by Corrie ten Boom.** In this book recounting her time in a German concentration camp, Corrie ten Boom tells of learning what Paul means when he says to "rejoice always, . . . give thanks in all circumstances" (1 Thess. 5:16–17), even in the face of a flea infestation. As they reflected on this passage, Corrie's sister Betsie prayed to thank God:

> "Thank You for the very crowding here.... Thank You . . . for the fleas and for—"
> The fleas! This was too much. "Betsie, there's no way even God can make me grateful for a flea."
> "'Give thanks in *all* circumstances,'" she quoted. "It doesn't say, 'in pleasant circumstances.' Fleas are part of this place where God has put us."
> And so we stood between tiers of bunks and gave thanks for fleas. But this time I was sure Betsie was wrong.[8]

But even the fleas turned out to be an encouragement from God. Corrie resumes the story:

> One evening I got back to the barracks late from a wood-gathering foray outside the walls. . . . Betsie was waiting for me, as always, so that we could wait through the food line together. Her eyes were twinkling.
> "You're looking extraordinarily pleased with yourself," I told her.
> "You know we've never understood why we had so much freedom in the big room," she said. "Well—I've found out."
> That afternoon, she said, there'd been confusion in her knitting group about sock sizes and they'd asked the supervisor to come and settle it.
> "But she wouldn't. She wouldn't step through the door and neither would the guards. And you know why?"
> Betsie could not keep the triumph from her voice: "Because of the fleas! That's what she said, 'That place is crawling with fleas!'"
> My mind rushed back to our first hour in this place. I remembered Betsie's bowed head, remembered her thanks to God for creatures I could see no use for.[9]

The fleas, which had been a source of discomfort and disgust to Corrie and her sister, turned out to be the very reason why the women were protected from abuse and allowed numerous opportunities to share the Scriptures.

This is the day.

Quote: **John Ortberg.** Ortberg reminds us that joy needs to be embraced today. "We all live with the illusion that joy will come someday when conditions change. We go to school and think we will be happy when we graduate. We are single and are convinced we will be happy when we get married. We get married and decide we will be happy someday when we have children. We have children and decide we will be happy when they grow up and leave the nest—then they do and we think we were happier when they were still at home."[10] There is a good reason why God says repeatedly in the Scriptures, "This is the day."

Notes

Introduction to 2 Corinthians

1. The phrase was first used by Murphy-O'Connor in his influential article "The Corinth That Saint Paul Saw," 147.

2. Concisely depicted by Vang, *1 Corinthians*, 1–7. For greater detail, see Savage, *Power through Weakness*, 19–53.

3. It is unclear if Chloe was a resident of Ephesus with connections to the church in Corinth, or a Corinthian who sent a message to Paul in Ephesus.

4. Most recently argued by Vegge, *2 Corinthians*.

5. Recent studies arguing for the unity of 2 Corinthians include Bieringer, "Plädoyer"; Young and Ford, *Meaning and Truth*; Amador, "Revisiting"; Vegge, *2 Corinthians*. Among commentaries, recent advocates include Witherington, *Conflict and Community*; Lambrecht, *2 Corinthians*; Barnett, *Second Epistle*; McCant, *2 Corinthians*; Hafemann, *2 Corinthians*; Garland, *2 Corinthians*; Matera, *2 Corinthians*; and Harris, *Second Epistle*.

6. On this, see Amador, "Revisiting," 94.

7. See Barrett, *Second Epistle*, 21–25; Furnish, *2 Corinthians*, 29–47; Thrall, *2 Corinthians*, 1:3–48.

8. Fitzmyer, "Qumran"; Dahl, "Fragment."

9. E.g., Beale, "Old Testament Background"; Webb, *Returning Home*; Adewuya, *Holiness and Community*.

10. Lambrecht, *2 Corinthians*, 122; Matera, *2 Corinthians*, 156–70.

11. Witherington, *Conflict and Community*, 402–4; McCant, *2 Corinthians*, 62–68; Long, *Ancient Rhetoric*, 168–72. Witherington and McCant regard 6:14–7:1 as a digression but justify this categorization as perfectly in keeping with rhetorical theory and practice.

12. Martin, *2 Corinthians*, xxxviii, 195; Harris, *Second Epistle*, 25, 497.

13. Barrett, *Second Epistle*, 194.

14. Sumney, *'Servants of Satan,'* 130–33.

15. Harris, *Second Epistle*, 79–80.

16. See Sumney, *Identifying Paul's Opponents*, for a detailed description of each profile, along with important advocates.

2 Corinthians 1:1–7

1. Matt Schneider, "Everything Is Not OK (on Parenthood) . . . the Bad Thing Is Already Happening," *Mockingbird*, October 4, 2012, http://www.mbird.com/2012/10/everything-is-not-ok-on-parenthood-the-bad-thing-is-already-happening/.

2 Corinthians 1:8–11

1. For imprisonment, see Thrall, *2 Corinthians*, 1:116–17; for mob violence, see Barnett, *Second Epistle*, 83–85.

2. John Chang, personal conversation with Jeff Porte, November 2010.

3. "Kayaker Rescued after Days at Sea," *ABC News*, accessed February 8, 2016, http://abcnews.go.com/GMA/story?id=125884; see also "Dialing God: The Miraculous Rescue of Kayaker Jon Stockton," *CBN*, accessed February 8, 2016, http://www1.cbn.com/700club/dialing-god-miraculous-rescue-kayaker-jon-stockton.

2 Corinthians 1:12–14

1. Garland, *2 Corinthians*, 83.

2. C. S. Lewis, *Mere Christianity* (New York: Macmillan, 1960), 109.

3. Erwin Raphael McManus, *Soul Cravings: An Exploration of the Human Spirit* (Nashville: Thomas Nelson, 2006), entry 17.

2 Corinthians 1:15–2:4

1. Garland, *2 Corinthians*, 101.
2. Hafemann, *2 Corinthians*, 85.
3. 1 Sam. 16:13; 1 Kings 19:16; Ps. 105:15; Zech. 4:14.
4. Quoted in James Hastings, ed., *The Great Texts of the Bible: II Corinthians and Galatians* (New York: Charles Scribner's Sons, 1913), 89.
5. Jane Austen, *Pride and Prejudice*, in *The Complete Novels of Jane Austen*, Wordsworth Library Collection (London: Wordsworth Editions, 2007), 353.

2 Corinthians 2:12–17

1. With Furnish, *2 Corinthians*, 171.
2. The Greek phrase can be understood as indicating agency, "*by* the Lord" (Thrall, *2 Corinthians*, 1:184; Martin, *2 Corinthians*, 41; NIV, NET) or sphere, "*in* the Lord" (Barnett, *Second Epistle*, 135; Barrett, *Second Epistle*, 94; NASB, ESV), or perhaps both (Furnish, *2 Corinthians*, 169).
3. So Barrett, *Second Epistle*, 94; Martin, *2 Corinthians*, 40.
4. Hafemann, *Suffering and Ministry*, 16–34.
5. See the Oxygen website, http://www.oxygen.com.
6. "The Rev. Kevin J. Gray Charged with 1st-Degree Larceny, Accused of Stealing Over 7 Years from Church," ECFA website, July 8, 2010, http://www.ecfa.org/Content/The-Rev-Kevin-J-Gray-Charged-With-1st-Degree-Larceny-Accused-Of-Stealing-Over-7-Years-From-Church.
7. Dr. White, "Four Lessons on Money," *Christianity History*, issue 19 (1988), http://www.christianitytoday.com/history/issues/issue-19/four-lessons-on-money.html.

2 Corinthians 3:7–11

1. On this issue, and the larger question of Paul's opponents in 2 Corinthians, see Sumney, *Identifying Paul's Opponents*.

2 Corinthians 3:12–18

1. Barrett, *Second Epistle*, 118–19; Furnish, *2 Corinthians*, 232; Hafemann, *2 Corinthians*, 153–56.
2. Following Harris, *Second Epistle*, 297–300.
3. E.g., 2 Cor. 3:7; Acts 3:4. See BDAG, "*atenizō*."
4. E.g., Harris, *Second Epistle*, 311–12; Thrall, *2 Corinthians*, 1:274; Barnett, *Second Epistle*, 199; all relying on Dunn's influential analysis in "2 Corinthians 3:17."
5. Harris, *Second Epistle*, 318.

6. John Newton, *The Life of the Rev. John Newton* (New York: American Tract Society, 1830), 45.
7. Ibid., 44.
8. For a brief narrative of Newton's life, see Chris Armstrong, "The Amazingly Graced Life of John Newton," *Christian History* no. 81 (Winter 2004):174–24, https://www.christianhistoryinstitute.org/magazine/article/amazingly-graced-john-newton/.

2 Corinthians 4:1–6

1. See Kim, *Origin of Paul's Gospel*, 136–238.
2. Quoted in Piper, *Supremacy of God*, 55.

2 Corinthians 4:7–15

1. Philip Yancey, *Disappointment with God: Three Questions No One Asks Aloud* (Grand Rapids: Zondervan, 1988), 227–28.
2. Thair Shaikh, "Amateur unearths 52,000 Roman Coins Worth $1m," CNN, July 9, 2010, http://www.cnn.com/2010/WORLD/europe/07/09/uk.roman.coin.treasure/.

2 Corinthians 4:16–5:5

1. Staff of Dr. Patt, "How Much Does America Spend on Plastic Surgery?," website of Dr. Bradford S. Patt, February 6, 2015, http://pattmd.com/cosmetic-surgery-2/much.

2 Corinthians 5:6–10

1. The Greek verb *ekdēmeō*, translated "away from" by the NIV, commonly means, "to leave one's country, take a long journey." See BDAG, "*ekdēmeō*."
2. BDAG, "*phaneroō*," 1.b.
3. "Hudson Taylor: Faith Missionary to China," *Christian History*, accessed June 6, 2016, http://www.christianitytoday.com/history/people/missionaries/hudson-taylor.html.
4. "Nuremberg Trials," History.com, accessed June 2, 2016, http://www.history.com/topics/world-war-ii/nuremberg-trials.

2 Corinthians 5:11–15

1. See Litfin, *St. Paul's Theology of Proclamation*.
2. Hubbard, *Christianity in the Greco-Roman World*, 78–80.
3. Hubbard, "Was Paul Out of His Mind?"
4. See BDAG, "*synechō*," 6.
5. This is called the anaphoric use of the article, and in this instance the emphasis is not easily replicated in English. An imperfect attempt would be to translate this clause, "One died for all, therefore *this* 'all' died."

2 Corinthians 5:16–21

1. Hubbard, *New Creation*, 2–8.

2. "Updating the New International Version of the Bible: Notes from the Committee on Bible Translation," NIV website, August 2010, http://www.thenivbible.com/wp-content/uploads/2014/11/2011-Translation-Notes.pdf.

3. Mitchell, "New Testament Envoys."

4. This is probably not an appeal to the Corinthians specifically but a concise summary of Paul's evangelistic message. This fits the context well, especially as a recapitulation of 5:11, "we persuade people." The NIV gives the impression that this appeal is directed toward the Corinthians by supplying "you" as the object of the appeal, "We implore you . . . : Be reconciled." However, this pronoun is not found in the Greek text.

5. Victor Hugo, *Les Misérables*, trans. Julie Rose, Modern Library Classics (New York: Modern Library, 2009), 90.

2 Corinthians 6:1–13

1. Arius Didymus, *Epit*.11g.

2. Although "with God" is not explicitly expressed, the verb requires an associated object, and the immediately preceding verses indicate that God is the implied co-worker.

3. *Disc*. 6, "On Training."

4. *Disc*. 7, "That One Should Endure Hardships."

5. Harris, *Second Epistle*, 467.

6. Mark Buchanan, *Your Church Is Too Safe* (Grand Rapids: Zondervan, 2012), 88–89.

7. Quoted in Jill Briscoe, *Spiritual Arts: Mastering the Disciplines for a Rich Spiritual Life* (Grand Rapids: Zondervan, 2007), 73.

2 Corinthians 6:14–7:1

1. Tacitus, *Ann*. 15.44.

2. E.g., 1QS 1.18; 1Q33 13.2; *T. Sim*. 5.3.

3. Bel 1–6; 2 Macc. 7:33; *Jos. Asen*. 11.10; *T. Job* 37.2; Philo, *Posterity* 168 (and throughout Philo).

4. Max Lucado, *In the Grip of Grace* (Nashville: Thomas Nelson, 1996), 87; Lucado quotes Paul Faulkner, *Achieving Success without Failing Your Family* (West Monroe, LA: Howard, 1994), 143–44.

2 Corinthians 7:2–4

1. Furnish refers to Athenaeus, *Deipnosophistae* 6.249b; Horace, *Odes* 3.9.24; and others (*2 Corinthians*, 367).

2 Corinthians 7:5–16

1. Thrall notes that Paul's "neither . . . nor" in this verse probably reflects a Hebraic idiom and should not be construed absolutely but should be understood to communicate, "not *primarily* on account of the offender, nor *primarily* on account of the person wronged" (*2 Corinthians*, 1:496).

2 Corinthians 8:1–7

1. Furnish, *2 Corinthians*, 413.

2. Barrett, *Second Epistle*, 211.

3. Gordon MacDonald, "Transforming Scrooge," *Leadership Journal*, April 15, 2013, http://www.christianitytoday.com/le/2013/spring/transforming-scrooge.html.

4. Andy Stanley, *Fields of Gold* (Carol Stream, IL: Tyndale, 2004), 72.

5. David Crary, "Wealthy Have Gotten Less Generous as Poor Give More to Charity," *Huffington Post*, December 6, 2014, http://www.huffingtonpost.com/2014/10/06/wealthy-charity-giving-greedy_n_5937100.html.

2 Corinthians 8:8–15

1. Harris, *Second Epistle*, 577.

2. BDAG, "*charis*," 3.a.

3. Barrett, *Second Epistle*, 222.

4. Compare the entries in LSJ and BDAG, "*isotēs*."

5. John Ortberg, *When the Game Is Over, It All Goes Back in the Box* (Grand Rapids: Zondervan, 2007), 86.

2 Corinthians 8:16–24

1. The NIV rightly renders the aorist tense verb as a present, "we are sending," and not as a past, "we sent." Grammarians refer to this as an epistolary aorist, where the writer adopts the temporal perspective of his readers as they are reading the letter. Although the sending of Titus was in the immediate future for Paul as he was writing, it would be in the past when the letter was read.

2. BDAG, "*hadrotēs*."

3. See Seth Dowland, "The 'Modesto Manifesto,'" Christian History Institute, accessed April 4, 2016, https://www.christianhistoryinstitute.org/magazine/article/the-modesto-manifesto/.

4. "Basic Training for Employees: Ethics in the Workplace," HRhero.com, accessed June 3, 2016, http://www.hrhero.com/basictraining/BTE_Ethics_6.pdf.

2 Corinthians 9:1–5

1. As argued by Betz, *2 Corinthians 8 and 9*.

2. Harris, *Second Epistle*, 624.

3. See Furnish, *2 Corinthians*, 427, 437.

4. This interpretation is also supported by a significant variant in the Byzantine textual tradition that reads, "in this matter of boasting."

5. Samuel Taylor Coleridge, *The Statesman's Manual*, in *The Complete Works of Samuel Taylor Coleridge*, vol. 1 (New York: Harper & Brothers, 1871), 433.

6. Jeff Slate, "Brian Wilson on the Beach Boys' 'Rivalry' with the Beatles and Flying Solo," *The Daily Beast*, April 4, 2015, http://www.thedaily beast.com

/articles/2015/04/04/brian-wilson-on-the-beach-boys-rivalry-with-the-beatles-and-flying-solo.html.

2 Corinthians 9:6–15

1. Barrett, *Second Epistle*, 237.
2. Quoted in Alan de Bolton, *Status Anxiety* (New York: Pantheon, 2004), 199.

2 Corinthians 10:1–6

1. BDAG notes that this construction with the Greek preposition *dia* is used "in wording of urgent requests" ("*dia*," A.3.f.).
2. Author's rendering. See Harris, *Second Epistle*, 676, who has compiled the suggestions of several commentaries regarding the imagery of 10:3–6.

2 Corinthians 10:7–11

1. For a full exposition of this topic, see Litfin, *St. Paul's Theology of Proclamation*.

2 Corinthians 10:12–18

1. This is the translation of the conjunction suggested by BDAG, "*gar*," 2, for 2 Cor. 10:12.
2. Dio Chrysostom, *Or.* 8.9. Although Dio purports to describe Corinth of Diogenes's day, current scholarship agrees that he is actually depicting Corinth of his own day, the late first century.
3. The "Second Sophistic" refers to an era from the first century AD through the middle of the third century, which witnessed the revival of the sophistic-styled oratory that was so roundly criticized by Plato. See Hubbard, *Christianity in the Greco-Roman World*, 75–82.
4. So Harris, *Second Epistle*, 714.
5. Frederic J. Brown, "Green the 'GOAT' Set for Pastures New," ABC News (Australian Broadcasting Company), February 4, 2008, http://www.abc.net.au/news/2008-02-05/greene-the-goat-set-for-pastures-new/1033168.

2 Corinthians 11:1–6

1. The proposals are succinctly outlined by Thrall, *2 Corinthians*, 2:667–70.
2. Bieringer, "Paul's Divine Jealousy."
3. Timothy Keller with Kathy Keller, *The Meaning of Marriage: Facing the Complexities of Commitment with the Wisdom of God* (New York: Dutton, 2011), 145.
4. Ibid., 146.
5. David Crowder Band, "How He Loves," written by John Mark McMillan, on *Church Music*, Six Steps Records, 2009.
6. James Dobson, *Life on the Edge* (Waco: Word, 1995), 24–25.

2 Corinthians 11:7–15

1. Hock, *Social Context*, 50–68.

2. Harris, *Second Epistle*, 761–62.
3. Furnish argues that they were boasting in their accomplishments and not in the Lord (*2 Corinthians*, 510). Lambrecht assumes the opponents were concerned with their social standing in Corinth (*2 Corinthians*, 178). Thrall argues that they boasted of their right to minister in Corinth (*2 Corinthians*, 2:691–93). Bruce believes they boasted of the financial support they received, which they saw as proof of their apostolic status (*2 Corinthians*, 2:690–93).
4. Against Matera, *2 Corinthians*, 254.
5. E.g., *T. Job* 6.4–7.13; 17.2; 23.1, 5, as noted by Harris, *Second Epistle*, 774.
6. David Garrison, *Church Planting Movements* (Midlothian, VA: WIGTake Resources, 2004), 33–36.

Additional Insights, pp. 187–88

1. For a full account of this perspective, see Marshal, *Enmity in Corinth*.
2. This is especially prominent in the *Odyssey* and is aptly illustrated in the first-century Jewish document *Testament of Job*. In this apocryphal retelling of Job's story, the protagonist not only provides hospitality to strangers, he insists that no one leaves his home "with an empty pocket" (10.4).
3. Some Stoics, however, advocated a similar policy of self-support rather than depending on others. See Hubbard, *Christianity in the Greco-Roman World*, 148–49.

2 Corinthians 11:16–21a

1. "The Good Shepherd," *Grimm*, season 2, episode 5, directed by Steven DePaul, aired September 28, 2012, NBC.
2. Sarah Pulliam Bailey, "Harold Camping Dead: Judgment Day 'Family Radio' Host Dies at 92 after Controversial Career," *Huffington Post*, December 17, 2013, http://www.huffingtonpost.com/2013/12/17/harold-camping-dead-dies_n_4459716.html.

2 Corinthians 11:21b–29

1. See Hubbard, *Christianity in the Greco-Roman World*, 121–22.
2. *Mor.* 147C, *Dinner of the Seven Wise Men*.
3. Thrall's analysis is the most convincing. She sees the list structured in terms of two couplets, one triplet, and the final danger "standing alone to give climactic emphasis" (*2 Corinthians*, 2:742–43): rivers, bandits; Jews, gentiles; city, country, sea; false brothers.
4. "Bishops Ridley and Latimer Burned," Christianity.com, July 2007, http://www.christianity.com/church/church-history/timeline/1501-1600/bishops-ridley-and-latimer-burned-11629990.html.
5. Victoria Barnett, "Dietrich Bonhoeffer: Resistance and Execution," United States Holocaust Memorial Museum, accessed April 4, 2016, https://www.ushmm.org/information/exhibitions/online-features

/special-focus/dietrich-bonhoeffer/resistance-and-execution.

2 Corinthians 11:30-33

1. For a comprehensive (and somewhat technical) discussion of the historical and chronological issues surrounding Paul's flight from Damascus, see Riesner, *Paul's Early Period*, 75–89, 256–62.

2. The expression "after three years" in Galatians 1:18 probably refers to the time that had elapsed since his conversion (1:16); it need not be interpreted to mean Paul spent three years in Arabia.

3. This reference was brought to my attention by Guttenberger, "Klugheit," 87.

4. Garland, *2 Corinthians*, 504.

5. Barrett, *Second Epistle*, 303.

6. Garland, *2 Corinthians*, 506; Witherington, *Conflict and Community*, 458–59; Martin, *2 Corinthians*, 384–85. I also adopted this interpretation in an earlier commentary (Hubbard, "2 Corinthians" [2002], 155), though I no longer consider it viable.

7. Judge, "Conflict of Educational Aims."

8. Harris also notes that "in [Paul's] supposed reversal of the imagery the crucial element of 'firstness' is missing" (*Second Epistle*, 824). Judge believes his interpretation is supported by a statue of the Greek goddess Tyche ("good fortune" = the Roman goddess Fortuna) found in Corinth adorned with a crown fashioned like city walls. However, this was a nearly universal depiction of the goddess, symbolizing her patronage of a city for its prosperity. It has nothing to do with the Roman military honor. We have scores of representations of the goddess wearing a wall crown and holding a cornucopia from a variety of locales and in a variety of archaeological media: coins, wall frescoes, tiled floors, and statuary.

9. Evan Andrews, "5 Daring Slave Escapes," September 23, 2014, http://www.history.com/news/history-lists/5-daring-slave-escapes.

10. M. Craig Barnes, *Yearning: Living between How It Is and How It Ought to Be* (Downers Grove, IL: InterVarsity, 1991), 81.

2 Corinthians 12:1-10

1. Harris, *Second Epistle*, 821.

2. Ibid., 831–32.

3. With Lambrecht, *2 Corinthians*, 200; Matera, *2 Corinthians*, 277.

4. Rowland, *Open Heaven*, 384–85.

5. Barnett, *Second Epistle*, 559–62.

6. Matera, *2 Corinthians*, 278.

7. Thrall, *2 Corinthians*, 2:782.

8. One heaven: *1 Enoch, 4 Ezra, 2 Baruch*; three heavens: *T. Levi* 3.1; five heavens: *3 Bar.* 11.1–2; seven heavens: *2 En.* 20.1; *Ascen. Isa.* 9.1; *Jos. Asen.* 22.9; ten heavens: *2 En.* 21–22.

9. Philip Yancey, *The Jesus I Never Knew* (Grand Rapids: Zondervan, 1995), 182.

10. Ingetraut Ludolphy, "Rinkart, Martin," in *The Encyclopedia of the Lutheran Church*, ed. Julius Bodensieck (Minneapolis: Augsburg, 1965), 3:2065.

2 Corinthians 12:11-13

1. Barrett, *Second Epistle*, 323.

2. Dan Allender, *Leading With A Limp: Take Full Advantage of Your Most Powerful Weakness* (Colorado Springs: Waterbrook, 2006), 4.

3. Philip Yancey, "The Good News Hiding beneath the Headlines," *Christianity Today*, January 15, 2015, http://www.christianitytoday.com/ct/2015/january-web-only/good-news-hiding-beneath-headlines.html.

4. David Platt, *Follow Me: A Call to Die. A Call to Live* (Carol Stream, IL: Tyndale, 2013), 68.

2 Corinthians 12:14-21

1. This reading is capably argued by Fee, *God's Empowering Presence*, 357–58. For an equally capable response, see Harris, *Second Epistle*, 892.

2. For a fuller explanation, see Hubbard, *Christianity in the Greco-Roman World*, 221–23.

3. E.g., Martin, *2 Corinthians*, 464–65; Thrall, *2 Corinthians*, 2:865; Barrett, *Second Epistle*, 326; Furnish, *2 Corinthians*, 562; Harris, *Second Epistle*, 901.

4. Dietrich Bonhoeffer, *The Cost of Discipleship* (New York: Touchstone, 1995), 89.

2 Corinthians 13:1-4

1. Garland, *2 Corinthians*, 542.

2. Thrall, *2 Corinthians*, 2:881.

3. Kevin Harney, "Truth-Telling and Church Discipline," *Preaching*, January 1, 2008, http://preaching.com/leadership/11562924.

4. Chuck Lawless, "12 Reasons Churches Don't Practice Church Discipline," *Thom S. Rainer* (blog), April 9, 2015, http://thomrainer.com/2015/04/12-reasons-churches-dont-practice-church-discipline/.

5. "Church Discipline Really Works When You Make It Loving and Redemptive: An Interview with Ken Sande of Peacemaker Ministries," *Leadership Journal*, July 2007, http://www.christianitytoday.com/le/2007/july-online-only/071305.html.

2 Corinthians 13:5-10

1. See Barnett, *Second Epistle*, 608; Barrett, *Second Epistle*, 338; Martin, *2 Corinthians*, 478; Lambrecht, *2 Corinthians*, 222. Thrall (*2 Corinthians*, 2:871) and Harris (*Second Epistle*, 921) suggest that the Greek expression *en hymin* might include both a communal and a personal sense: "Christ is in and among you."

2. Garland, *2 Corinthians*, 550.

3. E.g., Thrall, *2 Corinthians*, 2:899–900; Furnish, *2 Corinthians*, 580.

4. E.g., Matera, *2 Corinthians*, 310; Barnett, *Second Epistle*, 614; Lambrecht, *2 Corinthians*, 223.

5. Dictionary.com, *Dictionary.com Unabridged*, Random House, accessed May 9, 2016, http://www.dictionary.com/browse/magnanimous.

6. Plutarch, *Plutarch's Lives*, trans. John Dryden, ed. Arther Hugh Clough (New York: Modern Library, 2001), 2:188.

2 Corinthians 13:11-14

1. See Weima, *Neglected Endings*, 209.

2. So Martin, *2 Corinthians*, 500; Barnett, *Second Epistle*, 617.

3. Thrall, *2 Corinthians*, 2:911; Matera, *2 Corinthians*, 313.

4. It is possible that this expression *koinōnia tou hagiou pneumatos* should be understood as an objective genitive and rendered, "participation in the Spirit" (Furnish, *2 Corinthians*, 584). However, given the prominence of reconciliation in 2 Corinthians, as well as the reprimand for discord and jealousy (12:20) and the appeal for restoration (13:11), a subjective genitive seems preferable (see Hubbard, "2 Corinthians" [2014]).

5. Weima, *Neglected Endings*, 214.

6. For a full presentation of this subject see Hubbard, "2 Corinthians" (2014).

7. Ray Ortlund, "'One Another's' I Can't Find in the New Testament," *The Gospel Coalition Blog*, May 24, 2014, http://blogs.thegospelcoalition.org/rayortlund/2014/05/24/one-anothers-i-cant-find-in-the-new-testament-2/.

8. Corrie ten Boom with Elizabeth and John Sherrill, *The Hiding Place*, 35th anniversary ed. (Grand Rapids: Chosen, 2006), 210.

9. Ibid., 220.

10. John Ortberg, *The Life You've Always Wanted: Spiritual Disciplines for Ordinary People* (Grand Rapids: Zondervan, 1997), 68.

Bibliography

Recommended Resources

Barnett, Paul. *The Second Epistle to the Corinthians*. New International Commentary on the New Testament. Grand Rapids: Eerdmans, 2008.

Barrett, C. K. *The Second Epistle to the Corinthians*. Black's New Testament Commentary. Peabody, MA: Hendrickson, 1973.

Furnish, Victor Paul. *2 Corinthians*. Anchor Yale Bible 32A. New Haven: Yale University Press, 2005.

Garland, David E. *2 Corinthians*. New American Commentary. Nashville, TN: Broadman & Holman, 1999.

Harris, Murray J. *The Second Epistle to the Corinthians*. New International Greek Testament Commentary. Grand Rapids: Eerdmans, 2005.

Lambrecht, Jan. *2 Corinthians*. Sacra Pagina 8. Collegeville, MN: Liturgical Press, 1999.

Martin, Ralph P. *2 Corinthians*. Word Biblical Commentary 40. Waco: Word, 1986.

Matera, Frank J. *2 Corinthians: A Commentary*. Louisville: Westminster John Knox, 2003.

Thrall, Margaret E. *2 Corinthians*. 2 vols. International Critical Commentary. Edinburgh: T&T Clark, 1994, 2000.

Select Bibliography

Adewuya, J. Ayodeji. *Holiness and Community in 2 Cor 6:14–7:1: Paul's View of Communal Holiness in the Corinthian Correspondence*. New York: Lang, 2001.

Amador, J. D. H. "Revisiting 2 Corinthians: Rhetoric and the Case for Unity." *New Testament Studies* 46, no. 1 (2000): 92–111.

Beale, G. K. "The Old Testament Background of Reconciliation in 2 Corinthians 5–7 and Its Bearing on the Literary Problem of 2 Corinthians 6:14–7:1." *New Testament Studies* 35 (1989): 550–81.

Betz, H. D. *2 Corinthians 8 and 9: A Commentary on Two Administrative Letters of the Apostle Paul*. Edited by George W. MacRae. Hermeneia. Philadelphia: Fortress, 1985.

Bieringer, Reimund. "Paul's Divine Jealousy: The Apostle and His Communities in Relationship." In *Studies on 2 Corinthians*, edited by R. Bieringer and J. Lambrecht, 223–53. Leuven: Leuven University Press, 1994.

———. "Plädoyer für die Einheitlichkeit des 2. Korintherbriefes: Literarkritische und inhaltliche Argumente." In *Studies on 2 Corinthians*, edited by R. Bieringer and J. Lambrecht, 131–79. Leuven: Leuven University Press, 1994.

Bruce, Frederick Fyvie. *1 and 2 Corinthians*. New Century Bible Commentary. Grand Rapids: Eerdmans, 1980.

Dahl, Niels. "A Fragment in Its Context: 2 Corinthians 6:14–7:1." In *Studies in Paul*, 62–69. Minneapolis: Augsburg, 1972.

Dunn, James D. G. "2 Corinthians 3:17: The Lord Is the Spirit." *Journal of Theological Studies* 21 (1970): 309–20.

Fee, Gordon. *God's Empowering Presence: The Holy Spirit in the Letters of Paul.* Peabody, MA: Hendrickson, 1994.

Fitzmyer, J. A. "Qumran and the Interpolated Fragment in 2 Cor. 6:14–7:1: An Anti-Pauline Fragment?" In *Essays on the Semitic Background of the New Testament,* 205–17. London: Chapman, 1971.

Friesen, Steven. "Poverty in Pauline Studies: Beyond the So-Called New Consensus." *Journal for the Study of the New Testament* 26, no. 3 (2004): 323–61.

Guttenberger, Gudrun. "Klugheit, Besonnenheit, Gerechtigkeit und Tapferkeit: Zum Hintergrund der Vorwürfe gegen Paulus nach 2 Kor 10–13." *Zeitschrift für die neutestamentliche Wissenschaft und die Kunde der älteren Kirche* 96, no. 1–2 (2005): 78–98.

Hafemann, Scott J. *2 Corinthians.* NIV Application Commentary. Grand Rapids: Zondervan, 2000.

———. *Suffering and Ministry in the Spirit: Paul's Defense of His Ministry in 2 Corinthians 2:14–3:3.* Grand Rapids: Eerdmans, 1990.

Hock, Ronald F. *The Social Context of Paul's Ministry: Tentmaking and Discipleship.* Minneapolis: Fortress, 1980.

Hubbard, Moyer V. *Christianity in the Greco-Roman World: A Narrative Introduction.* Grand Rapids: Baker, 2010.

———. *New Creation in Paul's Letters and Thoughts.* Society for New Testament Studies Monograph Series 119. Cambridge: Cambridge University Press, 2002.

———. "2 Corinthians." In *A Biblical Theology of the Holy Spirit,* edited by Trevor J. Burke and Keith Warrington, 160–74. London: SPCK, 2014.

———. "2 Corinthians." In *Zondervan Illustrated Bible Backgrounds Commentary,* edited by Clinton E. Arnold, 3:194–263. Grand Rapids: Zondervan, 2002.

———. "Was Paul Out of His Mind? Re-reading 2 Corinthians 5.13." *Journal for the Study of the New Testament* 70 (1998): 39–64.

Judge, E. A. "The Conflict of Educational Aims in NT Thought." *Journal of Christian Education* 9 (1966): 32–35.

Kim, Seyoon. *The Origin of Paul's Gospel.* 2nd ed. Wissenschaftliche Untersuchungen zum Neuen Testament 2.4. Tübingen: Mohr, 1984.

Litfin, Duane. *St. Paul's Theology of Proclamation: 1 Corinthians 1–4 and Greco-Roman Rhetoric.* Society for New Testament Studies Monograph Series 79. Cambridge: Cambridge University Press, 1994.

Long, Frederick J. *Ancient Rhetoric and Paul's Apology: The Compositional Unity of 2 Corinthians.* Society for New Testament Studies Monograph Series 131. Cambridge: Cambridge University Press, 2004.

Longenecker, Bruce E. *Remembering the Poor: Paul, Poverty and the Greco-Roman World.* Grand Rapids: Eerdmans, 2010.

Marshall, Peter. *Enmity in Corinth: Social Conventions in Paul's Relations with the Corinthians.* Wissenschaftliche Untersuchungen zum Neuen Testament 2.23. Tübingen: Mohr Siebeck, 1987.

McCant, Jerry W. *2 Corinthians.* Readings—A New Biblical Commentary. Sheffield: Sheffield Academic Press, 1999.

Mitchell, Margaret. "New Testament Envoys in the Context of Greco-Roman Diplomacy and Epistolary Conventions: The Example of Timothy and Titus." *Journal of Biblical Languages* 111, no. 4 (1992): 641–62.

Murphy-O'Connor, Jerome. "The Corinth That Saint Paul Saw." *Biblical Archaeologist* 47, no. 3 (1984): 147–59.

Piper, John. *The Supremacy of God in Preaching.* Grand Rapids: Baker, 1990.

Riesner, Rainer. *Paul's Early Period: Chronology, Mission Strategy, Theology.* Grand Rapids: Eerdmans, 1998.

Rowland, Christopher. *The Open Heaven: A Study of Apocalyptic in Early Judaism and Christianity.* New York: Crossroad, 1982.

Savage, Timothy. *Power through Weakness: Paul's Understanding of the Christian Ministry in 2 Corinthians.* Cambridge: Cambridge University Press, 1996.

Sumney, Jerry L. *Identifying Paul's Opponents: The Question of Method in 2 Corinthians.* Journal for the Study of the New Testament Supplement Series. Sheffield: JSOT Press, 1990.

———. *'Servants of Satan,' 'False Brothers' and Other Opponents of Paul.* Journal for the Study of the New Testament Supplement Series. Sheffield: JSOT Press, 1999.

Vang, Preben. *1 Corinthians.* Teach the Text Commentary Series. Grand Rapids: Baker Books, 2014.

Vegge, Ivar. *2 Corinthians: A Letter about Reconciliation.* Tübingen: Mohr Siebeck, 2008.

Webb, William J. *Returning Home: New Covenant and Second Exodus as the Context for 2 Corinthians 6.14–7.1.* Journal for the Study of the New Testament Supplement Series. Sheffield: JSOT Press, 1993.

Weima, Jeffrey A. D. *Neglected Endings: The Significance of the Pauline Letter Closings.* Journal for the Study of the New Testament Supplement Series. Sheffield: JSOT Press, 1994.

Witherington, Ben, III. *Conflict and Community in Corinth: Socio-Rhetorical Commentary on 1 and 2 Corinthians.* Grand Rapids: Eerdmans, 1995.

Young, Frances M., and David Ford. *Meaning and Truth in 2 Corinthians.* Grand Rapids: Eerdmans, 1988.

Contributors

General Editors
Mark. L. Strauss
John H. Walton

Associate Editors, Illustrating the Text
Kevin and Sherry Harney

Contributing Author, Illustrating the Text
Jeff Porte

Series Development
Jack Kuhatschek
Brian Vos

Project Editor
James Korsmo

Interior Design
Brian Brunsting

Cover Direction
Paula Gibson
Michael Cook

Index

Abraham, 17, 197
  descendants, 194
abuse, 191
accessibility, 116
accountability, 84–85
Achaia, 1, 144
acquittal, 54
Adam vs. Christ, 29
admonition, 222
adoption, 112
Aelius Aristides, 176
Aequitas, 133
affection, 104, 105, 113, 114
afflictions, 69, 75, 78
afterlife, 81–82
agricultural imagery, 148–49, 152
Alexander the Great, 236
almsgiving, 152
already–not yet dialectic, 76, 78
ambassadors, 96, 101
Ananias, 198–99
anointing, 28
Apocalypse of Moses, 207
apostle
  character and works of, 213
  as father, 219
  See also false apostles; Paul: apostolic calling and credentials
apostles in Jerusalem, 162, 175
Arabia, 200–201
Aretas IV, King, 200–201, 202
Arius Didymus, 27
"aroma of Christ," 40, 42–43, 47

aroma of death, 70
arrogance, 191
atonement, 96, 97, 98
authority, disciplinary, 158–59

banditry, 196
Barrett, C. K., 6, 33, 57, 149, 194, 201, 214
beatings, 195, 196
Belial, 108
benefactions, 187
Berea, 125, 144
blamelessness, 222
blessing, 13, 146, 149–50, 153
boasting, 8, 21, 168–70, 171–72, 191, 220
  in the Lord, 167, 170, 172
  of Paul's opponents, 163, 167
  proper, 4, 25, 171–72
  See also Paul: boasting
bodies, redemption of, 76
bodily resurrection, 82
body and soul, 85
boldness, 56, 62–63, 70, 158–59. *See also* Paul: boldness
Bonhoeffer, Dietrich, 199, 222–23
brothers, 138–40, 143
brothers and sisters, 238
burden, 182, 185

calling and qualifications, 47
captives, 40
Cenchreae, 10
character, 31, 206, 213
charity, 134, 147
charlatans, 208

Chloe, 2
Christian life, as a journey, 84
church, as temple of God, 109, 110
church discipline, 33–34, 35–37, 228, 229, 233–34
church finances, 141–42
church unity, 145
circumcision, 7
collection, as a service, 145–46
collection for poor, 118, 124
comfort, 34, 238
  in affliction, 9, 11, 15, 118–19, 121–22
commendation, 4, 44–45, 214
communion with God, 111–12
comparison, 168
condemnation, 54
confidence, 21, 84
  of Paul, 55
  regarding personal destiny, 82
  in self, 17
  in spite of weakness, 55
conflict, corporate dimension of, 33
confrontation, 30
conscience, 21–22, 24, 64
consecration to the Lord, 127, 128–29
contentment, 104
conversion, 65–66
Corinth, 1–2, 202
Corinthians
  deception of, 177
  as fleshly, 94
  help for poor in Jerusalem, 144–45
  as infantile, 94
  pride of, 190
corruption, 141
courage, 122
co-workers, 101
creation, 65, 95
cross bearing, 227
Cynics, 101, 157, 197

Damascus, 200
  road to, 65, 200, 206
David, 197
day of the Lord, 24
deception, 64
deliverance, 19
Demeter, 150
Dio Chrysostom, 63, 88, 157, 164, 190, 197, 202
Diogenes, 197
discipleship, cruciform, 42, 70–71. *See also* Paul: cruciform life
discord, 220–21, 226, 240
disobedience, 157–58, 159
due process, 228
dying and rising with Christ, 71, 90, 93, 94–95, 114

earnestness, 120
ecstatic speech, 89
Eighteen Benedictions, 17
eloquence, 88–89, 176
Elysium, 81
encouragement, 241
endurance, 70, 101, 102
enlightenment, from turning to Christ, 59
enthusiasm, 147
Epaphroditus, 127
Epictetus, 197
Epicureans, 82
equality, 133
eschatology, 72, 82–83
ethnarch, 202
Eve, deception of, 174–75
exhortations, 237–38
exodus, 95
exploitation, 190, 191
Ezekiel, 209

factionalism, 220
fairness, 133–34
faith, 127
  and works, 85, 151
false apostles, 169, 183–84
false prophets, 6, 8, 184, 192
false teachers, 184–85, 191
false witness, 225
familial affection, 241
fear of the Lord, 87–88, 90, 91
fellowship, 240
finances
  exploitation, 114, 190, 191, 219
  financial support, 218
  integrity, 42, 114, 139–41
  ministry, 185
1 Corinthians, 2
flank attack, 159
flesh vs. spirit, 29
flogging, 195
folly, 155, 173–74, 189–90, 194
Fool's Speech, 155, 173, 174, 180, 200, 203, 212, 214
forgiveness, 34
fortitude, 101, 104
freedom, 58
freewill offerings, 152
Furnish, Victor Paul, 57, 109

Garland, David, 33, 233–34
generosity, 124–29, 132–34, 146, 149–50, 218, 222
generous-versus-grudging antithesis, 146, 148–49
giving
  as generous, 134
  inward dimension of, 133

as joyful, 134
  as regular and orderly, 134
  as voluntary, 134–35, 147, 152
glory, 75
  ever-increasing, 58
  of Moses, 57
  of new covenant, 52, 53
  and suffering, 68
glossolalia, 89
God
  comfort of, 11, 12–13, 15
  faithfulness, 18, 28, 29
  fatherly presence, 110
  holiness, 90
  jealousy, 176, 178–79
  living, 109
  power, 90, 101, 103, 203
  righteousness, 96–97, 98, 108
godly jealousy, 174, 176–77
godly leadership, 215
godly sorrow, 119, 122–23
god of this age, 64, 175
good works, 111, 235
gospel
  "different gospel," 175
  hindrance to, 182, 185
  partnership in, 182
  suffering and, 74
grace, 22–23, 27, 239
  of giving, 127, 132
  to Macedonian churches, 125
  and peace, 10
  priority of, 24
  received in vain, 105
  sufficiency of, 209
greed, 141
groaning, 76
guidance, divine, 42

Hafemann, Scott J., 28, 57
hardship, 19, 193, 198
hardship catalogs, 15, 16, 69, 100–104, 195, 199, 200, 201
harmony, 241
Harris, Murray J., 58, 103, 182, 194, 205
heart, 46, 89, 91, 114
  and giving, 133
  illumination of, 65
  of Titus, 137–38
Hebrews, 194
Heracles/Hercules, 201, 202
holiness, 110
holy kiss, 238, 239, 241
Holy Spirit, 220, 239–40
  as deposit, 28–29, 77
  freedom of, 58

Homer, 81
honoring Christ, 139
hope, 18, 19, 56, 83
Horace, 201
hospitality, 182, 188

idols, 109
if–then statements, 51
illumination, of human heart, 65
image of God, 64–65
imprisonment, 196
incarceration, 17
incest, 33
indicative and imperative, 162
indignation, 120
insight, 102
integrity, 22–23, 24, 30
intercession, 18
intermediate state, 82
internal and external, 75, 89, 90–91, 92
intimacy with the Father, 111–12
intruders, 3, 118, 155, 162, 163, 168, 177–78, 182–83, 191, 205, 208, 226. *See also* super-apostles
Isaiah, 209
Israelites, 194
Isthmian Games, 1, 202

jars of clay, 68, 72–73, 76
jealousy, 174, 176–77, 220
Jeremiah, 197
Jerusalem, poor in, 125, 131, 134, 139, 144, 151
Jesus Christ
  death of, 90, 92, 132
  glory of, 64
  as God's yes to his promises, 28
  humility and gentleness of, 155, 158
  incarnation, 132
  love of, 89–90
  made perfect through suffering, 19
  resurrection of, 132
  sacrificial love of, 87, 92
  as second Adam, 64
  sufferings of, 11–12, 19, 72, 226
  triumphal procession of, 40
  ultimate author of true life, 46
  weakness and strength of, 227–28
Jewish apocalypses, 206–7
Jews and gentiles, 151
Joseph and Aseneth, 95
Josephus, 39, 196
Joshua, 197
joy, 116, 134
Judaizers, 175
judgment, 24, 84
justice, 120

kissing, 239
knowledge, 24, 102, 128
  of God, 157

law
  vs. grace, 29
  as instrument of death, 51–52
leadership
  bold, 158
  emotional cost, 198
  responsibility of, 215
  as self-centered, 191
  self-sacrifice of, 116
Letter A, 2
Letter B (First Corinthians), 2
Letter C (painful letter), 3, 119, 120
letters of recommendation, 45, 47–48, 57, 138
letter-Spirit antithesis, 48, 50–52
life from death, 17–18
Life of Adam and Eve, 184
light from darkness, 65–66
living for Christ, 90
longing, 119, 120
losing heart, 63, 66
love, 128, 222
  bears fruit, 132
  of Christ, 89–90
Lucian, 64, 126, 168, 195

Macedonia, 27, 118
Macedonians, 124, 144
  generosity of, 124–29, 132, 133
  gift of, 182
  healthy competition with Corinthians, 144, 146–47
magnanimity, 235, 236
manual labor, 21
marriage, 111, 174
Martial, 187
Matera, Frank J., 206
maturity, 233
meekness, 158
Michael (archangel), 194, 207
military imagery, 103
ministry
  challenges of, 105
  conflict in, 30
  of death, 51–52, 53, 59, 240
  gravity of, 104–5
  relationships in, 115
  of the Spirit, 52, 54, 98, 240
  vicissitudes of, 103
miracles, 213–14
mob violence, 17, 196
money, power to corrupt, 141
Mosaic era of the law, 50–54, 59

Moses, 197
  meekness of, 158
  veiled face, 56–58
motivation, 91, 111–12
Musonius Rufus, 102
mutuality, 135
mystery religions, 81–82

nakedness, 76, 77
new covenant, 29, 46–47, 50, 52, 53–54, 62–66, 68–69, 92, 95, 110, 239, 240
new creation, 47, 55, 65, 93, 94–95, 98, 239
new life, 90

obedience, 91, 157
old covenant, 29, 68, 92, 121, 240
  veil of, 57–58
old era vs. new era, 29, 52
Old Testament
  Paul's use of, 227
  prophets, 221, 234
  reliability of, 227
"one another" statements, 241
opponents
  Jewish opponents, 7, 194
  in 2 Corinthians, 7–8
  See also intruders; super-apostles
orators, 89, 164, 176
Ortberg, John, 136, 242
outer person vs. inner person, 75, 78

pagan temples, 108, 109, 111
painful letter, 3, 119, 120
paradise, 207
parents, care for children, 218
patience, 228
  and kindness, 102
patronage, 180, 187–88
Paul
  alleged fickleness, 3, 22, 27, 135
  apostolic calling and credentials, 9–10, 21, 47, 163, 180, 212, 226
  authority, 165
  boasting, 163, 167, 168–70, 182, 200–203, 205
  boldness, 55, 56, 62–63, 155, 161, 163
  confidence in Corinthians, 6
  cruciform life, 197, 235
  escape from Damascus, 202–3, 205
  founding visit to Corinth, 225
  frankness, 114–15
  humor, 190
  impending (third) visit to Corinth, 218, 224–25, 227
  integrity, 113
  Jewish credentials, 194
  love for Corinthians, 38
  manual labor, 181, 196, 232
  near-death experiences, 195–96

"painful" (second) visit to Corinth, 2–3, 6, 27, 32, 118, 218, 221
pastoral heart, 115
physical appearance, 163, 164
as poor orator, 164, 226, 232
pride and joy over Corinthians, 115
as relief worker, 125
stern letter, 119
style and philosophy of preaching, 4
suffering, 3, 11–12, 101, 195–97, 198–99, 216, 226–27, 232
thanksgiving, 39, 40
timidity, 155, 161, 163
travel plans, 26–29
as unsparing in discipline, 228
weakness of, 3, 203, 226
peace, 238
peddling the word, 41, 218
perfection, 110
persecution, 17
perseverance, 19, 213
persuasion, 88
Philippian church, 125, 144, 182
Philo, 56, 190–91, 201
Phoebe, 188
Plutarch, 69, 103, 108, 168, 195, 236
poor, collection for, 118, 124
poverty, 125–27, 134, 139, 151, 152
    extreme, 126–27, 129
    relief of, 139, 151
    riches of, 128
    See also Jerusalem: poor in
power in weakness, 101, 209, 210, 228
prayer, 18, 209, 210
preaching Christ, 66, 67
present age, as evil, 64
pride, 25, 88–89, 210
promiscuity, 221
prosperity theology, 43
Publilius Syrus, 187
purity, 102, 107–12

Qumran, 6

reciprocity, 135
reconciliation, 3, 6, 36, 93, 96, 98, 100–104, 233
rejoicing, 238, 240
repentance, 119–20, 121, 122, 235
restoration, 3, 30, 230, 233–34, 238, 240–41
resurrection, 70–71, 72, 75
reward, 84, 111–12
rhetoric, 63, 88–89, 164–65, 176, 226
righteous, blessed state of, 149–50
righteous indignation, 177–78
righteousness
    ethical and forensic, 54
    of God, 96–97, 98, 108

harvest of, 150, 153
weapons of, 103
rival missionaries, 27
Roman Triumph, 38–39, 40

sacrificially living, 221–22
sacrificial system, 96
salvation, 12, 75–76
salvation history, 53
sanctification, 110
Satan, 64
    cunning, 34–35
    masquerades as angel of light, 184
    power, 66
    schemes, 36
    use of affliction, 208
Scripture, public reading of, 56
seals, 28
2 Corinthians
    Paul's opponents in, 7–8
    unity of, 4–7
    vocabulary, of, 6
secrecy, 235
seen vs. unseen, 76, 78, 83–84
self-commendation, 44–45, 168–69, 170, 213
self-examination, 230–31, 234–35
self-sufficiency, 101
Seneca, 104, 176
sentence of death, 16, 17, 18
separation from sin, 109–10, 111
servants of Christ, 163, 194
sexual immorality, 2
shalom, 10
shame, on Corinthians, 145
shipwrecks, 195
siege warfare, 156, 157
signs and wonders, 213–14
sincerity, 22–23
slave of Christ, 65, 67
Socrates, 201
sons and daughters, 110
sophists, sophistry, 63, 164, 168, 190
sowing and reaping, 148–49, 152
spiritual body, 77
spiritual experience, 206
spiritual fruit, 48
spiritual reciprocity, 13
stewardship, 134, 140–41
Stoics, 69, 101, 102, 103–4, 157, 176, 195, 197
stoning, 195
strength in weakness, 4, 42, 69, 71–72, 200, 202, 209, 210, 226–27, 239
strong and weak, 107
strongholds, 156–57
substitution, 98
success, in ministry, 198

suffering, 11–12, 41–42, 70, 72, 198
  advances the gospel, 74
  and eternal glory, 75, 78
  as light and momentary, 75
  produces perseverance, 19
sufficiency, from God, 48, 101
super-apostles, 162, 168, 175–76, 193, 212. See also intruders

tablets of stone, 46, 52, 59
temple, 108–10
temporary vs. eternal, 75–76, 79
tent image, 76
tentmakers, 185
thanksgiving, 18, 39, 40, 115, 150, 151
Theodotus inscription, 56
Thessalonica, 125, 144
thinking, and behavior, 160
third heaven, 205, 207
thorn in the flesh, 16, 208, 210, 211
Thrall, Margaret E., 33, 245n1 (2 Cor. 7:5–16), 246n3 (2 Cor. 11:21b–29)
Timothy, 2, 10, 27
tithing, 134, 135–36, 151–52
Titus, 3, 27, 30, 118–19, 120, 137–38, 140, 219
transformation, 55, 58, 60, 77–78, 94–95, 97–98
treasure, 69
Troas, 39

trust in God, 17
truth, 232

unbelievers, 22
understanding, 102
unrepentant sinners, 162
unseen things, as eternal, 76

veil image, 57–58, 64
vengeance, 120
Victoria, 202
virtue, 101
visions and revelations, 206, 209

walking, 220, 222
warfare metaphor, 156–57
weakness, 41–42, 69, 191, 200, 209, 210, 232. See also strength in weakness
wickedness, 108
wisdom, 90, 102, 190
witness, 176, 224–25
"Word of Faith" movement, 210
workplace, ethics in, 142
worldly point of view, 27, 92, 93, 94–95, 98, 156
worldly sorrow, 119, 122
worldly standards, 167
worldly wisdom, 22, 24

Yancey, Philip, 72–73, 211, 215

zeal, 120

Focused Biblical Scholarship to
TEACH THE TEXT EFFECTIVELY

"At last, a commentary series written by serious scholars who are seriously aiming at aiding teachers and preachers in the church. This puts whole worlds of biblical context and information in the hands that need it most."

—**John Ortberg,** senior pastor of Menlo Park Presbyterian Church

To see which titles are available, visit the series website at
teachthetextseries.com

Available wherever books are sold.

www.ingramcontent.com/pod-product-compliance
Lightning Source LLC
Chambersburg PA
CBHW030231170426
43201CB00006B/182